PRINCIPLES
AND PRACTICES
OF LIGHT CONSTRUCTION

Third Edition

RONALD C. SMITH

Structures Department
Southern Alberta Institute
of Technology (Retired)

PRENTICE-HALL, INC., *Englewood Cliffs, New Jersey 07632*

Library of Congress Cataloging in Publication Data

Smith, Ronald C
  Principles and practices of light construction.

  Includes index.
  1. Building. 2. Carpentry. I. Title.
TH145.S58   1980   690   79-20047
ISBN 0-13-701979-3

Editorial production supervision
and interior design by: JAMES M. CHEGE

Page Layout by: GENE SIEGEL

Cover design by: RL COMMUNICATIONS

Manufacturing buyer: GORDON OSBOURNE

Printed in the United States of America

10 9 8 7 6 5 4 3 2 1

PRENTICE-HALL INTERNATIONAL, INC., *London*
PRENTICE-HALL OF AUSTRALIA PTY. LIMITED, *Sydney*
PRENTICE-HALL OF CANADA, LTD., *Toronto*
PRENTICE-HALL OF INDIA PRIVATE LIMITED, *New Delhi*
PRENTICE-HALL OF JAPAN, INC., *Tokyo*
PRENTICE-HALL OF SOUTHEAST ASIA PTE. LTD., *Singapore*
WHITEHALL BOOKS LIMITED, *Wellington, New Zealand*

CONTENTS

iii

LIST OF TABLES

PREFACE

The demand for new buildings, large and small, continues to be heard throughout the world. Increases in population, a continuing rise in the standard of living in many areas, urban renewal and rural development plans all contribute to the demand.

New ideas and theories of construction are continually arising, while improved methods and techniques in building are being develloped. The concept of prefabrication, for example, has become widespread and applies to almost every facet of the construction industry. This book has been written with the hope that it will assist in developing competence in both the conventional and contemporary building arts for those who are, or will be, associated with the light construction industry.

The methods of achieving that purpose are basically fourfold. The author has endeavored to give an accurate, up-to-date account of conventional methods used in light construction. The second purpose is to elaborate on some of the new ideas in design and construction which have been put into practice. The third purpose is to help the student of construction realize the importance of construction planning. And finally, since the decision to adopt a metric system of measurement in North America—the S.I. system—this edition is written using that method. For those who still wish to relate to the imperial system, a list of approximate imperial equivalents to significant metric quantities is given at the end of each chapter.

I wish to acknowledge my debt and to express my gratitude to all those with whom I have worked through the years and to those who have so generously contributed illustrations and other material. Without their help and cooperation, this book would not have been possible.

RONALD C. SMITH

xi

Tools are an essential part of the woodworking trades and, until recent years, carpenters, cabinetmakers, millworkers and others who are involved in the craft of shaping wood have relied on hand tools to get the job done. Now some of these tools have been adapted to be run by electric power, which makes their operation faster and easier, while, with others, compressed air has been utilized to provide the power.

Over the years tools have been improved in many ways. They have been made lighter, stronger, of better material. Special tools have been developed to do specific jobs, while others have been re-designed to perform a number of operations.

Probably in no other trade may the workman be called upon to perform so many different operations in the course of his day's work as in the woodworking trades. Therefore he must have at his disposal and be familiar with a wide variety of tools, each with a specific use. It is the purpose of this chapter to describe and explain the use of the common tools—*hand, electric,* and *pneumatic*—which are available for use in modern light construction.

HAND TOOLS

Hand tools may be divided into the following groups, based on the type of work done with them:

1. Assembling tools
2. Boring tools
3. Cutting tools
4. Holding tools
5. Layout and marking tools
6. Leveling and plumbing tools
7. Measuring tools
8. Sharpening tools
9. Smoothing tools
10. Wrecking tools

On occasion we may find a tool which has a place in more than one of these groups. Such cases will be pointed out.

Assembling Tools

This group includes such tools as *hammers, screwdrivers, wrenches,* and *nail sets.*

1

TOOLS

(a) Claw hammer

(b) Ball peen hammer

FIGURE 1-1: *Hammers.*

(a) Regular claw

(b) Ripping claw

FIGURE 1-2: *Hammer claws.*

Hammers: These are classified first of all according to the type of work done with them. Two of the most common classifications are *nail* hammers and *peen* hammers. The one is used for driving and pulling nails, the other for metalwork (see Fig. 1-1, a and b).

Nail hammers are made with either curved claws for nail pulling or straight claws for ripping and wrecking (see Fig. 1-2, a and b). The face of a nail hammer may be made in either of two styles, bell face (see Fig. 1-3) or plain face. In the latter case the end of the hammer is not flared.

Nail hammer handles may be made of wood or steel. The wooden-handled hammer is preferred by some workmen; they feel it has more *give* or *spring*. Others prefer the steel-shanked hammer, which is very strong (see Fig. 1-3); it may be furnished with either a leather-bound or a plastic grip.

Nail hammers should never be used for other purposes than driving or pulling regular nails. Hardened nails, such as are used in concrete, should be driven with a peen hammer. The reason is that the metal in the nail may be harder than the hammer face and damage it. Also, extensions such as sections of pipe should never be slipped over the handle to give more pulling power. If the nail is very hard to pull, use a nail puller.

When a nail hammer is being used, the handle should be gripped near the end. This will allow a greater swing and provide for more power behind the drive, when required (see Fig. 1-4).

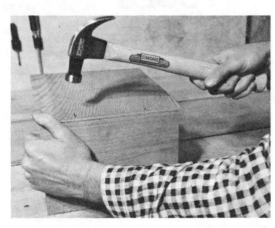

FIGURE 1-3: *Steel handle, plastic grip.*

FIGURE 1-4: *Hammer grip.*

Screwdrivers: Screwdrivers are made in three types: *flat blade,* for use with slotted screws, *Robertson,* for use with Robertson head screws, which have a square pocket in the head, and *Philips,* for use with Philips head screws, which have an indented cross in the head (see Fig. 1-5).

Slotted head

Robertson head

Philips head

FIGURE 1-5: *Screw head types.*

Flat blade screwdrivers are made with a plain handle (Fig. 1-6), a ratchet handle (Fig. 1-7), or with no handle but with a tapered end (see wood bit) to fit in a bit brace, to give the workman extra leverage for driving heavy screws.

The blades of screwdrivers are made in a number of widths and thicknesses to accommodate various sizes of screws (see Fig. 1-6). Some—called *"stubbies"*—are made with very short blades and handles for use in hard-to-get-at places (see Fig. 1-8). One of these is a handy addition to a tool kit.

Robertson screwdrivers are made in three sizes—small, medium, and large—to fit three standard sizes of screw pocket.

Philips screwdrivers are made a standard size, with a tapered drive end, to fit a variety of screw sizes.

Nail sets: Nail sets are designed to drive nail heads below the surface of wood. The diameter of the tip is the size, ranging from 1 to 5 mm. The shank is usually knurled for better grip (see Fig. 1-9).

Wrenches: Wrenches are not ordinarily considered to be carpenters' tools, but one or two can be very useful in a tool kit. Wrenches are classified as *open-end, box, adjustable, crescent, monkey* and *pipe*. The size of the latter three is designated by the length, varying from 150 to 600 mm. A 200 mm crescent wrench is considered to be a good general-purpose size. Open-end and box wrenches may be purchased in sets, and a set of small sizes will be a wise addition to the tool box.

FIGURE 1-7:   *Ratchet screwdriver.*

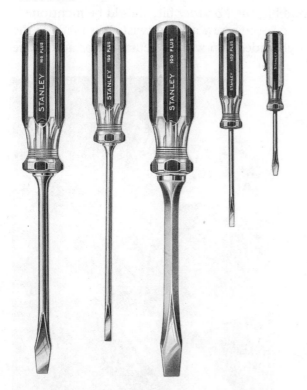

FIGURE 1-6:   *Plain-handled screwdrivers.*

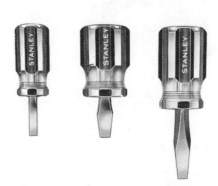

FIGURE 1-8:   *"Stubby" screwdrivers.*

FIGURE 1-9:   *Knurled shank nail set.*

Boring Tools

Included in this group are the tools which actually cut the holes in wood or metal—*bits* and *drills*—as well as the tools which hold and turn them—*bit braces* and *hand* and *breast drills*. In addition there are *countersink bits, push drills, bit extensions, bit depth gauges* and *expansive bits*.

Wood bits: Wood bits are made in several styles; two of the more common ones are illustrated in Fig. 1-10, an *auger* bit and a *solid center* bit, both of which have the same basic parts.

The small, threaded tip at the cutting end is the *feed screw,* which pulls the bit into the wood when it is turned. At the base of the feed screw are two *cutting lips,* which cut the wood from the bottom of the hole. At their outer ends are the two *spurs,* which cut the circumference of the hole. Above these is the *twist,* which carries the wood chips up out of the hole. At the end of the twist is the *shank* and, on the end of the shank, the *tang,* by which the bit is held in the brace.

Wood bits are commonly made in sizes ranging from 6 to 31 mm in diameter, increasing in size by increments of 1.5 mm. A common set, suitable for most tool boxes, will include bits from 6 to 24 mm. Holes over 24 mm in diameter are commonly bored with an *expansive bit* (see Fig. 1-11), in which an adjustable blade can be set to drill a hole of any size up to its maximum capacity. The bit is equipped with two blades, one boring up to 38 mm and the other from 38 to 75 mm.

Another type of wood bit, the *Forstner* bit, should be mentioned. It is unique in that it has no feed screw and no twist. It is made in the form of a shallow, straight-sided cup with the cutting lips across the

(a) Auger bit

(b) Solid center bit

FIGURE 1-10: *Wood bits.*

FIGURE 1-11: *Expansive bit.*

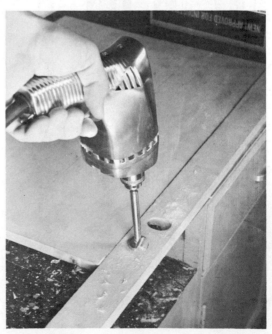

FIGURE 1-12: *Forstner bit in electric drill.*

open end (see Fig. 1-12). Since it bores a flat-bottomed hole, it is very useful when it is required to bore only part way through a board, as the feed screw of an ordinary bit might mar the underside of the surface. The type illustrated is for use in an electric drill, but Forstner bits are also made for use in hand braces.

Countersink bits: Countersink bits are used to widen the top of a screw hole so that the head of a flat head screw may be set flush with or slightly below the surface. The two illustrated in Fig. 1-13 do the same job, but one is intended for use in a hand brace and the other in a drill press.

FIGURE 1-13:   *Countersinks.*

Bit extension: Wood bits vary in length from 175 to 250 mm. If a very deep hole is required, such a bit may not reach far enough; then a bit extension may be used. It is a tool which will hold a wood bit in one end while the other end is held in a hand brace (see Fig. 1-14). It is made up to 600 mm long, so the possible depth of hole bored can be greatly increased.

FIGURE 1-14:   *Bit extension.*

Push drill: When holes smaller than 6 mm are required in wood, some other tool than a wood bit must be used. One such tool is a push drill. This is a spring-loaded tool, made so that when pressure is applied, the bit turns in one direction; when the pressure is released it turns in the opposite direction, cutting both ways. Bits are interchangeable, usually sold in sets of eight from 1.5 to 4.5 mm. The top is removable so that a set of bits may be stored inside (see Fig. 1-15).

FIGURE 1-15:   *Push drill.*

Bit depth gauge: Sometimes it is necessary to bore holes of the same depth or to bore a specified depth. In order to insure the proper depth, a bit depth gauge is used. It is clamped to a bit, measuring from the cutting lips to the flat lower end to get the required depth. It will fit any wood bit up to 24 mm (see Fig. 1-16).

Bit brace: Figure 1-17 illustrates two quite similar braces—tools used to hold and turn wood bits. One has a 250 mm sweep, and the other a 300 mm sweep. The *sweep* refers to the diameter of the circle

FIGURE 1-16:   *Bit depth gauge.*

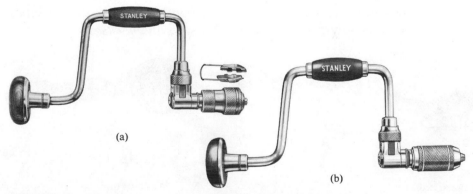

FIGURE 1-17:   *Bit braces: (a) 250 mm sweep; (b) 300 mm sweep.*

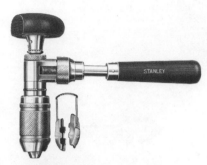

FIGURE 1-18: *Short brace.*

described by the handle as it turns. Both are *ratchet* braces which means that they can be set to drive in one direction only. This feature is very helpful when one is boring in a position where a complete turn of the handle cannot be made.

A specialized type of bit brace is the one shown in Fig. 1-18. It is called a short brace. It has two major advantages over an ordinary brace in some places. First, the distance from the head to the chuck is less, so it can be gotten into smaller spaces. Second, it is operated by a straight ratchet handle, so it may be used close to a wall or other flat surface.

Twist bits: Another method of drilling small holes is to use a *twist bit*. It is the same diameter from one end to the other, has no tang, and so requires a special chuck to hold it. The cutting end is tapered to a point, the cutting lips each forming an angle of about 60 degrees with the center line of the bit. This type of bit may be used for either wood or metal drilling (see Fig. 1-19).

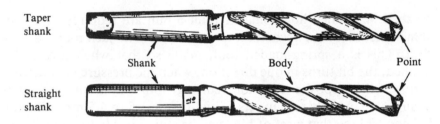

Taper shank

Straight shank

Shank   Body   Point

FIGURE 1-19: *Twist bits.*

Drills: Two of the tools used for holding and turning twist bits are illustrated in Fig. 1-20. One is called a *hand drill* and the other a *breast drill*.

Cutting Tools

Cutting tools include *saws, chisels, axes,* and *gouges.* In each of these major categories there are a number of styles or varieties, each adapted for a specific purpose.

Saws: Included in this category are *handsaws, backsaws, compass* and *keyhole* saws, *coping* saws, *utility* saws and *hacksaws.*

(a) Breast drill.   (b) Hand drill.

FIGURE 1-20: *Drills.*

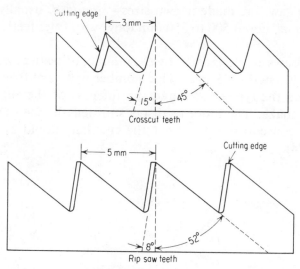

FIGURE 1-21: *Handsaw teeth.*

(a)

(b)

FIGURE 1-22: *Handsaw back styles: (a) skewback; (b) straightback.*

FIGURE 1-23: *Full tapered saw blade (Courtesy, Disston Inc.).*

Handsaws: Two types of handsaws are made: one designed to cut across the fibers of wood—a *crosscut* saw, and the other designed to cut along the fibers—a *rip saw.* The main difference between them is the method of shaping and sharpening the teeth.

Crosscut saws have teeth with the cutting edge sloped forward and filed at an angle, so that each tooth, as it is drawn across the wood, severs the fibers like a knife. Rip saws have the front of the teeth at right angles, or very nearly so, to the blade. As a result the top of each tooth is cutting edge and acts like a chisel (see Fig. 1-21).

Both crosscut and rip saws are made with curved—*skew*—backs and *straight* backs (see Fig. 1-22) and in some saws the blade is *tapered,* that is, it is made thicker at the cutting edge than it is at the back so that the saw will run more smoothly in the saw kerf (see Fig. 1-23).

7

Crosscut saws are made in two sizes—*standard,* usually 650 mm long, and *panel,* about 500 to 550 mm long, with finer teeth for finish work.

All handsaws are designated by the number of teeth or *points* they have per unit length—25 mm. This number will vary from 5 to 14, depending on the type of saw and the fineness of the cut that it is intended to make. The more teeth per unit length, the smaller they will be and consequently the finer the cut that should be obtained (see Fig. 1-24).

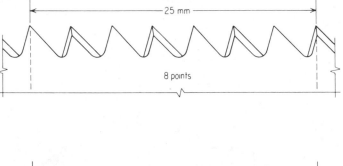

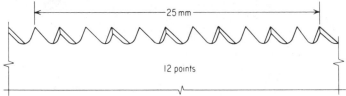

FIGURE 1-24: *Fine and coarse saw teeth.*

Backsaws: Backsaws are made with a stiff rib along the back and are intended for fine cutting and small work. Several styles are made, including the *standard* backsaw illustrated in Fig. 1-25, a *dovetail* saw, with a narrower blade than the standard, used for cutting dovetail joints (see Fig. 1-26) and a *miter* saw, a long saw made to fit in a frame with guides to hold it in place (see Fig. 1-27). Its purpose is to cut angles or miters and so the saw and its guides are on an adjustable arm which can be swung through an arc of 90 degrees, up to 45 degrees on either side of the right-angle position. It may be locked in any position to insure an accurate miter cut.

Compass and keyhole saws: Compass and keyhole saws are made with narrow, tapered blades and teeth designed to cut either along or across the grain. They are used for cutting holes or sawing along curved or irregular lines. The keyhole saw has the narrower blade of the two (see Fig. 1-28).

Coping saw: A coping saw consists of a bow frame fitted with a very fine blade and is used for cutting thin, curved work. It is very useful in interior finishing work for making *coped* joints in small moldings, casing, baseboard, etc. (see Chapter 12).

FIGURE 1-26: *Dovetail saw.*

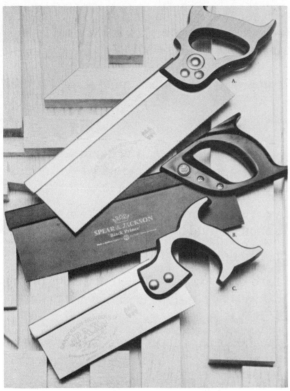

FIGURE 1-25: *Standard back saw.*

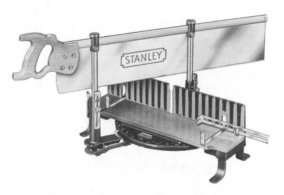

FIGURE 1-27: *Mitre saw and frame (Courtesy, Stanley Tool Co.).*

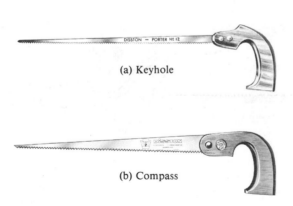

(a) Keyhole

(b) Compass

FIGURE 1-28: *Keyhole and compass saws.*

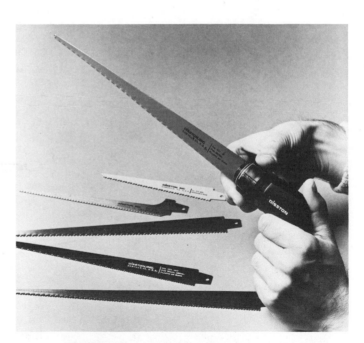

FIGURE 1-29: *Utility saw with detachable handle.*

Utility saw: A utility saw consists of a thin, hard blade with small teeth, which is useful for cutting hard materials such as metal, plastic laminates, or for gypsum board or similar materials which tend to dull normal saw teeth. The one shown in Fig. 1-29 has a detachable handle which can be rotated into any position.

Hacksaw: The hacksaw is somewhat similar in design to the coping saw, but is longer and not so deep. It is equipped with a thin cutting blade and is used for cutting metal (see Fig. 1-30).

Features of a good handsaw: There are a number of features that should be found in a handsaw if one expects to produce good results with it. They include:

1. A straight blade. Sight along the saw from handle to tip as it is held with the teeth up and the blade pointed downward. The blade should follow a perfectly straight line.

2. The teeth should be evenly set. When sighting down the blade held as above, the points should be in two straight lines.

3. The blade and handle should be in alignment.

4. The saw should have good *balance*. When it is held by the handle in a normal sawing position, it should handle comfortably and *feel* right.

5. The saw should be checked for taper from cutting edge to back, for a uniform taper is the secret of easy cutting action.

6. There should be sharp edges on the teeth. When teeth are sharp, they show a shining surface. When they are dull, the tips will show shiny ends.

7. Crosscut saw teeth should be filed to a front bevel of from 20 to 35 degrees; rip saws are filed at 90 degrees (see Fig. 1-31).

FIGURE 1-30: *Hacksaw.*

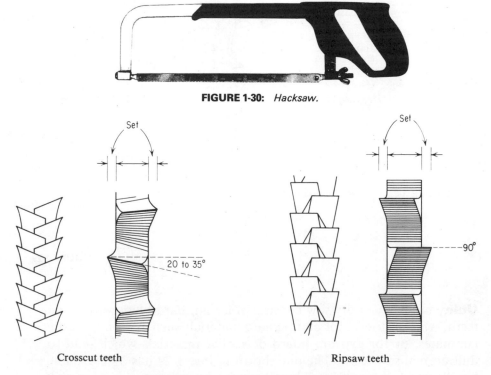

Crosscut teeth   Ripsaw teeth

FIGURE 1-31: *Handsaw teeth set and bevel.*

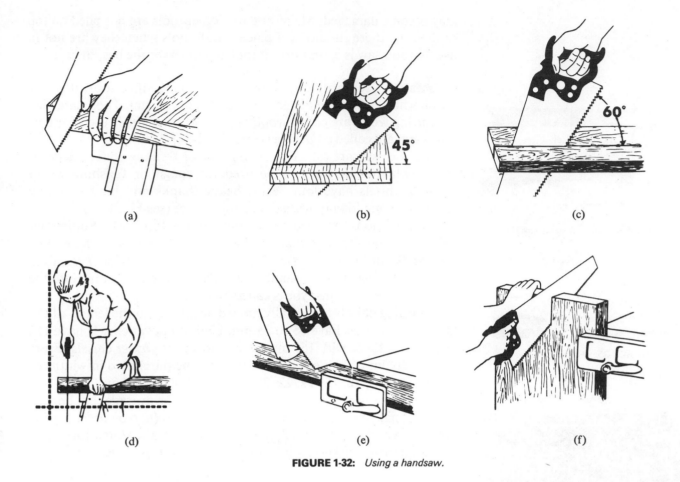

(a)   (b)   (c)

(d)   (e)   (f)

FIGURE 1-32: *Using a handsaw.*

How to use a handsaw: To begin a cut with a handsaw, rest the blade on the edge of the work, on the waste side of the cutting line. Steady the blade with your thumb (see Fig. 1-32a). Draw the saw toward you slowly and carefully several times until a slight groove is formed. After the cut is started, use long, easy strokes with light pressure on the forward stroke. You will cut most easily with a crosscut if the saw is held at an angle of 45 degrees to the work (see Fig. 1-32b). After cutting has been started, be sure to place your body in a position that will enable you to see the cutting line. The saw, the forearm, and the shoulder should form a straight line at right angles to the work. Be sure to support the work properly (see Fig. 1-32d). Resting it on sawhorses is preferable, but if they are not available, the work may be held in a vise (see Figs. 1-32e, and f). Be sure to support the piece that is being cut off so that it does not break away and splinter the underside of the stock.

When ripping is done, the saw should be held at an angle of 60 degrees to the work (see Fig. 1-32c). If the saw binds when you are ripping long stock, insert a wedge into the cut some distance from the blade.

When it is not being used, a saw should be hung up or placed in a bench rack, like that illustrated in Fig. 1-33. It should not be dropped on the floor or left leaning against a sawhorse or wall. If it slips, it

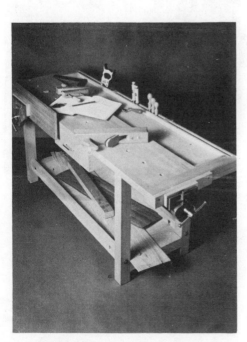

FIGURE 1-33: *Saw rack on work bench.*

11

may become damaged. Make sure that other tools are not piled on top of the saw; there should be a place for all tools when they are not in use. A good saw is an important tool and deserves the best of care.

Chisels: Chisels are divided into two main classifications, depending on whether they are designed to cut wood or metal. Those intended for cutting wood are called *wood* chisels, whereas those used for cutting metal are called *cold* chisels (see Fig. 1-34).

Wood chisels are classified as *finishing* or *framing* chisels, depending on whether they are to be used for rough or finishing work. Framing chisels have long, extra heavy shanks and blades usually at least 200 mm long to withstand rough usage (see Fig. 1-35).

Two methods are used for fitting handles to chisels. Sometimes the end of the shank is shaped like a hollow cone, with the end of the handle fitting into it (see Fig. 1-34b). This is the *socket* chisel. Sometimes the end of the shank is shaped like a spike and fits into the end of the handle. This type is called a *tang* chisel.

Finishing chisels are usually named according to the length of the blade. *Butt* chisels have 65 to 75 mm blades; *pocket* chisels have 112 mm blades; those with 165 mm blades are called *firmer* chisels. From the standpoint of blade width, chisels may be purchased in widths of 3, 4.5, 6, 8, 10, 12, 16, 19, 22, 26, 30, 34, 38, and 44 mm. Figure 1-36 illustrates a very satisfactory set of chisels for the average tool box.

A special chisel is made for cutting mortises (narrow, rectangular holes) in wood. It has a thick, narrow blade, ideally suited for reaching into narrow pockets to cut or remove wood. It is called a *mortising* chisel.

Figure 1-37 illustrates the parts of a chisel. Notice particularly the bevel. This is the area which is in contact with the stone when the chisel is being ground. It should be perfectly straight across, slightly hollow ground, and should form an angle of between 20 and 30 degrees with the back. If the chisel is to be used for softwood only, the angle may be 20 degrees. This angle gives a thin cutting blade which is capable of taking a very fine edge, but which will break down rather readily under heavy usage. For hardwood cutting, the bevel should be ground to 30 degrees. For the average chisel, which may be used for either hardwood or softwood, you should compromise with a 25 degree bevel.

The companion tool for a chisel is a *mallet*—never a hammer. The softer head of a wooden or plastic mallet will not damage the

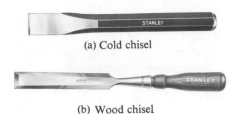

(a) Cold chisel

(b) Wood chisel

FIGURE 1-34:   *Chisel types.*

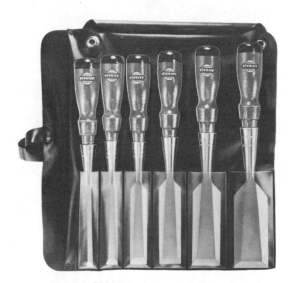

FIGURE 1-35:   *Framing chisel.*

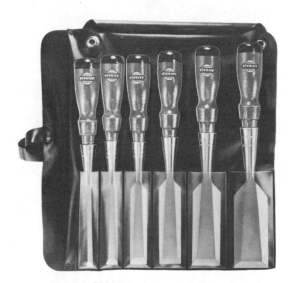

FIGURE 1-36:   *Chisel set.*

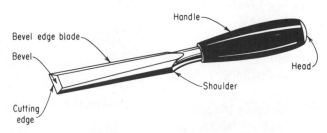

FIGURE 1-37:   *Parts of a chisel.*

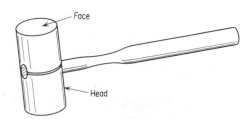

FIGURE 1-38:   *Mallet.*

(a) Bench ax

(b) Wrecking hatchet

(c) Lathing hatchet

FIGURE 1-39: *Hatchets.*

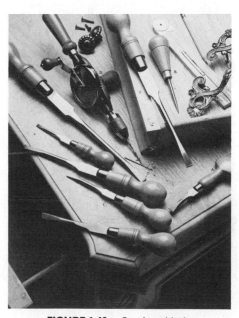

FIGURE 1-40: *Carving chisels.*

head of your chisel as a hammer will. Also, remember that when you are working your chisel with your hand only, you must make sure that your other hand is not in a dangerous position. A little slip could mean a very serious cut (see Fig. 1-38).

Axes: In more primitive types of construction the ax was a very useful tool. It was used for felling timber, hewing surfaces flat, cutting notches in logs, and many similar jobs. Today, however, with some changes in size, shape, and weight, the ax is being put to quite different uses. One type, short-handled and broad-bladed, is known as a *bench ax* or *hatchet*. It is used for rough cutting, stake sharpening, etc. (Fig. 1-39a). Another of similar style has had ripping claws added to the back of the head and is used for wrecking purposes (Fig. 1-39b). An ax of different style, which has a narrow blade and slim head, is used for lathing (Fig. 1-39c). An almost identical type is used for laying wooden shingles. The only difference is that sometimes a metal pin, which threads into one of four evenly spaced holes along the head, is included in the latter. The distance between the back of the head and the pin in any of its positions is a standard exposure distance for wooden shingles. Still another type, similar to a bench ax, but with a nail slot in the back edge of the blade, is a *flooring hatchet*.

Gouges: Gouges and other carving tools are similar to chisels in many respects but are produced in a variety of sizes and shapes, with straight or bent shanks and curved or beveled blades. They are not carpentry tools but are used in wood carving, etching and sculpting (see Fig. 1-40).

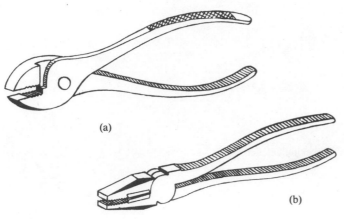

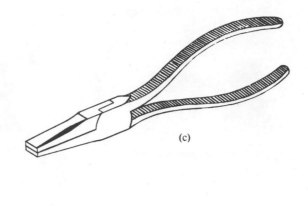

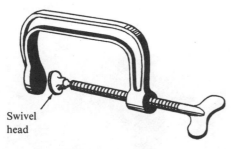

FIGURE 1-41: *Pliers: (a) adjustable; (b) side cutters; (c) flat-nosed.*

Swivel head

FIGURE 1-42: *C-clamp.*

Holding Tools

Included in this group are *pliers, C-clamps, bar* or *pipe* clamps, *adjustable hand screws,* and *vises.*

Pliers: Pliers are made in many sizes, shapes, and styles. Two of the most common are *adjustable* and *side-cutting* pliers. The adjustable pliers may be put to any one of a large number of holding uses; the side-cutters are particularly useful for cutting wire (see Fig. 1-41).

C-clamps: The C-clamp is useful for holding small sections of lumber together, perhaps for gluing. They are made in a number of common sizes from 75 to 400 mm, the size indicating the depth of the throat opening (see Fig. 1-42).

Adjustable hand screw: This tool is made of two parallel wooden jaws operated by two long screws. They too are made in a number of sizes, the size indicating the length of the jaw (see Fig. 1-43).

Bar and pipe clamps: These consist of a screw head and a movable tail block mounted on a bar or pipe. They are most useful for gluing pieces together, edge to edge. If pipe is used, almost unlimited lengths may be obtained by joining pieces of pipe together with couplings. A good set of tools should include at least two 150 mm C-clamps and a pair of 1 m bar or pipe clamps (see Fig. 1-44).

Woodworkers' vise: This is a small, sturdy vise that may be clamped to a bench or sawhorse to hold work. It is particularly useful on a sawhorse to hold doors or window sash while they are being dressed to size (see Fig. 1-45).

FIGURE 1-43: *Woodworker's clamps.*

Layout and Marking Tools

This group includes among its members the *framing square,* the *combination square,* the *try square,* and the *sliding T-bevel.* Others are *dividers, scriber, marking gauge, mortise gauge, marking knife, butt gauge,* and *straightedge.*

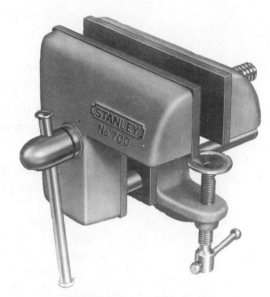

FIGURE 1-44: *Bar clamp.*

FIGURE 1-45: *Woodworker's vise.*

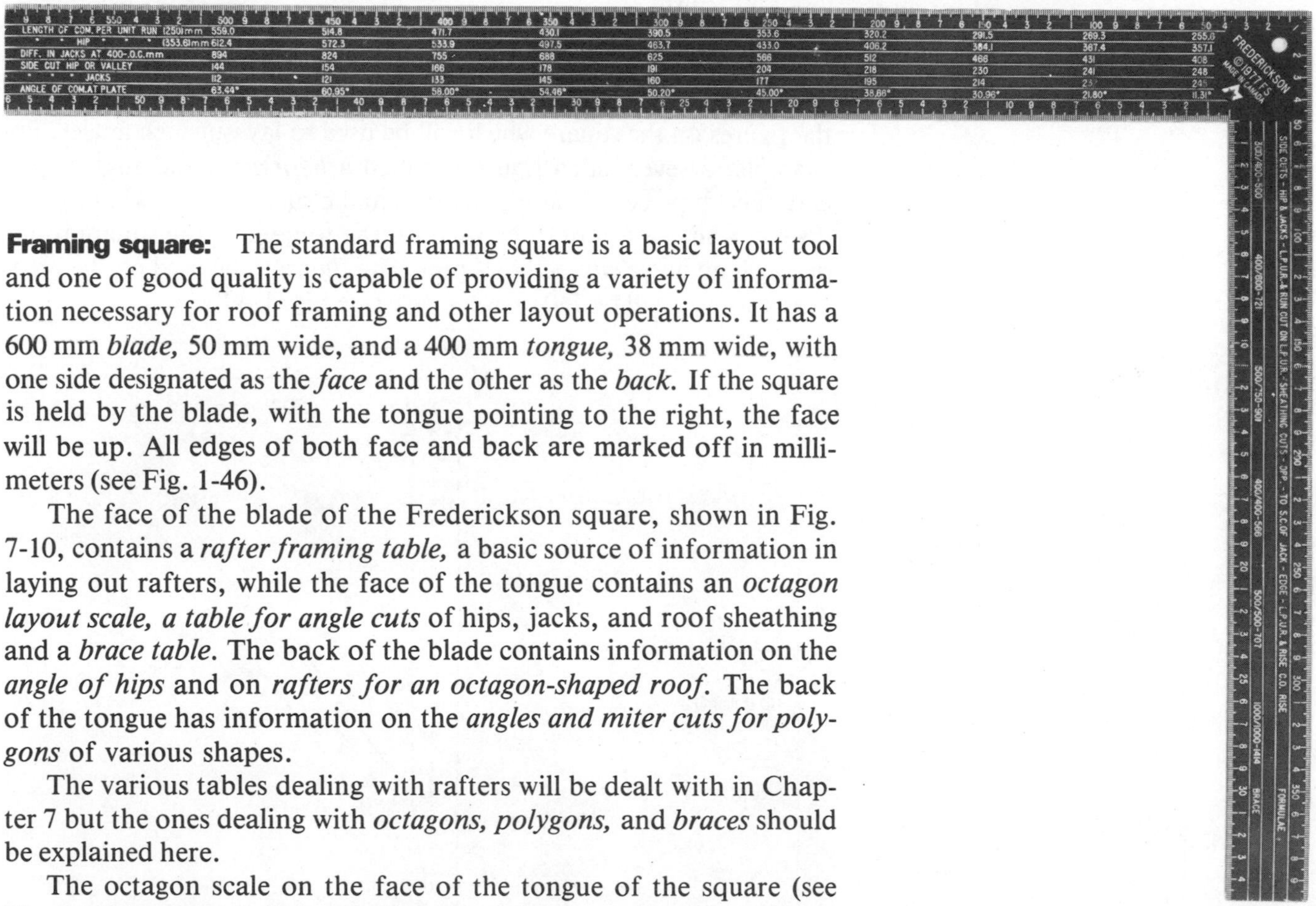

FIGURE 1-46: *Framing square.*

Framing square: The standard framing square is a basic layout tool and one of good quality is capable of providing a variety of information necessary for roof framing and other layout operations. It has a 600 mm *blade,* 50 mm wide, and a 400 mm *tongue,* 38 mm wide, with one side designated as the *face* and the other as the *back.* If the square is held by the blade, with the tongue pointing to the right, the face will be up. All edges of both face and back are marked off in millimeters (see Fig. 1-46).

The face of the blade of the Frederickson square, shown in Fig. 7-10, contains a *rafter framing table,* a basic source of information in laying out rafters, while the face of the tongue contains an *octagon layout scale, a table for angle cuts* of hips, jacks, and roof sheathing and a *brace table.* The back of the blade contains information on the *angle of hips* and on *rafters for an octagon-shaped roof.* The back of the tongue has information on the *angles and miter cuts for polygons* of various shapes.

The various tables dealing with rafters will be dealt with in Chapter 7 but the ones dealing with *octagons, polygons,* and *braces* should be explained here.

The octagon scale on the face of the tongue of the square (see Fig. 7-10) is marked off in equal spaces of 5 units and numbered from the left by 5, 25, 50, etc. Those numbers relate to distances in mm; thus 5 units relates to 50 mm, 25 units to 250 mm, 75 units to 750 mm, etc., enabling the scale to be used to lay out an octagon of any required diameter, from a square of the same diameter. For example, suppose that it is required to draw an octagon with a diameter of 100 mm. The procedure is as follows:

1. Lay out full-scale a 100 × 100 mm square and draw both horizontal and vertical center lines (see Fig. 1-47).

2. With a divider (see Fig. 1-54) take a distance equal to *10 units* from the scale and lay off this distance on both sides of each end of both center lines (see Fig. 1-47).

3. Join these points in order, to produce an octagon with a diameter of 100 mm.

The brace table on the face of the tongue gives the *line length* of brace required for various horizontal and vertical distances of the ends of the brace from the corner to be braced. For example, the first figures indicated on the left are 300-400—500. This means that if one end of the brace is to be 300 mm from a corner and the other 400 mm from the corner, the line length of the brace will be 500 mm (see Fig. 1-48).

The polygon table on the back of the tongue lists names of the polygons from three-sided to twelve-sided, the size of the angle at the ends of pieces used to make a form with one of those shapes and the figures on the square which will be used to lay out such angles. For example, a seven-sided figure is called a *heptagon,* the angle at the end of each piece of material used to make such a figure will be 64.29 degrees and the figure to be used on the tongue of the square to lay out such an angle will be 120.4 mm. The figure to be used on the blade of the square will be 250 in every case (see Fig. 1-49).

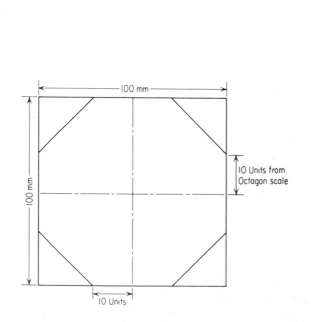

FIGURE 1-47: *Octagon layout.*

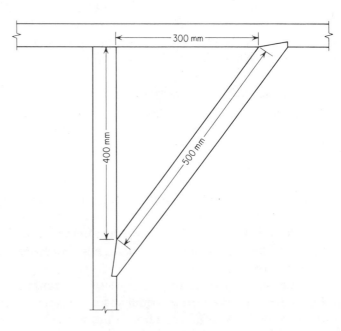

FIGURE 1-48: *Brace dimensions.*

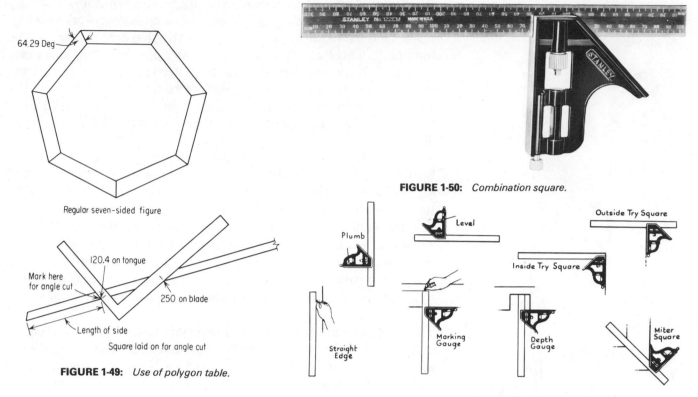

FIGURE 1-49: *Use of polygon table.*

64.29 Deg

Regular seven-sided figure

120.4 on tongue

Mark here for angle cut

250 on blade

Length of side

Square laid on for angle cut

FIGURE 1-50: *Combination square.*

Plumb

Straight Edge

Level

Marking Gauge

Depth Gauge

Inside Try Square

Outside Try Square

Miter Square

FIGURE 1-51: *Combination square uses.*

Combination square: This tool is a versatile one and, as its name implies, does the work of several simple tools. The blade slides in a slot in the head and may be locked in any position (see Fig. 1-50). One edge of the head is at right angles to the blade; another is at an angle of 45 degrees. Some manufacturers include in the head two spirit bubbles so that the tool may be used for plumbing and leveling. The illustrations in Fig. 1-51 depict some of the uses to which the tool may be put.

Two more heads are available that will take the same blade. They are a *protractor* head and a *centering* head. With the protractor head on, the tool is used to measure and lay off angles by degrees. With the centering head, the tool is used to locate the center of a circular surface.

Try square: The basic purpose of a try square is to check inside or outside angles for squareness. They are small and sturdily built, with blades ranging from 150 to 300 mm in length and steel or wooden handles from 75 to 200 mm long (see Fig. 1-52).

Sliding T-bevel: The T-bevel, or bevel square, has an adjustable blade which makes it possible to set the tool to any angle desired. Once set, the angle may be duplicated as many times as necessary. The T-bevel is particularly useful in rafter cutting. Once a pattern is laid out and cut, the bevel is set to the exact angle and used to mark all the other rafters (see Fig. 1-53).

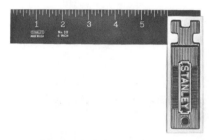

FIGURE 1-52: *Try square.*

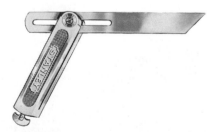

FIGURE 1-53: *Sliding T-bevel square.*

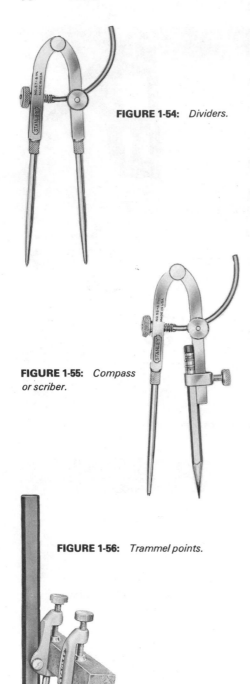

FIGURE 1-54: *Dividers.*

FIGURE 1-55: *Compass or scriber.*

FIGURE 1-56: *Trammel points.*

Dividers: A pair of dividers is a very useful tool when it is necessary to lay out a number of equal spaces, as in stair layout work (see Fig. 1-54). One leg has a metal guide bar in the shape of an arc passing through it. This leg may be clamped at any position along this guide bar when the desired step size has been determined. Notice that the end of the guide bar is threaded, passes through the other leg, and has a knurled nut at the end. This arrangement enables the workman to make very fine adjustments in the length of step he has set on the dividers.

Scriber: Very similar in design to dividers, a scriber has one metal leg, and a pencil clamped in place serves as the other (see Fig. 1-55). Its main purpose is to reproduce the curves or irregularities of a wall or other such surface on a board, which must be made to fit tightly against it. It is used by holding the piece which must be made to fit in the position which it is supposed to take. Then, by following the face of the wall with the fixed leg of the scriber, you draw out the shape to be formed. A scriber may also be used as a compass.

Trammel points: Sometimes it is necessary to describe arcs or circles much larger than could be described with a scriber or compass. Trammel points are made for just such a purpose. They consist of a pair of steel points with an attached clamp on each. One of them also has a clamp for holding a pencil. The two points are clamped to a wooden bar, one acting as the pivot while the one holding the pencil traces the arc or circle desired (see Fig. 1-56).

Marking gauge: This tool is used to lay out lines parallel to the edges of stock. It consists of a stem marked off in millimeters and an adjustable head. The face of the head is reinforced with brass for better wear (see Fig. 1-57). When it is being used, the gauge should be pushed away from you and held so that the marking pin trails rather than points straight down. A combination square may be used to do the same job, a pencil being held at the end of the blade to do the marking.

Mortise gauge: This tool is really a refinement of the marking gauge. The basic design is the same, but the mortise gauge has two stems and makes two marks at the same time. A further change is that in place of a pin, the mark is made by a little sharp-edged wheel (see Fig. 1-58). One stem is set to mark the distance from the edge of the

FIGURE 1-57: *Marking gauge.*

FIGURE 1-58: *Mortise gauge.*

stock to the edge of the mortise. The other is set to mark the width of the mortise. Either mortises or tenons may be laid out in this manner.

Utility knife: Any reasonably sharp knife may be used as a marking knife, but the one illustrated in Fig. 1-59 is particularly good, because it has an interchangeable blade. The reason for using a knife, rather than a pencil, for marking on the surface of wood is that a knife will produce a much finer line. Also, the knife makes a small cut in the surface which can be followed more exactly with a chisel than can a pencil mark.

FIGURE 1-59: *Utility knife.*

Butt gauge: Here is an example of a tool that has been designed for one specific purpose—to lay out the gains for butt hinges. It consists of a metal block containing two sliding pins (see Fig. 1-60). One pin has one marker attached, the other two. The single marker is set to gauge the depth of the hinge gain. The others mark the distance from the back edge of the door that the hinge will reach and the distance from the inner face of the door rabbet that the jamb leaf of the hinge will reach.

FIGURE 1-60: *Butt gauge.*

Straightedge: This is one tool which is usually made in the shop. Dimensions will vary according to the kind of work to be done with it. A satisfactory one for many jobs may be 1.8 m long with thickness and width in proportion. However, for some construction jobs a 3 or 3.6 m straightedge may be necessary.

The best straightedges are made by laminating strips of hardwood together, edge to edge, until the desired width is obtained, probably about 150 mm. The whole thing is dressed down to a thickness of 19 mm. The bottom edge is dressed perfectly straight, and the top edge is made parallel with it. The back is then tapered according to the illustration in Fig. 1-61, and a hand hole is cut.

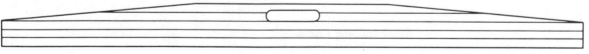

FIGURE 1-61: *Laminated straightedge.*

Leveling and Plumbing Tools

These are tools that are used to check the levelness or plumbness of structures being erected. In this category are the *spirit level, line level, level sights, plumb bob,* and *builder's level.* The latter is an expensive instrument and is not a regular part of a carpenter's tool kit.

Spirit level: This is really both a level and a plumb. The body is made from wood, aluminum, or magnesium, machined on top and bottom faces for accuracy. It contains three or more vial units, the

FIGURE 1-62:   *Spirit level.*

FIGURE 1-63:   *Line level.*

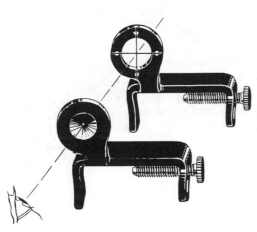

FIGURE 1-64:   *Level sights.*

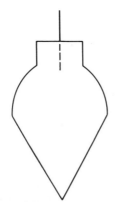

FIGURE 1-65:   *Plumb bob.*

bubbles in which indicate levelness or plumbness, depending on how the tool is held. Levels should be handled with great care to preserve their accuracy (see Fig. 1-62). For leveling or plumbing long lines, a straightedge should be used in conjunction with the spirit level.

Line level: This is really a very small model of the spirit level, containing only a level bubble. It is used to hang on a building line to check its levelness (see Fig. 1-63).

Level sights: A pair of level sights consists of a peephole piece and a cross-hair piece (see Fig. 1-64) to be attached to a spirit level. The level is set up on a solid base and leveled. Then the workman can sight to a distant object to determine its levelness. This is a good means of leveling window sills, door sills, headers, beams, forms, etc.

Plumb bob: The plumb bob is an ancient but very useful tool. It consists merely of a cone-shaped piece of steel or brass which hangs point down from a cord running from the center of the top (see Fig. 1-65). It is suspended from a point above and, when it comes to rest, will indicate a point on the earth directly below. It has many applications in construction when it is necessary to plumb down.

Builder's level: See Chapter 2 for a description of the builder's level.

Measuring Tools

Tools used for finding, laying out and checking distances are included among the measuring tools. The more common ones include the *fourfold boxwood rule* (see Fig. 1-66), the spring-loaded pocket tape, in lengths from 2 to 5 m (see Fig. 1-67), and the rolled steel tape, in lengths of 7.5, 15, and 30 m (see Fig. 1-68).

Sharpening Tools

This group of tools is not used in performing woodworking operations. Their function is to help keep the woodworking tools sharp. Included in this group are *triangualr files, mill files, saw sets, bit files, oilstones, slip stones, emery stones,* and *burnishers.*

Files: Triangular files are made specially for filing handsaw teeth. They are designated by length and by their cross-sectional size or taper. Lengths range from 125 to 250 mm and taper from *regular* to *double extra slim.*

Mill files are flat, made in single and double cut, in three sizes of teeth: *bastard, second cut,* and *smooth cut.* They are used for jointing handsaws and for general filing. They are available in lengths from 100 to 400 mm (see Fig. 1-69).

Bit files are made especially for filing the cutting lips and spurs of

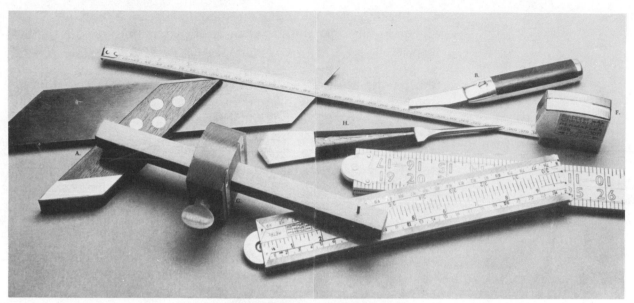

FIGURE 1-66: *Fourfold boxwood rule.*

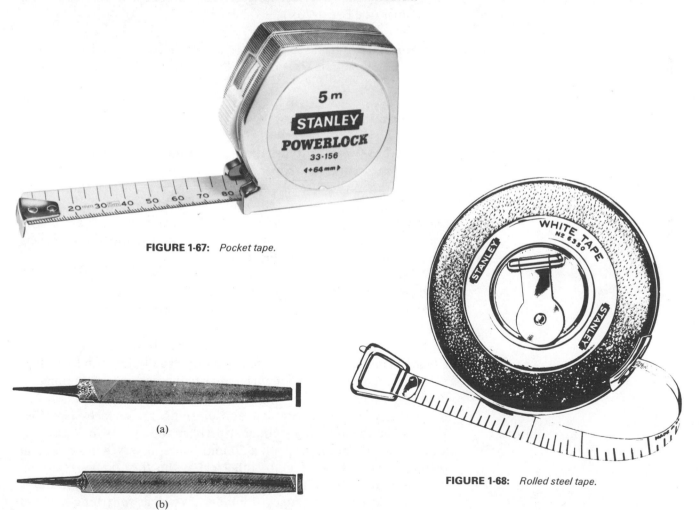

FIGURE 1-67: *Pocket tape.*

(a)

(b)

FIGURE 1-69: *Files: (a) double cut flat file; (b) single cut mill file.*

FIGURE 1-68: *Rolled steel tape.*

wood-boring bits. One end has teeth on the flat faces but none on the edges and the other end has teeth on the edges but none on the flat surfaces.

Sharpening stones: Of the three stones mentioned above, the slip stone is the finest, the oilstone is next, and the emery stone is the coarsest. A slip stone is used for sharpening gouges or other very fine edges and is sometimes used dry. The oilstone is used for sharpening plane blades and chisels and uses light oil as a lubricant. The emery stone is usually turned mechanically, either by hand or by electricity, and is used for grinding down plane blades, sharpening axes, and similar work. A small one which may be clamped to a bench or saw-horse is a useful addition to a tool kit.

Saw sets: A saw set is needed to set the teeth of a handsaw so that it will have clearance in the saw kerf. The set can be adjusted to set more or less, depending on the size of the saw teeth and the type of lumber being cut. Green lumber requires more set in the teeth than dry lumber (see Fig. 1-70).

Burnisher: A burnisher is simply a very hard, tapered steel shaft with a wooden handle. It is used to "turn the edge" of scraper blades (see Fig. 1-76).

Smoothing Tools

There are five main types of tools in this group: *planes, routers, scrapers, rasps,* and *sandpaper blocks.* The purpose of each is to produce smooth surfaces and each has some specific uses. Planes and scrapers work on exposed, flat surfaces, with the grain, while routers reach down into recesses below the surface and may work across the grain. Rasps are useful for curved surfaces and sandpaper performs the final smoothing operation.

Planes: Planes are of two main kinds, surfacing and special. The latter are among the tools, mentioned at the beginning of the chapter, that have been devised to do specific jobs.

Surfacing planes are made in five standard sizes, the smallest being a *block* plane, a small, light, one-hand tool usually 150 mm long (Fig. 1-71a). Its main uses are for surfacing small areas or for planing end grain. The next size is the *smooth* plane, a common style about 225 mm long, used for smoothing and cleaning up surfaces (see Fig. 1-71b). The third is the *jack* plane, perhaps the most widely used of all. About 350 mm long, with a 50 mm blade, it serves most general planing purposes (see Fig. 1-71c). Next is the *fore* plane, really an oversized jack plane. It varies from 450 to 550 mm in length, and is useful for straightening edges of lumber, as well as for truing surfaces (Fig. 1-71d). The largest surfacing plane is the *jointer,* which is 550 to 600 mm long, usually with a 60 mm blade. It is particularly useful

FIGURE 1-70:   *Saw set.*

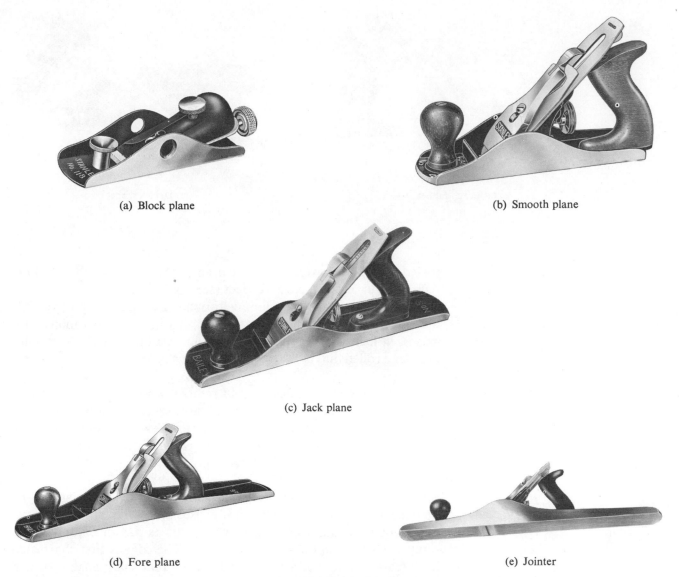

(a) Block plane

(b) Smooth plane

(c) Jack plane

(d) Fore plane

(e) Jointer

FIGURE 1-71: *Surface planes.*

for straightening the edges of doors, window sashes, or long boards. It is also used on large, flat surfaces (Fig. 1-71e).

Special planes, as the name implies, are used to perform operations not possible with regular surfacing planes. There are *rabbet* planes in various styles (see Fig. 1-72): *matching* planes, *bullnose* planes, *circular* planes, and *universal* planes (see Figs. 1-73 and 1-74).

Rabbet planes are designed to cut a rabbet—or groove—extending to the edge of a board, along its length. Two styles are illustrated, but there are several others on the market. A matching plane is used to cut a tongue on the edge of one board and a groove in the edge of the next so that the two will fit together, or match (Fig. 1-73a). The bullnose plane has its blade placed close to the front end of the body so that it can reach close to the obstructed end of a surface (Fig. 1-73b). A circular plane has a flexible steel bottom that can be ad-

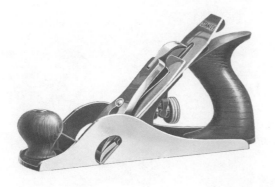

(a) Bench rabbet plane

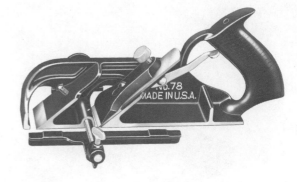

(a) Duplex rabbet plane

FIGURE 1-72: *Rabbet planes.*

justed to fit a convex or concave surface. It is used for planing regularly curved surfaces and edges (see Fig. 1-73c).

The universal plane is a unique tool having many interchangeable blades or cutters. As the name implies, it will do a great many jobs and is, in fact, a plow, rabbet, matching, beading, sash, and moulding plane rolled into one.

Routers: Routers are designed to remove wood in order to form a groove or to smooth the bottom of grooves and dadoes made by other means. The side cuts of grooves made with a router must be cut beforehand with a saw. Hand routers are usually supplied with three cutters of varying widths (see Fig. 1-75).

Scrapers: A scraper is used for the same general purpose as a plane —to make a surface smooth—but it is used in a different way. Whereas a plane blade has a sharp edge which cuts its way through wood, a scraper works with the action of a claw. The edge is first sharpened in the same manner as a plane blade. Then that sharp edge is turned over into the shape of a hook. This is done with the aid of a hard, steel instrument known as a *burnisher* (see Fig. 1-76d). When the scraper is then pushed or pulled across the surface of the wood, it scrapes off very thin shavings. Its work is limited to the final stages of smoothing a surface.

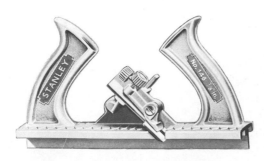

(a) Matching plane

(b) Bullnose plane

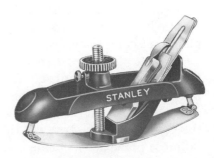

(c) Circular plane

FIGURE 1-73: *Special planes.*

FIGURE 1-74: *Universal plane.*

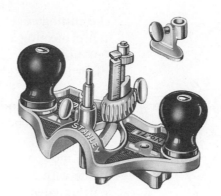

FIGURE 1-75: *Hand router.*

The simplest type of scraper is a thin piece of alloy steel with one sharpened edge. It may be held in one or both hands (see Fig. 1-76a). Another type has a frame in which the steel blade is held (Fig. 1-76b). It is used with both hands and is normally pushed away from the operator. Still another type is a somewhat specialized version. It consists of a frame in which a narrow, adjustable steel blade is held. It is intended to scrape curved edges and surfaces, and is called a *spokeshave* (Fig. 1-76c).

A good plane is a very important tool and the student should, first of all, be acquainted with the names of the parts, which are illustrated in Fig. 1-77. He should also know how to sharpen and adjust the plane in order to do a good job with it.

The plane iron and cap iron assembly must be removed first; then the cap iron can be removed from the plane iron. After sharpening, it is ready for assembly and adjusting (for sharpening procedures, read the section later in this chapter on sharpening of tools). Replace the cap iron. See that the edge of the cap iron is back about 1.5 mm from the cutting edge of the plane iron. Tighten the cap iron screw and replace the assembly in the plane, beveled edge down. Set the lever cap in place and snap down the cam. If the cam does not snap readily into place, adjust the lever cap screw until it does. Now the blade can be adjusted in the plane. Hold the plane upside down and sight along the bottom, as in Fig. 1-78. Turn the adjusting nut until

(a) Handscraper

(b) Cabinet scraper

(c) Spokeshave

(d) Burnisher

FIGURE 1-76: *Scrapers and burnisher.*

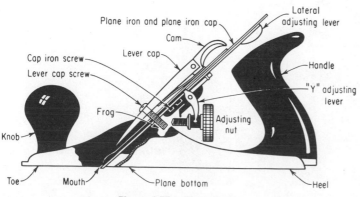

Figure 1-77: *Plane parts.*

25

the cutting edge projects from the mouth very slightly. If the edge is not projecting evenly, move the lateral adjusting lever to the right or left until both corners of the blade project the same amount. The plane is now ready for use.

Rasps: A wood rasp is a file-like tool, used to shape and smooth surfaces which are irregular or difficult to reach with a plane or scraper.

A modern version of the rasp is known as a *Surform* tool. It has a blade with a large number of small, razor-sharp cutting edges. Each cutting edge has its individual throat which allows the shavings to pass through the blade, thus eliminating clogging. These tools are made in several styles, each suited to a particular purpose (see Fig. 1-79). A couple of the uses to which these tools may be put are illustrated in Fig. 1-80.

Another new version of a rasp is known as an *abrader*. It operates much like sandpaper but is made from a stainless steel sheet in five different shapes (see Fig. 1-81). Figure 1-82 illustrates operations which may be performed with abraders of different shapes.

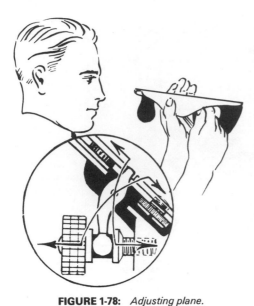

FIGURE 1-78: *Adjusting plane.*

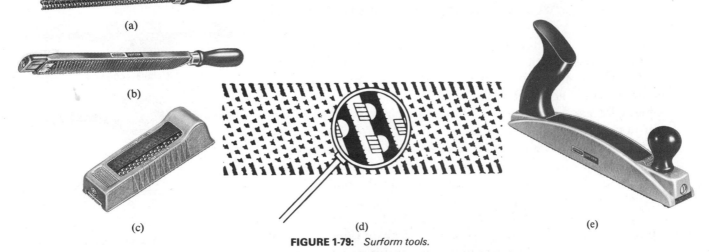

(a)

(b)

(c)

(d)

(e)

FIGURE 1-79: *Surform tools.*

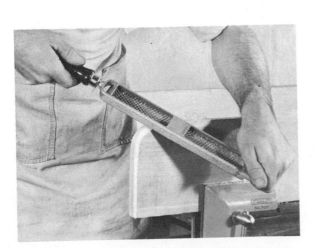

(a) Using "surform"

(b) Trimming top of door

FIGURE 1-80: *Using surform tools.*

FIGURE 1-81: *Abraders (Courtesy, Disston, Inc.).*

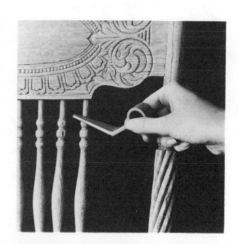

FIGURE 1-82: *Abraders in use.*

Wrecking Tools

Tools belonging to this group are used to dismantle structures that have served their purpose. For example, concrete forms that have been used are taken apart with wrecking tools. The group includes the *rip claw hammer, ripping bar, nail puller, axe,* and *side-cutting pliers.*

27

FIGURE 1-83:   *Ripping bar.*

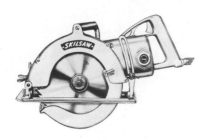

(a) One style of saw

(b) Saw in use

FIGURE 1-84:   *Hand electric saws.*

(a) Belt sander

(b) Orbital sander

FIGURE 1-85:   *Power sanders.*

Rip claw hammer: The claws on this style of hammer are made for ripping or prying (see Fig. 1-2). It may also be used, of course, for the same purposes as other hammers.

Ripping bar: This tool, sometimes called a "goose neck" bar, is made both for pulling nails and for prying. It is made in several lengths, ranging from 300 to 900 mm (see Fig. 1-83).

Nail puller: A nail puller is made for one purpose only—pulling nails. It has a pair of movable jaws that clamp below the nail head and a curved lever arm that gives great pulling advantage. It is also fitted so that the jaws may be driven into wood to reach below the surface for nails whose heads do not protrude above.

POWER TOOLS

In an age of speed and mass production, more and more power tools are being introduced into construction. There are power tools for every conceivable kind of job today, powered by electricity, compressed air, gasoline or explosive powder. Some of them will do the job faster, some will do it more accurately than can be done by hand; all lighten the load of manual labor involved.

All these tools are high-speed, and great care must be taken in their operation. Detailed instructions on how to set up and operate each one are issued by the manufacturer, and they should be followed explicitly.

With a couple of exceptions, the tools described here are held in the hand while being operated and it cannot be stressed too strongly that *great care and attention are necessary* in their handling and operation.

Electric Power Tools

Hand electric saw: This tool is a quite versatile one. It may be used almost anywhere that an ordinary hand saw may be used. It will both crosscut and rip. The depth of cut is adjustable and the bed may be tipped to permit angle cutting. It is available in a number of sizes, based on the diameter of the blade—from 150 to 250 mm (see Fig. 1-84). One of the many uses of the tool is illustrated in Fig. 1-84b.

Electric sanders: Illustrated here are two of the many types of sanders on the market today (see Fig. 1-85). Figure 1-85a illustrates a belt sander, for which belts of varying degrees of fineness are available. When this type of sander is being used, it must be kept constantly on the move, or it may leave deep depressions on the surface being sanded.

Figure 1-85b is an orbital sander, designed to do fine sanding, although various grades of paper may be used. In the case of these and other types of sanders, they should be allowed to sand by their own weight only. Never press down on them while they are in operation.

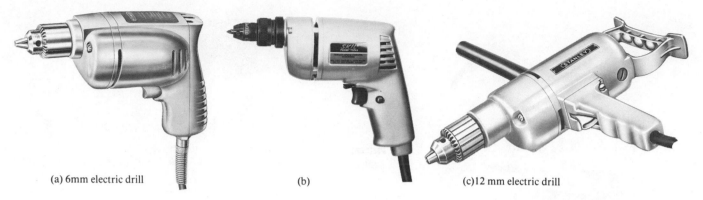

(a) 6mm electric drill   (b)   (c)12 mm electric drill

FIGURE 1-86: *Electric drills.*

Electric drills Electric drills are usually designed to receive straight-shanked bits and are made in several sizes, depending on the maximum diameter bit they will take. Figure 1-86a illustrates a drill that can be handled with one hand and will take bits up to 6 mm diameter. Figure 1-86b illustrates another light drill with trigger speed control and a reversing switch. Figure 1-86c shows a larger drill which is operated with both hands. It takes bits up to 12 mm in diameter and extra pressure may be exerted by pushing against the drill with the chest.

Routers: Electric routers are versatile tools because they will do many operations: *dadoing, rabbetting, bullnosing, fluting,* to mention only a few. Such a variety of operations is possible because a great many different bits may be used in the machine. Routers are made in a number of sizes, ranging from 0.37 to 1.85 kW. Two common styles are illustrated in Fig. 1-87, one a 0.37 kW and the other 0.56 kW.

Saber saw: This is an electric saw that can do all manner of jobs. It can do the work of a crosscut or rip saw, band saw, keyhole saw, hacksaw or jig saw. It is particularly suited to jobs that are hard to get at with any other type of saw (see Fig. 1-88). Although it is quite light, it will cut lumber up to 38 mm. thick. Three blades of different sizes fit in the chuck.

Electric plane: The electric plane is intended for jointing purposes, straightening edges, etc. It is particularly useful for working on doors or large window units. The fence may be tilted so that a bevel can be planed on an edge, as is necessary on the closing edge of a door (see Fig. 1-89).

Hammer drill: A hammer drill is used to penetrate hard material such as concrete or stone and operates in such a way that it hammers at the same time as it turns the bit. Figure 1-90 illustrates three styles of drills and two different kinds of drilling operations.

FIGURE 1-87: *Electric routers.*

29

FIGURE 1-88: *Sabre saws (Courtesy, Skil Power Tools).*

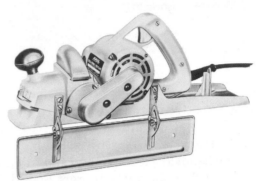

FIGURE 1-89: *Electric plane (Courtesy, Skil Power Tools).*

FIGURE 1-90: *Hammer drills (Courtesy, Skil Power Tools).*

Power screwdriver: Various types of power screwdrivers are in use, some of them as attachments to an electric drill. The one shown in Fig. 1-91 is operated by rechargeable batteries.

Radial arm saw: The radial arm saw is not a hand electric tool, but is operated from a table or bench and gets its name from the fact that the saw is suspended on a horizontal arm which allows a great variety of movement. The saw can travel along the arm, pivot on the arm, and turn into a horizontal position; the arm itself will turn (see Fig. 1-92). The versatility of the tool is illustrated in Fig. 1-93, which shows it being used for dadoing, inboard ripping, and double mitering, as well as having a dado head mounted instead of a saw blade.

FIGURE 1-91: Battery-powered screwdriver (Courtesy, Disston, Inc).

FIGURE 1-92: Radial arm saw with extension tables.

(a) Straight dadoing with the delta 300—350 mm radial saw

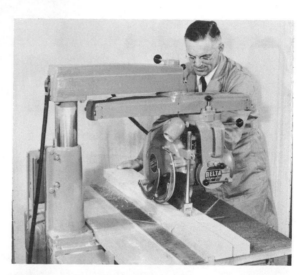

(b) Inboard ripping with the delta 300—350 mm radial saw

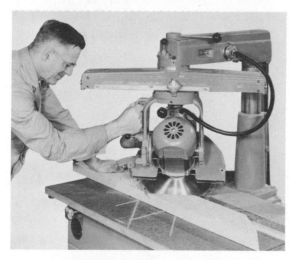

(c) Cutting a left-hand double miter with a delta 300—350 mm radial saw

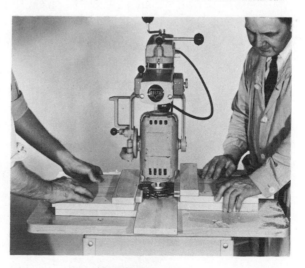

(d) With dado head

FIGURE 1-93: Radial arm saw in use.

31

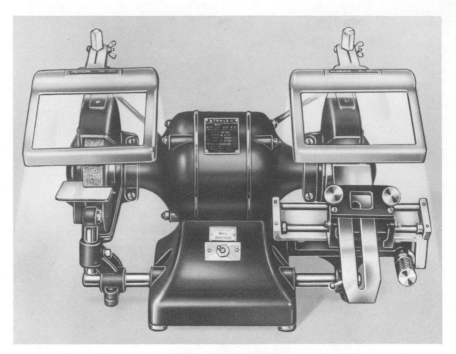

FIGURE 1-94: *Bench grinder.*

Bench grinder: This is another tool which is not a hand electric one but is fastened to a bench. The one illustrated in Fig. 1-94 is equipped with a device which holds plane blades at the proper angle while they are being sharpened.

Gasoline-Powered Tools

A number of tools are run by small gasoline engines, including *paint sprayers, soil compactors* and *chainsaws.* The latter are made in a variety of sizes, the size being determined by the length of the bar on which the saw chain runs. The one illustrated in Fig. 1-95 is a 350 mm saw. Such saws are useful for cutting heavy timbers, posts, piles, etc.

FIGURE 1-95: *Gas powered chainsaw (Courtesy, Skil Power Tools).*

FIGURE 1-96: *Using tacker for applying shingles (Courtesy, Bostitch Textron).*

FIGURE 1-97: *Using stapler for applying sheathing (Courtesy, Bostitch Textron).*

FIGURE 1-98: *Using nailer to assemble lintel (Courtesy, Bostitch Textron).*

Pneumatic Tools

The most common pneumatic tools—those operated by compressed air—are *tackers, staplers* and *nailers.* Tackers and staplers are both designed to drive staples, the main difference between them being in the size of fastener used. Normally, tacker staples will have a maximum length of 30 mm and a maximum crown width of 11 mm. The tool is used for upholstering, and for fastening paneling, building paper and asphalt shingles (see Fig. 1-96).

The fasteners used in staplers may be up to 40 mm in length, with a maximum crown width of 25 mm. Such tools may be used for paneling, subflooring, sheathing, sash and door assembly, etc. (see Fig. 1-97).

Nailers are designed to drive various sizes and styles of nails, up to a maximum of about 95 mm in length and 3.75 mm diameter. They may be used almost anywhere that nails are required (see Fig. 1-98).

Powder-Actuated Tools

In many situations, it becomes necessary to attach some object or material to a masonry or steel surface. Not only is a special fastener necessary—one that is hard enough to penetrate the surface without bending—but special power is required to drive such a fastener into a hard material.

Tools designed to do such a job use an explosive charge contained in a small cartridge similar to a 22 caliber rifle cartridge. By this means several types of pins and threaded fasteners (see Fig. 1-99) are driven into steel and concrete or other masonry materials.

Cartridges of various energy levels are produced for use with fasteners of various lengths and materials of various densities. The energy level is designated by color: green, yellow, red, purple, gray and brown denoting energy levels from low to high.

In Fig. 1-100, a powder-actuated tool is being used to apply wood strapping to a concrete wall. Notice the safety glasses being worn by the operator.

Headed fastener

Eyed fastener

Threaded fastener

Knurled shank fastener

FIGURE 1-99: *Powder-actuated fasteners.*

FIGURE 1-100: *Powder-actuated tool in use.*

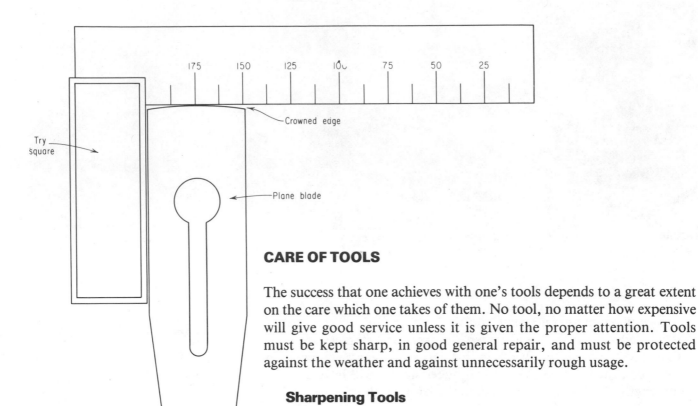

FIGURE 1-101: *Testing shape of blade edge.*

CARE OF TOOLS

The success that one achieves with one's tools depends to a great extent on the care which one takes of them. No tool, no matter how expensive will give good service unless it is given the proper attention. Tools must be kept sharp, in good general repair, and must be protected against the weather and against unnecessarily rough usage.

Sharpening Tools

While all cutting tools must be kept sharp, the ones which will probably need the most careful and constant attention are plane blades, chisels, and saws. Therefore, let us consider the sharpening procedures for these rather carefully.

Plane blade: The first step is to shape the cutting edge. It may be square or there may be a slight crown in it, depending on how it is to be used. If a surface is to be dressed flat, a crowned edge will be best but for straightening an edge, a square edge is preferable.

Hold the iron at right angles to the grinding wheel, use light pressure and grind slowly. If the edge is to be crowned, increase the pressure slightly at the ends of the blade. Test with a try square (see Fig. 1-101).

At the same time the blade must be ground at the correct bevel, which, for general purpose blades will be 25 degrees. Adjust the rest shown on the bench grinder in Fig. 1-94 so that when the plane iron is held on it, the correct angle will be ground. A simple gauge can be made to check the angle of the bevel (see Fig. 1-102 for particulars). When grinding, work the plane iron back and forth across the face of the stone using light, uniform pressure. Check the edge frequently and try to insure that it becomes sharp throughout its entire length at the same time. The grinding operation leaves a burr on the back of the blade which must be removed by *whetting*. This, the next step in the sharpening process, is often done in two stages.

Two stones are generally used for whetting—an oilstone and a finer, harder Arkansas stone. Use the oilstone first. Apply a few drops of lubricant to start. A mixture of equal parts of light machine oil

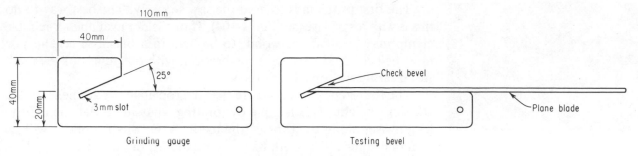

FIGURE 1-102: *Grinding gauge.*

and kerosene is recommended. Now set the bevel of the blade on the stone and raise the heel of the iron about five degrees. Only the cutting edge of the bevelled surface is in contact with the stone (see Fig. 1-103). Using a circular motion, whet the edge, taking care to hold the iron at a constant angle. After a few strokes, turn the blade over and rub it over the stone a few times, holding it perfectly flat. This action removes the burred edge which forms in whetting. Repeat this procedure until you have produced as sharp an edge as the stone will allow. The edge may be improved with a finer stone, so you repeat the whetting on the Arkansas stone.

The final step is *stropping* the edge on a piece of leather in much the same way that a barber would do with a razor blade. Glue a piece of heavy leather about 75 by 100 mm to a wooden block. Strop the cutting edge back and forth across the leather several times. The last remnants of the burr are removed, leaving an extremely fine, sharp, cutting edge.

Chisel: The same procedure is used for sharpening a chisel as was used for a plane blade. The only difference is that the cutting edge of the chisel is always square. Try square and bevel gauge may be used in the same way as for plane blades.

Handsaws: Four operations, namely, *jointing, shaping teeth, setting,* and *finish filing,* are required to make saws cut efficiently. Sometimes shaping is not necessary; setting is usually only needed for every three or four finish filings. The first three operations are similar for both crosscut and rip saws, whereas the fourth differs slightly from one to the other.

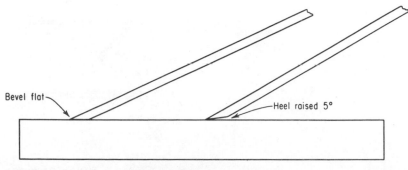

FIGURE 1-103: *Whetting a blade.*

35

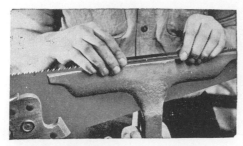

FIGURE 1-104:   *Saw vise.*

(a) Cross cut teeth set

(b) Rip teeth set

FIGURE 1-105:   *Saw teeth set.*

The first problem is to hold the saw securely. The best way to do this is with a saw vise (see Fig. 1-104). If one is not available, a suitable clamp may be made of wood, to be held in a bench vise. The saw must be held rigidly to prevent vibration, with the gullets of the teeth just clearing the top edge of the vise.

The first step is to make sure that the top edges of all the teeth are the same height. This is done by jointing—passing a flat file lightly, lengthwise, along the tops of the teeth. After this is done it will be seen that some of the teeth have been flattened on top, whereas others may have just barely been touched. Obviously, the former require the most filing.

After jointing, the teeth must be all filed to the same size and shape. Do not bevel the teeth now—beveling is done after setting. To shape the teeth, file in each gullet straight across, at right angles to the saw, using a slim or extra slim taper, three-cornered file. Use light pressure until the file is well seated in the gullet, and hold the file so as to produce teeth with the proper *rake,* as shown in Fig. 1-21. If the teeth are of uneven size, file in each gullet until you reach the center of the flat made by jointing. All gullets must be filed to the same depth, and all teeth to the same size, as shown in Fig. 1-21.

For setting the teeth, a *saw set* is used (see Fig. 1-70). It bends the top portion of each tooth outward, so that the width of the cut made will be greater than the blade which keeps the saw from "binding" in the saw kerf. Notice that alternate teeth are set in opposite directions on both crosscut and rip saws to about half the thickness of the tooth (see Fig. 1-105).

In filing the teeth of the crosscut, it must be remembered that they cut with both edges and points. Consequently, edges must be bevel-sharpened. There are two methods of bevel filing, that of filing toward the point of the saw and that of filing toward the handle. As the first is perhaps easier for the beginner, let us look at that method.

Begin at the point of the saw and work toward the handle. Tilt the saw vise slightly away from you, not more than 10 degrees. Place the saw in the vise with the handle to the right, and, starting at the point of the saw, place the file in the gullet to the left of the first tooth set away from you. Swing the handle of the file toward the handle of the saw, to about the angle shown in Fig. 1-106. Keep the file level

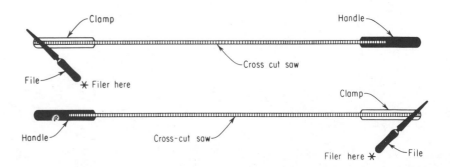

FIGURE 1-106:   *Bevel filing (Courtesy, Nicholson File Co.).*

throughout the entire stroke—don't "rock" it. In order to get all the teeth of equal size, you will have to "crowd," or put a little extra pressure toward the backs of the teeth being filed. Skip the next gullet and every other one thereafter. Then reverse the saw in the vise and file the other half of the teeth, beginning again at the point of the saw. Place the file in the gullet to the right of the first tooth set away from you. Swing the handle of the file toward the handle of the saw as before. Proceed as previously explained, remembering that a little "crowding" to the back is necessary to secure even teeth.

A three-cornered file is used for saw filing, its size depending on the size of the saw teeth. For a saw with five or six points per 25 mm, use a 150 mm slim taper or 175 mm extra slim taper file. For seven or eight points, use a 150 mm slim taper, a 175 mm extra slim taper or a 200 mm double extra slim taper. For nine or ten points, use a 150 mm extra slim taper or a 175 mm double extra slim. For eleven or twelve points, use a 125 mm extra slim taper or a 150 mm double extra slim.

FIGURE 1-107: *Filing rip saw (Courtesy, Nicholson File Co.).*

The rip saw must not be tilted at an angle while being filed. Place the saw in the vise with the handle toward the right. Starting at the point, place the file in the gullet to the left of the first tooth set away from you. File in every second gullet, filing straight across as in Fig. 1-107. Try to keep the shape of the teeth as near to those shown in Fig. 1-21 as possible. When you have reached the handle, reverse the saw and, beginning at the point again, file in those gullets you skipped in filing from the other side. Be sure to prevent vibration of the saw when filing.

Saw filing is an operation which takes practice to perfect. Do not be discouraged if your first job is not all that you would like it to be. The next one should be better, and you should become progressively more proficient as you practice.

Storing Tools

Proper storage facilities contribute considerably to the life of tools. Sharp-edged tools such as saws or chisels should be so placed in the tool box that the edges do not become damaged from contact with other tools. An excellent way to carry chisels or auger bits, for example, is to have them in a cloth roll with separate compartments for each bit or chisel. A wooden cap may be made for the saw blades, or they may be held separately, teeth down, in the tool box or kit. Take care of all your tools in some such manner, and you will be rewarded with longer use and better results.

Handling Tools

Equally important is how you handle and care for your tools *while on the job.* Saws and squares should never be dropped on the floor. Also, they should not be leaned against the leg of a sawhorse or bench unless you are sure that they are not going to slip and fall to the floor. Use some means of holding them securely. Planes should always be laid on the side—never on the bed of the plane. Don't let a great variety of tools get stacked up around you at work on the bench. When you have finished with one tool for a time, put it away where it will not be damaged.

Care in the handling of power tools is very important. This is true not only from the standpoint of damage to the tool but also from the possibility of danger to you. Careless or improper handling of a power tool may result in serious injury.

Develop a pride in your tools—in their appearance and condition —and you will find that you will be able to do a better job, that tool replacement will be less costly, and that you will be looked upon as a workman worthy of the name.

Approximate Imperial Equivalents to Metric Quantities

1 mm	—	$\frac{1}{32}$ in.	75 mm — 3 in.
5 mm	—	$\frac{5}{32}$ in.	150 mm — 6 in.
6 mm	—	$\frac{1}{4}$ in.	200 mm — 8 in.
8 mm	—	$\frac{5}{16}$ in.	250 mm — 10 in.
12 mm	—	$\frac{1}{2}$ in.	300 mm — 12 in.
19 mm	—	$\frac{3}{4}$ in.	500 mm — 20 in.
25 mm	—	1 in.	550 mm — 22 in.
31 mm	—	$1\frac{1}{4}$ in.	600 mm — 24 in.
38 mm	—	$1\frac{1}{2}$ in.	650 mm — 26 in.
50 mm	—	2 in.	

REVIEW QUESTIONS

1-1. Name two *basic* differences between crosscut and rip-saw teeth in saws.

1-2. What is the advantage of having a handsaw with a tapered blade?

1-3. How many teeth per 25 mm are there in an *eight-point* saw?

1-4. How does a back saw differ from most other handsaws?

1-5. For what type of work are *framing* chisels intended?

1-6. *Firmer* chisels have what length of blade?

1-7. What is the basic difference between a mortising chisel and other wood chisels?

1-8. Why should the cutting angle of a chisel that is to be used for cutting hardwood be ground to 30°?

1-9. What are the two main differences between a lathing hatchet and a bench ax?

1-10. List four tables found on a framing square.

1-11. What is the main purpose of a sliding T-bevel square?

1-12. For what purpose are trammel points used?

1-13. List three main differences between a Forstner bit and an auger bit.

1-14. Why should hardened nails not be driven with a nail hammer?

1-15. What two tools would you use to level across an eight-foot distance?

1-16. Matching Test

Place the number found beside each item in *Column 1* in the blank space to the left of each phrase in *Column 2* with which it matches.

Column 1	*Column 2*
1. Bit extension	_____Acts as a depth gauge
2. Push drill	_____Mounted on a spirit level
3. Bit file	_____For drilling deep holes
4. Jointer blade	_____Has 450 mm tongue
5. Butt gauge	_____Cutting irregular lines
6. Burnisher	_____Ground straight across
7. Combination square	_____Has one safe edge
8. Level sights	_____For turning scraper edge
9. Compass saw	_____To lay out hinge gains
10. Framing square	_____Has an interchangeable blade
	_____A spring-loaded tool

1-17. Tool Manipulation Test

See test drawing No. 1 below for plan and elevation of project. Carry out operations as follows:

(a) Saw rough stock to 25 × 125 × 325 mm.

(b) Plane all surfaces and square ends. Use no sandpaper.

(c) Lay out butt gain and complete.

(d) Lay out and drill holes.

(e) Mark chamfers and complete them in order A, B, C.

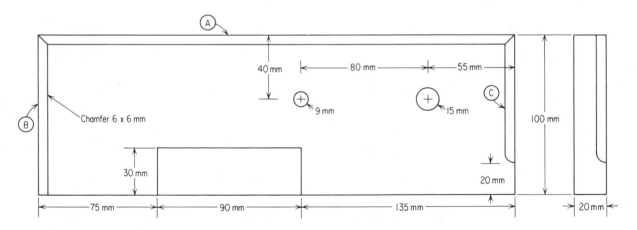

1-18. Chisel Test

See test drawing No. 2 for isometric view of project. Carry out operations as follows:

(a) Cut rough stock to 25 × 100 × 250 mm.

(b) Plane to 20 × 90 × 240 mm.

(c) Lay out and make cuts as indicated:

    (1) 20 × 20 × 30 mm cut.

    (2) 10 × 25 × 30 mm blind mortise.

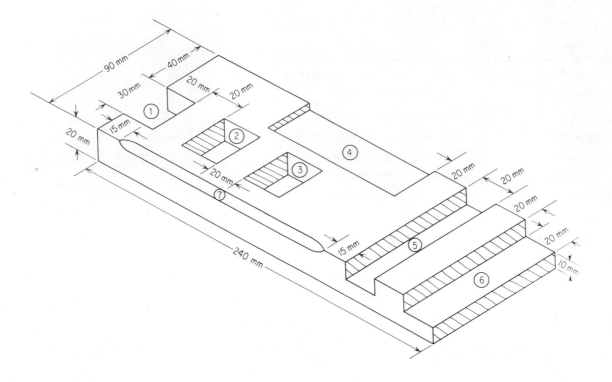

(3) 20 × 25 × 30 mm through mortise.

(4) Gain for leaf of 89 mm butt hinge, 31 mm wide.

(5) 10 × 20 × 90 mm dado.

(6) 10 × 20 × 90 mm rabbet.

(7) 6 mm stopped chamfer.

2

THE BUILDING SITE

SITE INVESTIGATION

The erection of a building, large or small, necessitates a good deal of prior study and planning, both in connection with the building itself and with the site on which it will be built.

This study, commonly referred to as *site investigation,* will vary widely as to method and degree, depending on the type, size, and proposed use of the building to be constructed. Planners in the light construction area are likely to be most interested in surface aspects of the site and the subsoil at relatively shallow depths. On the other hand, planners of large, heavy buildings are usually deeply interested in the nature of the subsoil at considerable distance below the surface and are concerned with the surface chiefly from the standpoint of site area and adjacent buildings.

Site Investigation in Light Construction

The surface aspects of the site with which planners in the light construction field will be concerned include:

1. Presence or absence of trees and shrubs.

2. Contours of the site.

3. Elevation of the site in relation to the surrounding area.

4. The size, shape, and proximity of surrounding buildings.

Particularly in the case of planning for residential construction, the presence of trees and their size often influence the design of the building. The number and kinds of trees and shrubs present will also help to determine the type of equipment necessary to clear the site. In some cases, it may be deemed necessary to remove all the trees, while in others the architect may wish to retain some trees as part of the overall design.

Whether the site is flat or rolling, whether it slopes in one direction and, if so, in what direction in relation to the front of the building are important questions for the designer. For example, a slope or small hill may enable him to introduce ground level entrances to the building at different levels of the building. The amount of slope and its direction will also determine the amount and disposition of fill which may have to be brought to the site.

The level of the area under study, in relation to that of the surrounding area, requires consideration. If it is low in comparison to the surrounding land, the level will probably have to be raised by adding fill. On the other hand, care must be taken that run-off from elevated land does not cause damage to surrounding property.

In the case of residential buildings particularly, it is usually desirable that they conform in a general way to those around them. For example, a tall, narrow building in the midst of a group of low, rambling ones would probably look out of place.

SOIL INVESTIGATION

Soil investigation, carried out in connection with light construction projects, will consist basically of tests to determine the kinds of soil to a depth of 2 to 3 m below the surface, the level of the water table in the soil, where frost is a problem, the depth of frost penetration and any very unusual soil characteristics.

The type or types of soil present will indicate the bearing strength of the material and will help to determine what sort of excavating equipment is best suited for the job at hand and what measures, if any, must be taken to prevent cave-in of the excavation. Depending on the type of soil, the excavated material will either have to be removed from the site and replaced by other soil or it must be stored to be used for backfilling and landscaping. Soil type will also be an indication as to whether or not frost penetration is a serious problem. Some very fine clay soils expand substantially when subjected to moisture and care must be taken when these are encountered at the foundation level of a building.

The level of the water table—the natural water level in the soil—will determine whether particular precautions, e.g., the installation of weeping tile, must be taken to drain water away from around the foundation. It may also influence the waterproofing techniques employed on the exterior of the foundation walls.

Testing for the presence of a number of aggressive chemical substances, particularly sulphates of calcium, sodium, or magnesium, in the ground water or soil are important considerations in the study of soils on the site. When soil or water containing appreciable amounts of these sulphates comes in contact with concrete, the sulphates react chemically with hydrated lime and hydrated calcium aluminate in the cement paste. This causes considerable expansion in the paste, resulting in corrosion and disintegration of the concrete.

To prevent this deterioration from taking place, concrete which will be in contact with these sulphates should be made using cement which has a low content of calcium aluminate. If the soil contains from 0.10 to 0.20% sulphates or water contains from 150 to 1000 ppm (parts per million) water-soluble sulphate, modified (Type 20) cement should be used. If the concentration of sulphates in soil or water is above the limits specified above, sulphate-resistant (Type 50) cement should be used.

Penetration of the soil by frost may have serious consequences under certain conditions. When moisture is present in any of several fine-grained soils, freezing may result in the formation of ice lenses and consequent heaving of the soil. Under these conditions, it is desirable to have the footings for a building below the frost line. Possible alternatives are to eliminate the soil moisture by draining it away or to replace the offending soil with one which is not affected by frost action—gravel or coarse sand.

One of the simplest and most practical methods of carrying out soil investigation to limited depths is by means of a test pit, dug either by machine or by hand. By this method, the soil strata may be observed in place, the water table level readily detected if the pit reaches that depth, and the stability of the soil checked. It should be borne in mind that soil stability may vary greatly, depending on the amount of moisture present in the soil. For example, subsurface soils that appear to be quite stable when freshly cut and in a moist condition may be very unstable when dried out.

Typical soil samples may be taken for analysis and bearing strength tests carried out on soil at any level in a test pit.

The other method of soil testing commonly used in this type of construction work is done by boring. Either hand or machine augers may be used and soil is brought to the surface for analysis in a *disturbed* condition (see Fig. 2-1).

FIGURE 2-1:   *Earth auger being set up.*

Another danger which must be considered, although it is sometimes very difficult to detect without special equipment, is the presence of underground watercourses or springs. Such watercourses normally flow to some natural outlet but when the soil is disturbed and natural outlets dammed off, the result is often trouble. Water begins to collect underground, the hydrostatic pressure builds up and eventually the water must break out somewhere. Often it will be through the basement floor. If there is the slightest hint of an underground water flow, drainage tile must be installed to take care of it.

AVAILABLE SERVICES

Are services such as electricity, sewer, water, gas, and telephone available? The answer will affect plans and preparations for the building. If a sewer line is already installed, it will be necessary to know its depth in order to get a drop from the building to the sewer line. A trench will have to be dug across the property to the building. If no sewer line is in, it will be necessary to find out what the level of a future line will be, or, if none is available, to make plans for a private sewage disposal system.

Is there a water main in the immediate area? If so, what is, or will be, the location of the water connection for the site concerned? This location will determine where the water line will enter the building. If there is no main, plans must be made for a well or other water supply.

The availability of electricity will have an effect on the actual construction work. If there is none, the work will all have to be done by hand or by gasoline engine power. If there is electricity near at hand, a number of power tools may be used which could substantially reduce the time required for building.

If there is gas in the area, it should be ascertained where it is likely to enter the building, so that gas appliances may be located as conveniently as possible. If there is no gas, some other means of supplying heat must be found. It may be that more electrical power must be provided.

It will be necessary to find out from some civic authority the grade level at the site. The level at which the street and sidewalks will be put in must be known before the excavation and landscaping are planned. The grounds in front of the building should be level with or slope toward the sidewalk or street.

ZONING RESTRICTIONS

Most urban areas have zoning laws which restrict specified areas to certain uses. They may be industrial, business, local commercial, multiple-family dwelling area, or single-family dwelling area. In addition, a building in a particular area may be required to have a specified minimum number of square feet of floor space. Regulations stipulate how far back from the front property line the house must be and the minimum distance it must be away from the side property line. Often minimum lot areas are defined and the maximum area of a lot which a building may cover. The setback for garages, whether front-drive or lane-drive, is specified in many cases.

These regulations will vary to some degree from city to city and from community to community. However, the basic reasons for having these restrictions are the same, namely, the preservation of certain standards and the protection of the citizens to whom they apply. Therefore, it is quite essential, when one is contemplating the erection of a building, that he familiarize himself with the regulations which apply to that community and the particular area being considered.

BUILDING LAYOUT

When the design work for a building has been completed, plans are drawn to indicate in detail how the building is to be constructed. In many cases a *site plan* is included to show the exact location of the building on the property. When no site plan is included, more freedom of location may be possible, subject to the local or regional building regulations that will specify the minimum allowable proximity of the building to front and side property lines. In residential construction, for example, the front *set-back* is frequently a minimum of 6 m while the side clearance might be 10 percent of the width of the lot. These regulations should be checked before proceeding with any proposed construction.

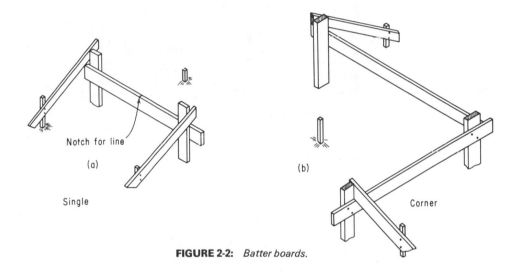

Notch for line

(a)

(b)

Single

Corner

FIGURE 2-2: *Batter boards.*

Armed with a set of plans, the builder must first lay out the position of the building on the site. If it were to be built on the surface of the ground, it would be a relatively easy matter to set stakes at the corners and other important points in the building by accurate measurements from the property lines, but in most situations some soil at least will be removed from the surface and stakes would be lost during excavation. The alternative is to establish the necessary positions on *batter boards* (see Fig. 2-2), which are kept back some distance from the actual building location and so are not disturbed during excavation work. Then, when excavating is complete, building lines are strung from one batter board to another and each intersection of two building lines represents a point on the building. These points can be established in the excavation by dropping a plumb bob from the line intersections to the ground below.

A batter board consists of a pair of stakes driven into the ground and braced, if necessary, to which is fastened a horizontal bar in a level position. Not only must the bar be level but all batter boards should be at the *same* level. Two batter boards may be combined, as in Fig. 2-2b, for use at the corner of a building. They may be simple wooden structures, such as those shown in Fig. 2-2 or, where larger buildings requiring longer lines with more tension are involved, they may be made from heavier timbers or even from steel members.

A batter board is located by driving a stake at the approximate position of each point to be established and then building a batter board to cover each position, placed well back from the area to be excavated. Then by accurate measurements and sometimes with the aid of leveling instruments (see Figs. 2-5 and 2-6), the necessary reference points are placed on the batter boards where they may be marked by a nail or by making a shallow saw kerf on the top edge of the bar.

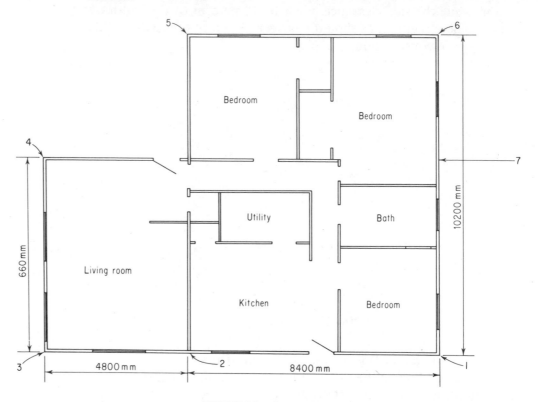

FIGURE 2-3: *House plan.*

A Simple Building Layout

Suppose that a house with a plan as shown in Fig. 2-3 is to be built on a lot measuring 22.86 m × 38.1 m. It is to be set back 9 m from the front property line and in 2.5 m from the east boundary. If the layout is to be done without the aid of a leveling instrument, proceed as follows:

1. Locate the four corners of the lot and stake them.

2. Run tight lines across the front and down both sides of the lot.

3. Measuring from these lines, drive stakes at approximately the positions indicated as (1) to (7) in Fig. 2-4.

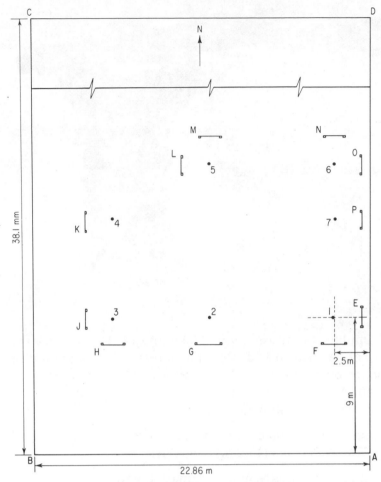

FIGURE 2-4: *Batter board layout.*

4. Erect batter board marked "E" on Fig. 2-4 to cover the stake at position (1), placing the horizontal bar at some convenient height.

5. Drive the stakes for batter board "F."

6. Run a line from the top of the bar on batter board "E" to the side of one of the stakes at "F" and hang a line level from it. Adjust the line up or down against the stake till it is level and mark that position on the stake.

7. Attach the bar at that point and level it. The bars at "E" and "F" will now be level with one another.

8. Erect the remainder of the batter boards indicated in Fig. 2-4 and level them all from "E."

9. Measuring accurately from property line AD (see Fig. 2-4), mark the top of batter board "F" at 2.5 m (2500 mm) from AD. At the same time, mark the top of batter board "G" at 2500 + 8400 = 10,900 mm (10.9 m) from AD and the top of batter board "H" at 10,900 + 4800 = 15,700 mm (15.7 m) from AD (see dimensions on Fig. 2-3).

FIGURE 2-5: *Builder's level.*

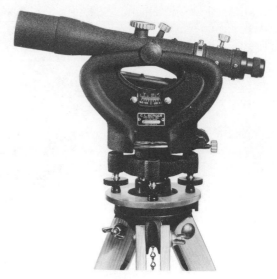

FIGURE 2-6: *Transit level.*

10. From line AB measure 9 m (900 mm) exactly and mark the top of batter board "E." At the same time mark the top of batter board "P" at 9000 + 6600 = 15,600 mm 15.6 m) from AB and the top of "O" at 15,600 + 3600 = 19,200 mm (19.2 m) from AB.

11. From an appropriate position on line AB, mark batter board "L" at 19,200 mm (19.2 m) from AB.

12. From another position on AB, mark the top of "J" at 9000 mm and the top of "K" at 9000 + 6600 = 15,600 mm (15.6 m) from AB.

13. From an appropriate position on AD, mark the top of batter board "N" at 2.5 m (2500 mm) and, from the same position, the top of "M" at 2500 + 8400 = 10,900 mm (10.9 m).

14. Cut a shallow saw kerf across the top of each batter board at each location marked.

All the points required to lay out the building are now established on the batter boards and excavating work may proceed as required.

LEVELING INSTRUMENTS

The alternative to laying out as described above involves the use of a leveling instrument. There are two basic types commonly used in construction work, the builder's or *dumpy* level (see Fig. 2-5) and the transit level, illustrated in Fig. 2-6. An engineer's level (see Fig. 2-7) may be used in place of either one of these.

The dumpy level turns in a horizontal plane only, while the transit level and engineer's level move in both horizontal and vertical planes,

FIGURE 2-7: *Engineer's level.*

making them much more versatile. Some instruments are leveled by means of leveling screws (see Fig. 2-5) while others are automatic—they simply require a small bubble to be centered in a circular dial by means of a single adjustment in order to level them.

Builder's Level

The leveling instrument illustrated in Fig. 2-5 consists of a *telescope tube* containing an *objective lens* in front, which can be focused by means of a *focusing knob* on top. The telescope is mounted in a *frame* and has attached to it a *bubble tube* very similar to a small spirit level. The telescope and bubble tube are leveled by means of four *leveling screws,* turned against a *leveling head.* The screws are adjusted in opposing pairs until the bubble is centered in the tube, regardless of the direction in which the instrument points.

At the rear end of the telescope there is an *eyepiece,* containing a small lens and an *eyepiece ring* which can be turned to focus the lens. A pair of *cross-hairs* are mounted in front of the eyepiece lens and they are brought into sharp focus by the adjustment of the eyepiece ring.

At the bottom of the frame there is a *graduated horizontal circle* and a *vernier scale,* used to read horizontal angles accurately. The instrument may be held in any horizontal position by tightening a *horizontal motion clamp screw.* It can then be brought into fine adjustment by a *horizontal motion tangent screw.*

Transit Level

A transit level telescope is pivoted in the frame and held in the horizontal position by a *locking lever.* When it is unlocked, the telescope may be tilted through a vertical arc and held in a tilted position by a *vertical motion clamp screw.* A fine adjustment to the position can then be made by the *vertical motion tangent screw.*

Attached to the telescope is a *graduated vertical arc* which moves as the telescope is tilted. Fixed to the frame is a *vertical vernier scale,* used to read the degree of tilt accurately.

The entire instrument is carried on a *centering head* which sits in a circular opening in the leveling head and allows lateral movement of the instrument within the confines of the opening when the leveling screws are loosened slightly. With some instruments a *plumb bob* is hung from the underside of the centering head and this lateral movement aids in the final centering of the instrument over a pin in the ground. Other instruments use an *optical plummet* (a visual sighting arrangement) to center over a pin.

Setting Up Level

When in use in the field, a level is set on a tripod which has a threaded top plate protected by a cap. To mount the instrument and adjust it in preparation for use, the following steps are suggested:

1. Set the tripod in the desired position and spread the legs so that when the instrument is mounted, the eyepiece will be at a comfortable height for the user. The legs should have a spread of about 1 m. Try to set it so that the tripod head is as level as you can judge by eye.

2. Set the leg tips firmly in the ground. On a hard surface, it may be desirable to use a wooden pad under the tips. Some tripods have telescoping legs so that on uneven ground the tripod head can be kept level by lengthening or shortening one of the legs.

3. Tighten the wing nuts at the top of the tripod legs into a firm position.

4. Remove the screw cap from the tripod and, lifting the instrument by the frame, set it on the tripod head. Be sure that the horizontal clamp screw is loose.

5. Hold the level by the frame and screw the leveling head firmly into place.

Leveling an Instrument

The instrument is now ready to be leveled. This operation must be carried out carefully and precisely, not only to obtain accurate results but also to ensure that the screw threads are not damaged by too much pressure. The following procedure may be adopted for this purpose:

1. Check to see that, with a transit level, the locking lever is in the *locked* position and that the horizontal motion clamp screw is loose.

2. Turn the instrument so that the telescope tube is parallel to one pair of leveling screws.

3. Turn the screws simultaneously with the thumb and forefinger of each hand, one clockwise and the other counter-clockwise until the bubble is centered in the tube. Be sure that both screws are exerting light pressure against the leveling head but *do not* exert excess pressure on them.

4. Turn the instrument until the telescope is parallel to the second pair of screws and repeat step No. 3.

5. Turn back over the first pair and recenter the bubble. Return to the second pair and check the levelness.

6. Now turn the instrument 180° and check to see that the bubble is still centered as it should be in this or any other position of the telescope.

7. Check to see whether the cross-hairs appear sharp and clear. If they do not, turn the eyepiece ring to bring them into focus for you.

Level Sights

The instrument is now ready to take a level sight and, in order to do so, a *leveling rod* or a thin wooden pole is required. A leveling rod, usually made in two or more sections, is marked off in *meters* and subdivided into *decimeters, centimeters* and *half-centimeters* (see Fig. 2-8).

Some rods are equipped with a sliding *target* (see Fig. 2-9) which is adjusted until the horizontal line coincides with the horizontal cross-hair and then locked in position. The reading is then taken *at the horizontal line.* To take a level sight on a rod with target, proceed as follows:

1. Have a colleague hold a leveling rod with target at some convenient distance away (15–30 m) from the leveled instrument.

2. Aim the telescope at the rod by sighting along the top.

3. Now sight through the eyepiece and adjust the focus by turning the focussing knob. Adjust the instrument until the object is centered as closely as possible. Tighten the horizontal motion clamp screw and adjust with the horizontal motion tangent screw till the vertical cross-hair is centered on the rod.

4. Have the rod man adjust the target up or down until the horizontal cross-hair coincides with the horizontal line on the target. He can now take the reading indicated on the rod.

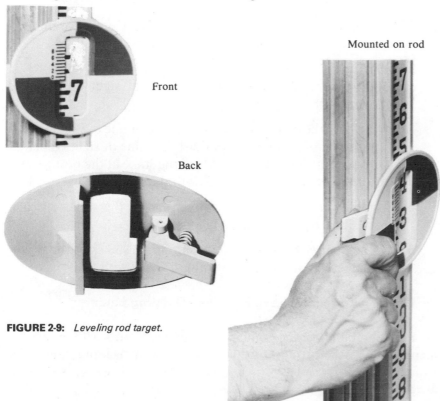

Front

Mounted on rod

Back

FIGURE 2-9: *Leveling rod target.*

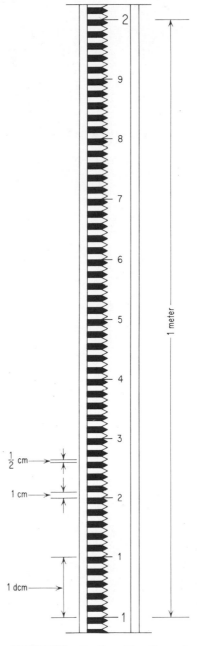

FIGURE 2-8: *Section of levelling rod.*

51

If, for example, the reading taken in the procedure outlined above was 1.105 m, it would mean that the horizontal cross-hair is that distance above the ground on which the rod is standing. This is commonly known as the *height of instrument* (H.I.) for that position.

Now have the rod moved to a second position and again obtain a reading, e.g., 1.447 m. Since the *line of sight* of the instrument is level, the bottom end of the rod must be $1.447 - 1.105 = 0.342$ m lower in the second position than it was in the first. In other words, the *difference in elevation* of the ground between those two positions is 0.342 m (342 mm).

Use of a Level to Establish Batter Board Heights

In order to use a level in building layout, there are a number of basic operations that must be understood. One is the establishment of a common level at a number of different locations. A second is the determination of the elevation of a point or series of points, relative to a point of known elevation—a *bench mark*. A third is the running of a straight line and a fourth the measurement of a given angle or the establishment of an angle of given size.

An example of how to set a common level at a number of positions may be shown by referring to Fig. 2-4 again, where batter boards are to be set at a common level—the level of the bar at "E." To set the remainder of the bars at the same level with a leveling instrument, proceed as follows:

1. Set up the instrument at some convenient point, preferably within the confines of the batter boards and level it.

2. Have a wooden pole held vertically on top of the bar at "E." Sight on the pole and have your line of sight on the pole marked with a pencil.

3. Now have the pole held against the side of one of the stakes at "F" and moved up or down until your line of sight coincides with the pencil mark again. Mark the stake at the bottom end of the pole. That point is level with the top of the bar at "E."

4. Establish a similar level mark on one of the stakes at each batter board position in the layout.

5. Attach batter board bars to each pair of stakes at the established level. All will be on a common level with "E."

Use of a Transit Level to Establish Building Lines

Locating building line points on the batter boards with an instrument involves the turning of an angle of given size and running a straight line. A transit level is required for the job. The suggested steps are as follows:

1. Measure accurately along AB (see Fig. 2-4) distances of 2.5,

10.9, and 15.7 m from A; drive a stake at each location and set a pin in the top of each stake, on the AB line and the exact distance from A.

2. Similarly, set up stakes along AD at distances of 9, 15.6, and 19.2 m from A.

3. Set up the instrument with plumb bob attached over the stake at 2.5 m from A. Adjust the tripod legs until the plumb bob point is as close as possible to being directly over the pin.

4. Slack off the leveling screws and move the instrument on the centering head until the plumb bob is exactly over the pin.

5. Level the instrument.

6. Unlock the horizontal locking lever, tilt the telescope downward, sight on the center of the stake at B and tighten both the horizontal and vertical motion clamp screws.

7. Now turn the horizontal circle (it is knurled on the underside for this purpose) until 0° coincides exactly with the center mark on the vernier.

8. Loosen the clamp screw, turn the instrument 90° clockwise and tighten the clamp screw again. Make the final adjustment to 90° with the tangent screw, if necessary.

9. Loosen the vertical motion clamp screw, adjust the tilt of the telescope and sight across the top of the bar at "F." Have the intersection of the vertical cross-hair with the top edge of the batter board marked with a pencil and later indented with a saw kerf.

10. From the same position, mark the batter board at "N" in similar fashion.

11. From the other positions established along AB and AD, mark the remainder of the batter boards by the same method.

How to Establish Building Corners from Batter Boards

1. After excavating has been completed, string building lines tightly on the batter boards from one marked point to another.

2. Drop a plumb bob from a line intersection to the bottom of the excavation (see Fig. 2-10) and drive a short stake at that point. Set a pin in the stake at the point of the plumb bob.

3. Repeat this procedure at each line intersection involved. The building corners are now established.

4. Check the diagonals of the layout—they should be exactly equal—and check the angles to make sure that they are right

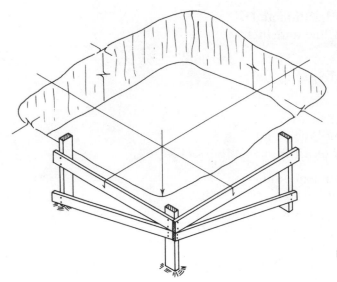

FIGURE 2-10: *Locating building corner in excavation.*

angles by using the 3–4–5 right triangle method (see Fig. 2-11). The angles may also be checked by measuring them with the level transit.

The site is now ready and the work of building a foundation can begin.

Approximate Imperial Equivalents to Metric Quantities

2 m	— 6 ft	9 m	—	29½ ft
2.5 m	— 8 ft	10.9 m	—	35¾ ft
4.8 m	— 15¾ ft	15.6 m	—	51 ft
6 m	— 19½ ft	19.2 m	—	63 ft
6.6 m	— 21½ ft	22.86 m	—	74⅓ ft
8.4 m	— 27½ ft	38.1 m	—	125 ft

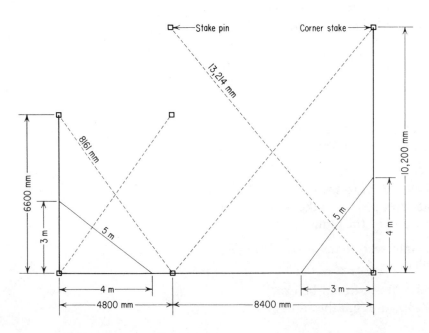

FIGURE 2-11: *Checking diagonals and angles.*

REVIEW QUESTIONS

2-1. Give two reasons for inspecting a residential building site before any plans are drawn.

2-2. Who is responsible for the location of property corner stakes?

2-3. Explain what is meant by "front setback."

2-4. What do National Housing Standards say about:

    (a) the retention of existing trees on a lot on which a building is to built?

    (b) the handling of topsoil on a lot?

2-5. Explain how the approximate corners of a building are located.

2-6. Give two reasons why batter boards should be set to a common level.

2-7. What do the lines strung on batter boards usually represent?

2-8. Why is it important to keep batter boards back several feet from approximate building corners?

2-9. Explain how a corner is located in the excavation from building lines.

2-10. What is the purpose of each of the following parts of a transit level?

    (a) objective lens.

    (b) eyepiece ring.

    (c) a vernier scale.

    (d) horizontal motion tangent screw.

    (e) centering head.

2-11. Explain how you would use a leveling rod with target to set batter board bars.

2-12. A leveling instrument is set up in the center of the building site illustrated in Fig. 2-4. A rod reading taken at position A is recorded as 1.125 m. Readings taken at positions B, C, and D are recorded as 1.187, 1.904, and 1.988 m, respectively.

    (a) What is the difference in elevation between point A and each of the other three points?

    (b) In what direction does the lot slope?

    (c) What is the average amount of drop per 30 m?

3

THE
FOUNDATION

The foundation is the supporting base upon which the superstructure of a building is built; it anchors the building to the earth and transmits the loads of that building to the soil beneath. It is therefore of the utmost importance that the foundation be strong, accurately built to size, plumb and level, and of such dimensions that its loads are spread over an area of undisturbed soil large enough to support them safely. Any errors made in the size, shape, or strength of the foundation may lead not only to construction difficulties but may also contribute to instability and future movement.

A building falling into the category of light construction may be constructed on any one of a number of types of foundation, depending on its size, use, location, the prevailing climatic conditions and the type of soil in the area.

FOUNDATION TYPES

The types of foundation most commonly used include: *concrete full basement foundation, concrete surface foundation, slab-on-ground foundation, pier foundation, preserved wood foundation,* and *pressure-treated pole foundation.*

FOUNDATION EXCAVATION

Regardless of the type of foundation to be used, some earth removal will be necessary, the amount depending on the type of foundation, type of soil, depth of frost penetration, soil drainage conditions and the proposed use of the building.

For a full concrete basement or preserved wood foundation, the excavation may be of some considerable depth, while for a slab-on-ground, relatively little earth removal may be required. For a surface, pier, or treated-pole foundation, the excavating may be confined to holes or trenches.

In any case, the top soil and vegetable matter must be removed and, in localities in which termites occur, all stumps, roots, and other wood debris must be removed to a minimum depth of 300 mm, in unexcavated areas under a building.

National building codes specify the *minimum depths* of foundations, based on the type of soil encountered and on whether or not the foundation will contain enclosed heated space. In general, for rock or soils with good drainage, there is no depth limit but for soils with poor drainage and where there will be no heated space, the minimum depth will normally be 1200 mm or the depth of frost penetration, whichever is greater. The depth of frost penetration in a particular area is established by the local building authority.

The first step in carrying out an excavation is to stake out the area to be excavated. This will include not only the area covered by the building, already established (see Chapter 2), but enough extra space that men may move about outside the foundation forms (see Fig. 3-1). The deeper the excavation, the more necessary it is to allow outside working room. Generally, 600 to 900 mm on all sides will be sufficient.

The type of soil involved will also have an influence on the excavation limits. If it is firm, well packed, and has good cohesive qualities, it may be possible to excavate and leave perpendicular earth walls standing at the outlined limits. However, if the soil is loose or becomes loose as it dries out, it will be necessary either to *slope the sides* of the excavation, up to about 45 degrees, depending on the type of soil, thus increasing the excavation limits, or to *shore* the sides.

If space does not permit sloping, then shoring becomes necessary. If the excavation walls will hold up, then temporary walls—*cribs*—of plywood or planks may be placed against them and held in place by *cribbing studs,* with one end driven into the bottom of the excavation and the other tied back to a stake driven into solid ground (see Fig. 3-2).

If the soil is very loose, it may be necessary to drive cribbing into the ground around the perimeter of the area and excavate inside it. This type of cribbing may be interlocking sheet piling or wooden or steel piles behind which some type of sheathing is placed as the excavating proceeds.

Another problem involved is the disposal of the earth from the excavation. If the top soil is good loam, it may be required for landscaping on the site after construction, in which case it should be stripped and piled by itself. The remainder of the earth must be disposed of according to circumstances. If some of it is required for backfilling, it should be piled at the site, out of the way of construction. If space does not permit storage, excavation machinery should be used which will allow direct loading onto trucks for removal (see Fig. 3-3).

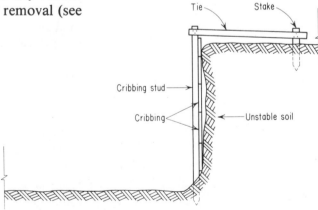

FIGURE 3-2: *Side of excavation cribbed.*

FIGURE 3-1: *Excavation with space outside the foundation forms.*

EXCAVATING PROCEDURES

The type of machinery used to do the excavating work will depend on the area and depth of the excavation, the type of soil involved and the available space outside the excavation.

Shallow excavations may be dug with a *bulldozer blade* (see Fig. 3-4), provided that there is room around the excavation to deposit the soil or another machine to load it onto trucks. Deeper excavations may be carried out with a *power shovel* (see Fig. 3-5) or a digging bucket on a tracked or wheeled tractor (see Fig. 3-3).

FIGURE 3-3: *Excavating with bucket on wheeled tractor (Courtesy, Hough Machine Co.).*

FIGURE 3-4: *Dozer blade in shallow excavation.*

Another excellent machine for excavating, particularly for light construction, is the *pull shovel* (back hoe). It can dig either shallow or deep excavations (see Fig. 3-6) with straight, vertical walls and a level floor, with the machine always resting on solid ground. By following a prearranged plan, such as that outlined in Fig. 3-7, a fast and efficient excavating operation may be carried out. The procedure is as follows.

Area 1 (see Fig. 3-7) is excavated first from position A and area 2 is then done from position B. The machine is then moved to positions C, D and E in succession to excavate areas 3, 4, and 5 and then turned in the opposite direction to excavate areas 6, 7, and 8. Area 9 is done from position I and the final portion, area 10 is completed with the machine in position J, moving as indicated.

FOUNDATION CONSTRUCTION

When the excavation has been completed, the work of constructing the foundation can begin. For foundations involving cast-in-place concrete, forms have to be built. For others, gravel must be laid and

58

FIGURE 3-5: *Power shovel.*

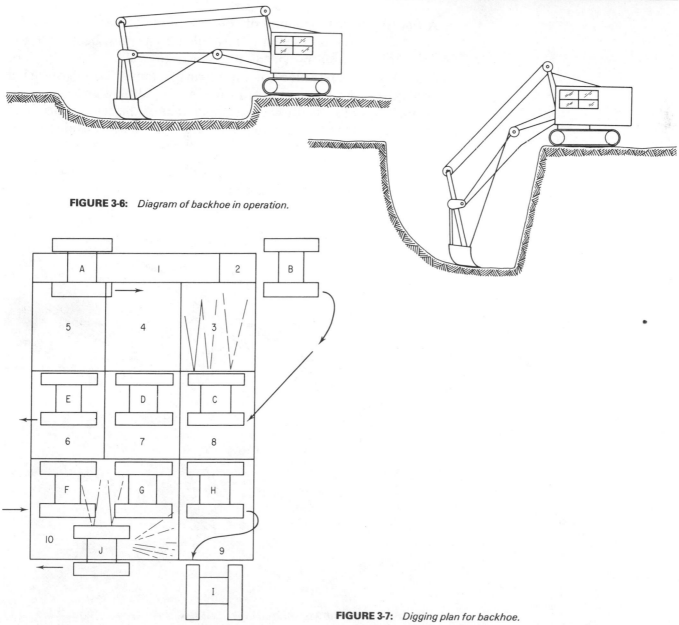

FIGURE 3-6: *Diagram of backhoe in operation.*

FIGURE 3-7: *Digging plan for backhoe.*

compacted. In each case, the building lines must be established on the excavation floor. Proceed as follows:

1. String the building lines on the batter boards as tightly as possible.

2. From each intersection of lines, drop a plumb bob to the excavation floor (see Fig. 2-10) and drive short stakes to mark each location.

3. In the top of each stake, drive a small nail at the *plumb bob point, to pinpoint each location exactly.*

CONCRETE FULL BASEMENT FOUNDATION

A *full basement* foundation of concrete is one of the most common types of foundation used in residential construction, because of the extra usable space provided. It consists of walls of cast-in-place concrete or concrete block, not less than 150 mm thick and of such a height that there will be at least 1950 mm of headroom under the main beam. The walls usually encompass an area of the same dimensions as the floor plan of the building and enclose a floor and livable space.

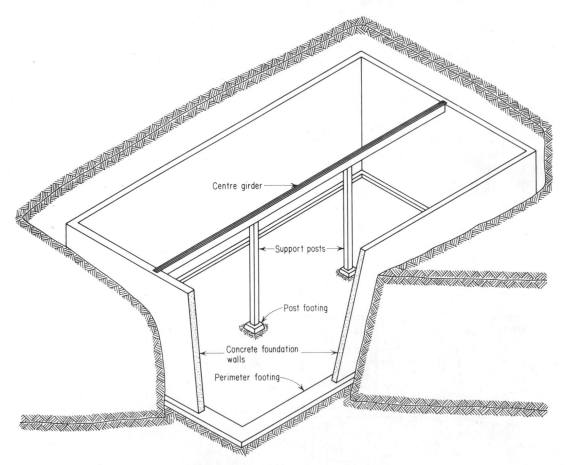

FIGURE 3-8: *Full basement foundation.*

The walls are supported on *continuous footings* wide enough that the building loads are supported safely by the soil beneath them. Interior loads are carried on one or more *girders,* supported on posts resting on individual *post footings* (see Fig. 3-8).

Footing Forms

Forms for the continuous perimeter footings and the interior post footings are the first requirement in the construction of a full basement foundation.

Minimum footing widths for light buildings are given in Table 3-1. The thickness of the footing must not be less than the projection beyond the supported wall or post, except where the footing is suitably reinforced and, in any case, must not be less than 100 mm.

TABLE 3-1:   *Minimum footing widths for light construction*

Number of floors supported	Minimum widths of strip footings (mm)		Minimum area of column Footings (m²)
	Supporting external walls	*Supporting internal walls*	
1	250	200	0.4
2	350	350	0.75
3	450	500	1.0

(Courtesy National Research Council)

NOTES: 1. For each story of masonry veneer over wood-frame construction, width of footings supporting exterior walls are to be increased by 65 mm.

2. For each story of masonry construction other than the foundation walls, width of footings supporting exterior walls must be increased by 130 mm.

3. For each story of masonry supported by the footing, the width of footings supporting interior walls must be increased by 100 mm.

4. Sizes of column footings shown in the table are based on columns spaced 3 m o.c. For other column spacing, the footing areas must be adjusted in proportion to the distance between columns.

The type and thickness of material required for footing forms will depend on their size and on whether they are to be constructed above or below ground level (see Fig. 3-9). If they are to be set above the ground level, they should be built of 38mm lumber, to withstand the pressure of the freshly placed concrete. Footings below ground level may be made from lighter material.

To lay out and construct footing forms for footings above grade level (see Fig. 3-9a), proceed as follows:

1. At each located corner, measure *out in two directions* (see Fig. 3-10) the width of the footing projection plus the thickness of the form material and drive one or two 38 mm stakes (depending on whether external or internal corner) firmly into the excavation floor.

2. Mark the level of the top of the footing form on one external corner stake, tack a 19 mm block to the stake at that point and secure one end of a building line at that level.

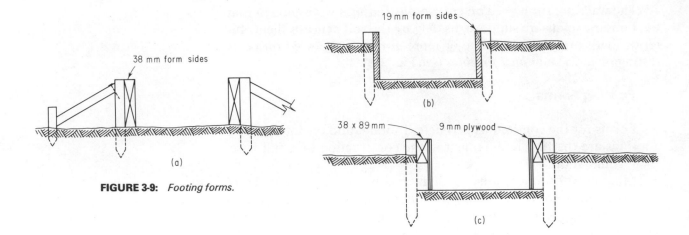

FIGURE 3-9: *Footing forms.*

19 mm form sides

(b)

38 x 89mm   9 mm plywood

(c)

38 mm form sides

(a)

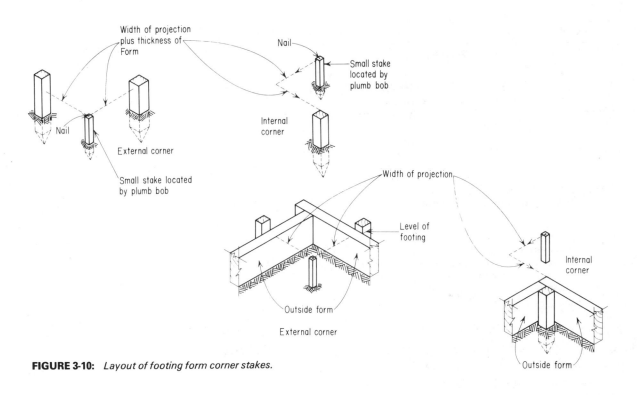

Width of projection
plus thickness of
Form

Nail

Small stake
located by
plumb bob

Nail

Internal
corner

External corner

Small stake located
by plumb bob

Width of projection

Level of
footing

Internal
corner

Outside form

External corner

Outside form

FIGURE 3-10: *Layout of footing form corner stakes.*

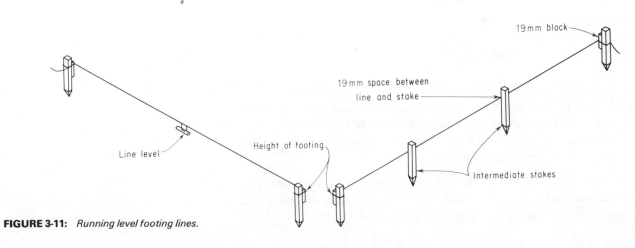

19mm block

19mm space between
line and stake

Line level

Height of footing

Intermediate stakes

FIGURE 3-11: *Running level footing lines.*

3. Stretch the line to the other corner stake on the same side, level it with a *line level* (see Fig. 3-11), pull it as tight as possible, and secure it to the second corner stake (see Fig. 3-11).

4. Run similar lines for each side.

5. Drive a series of stakes to support the forms, about 1 to 1½ m apart, outside the line and 19 mm away from it.

6. Check the position of each with a 19 mm test block and, when all are in position, remove the lines.

7. Attach one end of a piece of form material to an external corner stake at the marked level (see Fig. 3-10b). Level it with straightedge and spirit level or with a leveling instrument and nail the other end to an intermediate stake (see Fig. 3-12). Attach by nailing *through the stake* into the form side.

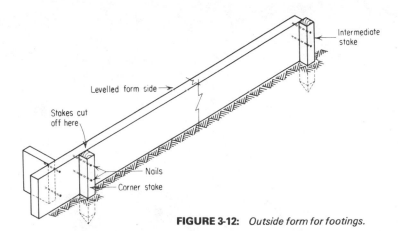

FIGURE 3-12: *Outside form for footings.*

8. Continue with one or more pieces of material to the end of that side.

9. Butt a piece of form material to that already in place at a corner (see Fig. 3-10b) to start the outside form for another side of the footing.

10. At an internal corner, form ends will lap as indicated in Fig. 3-10b.

11. When all outside forms are in place, check them for being level, make any necessary adjustments, nail to all intermediate stakes and cut off stake tops level with the top of the form (see Fig. 3-13).

12. At one external corner, measure *in* the width of the footing plus the thickness of the form material and drive a 38 mm stake so that two faces are parallel to side and end (see Fig. 3-14).

13. Repeat at all external corners.

14. At internal corners, measure *in* the width of the footing plus the thickness of the form material in two directions (see Fig. 3-14) and drive two stakes as indicated.

15. Run level lines between pairs of stakes and set the intermediate stakes as before.

16. Remove the lines and attach the form sides. Use a spirit level to level the inside form with the outside one (see Fig. 3-15).

17. Finally, cut off the tops of all the stakes level with the form.

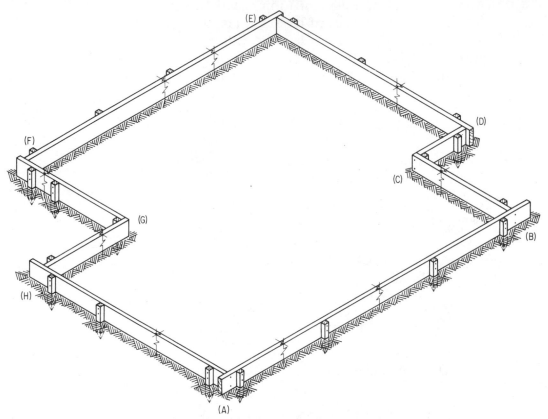

FIGURE 3-13

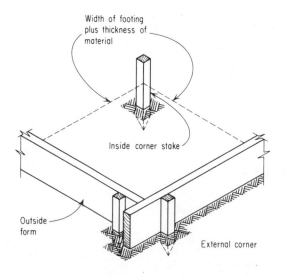

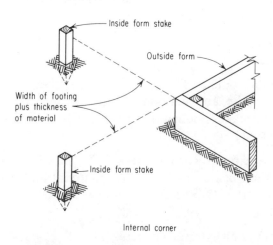

FIGURE 3-14: *Setting inside form corner stakes.*

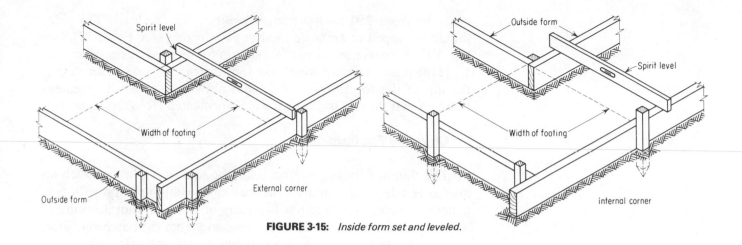

FIGURE 3-15: *Inside form set and leveled.*

Footing-to-Wall Ties

Some means must be provided for tieing together the footing and the wall which will rest on it. One method is to insert short *steel dowels* into the footing concrete along the center line at about 1300 mm intervals, when it is first placed. Dowels should project about 75 to 100 mm above the footing. Another method is to set *bricks on edge* into the fresh concrete, to about one-half their depth at approximately the same intervals. A third method involves setting an *oiled, tapered wooden keyway* form into the top of the footing, suspended in place by straps nailed across the top of the footing form (see Fig. 3-16).

If the keyway thus formed is coated with a thick coating of asphalt before the wall is cast, it will provide a barrier against penetration of moisture between wall and footing.

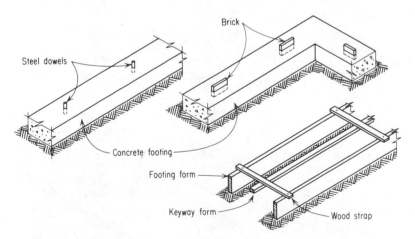

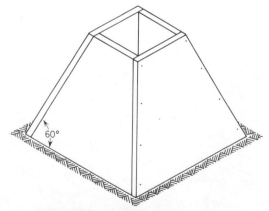

FIGURE 3-16: *Footing-to-wall ties.*

Post Footings

Individual footings, usually square in plan are required for the posts which will support the center girder (see Fig. 3-8). The minimum area of such footings is given in Table 3-1 and the depth will nor-

FIGURE 3-17: *Tapered post footing form.*

mally be from 250 to 300 mm, depending on the load. The sides should be sloped at an angle of about 60 degrees (see Fig. 3-17). See Fig. 3-47 in the section on pier foundation for method of construction.)

If the post is to be of wood, the footing form should be set so that the top of the footing will be 75 mm above the finished basement floor, so that the end of the post will be protected from moisture.

Chimney Footings

The chimney footing will normally be square in plan, of such an area as to adequately support the load of the chimney and with perpendicular sides. The depth will usually be not less than 300 mm. It must be isolated from the other footings and from the basement floor, so that any settlement which takes place will not affect the other structural members.

Bearing Wall Footing

In place of the conventional center girder, supported by posts, it is common practice to use a *bearing wall,* normally made of a 38 × 140 mm wood frame (see Chapter 4 for framing details).

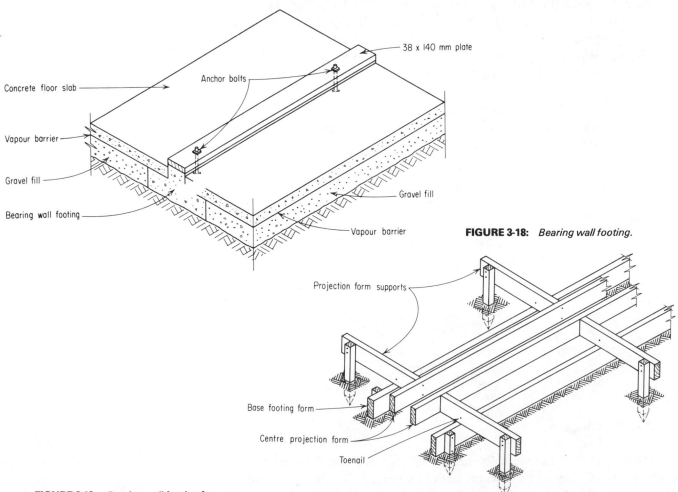

FIGURE 3-18: *Bearing wall footing.*

FIGURE 3-19: *Bearing wall footing forms.*

The wall is supported on a continuous footing, similar in dimensions to the outside wall footings but with a raised center portion, to keep the bottom of the bearing wall plate above the level of the basement floor (see Fig. 3-18).

The bottom part of the form is similar to that used for sidewall footings, while the center section is formed by suspending a narrow form the same width as the bearing wall (see Fig. 3-19).

In residential construction, loads are seldom heavy enough that reinforcement is necessary in the footings. But other types of light construction may require reinforced footings and, in such cases, the reinforcement should be in the form of *deformed rods* with hooked ends, placed *across the width* of the footing. There should be about 75 mm of concrete below the reinforcement and the ends of the hooks should not be closer than 25 mm to the side form (see Fig. 3-20). Post footings are reinforced in the same manner, except that in some cases, two layers of bars may be placed, to run at right angles to one another —*two-way reinforcement.*

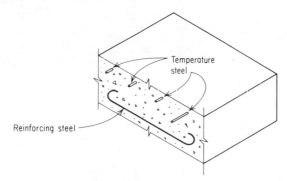

FIGURE 3-20:   *Reinforced footing.*

Wall Forms

When the footing concrete has hardened and at least partially cured, the forms are removed and the job is ready for the erection of wall forms. There are many methods of building them and here only a few of the well-known ones will be discussed.

Wall forms all contain the same basic features, although they may vary as to the details of construction and hardware required. The main components include a *framework* to support the *sheathing* which will give the concrete its desired shape. The frame is stiffened and aligned by horizontal *walers,* which, in turn, are supported by *bracing.* The two sides of the form are fastened together by a system of *ties* and are held at their proper spacing by *spreaders* (see Fig. 3-21).

Framed Panel Forms

One of the most common methods of wall forming involves the use of reusable sections or *panels,* fastened together to form a complete wall. Panels are made with a 38 × 89 mm frame, faced with 15 or 18 mm plywood. Common panel sizes are 600 × 2400 and 1200 ×

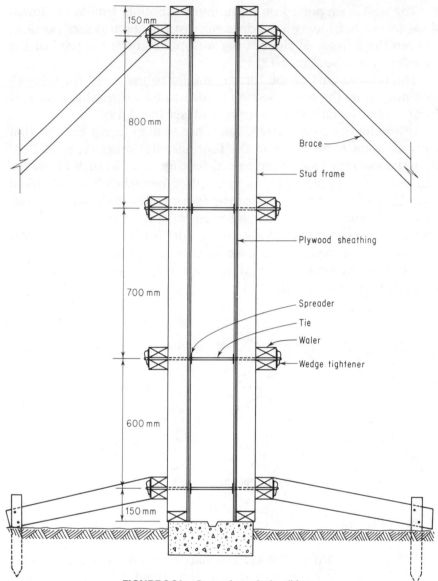

FIGURE 3-21: *Parts of a typical wall form.*

2400 mm (see Fig. 3-22); odd sizes may be made as required to fill spaces not accommodated by the regular panels.

Panels are held together, *edge to edge,* to form a continuous wall by *nailing,* by *bolts* or by *panel ties* and *wedges* (see Fig. 3-23).

Form Ties

The inner and outer walls of forms must be tied together to produce a concrete wall which will be the proper thickness and this is done by means of *form ties*. A number of types are in common use, including *rod ties, bolt ties, bar ties,* and *wire ties* (see Fig. 3-24).

The rod and bolt ties illustrated in Fig. 3-24 are intended for use in forms in which the ties span the wall thickness plus sheathing, panel frame, and walers on each side (see Fig. 3-25), while the bar

68

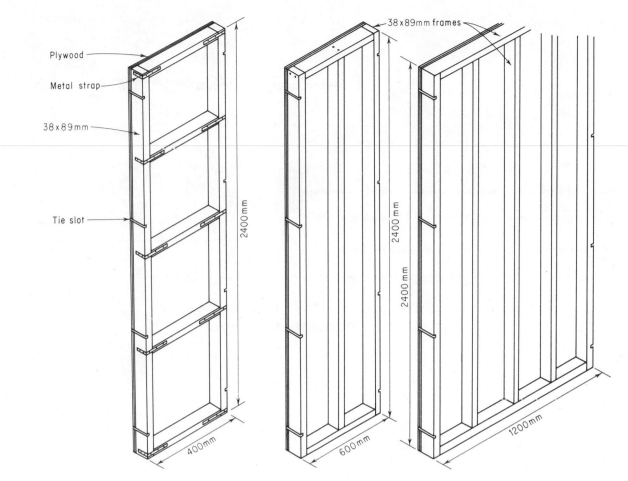

FIGURE 3-22: *Typical form panels.*

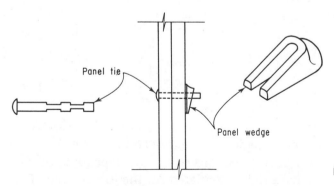

FIGURE 3-23: *Tying panels edge to edge.*

and wire ties are intended for forms in which the ties span the wall thickness and sheathing only.

Corner Forming

Careful construction at form corners is of particular importance because the corners are potential points of weakness in the form. One method is to build interior and exterior corner sections of such dimensions that regular 600 mm or 1200 mm panels may be used, inside

69

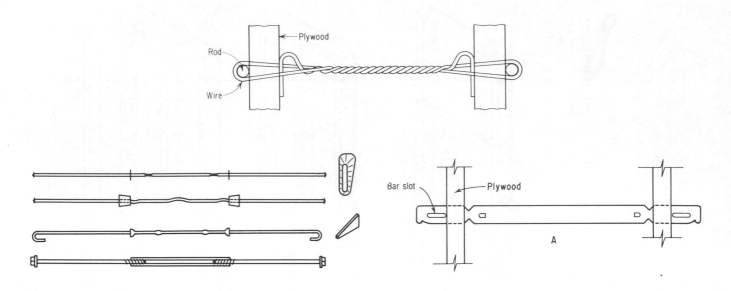

FIGURE 3-24: *Typical form ties.*

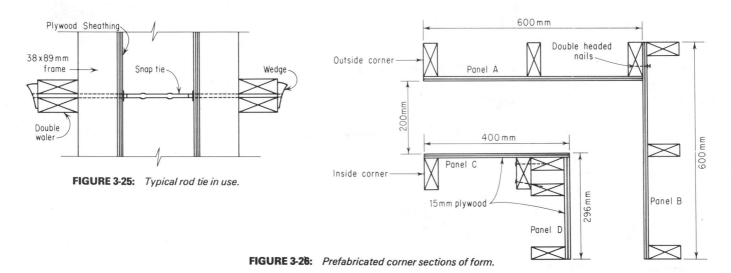

FIGURE 3-25: *Typical rod tie in use.*

FIGURE 3-26: *Prefabricated corner sections of form.*

and out, when continued from the corner sections. Figure 3-26 illustrates such corner panels, made to form a 200 mm thick wall.

Dimensions of these corner sections will vary, depending on the wall thickness and will have to be calculated for the job at hand. The corners are locked in position by overlapping the outside walers and either pinning them together or nailing on vertical blocking (see Fig. 3-27).

Panel Erection

When wall forms are to be built by the panel method, the first step is to prefabricate and oil the panels. The procedure is as follows:

1. Check the plan to determine the outside dimensions of the

70

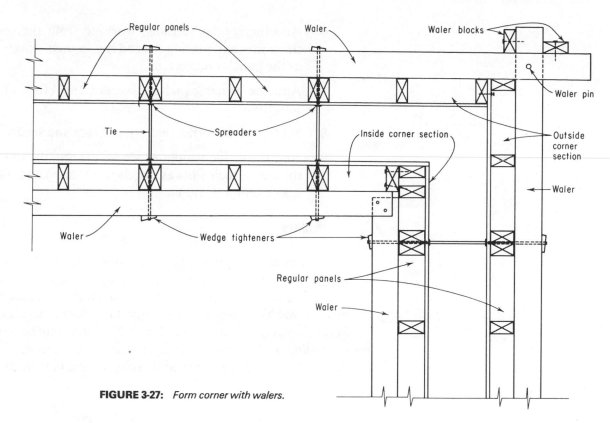

FIGURE 3-27: *Form corner with walers.*

foundation walls, calculate the number of regular 600 or 1200 mm panels that can be used and build them.

2. Calculate the width of any odd-sized panel required and make two, one for the outside and one for the inside wall.

3. Make up inside and outside corner sections as required for the designated wall thickness (see Fig. 3-26).

4. Snap a chalk line on the footing at the location of the outside of the foundation wall.

5. Set the outside corner sections in place, with the inside face of the sheathing to the line, nail them together and secure them to the footing with *concrete nails* or *powder-driven pins* through the bottom plate (see Fig. 3-28) or with *stakes, braces,* and *wedges* against the outside of the plate.

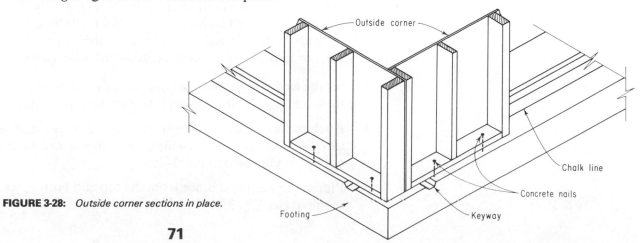

FIGURE 3-28: *Outside corner sections in place.*

71

6. Add the regular sections, working from the corners toward the center and placing the rod ties in their slots (see Fig. 3-22), as the panels are erected.

7. Add the center panel and secure and brace all panels temporarily.

8. Set the inside corner sections in place and secure them.

9. Add the inside regular sections, placing the opposite ends of the ties in their slots as panels are erected and, lastly, add the inside center sections.

Walers

Walers are horizontal members (see Fig. 3-21), usually 38 × 89 or 38 × 140 mm, depending on the size of the wall, placed on the outside of the form walls to keep them straight. There will normally be *four double walers* on a 2400 mm high, 200 mm thick wall, spaced approximately as indicated in Fig. 3-21. They may be held in place by *toenailing* to the panel studs or by using *waler brackets,* as illustrated in Fig. 3-29. The procedure for placing walers may be as follows:

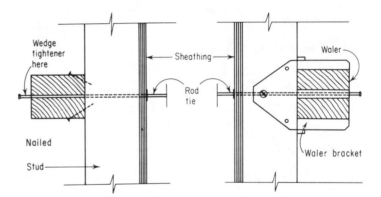

FIGURE 3-29:   *Double walers secured to form panels.*

1. If waler brackets are being used, locate them in their proper places.

2. Set the two sections of each waler in place, one at a time, either in the waler brackets or by toenailing to the studs. Allow the ends of outside walers to project at the corners far enough to overlap the ends of those on adjacent walls (see Fig. 3-27).

3. Set the wedge tighteners over the tie ends and drive them tight, thus drawing the inside form into its proper position.

4. Anchor the overlapping waler ends together, either by *nailing* through the ends or by nailing on *vertical blocking* in the poisitions indicated in Fig. 3-27.

5. Plumb the walls and brace from the top and bottom walers as required (see Fig. 3-21).

Tie Spacing

The spacing of ties in the form depends on a number of factors, including the designated safe load of the tie, the thickness and type of form sheathing, the size and spacing of studs, the size of walers, the vertical rate of placement of concrete and the temperature of the concrete and atmosphere. Table 3-2 indicates the horizontal and vertical spacing of ties under a variety of these conditions.

TABLE 3-2: *Snap tie spacing table*

	H	V	Sheathing	Studs	Wales
	800 mm	750 mm	15 mm plywood	38 × 89 @ 400 mm o.c.	Dbl 38 × 89
			19 mm sheathing	38 × 89 @ 475 mm o.c.	
1360 kg	600 mm	750 mm	as above	38 × 89 @ 350 mm o.c.	
			as above	38 × 89 @ 425 mm o.c.	Dbl 38 × 89
	600 mm	600 mm	as above	38 × 89 @ 325 mm o.c.	Dbl 38 × 89
			as above	38 × 89 @ 400 mm o.c.	
	800 mm	800 mm	15 mm plywood	38 × 89 @ 350 mm o.c.	Dbl 64 × 89
			19 mm sheathing	38 × 89 @ 400 mm o.c.	
	800 mm	675 mm	as above	38 × 89 @ 325 mm o.c.	Dbl 64 × 89
2668 kg			as above	38 × 89 @ 400 mm o.c.	
	750 mm	600 mm	as above	38 × 89 @ 300 mm o.c.	Dbl 64 × 89
			as above	38 × 89 @ 350 mm o.c.	
	600 mm	600 mm	as above	38 × 89 @ 300 mm o.c.	Dbl 38 × 89

NOTES: H = horizontal spacing; V = vertical spacing; 1360 kg = tie with a safe load of 1360 kilograms; 2668 kg = tie with a safe load of 2668 kilograms

Rate of placement of concrete in m/hr, with temp (°C) of:					Concrete pressure (kPa)
5°	10°	15°	20°	25°	
400 mm	500 mm	600 mm	700 mm	800 mm	24
600 mm	750 mm	900 mm	1050 mm	1200 mm	32
800 mm	1000 mm	1200 mm	1400 mm	1600 mm	40
650 mm	825 mm	1000 mm	1150 mm	1325 mm	35
825 mm	1025 mm	1250 mm	1450 mm	1650 mm	41.5
1025 mm	1275 mm	1550 mm	1800 mm	2050 mm	50
1325 mm	1625 mm	2000 mm	2325 mm	2675 mm	62

Unframed Panel Forms

Another commonly used forming system involves the use of 18 mm *plywood panels without any framework, ties* with loops or slots in their ends and *rods or bars* which are inserted through the tie ends on the outside of the forms. Single *walers* are used to align the forms. The bar and wire ties shown in Fig. 3-24 are commonly used in this type of form.

Panels are held together at the corners by a vertical rod running through a series of metal straps with looped ends, which are bolted or screwed along the panel edges, as illustrated in Fig. 3-30.

The erection of a wall form by this method is quite simple. First, the plywood panels are slotted to receive the tie ends. The number of ties required will depend on the rate of placement and the temperature but commonly accepted tie spacings for a 1200 mm rate of placement at 21 °C are as follows:

For a 600 × 2400 mm panel, the *two* end slots are 200 mm from the top and bottom of the panel and 150 mm from the edges. The remainder are in line, 500 mm o.c.

For a 1200 × 2400 mm panel, the *three* end slots are spaced 400 mm o.c., 200 mm from top and bottom and 200 mm from the edges. The remainder are in line, 400 mm o.c. All panels are treated with oil or other form coating.

The panels are erected as follows:

1. Snap a chalk line on the footing 19 mm outside the foundation wall line.

2. Nail a 38 × 89 mm plate to the footing on that line with concrete nails.

3. Hinge the outside corner panels together with a rod and stand them in place.

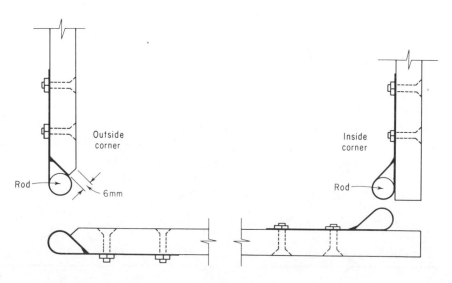

FIGURE 3-30: *Corner straps for plywood forms.*

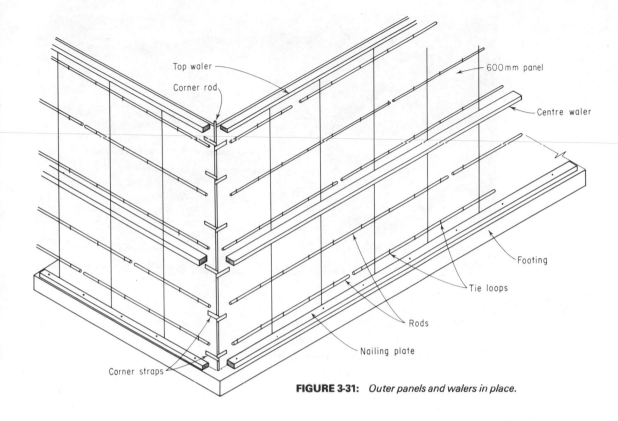

Top waler
Corner rod
600mm panel
Centre waler
Footing
Tie loops
Rods
Nailing plate
Corner straps

FIGURE 3-31: *Outer panels and walers in place.*

4. Nail them to the plate with 50 mm nails and plumb and brace them temporarily.

5. Set all the outside panels in place and nail two 38 × 89 mm members to them horizontally, one at the top and one at the center (see Fig. 3-31).

6. Place the ties in the slots and insert the rods or bars as shown in Fig. 3-31.

7. Put inside corners together and set them in place, using temporary wooden spreaders to maintain proper spacing.

8. Place the remainder of the inside panels, guiding the tie ends through the slots as each is erected.

9. Insert the inside rods or bars.

10. Finally, align the outside form and brace it as required from the two single walers.

Prefabricated Forms

A number of types of prefabricated forms are in common use for light construction. One consists of sections or *panels* made with steel frames and sheathed with plywood (see Fig. 3-32). Sections are made in various widths and heights, with special pieces to form corners and pilasters. The units are held together by a system of bar ties and

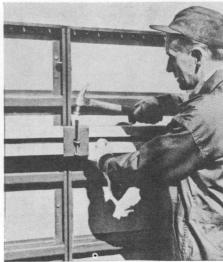

wedges which give the completed form great rigidity. A minimum of walers and bracing is required with this type of form.

Another prefabricated forming system is made entirely of steel. Again, a variety of pieces is available, including standard 600 mm wide wall sections, 1200 mm high, inside and outside corners, angle corners, radius corners, inside fillets, flexible panels for odd-sized spaces, insert angles, spreader ties, spreader tie pins, plate clamps and aligner clamps. Again, as illustrated in Fig. 3-33, a minimum of walers and bracing is necessary.

Girder Pocket Form

In designs in which the floor frame is to be built on top of the foundation (box sill) it is necessary to provide a pocket in two opposite foundation walls, in which the ends of the center girder may

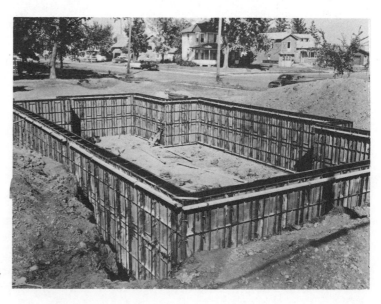

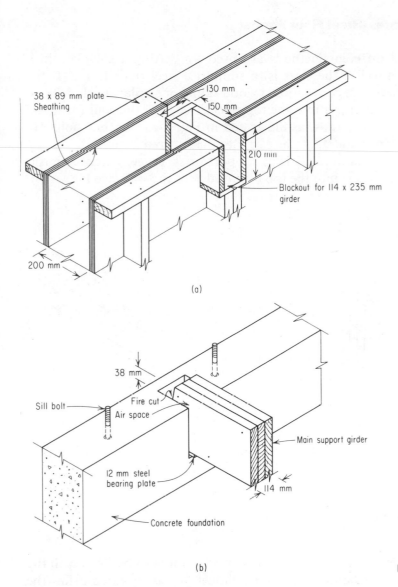

(a)

(b)

FIGURE 3-34: *Girder pocket in concrete foundation.*

rest (see Fig. 3-34b). It is formed by a box, wide enough to allow for an air space around the end of the girder (see Fig. 3-34a) and deep enough to allow for a 12 mm bearing plate under the end of the girder and for the top of the girder to be 38 mm above the top of the foundation wall.

Still Plate Bolts (Wood Floor Frame)

Also, in cases where box sill construction is used, the floor frame must be anchored to the foundation walls. This is done by bolting a 38 × 140 or 38 × 186 mm *sill plate* to the top of the foundation and nailing the floor frame to it. The anchors are 15 mm bolts, spaced approximately 1200 mm o.c., set into the concrete (see Fig. 3-34b) to hold the sill plate in position. They may be set after the concrete has been placed and before it has hardened or they may be suspended from wood straps nailed across the top of the form before concrete is placed.

77

Sill Plates (Steel Floor Frame)

Several different methods are used for setting a sill plate in a foundation wall if the plate is to support a steel floor frame. If the building is to have conventional wood siding or similar finish, a 38 × 89 mm sill plate is set into the top *outside* edge of the wall form and held in place by straps, as illustrated in Fig. 3-35. Anchor bolts are suspended from the sill, to be cast into the concrete.

If the foundation wall is to support brick veneer exterior finish, the sill plate is cast into the top *inside* edge of the wall (see Fig. 3-36).

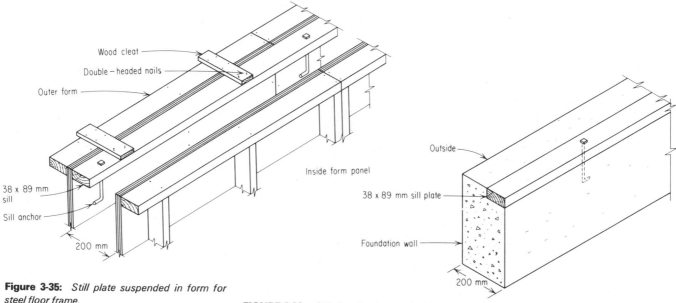

Figure 3-35: *Still plate suspended in form for steel floor frame.*

FIGURE 3-36: *Sill plate in place on inside edge of wall.*

The design may call for the top of steel joists to be flush with the top of the foundation. The sill plate must then be *recessed* below the top of the wall by the depth of the joists (see Fig. 3-37).

Steel Joists Pockets

Another method of setting steel joists flush with the top of the foundation wall is to provide pockets for the joist ends, as illustrated in Fig. 3-38. Pockets should project into the wall about one-half its width, should be 48–50 mm wide and as deep as the depth of joist, commonly 140 mm. Anchor bolts are located in the wall to tie down the subfloor and the sole plate.

"Cast-in" Wood Floor Frame

One of the most common methods of anchoring the floor frame to the foundation is to use the *cast-in joist* system. Instead of resting on top of the foundation, the ends of the floor joists and the girder ends are embedded in the concrete (see Fig. 3-39).

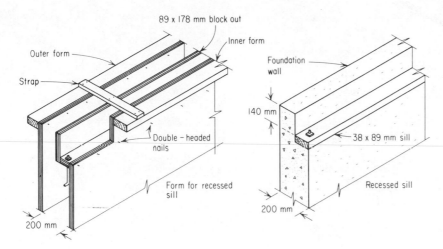

FIGURE 3-37: *Recessed sill plate for steel floor frame.*

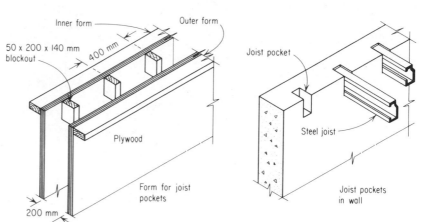

FIGURE 3-38: *Steel joists recessed in top of foundation.*

As a result, the girder and floor joists must be set in place before concrete is placed. The procedure is as follows:

1. Treat the ends of the girder and one end of each joist with wood preservative.

2. Cut notches in two opposite inside wall forms, the width and depth of the girder and nail a support block at the bottom of each notch (see Fig. 3-39a).

3. Cut a *fire cut* (see Fig. 3-39a) at each end of the girder and set it in place, with at least 25 mm clearance between the ends and the outer form. Support the girder between walls with posts as required.

4. Lay out the joists with one end resting on the center girder and the other on the wall forms.

5. Lay off the header joists according to the specified joist centers and nail the joists to them at these locations (see Fig. 3-40).

6. Position the joist assembly so that (a) the outer face of the header joists is flush with the inner face of the outside form or

79

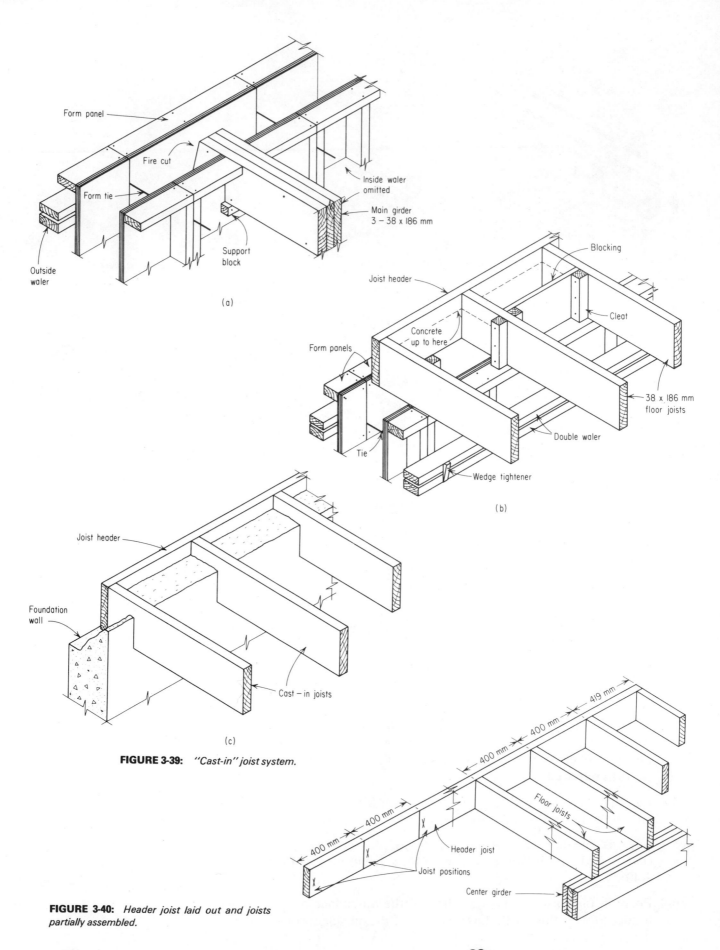

FIGURE 3-39: *"Cast-in" joist system.*

FIGURE 3-40: *Header joist laid out and joists partially assembled.*

80

(b) the outside face of the header joists is *set in* the thickness of the exterior sheathing (see Fig. 3-39b). Nail 50 mm cleats to the sides of the joists, as illustrated in Fig. 3-39b.

7. Nail *blocking* inside the cleats, flush with the inner face of the form sheathing.

"Cast-in" Steel Floor Frame

Steel joists may be "cast-in" in much the same way as wood ones except that steel joist ends are let into the inside form, as shown in Fig. 3-41. Wood or polystyrene blocks are fitted into the ends of the joists where they protrude through the form, to prevent concrete from flowing out through the opening.

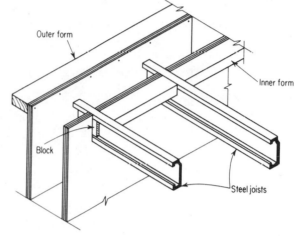

FIGURE 3-41: *Steel joists cast in.*

Door and Window Openings

Openings for doors and windows may be blocked out in two ways. One method is to secure the door or window *frame* into the form in its correct position. Wood frames must be made to coincide with the wall thickness and metal frames are produced to fit various wall thicknesses. Wood frames should have *keys* secured to their outside surface so that they will not be able to move in the wall (see Fig. 3-42).

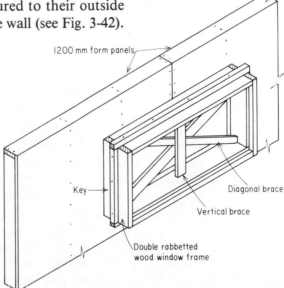

FIGURE 3-42: *Wood window frame secured to outside form panels.*

Wood frames must also be braced diagonally, horizontally, and vertically so that the pressure of the concrete will not change their shape during placing.

Another method of forming openings is to set *rough bucks* into the form. A rough buck is a frame made from 38 mm material, with *outside dimensions* equal to those of the frame to be used. *Wedge-shaped keys* are nailed to the outside of the buck as illustrated in Fig. 3-43. After the concrete is placed and hardened and the forms removed, the rough buck is also removed, leaving the key embedded in the concrete. The door or window frame is then inserted into the opening and held in place by nailing it to the key.

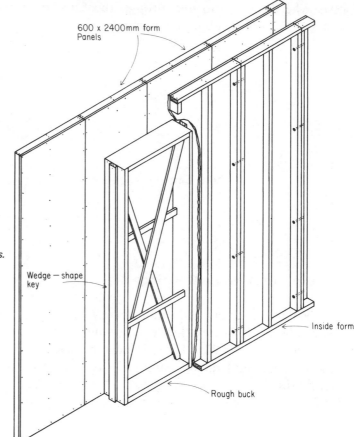

FIGURE 3-43: *Rough buck for door secured in forms.*

CONCRETE SURFACE FOUNDATION

A surface foundation also consists of concrete or concrete block walls but they extend into the earth only far enough to reach below the frost line. The earth may or may not be excavated from within the walls and, in many cases, the space is not great enough to be livable. A concrete floor may or may not be included, depending on the proposed use of the space. The walls rest on footings, similar to those used for full basement foundations.

Forms for a concrete surface foundation will be the same as those for a full basement, except that the wall forms normally will not be as high. The footing forms may be built in trenches, rather than in a full scale excavation, as illustrated in Fig. 3-44, but otherwise, procedures will be very similar to those described for full basement forms.

The only openings in the wall will usually be *crawl space* openings, which will be formed in the same way as those for doors or windows.

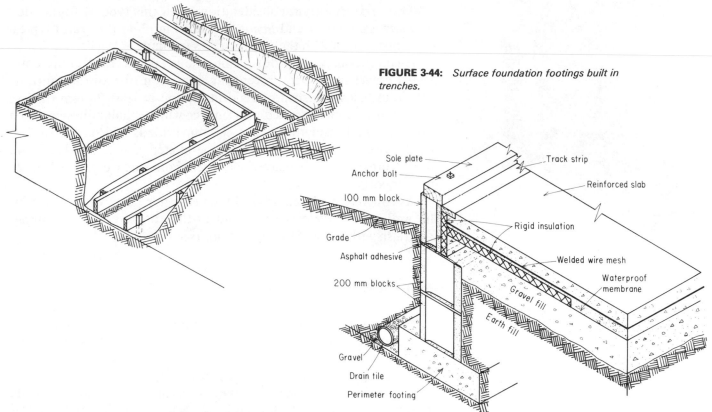

FIGURE 3-44: *Surface foundation footings built in trenches.*

FIGURE 3-45: *Typical slab-on-ground foundation.*

SLAB-ON-GROUND FOUNDATION

A slab-on-ground foundation consists of perimeter footings and stub walls, surrounding a reinforced concrete slab cast directly on the ground. The walls will extend down only to solid, undisturbed soil and, where possible, below frost level (see Fig. 3-45). However, in areas of deep frost penetration, it may be impractical to extend the footings down to below the frost line and instead, the footing is placed on a well-drained gravel pad at least 125 mm in depth.

The slab must not be less than 95 mm in thickness, supported by at least 125 mm of clean, coarse, well-packed gravel or similar granular material.

Forms for the footings for the perimeter bearing wall will be identical to those for a surface foundation and normally will be built in a shallow trench.

Walls may be cast-in-place concrete or concrete blocks and, in many cases, may not exceed 400 to 800 mm in height. If concrete walls are specified, forms for them will be similar to those for other concrete walls except for the height. Anchor bolts must be inserted into the top of the wall to secure the plate on which the walls will be erected.

FIGURE 3-46: *Power compactor at work (Courtesy Wacker Co.).*

When the walls are complete, the earth within them is leveled and compacted to within approximately 220 mm of the top of the wall. A layer of gravel is added and compacted to a level within 95 to 100 mm from the top. Compaction is usually carried out by a power-driven compactor, similar to that shown in Fig. 3-46.

Two very important considerations with this type of foundation are *moisture control* and *insulation* and Fig. 3-45 illustrates typical slab construction with these two factors in mind.

A continuous waterproof membrane is laid over the entire compacted gravel surface to prevent the migration of moisture into the slab from below. A strip of rigid insulation at least 25 mm thick is applied to the inner exposed wall surface with asphalt adhesive. Then a strip of rigid insulation about 600 mm wide is laid on the surface against the wall around the entire perimeter. Finally, welded wire mesh reinforcement is placed over the whole surface, carried on 20 mm supports.

As concrete is placed around the perimeter, level with the top of the wall, a *tack strip* is embedded in the concrete, with its upper face flush with the surface of the floor (see Fig. 3-45).

PIER FOUNDATION

A pier foundation is one in which the building is constructed on a number of beams, each of which is supported by several *piers* or posts of wood, steel, or masonry, each in turn resting on an individual concrete footing or pad (see Fig. 3-47). Piers are restricted in height to 3 times their least cross-sectional dimension at the base and normally are spaced not more than 3.6 m o.c.

Pier footings should be taken down to below the frost line or placed on well-drained gravel pads.

Forms for pier footings are usually built in individual excavations, square in plan, and may be *rectangular, stepped,* or *tapered.* The footing area is based on the amount of load carried by each one and

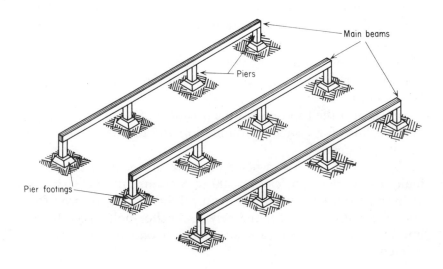

FIGURE 3-47: *Pier foundation.*

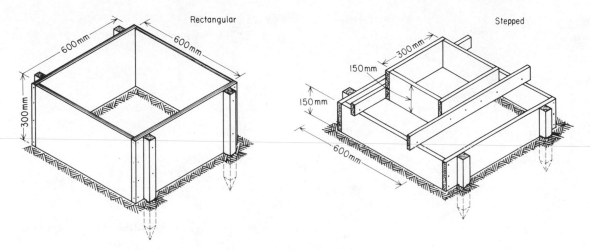

FIGURE 3-48: *Pier footing forms.*

the type of soil on which it rests. The construction of rectangular and stepped footing forms is illustrated in Fig. 3-48, while the tapered form, shaped like that shown in Fig. 3-17, requires some special planning.

Two opposing panels are made the exact dimensions of the footing face, while the other two must be long enough to accommodate the thickness of the form material and the width of the cleats used to hold the sides together (see Fig. 3-49).

There are three angle cuts to be made—a *butt joint cut,* across the edge; a *face angle cut,* across the face; and an *edge bevel,* along the upper and lower edges (see Fig. 3-49). These angles may be laid out by taking figures obtained from a *basic hopper layout* (see Fig. 3-49) and using them in combinations on the tongue and blade of a framing square to lay out the angles. The angles are laid out as follows:

Butt joint angle   —   Use C and D. Mark on D.

Face angle   —   Use A and C. Mark on C.

Edge bevel   —   Use A and B. Mark on A.

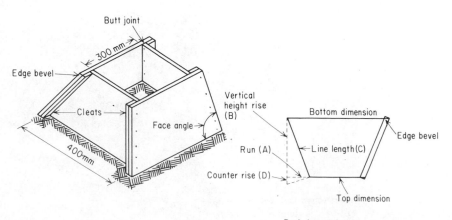

FIGURE 3-49: *Tapered pier footing form.*

Basic hopper layout

85

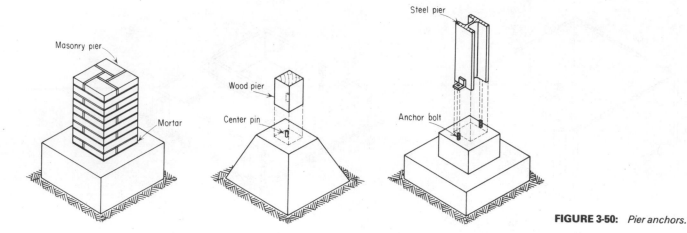

FIGURE 3-50: *Pier anchors.*

Footings which are to support wooden piers should have a *steel pin* set in the center of the top surface to anchor the pier in place (see Fig. 3-50). Steel piers usually require two *anchor bolts,* while the *mortar bond* provides the anchor for masonry piers.

PRESERVED WOOD FOUNDATION

A preserved wood foundation is a complete *wood-frame foundation* system, built with preservative-treated lumber and intended for buildings falling into the light construction category. In this system, all wood exposed to decay hazard is pressure-treated with chemical preservatives which permanently impregnate the wood cells to the degree that makes the wood resistant to attack by decay organisms and termites.

It can be built as a *full basement* foundation (see Fig. 3-51) with a

FIGURE 3-51: *Preserved wood foundation with pressure-treated plank footings. (Courtesy, Council of Forest Industries of B.C.).*

FIGURE 3-52: *Preserved wood surface foundation (Courtesy, Council of Forest Industries of B.C.).*

concrete slab floor, wood sleeper floor or *suspended wood floor* or as a *surface* foundation (see Fig. 3-52) with an excavated crawl space with no floor.

Site Preparation

After the excavation has been completed to the desired level, service and drain lines and a sump, if necessary, are installed and the trenches backfilled and compacted. In some localities, the sump pit may be replaced by a 100 mm perforated, vertical standpipe, at least 600 mm high, surrounded by 375 mm of washed, coarse gravel. The standpipe should extend up through the floor and be capped by a cleanout plug. No drainage system is required for unexcavated crawl spaces, if the final grade inside the crawl space is equal to or higher than the grade outside.

Next, 125 mm of clean gravel is laid on undisturbed soil over an area extending 150 mm beyond the dimensions of the building and leveled. The gravel under all *footing plates* is compacted at least 150 mm beyond the edges of the plates, to provide good bearing for loads.

Footings

Continuous wood footings, consisting of the *wood footing plates* and the *compacted gravel bed* beneath them, are the most practical and economical for this type of foundation, since they eliminate the building of forms and placement of concrete (see Fig. 3-51).

Wood footing plates are placed directly on the leveled, compacted gravel bed, butted together at end joints and wall intersections. The treated lumber can be ordered in specified lengths to suit the footing layout and members may extend beyond the line of the wall at corners, to avoid the cutting of plates wherever possible. However, if members must be cut, the exposed ends must be thoroughly saturated with wood preservative.

The sizes of plates required for various positions in the layout and conditions of loading, are given in Table 3-3.

TABLE 3-3:   *Wood footing plate sizes (bearing on gravel bed)*

Type of basement floor	Number of floors supported above the basement	Type of exterior finish	Minimum sizes of wood footing plates	
			Supporting exterior walls	Supporting interior walls
Slab	1	Wood	38 × 89	38 × 140
		Brick veneer	38 × 140	38 × 140
	2	Wood	38 × 140	38 × 235
		Brick veneer	38 × 184	38 × 235
Treated wood sleeper or Suspended wood floor	1	Wood	38 × 140	38 × 184
		Brick veneer	38 × 184	38 × 184
	2	Wood	38 × 184	38 × 286
		Brick veneer	38 × 235	38 × 286

(Courtesy Canadian Wood Council)

NOTES: 1. Width of footing plate supporting interior walls which bear on slab floors can be reduced by 50 mm from the values shown if concrete strength is 2017 MPa or greater.
2. Interior wood footing plate supporting only sleeper or suspended floor can be 38 × 89 mm.
3. Width of footing plate should be at least equal to the width of the foundation wall stud.

If continuous concrete footings are used under the wood foundation walls, they are placed on top of the gravel bed to allow drainage under the footing. The width of such concrete footings supporting exterior walls can be 75 mm less than the widths specified in Table 3-1, because wood foundation walls are lighter than conventional concrete walls. Concrete footings supporting interior walls should be the same width as those specified in Table 3-1.

When a girder and posts are used to support the interior loads, rather than a bearing wall, the post footings may be either concrete or preservative-treated wood. Concrete footings will be similar to those in conventional foundations and Fig. 3-53 illustrates the construction of wood post footings for various loading conditions.

Post footings may be set on undisturbed soil below the gravel bed in order to avoid the top of the footings interfering with the basement floor.

Foundation Walls

Wood foundation walls, consisting of a *frame* of *studs* with *single top and bottom plate, sheathed with plywood* and all treated with preservative, may be prefabricated in sections in a shop or completely assembled on site. Where plywood sheets are applied horizontally, *blocking* is required between studs at the plywood joint. In addition, all plywood joints are caulked with sealant (see Fig. 3-54).

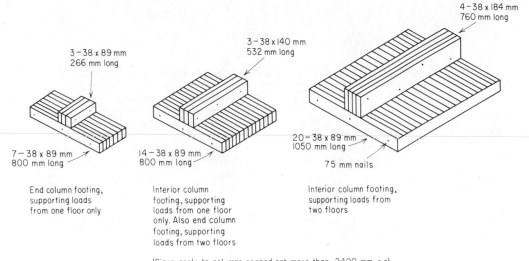

3 – 38 x 89 mm
266 mm long

3 – 38 x 140 mm
532 mm long

4 – 38 x 184 mm
760 mm long

7 – 38 x 89 mm
800 mm long

14 – 38 x 89 mm
800 mm long

20 – 38 x 89 mm
1050 mm long

75 mm nails

End column footing,
supporting loads
from one floor only

Interior column
footing, supporting
loads from one floor
only. Also end column
footing, supporting
loads from two floors

Interior column footing,
supporting loads from
two floors

(Sizes apply to columns spaced not more than 2400 mm o.c)

FIGURE 3-53: *Wood post footings.*

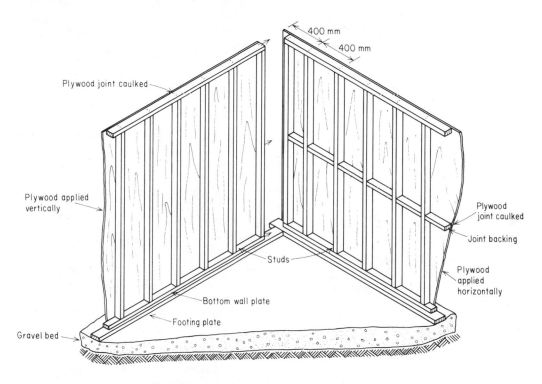

400 mm

400 mm

Plywood joint caulked

Plywood applied
vertically

Plywood
joint caulked

Joint backing

Plywood
applied
horizontally

Studs

Bottom wall plate

Footing plate

Gravel bed

FIGURE 3-54: *Typical preserved wood foundation walls.*

For full basement construction, walls are 2400 mm high for slab
and sleeper floors and 3000 mm high for suspended wood floors (see
section on floors, page 94). The size and spacing of studs depends
on the *building loads, species* and *grade of lumber* and the *height of
backfill* which, in turn, depend on the depth of the excavation. Table
3-4 gives the required stud size and spacing for foundation walls for
basements with slab and sleeper floors and Table 3-5, the same information for basements with suspended wood floors.

TABLE 3-4: *Foundation wall stud sizes (slab and sleeper floors)*

Type of house	Lumber species	Lumber grade	38 × 89 @ 400	38 × 140 @ 300	38 × 140 @ 400	38 × 184 @ 400
			Backfill heights (mm)			
One-story with conventional siding	Douglas fir	No. 1	1275	2250	1950	2250
	Larch (N)	No. 2	1125	2100	1950	2250
	Hem–Fir	No. 1	1050	2025	1725	2100
	(N)	No. 2	900	1800	1725	2100
	Hem–Tam	No. 1	975	2175	1875	1875
	(N)	No. 2	825	1950	1875	1875
	S–P–F	No. 1	900	1875	1725	2025
	(N)	No. 2	675	1725	1650	2025
	E. white pine,	No. 1	675	1800	1575	1875
	Red pine	No. 2	450	1650	1575	1875
One-story with brick veneer or 2 story with conventional siding	Douglas fir	No. 1	—	2250	1950	2250
	Larch (N)	No. 2	—	2025	1950	2250
	Hem–Fir	No. 1	—	1950	1725	2100
	(N)	No. 2	—	1725	1650	2025
	Hem–Tam	No. 1	—	2100	1875	2175
	(N)	No. 2	—	1875	1800	2175
	S–P–F	No. 1	—	1875	1725	2025
	(N)	No. 2	—	1650	1575	1950
	E. white pine,	No. 1	—	1800	1575	1875
	Red pine	No. 2	—	1575	1500	1875
Two-story with brick veneer on one and conventional siding on the other	Douglas fir	No. 1	—	2275	1950	2250
	Larch (N)	No. 2	—	2025	1875	2250
	Hem–Fir	No. 1	—	1950	1725	2100
	(N)	No. 2	—	1725	1575	2025
	Hem–Tam	No. 1	—	2025	1875	2175
	(N)	No. 2	—	1800	1725	2175
	S–P–F	No. 1	—	1800	1725	2025
	(N)	No. 2	—	1650	1500	1875
	E white pine,	No. 1	—	1725	1575	1875
	Red pine	No. 2	—	1575	1425	1800

NOTE: Backfill height measured from bottom edge of foundation wall sheathing.

TABLE 3-5: *Foundation wall stud sizes (suspended wood floors)*

Type of house	Lumber species	Lumber grade	38 × 89 @ 400	38 × 140 @ 300	38 × 140 @ 400	38 × 184 @ 400
			Backfill heights (mm)			
1 story with conventional siding	Douglas fir Larch (N)	No. 1	2100	2850	2850	2850
		No. 2	1725	2775	2700	2850
	Hem–Fir (N)	No. 1	1500	2700	2625	2850
		No. 2	1200	2475	2400	2850
	Hem–Tam (N)	No. 1	1575	2850	2775	2850
		No. 2	1125	2625	2550	2850
	S–P–F (N)	No. 1	1200	2625	2550	2850
		No. 2	900	2400	2325	2850
	E. white pine, Red pine	No. 1	1050	2550	2475	2850
		No. 2	750	2400	2325	2775
1 story with brick veneer or 2 story with conventional siding	Douglas fir Larch (N)	No. 1	—	2850	2850	
		No. 2	—	2700	2625	2850
	Hem–Fir (N)	No. 1	—	2625	2550	2850
		No. 2	—	2475	2400	2850
	Hem–Tam (N)	No. 1	—	2775	2700	2850
		No. 2	—	2550	2475	2850
	S–P–F (N)	No. 1	—	2550	2475	2850
		No. 2	—	2400	2325	2850
	E. white pine, Red pine	No. 1	—	2475	2400	2850
		No. 2	—	2325	2250	2700
2 story with brick veneer on one and conventional siding on the other	Douglas fir Larch (N)	No. 1	—	2850	2850	2850
		No. 2	—	2700	2625	2850
	Hem–Fir (N)	No. 1	—	2625	2550	2850
		No. 2	—	2400	2325	2850
	Hem–Tam (N)	No. 1	—	2775	2700	2850
		No. 2	—	2550	2400	2850
	S–P–F (N)	No. 1	—	2550	2475	2850
		No. 2	—	2325	2250	2775
	E. white pine Red pine	No. 1	—	2475	2400	2850
		No. 2	—	2325	2175	2700

NOTE: Backfill height measured from bottom edge of foundation wall sheathing.

The thickness of plywood used for sheathing depends on the *direction of face grain*—face grain parallel or perpendicular to the studs—the *stud spacing* and the *height of backfill.* The plywood thickness required, based on these factors, is given in Table 3-6.

TABLE 3-6: *Foundation wall plywood sheathing thickness (unsanded)*

Face grain direction	Stud spacing (mm)	Plywood thickness		
		12 mm	15 mm	18 mm
		Height of backfill (mm)		
Perpendicular to studs	300	2850	2850	2850
	400	1950	2400	2850
Parallel to studs	300	1950	2550	2850
	400	1200	1500	2250

(Courtesy Canadian Wood Council)

Plywood may be fastened to the frame with common nails or with 14 or 16 gauge staples, minimum length, 50 mm. Nails and 14 gauge staples are spaced 150 mm o.c. along outside edges and 300 mm o.c. along intermediate supports, while 16 gauge staples are spaced at 100 mm o.c. on outside edges and 200 mm o.c. on intermediate supports. Staples should be driven with the crown parallel to the framing.

Openings in foundation walls are framed in the same manner as those for conventional wall frames (see Fig. 5-9) page 142). Nailing requirements at openings are indicated in Fig. 3-55.

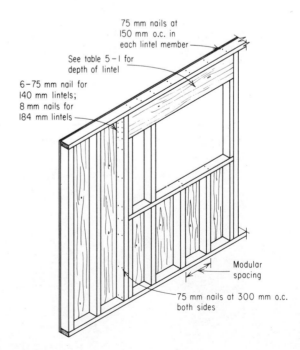

75 mm nails at 150 mm o.c. in each lintel member

See table 5–1 for depth of lintel

6–75 mm nail for 140 mm lintels; 8 mm nails for 184 mm lintels

Modular spacing

75 mm nails at 300 mm o.c. both sides

FIGURE 3-55: *Nailing requirements at openings in preserved wood foundation wall.*

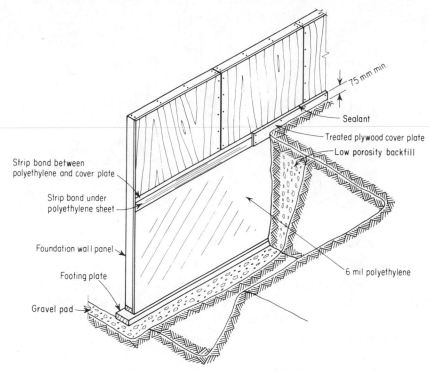

FIGURE 3-56: *Polyethylene moisture barrier on exterior of preserved wood foundation wall.*

All joints between plywood panels below grade are sealed by bedding the plywood edges in a sealant applied to the face of the framing member or by leaving a 3 mm gap between plywood edges and caulking it with a sealant.

The exterior of foundation walls below grade is also covered with a 6 mil polyethylene membrane, extending from a minimum of 75 mm above the finished grade line to the bottom of the footing plate, where it should be cut off. The membrane *should not* extend under the gravel pad or under the footing plate.

The polyethylene is cemented to the sheathing at the top edge by a 150 mm band of adhesive (see Fig. 3-56). It is also protected at the grade level by a 300 mm wide strip of treated plywood, set with its top edge at least 75 mm above the finished grade line. A strip of sealant about 75 mm wide is applied to the top inside face of the ply-wood before it is nailed to the foundation wall.

Concrete Slab Floors

Concrete slab floors used in conjunction with wood foundations are similar to those used for conventional basement floors. Basically, they consist of a minimum 95 mm concrete slab, placed over a 125 mm gravel bed, with a 6 mil polyethylene moisture barrier between con-crete and gravel.

In order to transmit lateral soil loads from the wall into the slab, the top edge of the slab must butt directly against the bottom ends of the wall studs. This may be done by fastening a continuous, treated

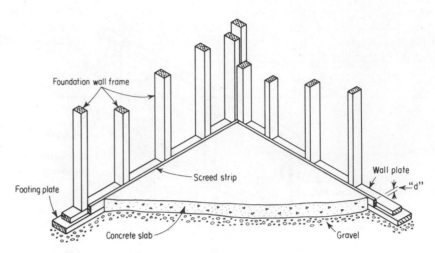

FIGURE 3-57: *Concrete slab floor in wood foundation basement.*

wooden strip, along the lower edge of the foundation wall (see Fig. 3-57) wide enough that distance "d" will be from 25 to 45 mm, depending on stud spacing and depth of backfill. This strip can be used as a screed to level the concrete slab and will remain in place after the concrete has hardened.

Wood Sleeper Floors

Wood sleeper floors (see Fig. 3-58) are damp-proofed by laying 4 mil, 1200 mm wide strips of polyethylene, overlapped 100 mm at the edges—not a continuous membrane—over the leveled gravel bed.

The 38 × 89 mm treated wood *sleepers* are placed on the polyethylene cover at spacings of from 1200 to 1800 mm, depending on the depth of the floor joists to be used. Then floor joists, 38 × 89 mm or wider, span between the footing plates and the sleepers with at least 38 mm bearing on the footing plate. To achieve this, it may be necessary to use wider footing plates than the design requires.

Joists are placed in line with foundation wall studs (see Fig. 3-58)

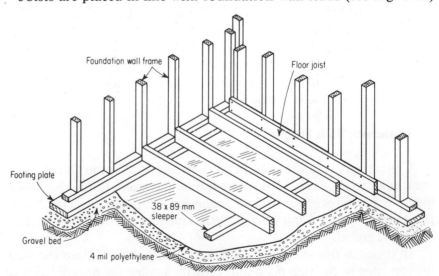

FIGURE 3-58: *Wood floor frame on wood sleepers.*

94

and butt in line over the sleeper supports. They are toenailed to the sleepers and to the wall studs with at least two 75 mm nails at each junction.

Plywood subflooring is installed over the floor joists and acts as a diaphragm to resist lateral earth loads. For thickness of plywood required, see Chapter 4, page 132.

To ensure the proper transfer of lateral soil loads from the *end* walls to the floor frame and plywood subfloor, it is necessary to provide additional nailing and, in some cases, additional framing. If the depth of backfill 1500 mm or less, the frame illustrated in Fig. 3-58 is sufficient, with the plywood nailed to the end joist with at least 50 mm nails at 150 mm centers (see Fig. 3-59a). If the backfill depth exceeds 1500 mm, an extra 38 × 89 mm member (a stiffener) is nailed to the end joist and 2 rows of 50 mm nails are used, at 75 mm centers (see Fig. 3-59b).

Suspended Wood Floors

Joists for a suspended wood floor are supported above the gravel base on a continuous 38 × 89 mm *ledger* at the foundation walls and by a low bearing wall at the inner end (see Fig. 3-60). Joist size and spacing is in accordance with Table 4-4, page 116.

Joists are placed directly in line with the foundation wall studs and butted in line over the bearing wall (see Fig. 3-60). Plywood subflooring is applied over the joists and nailed as required in the same manner as for sleeper floors. Again, consult, page 132 for plywood thickness.

As was the case with wood sleeper floors, additional framing and

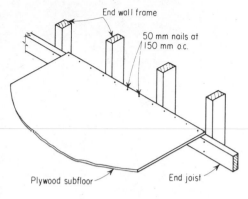

For sleeper floors with height of backfill 1500 mm or less

(a)

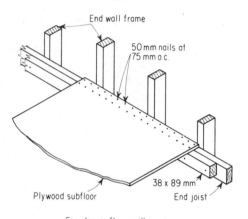

For sleeper floors with height of backfill greater than 1 500 mm
and
for suspended floors with height of backfill 1 950 mm or less

(b)

FIGURE 3-59: *Sleeper floors end nailing and extra framing.*

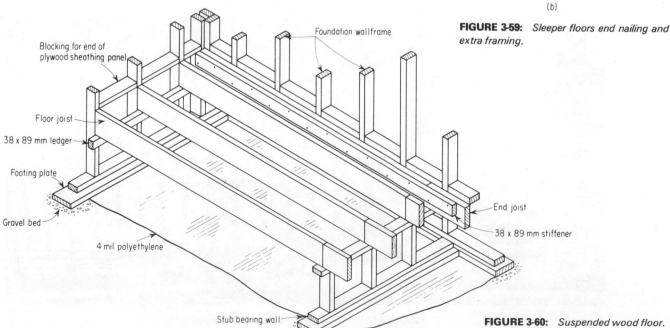

FIGURE 3-60: *Suspended wood floor.*

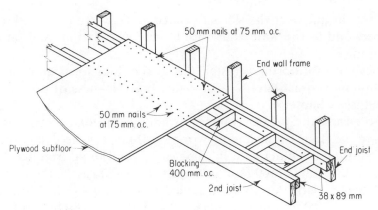

FIGURE 3-61: *Suspended floors end framing and nailing.*

nailing may be required to ensure the proper transfer of lateral soil loads to the floor. If the depth of backfill is 1950 mm or less, the end framing illustrated in Fig. 3-60 is sufficient, with the plywood nailed to the end frame as indicated in Fig. 3-59b. If the depth of backfill exceeds 1950 mm, the extra framing and nailing illustrated in Fig. 3-61 is required.

PRESSURE-TREATED POLE FOUNDATION

A pressure-treated pole foundation consists of two or more rows of wood poles, usually with at least a 125 mm top diameter, which have been *pressure-treated* with wood preservative to render them highly resistant to decay and insect attack.

The poles are set into the earth to a depth of 1200 to 1500 mm, on compacted gravel pads and project above the ground 3 to 5 m to form the frame for the type of building illustrated in Fig. 3-62.

FIGURE 3-62: *Typical pressure-treated pole building.*

Layout

After the site has been leveled off, stakes are driven at the approximate corners, sets of batter boards built around them about 900 mm beyond the outside dimensions of the building and exact dimensions marked on them (see Chapter 2).

The corners are located first and lines run from one to the next (see Fig. 3-63). The corners should be checked for squareness, using the 3–4–5 triangle.

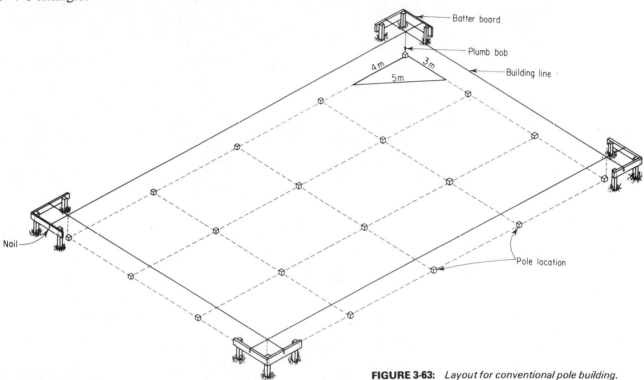

FIGURE 3-63: *Layout for conventional pole building.*

When the outline is square, the positions of all poles are located and holes dug. Holes must have a minimum diameter of 250 mm and preferably should have a 400 mm diameter. The depth of the holes will depend on the type of building and its height. If the building is *clear span,* the holes must be a minimum of 1200 mm deep and if it is clear span with an eave height over 4.2 m, the holes must be 1350 mm deep. For a *conventional* pole building with the eave height not over 3.6 m, holes may be 1050 mm deep.

Erection of Poles

The corner poles should be erected first. If the soil is firm—stiff to medium clay, sand or gravel and dense silt—the pole may be set directly on the bottom of the hole. If the soil is soft, a 250 mm pad of well-compacted coarse gravel should be placed in the hole first, which means that, in these cases, the holes must be made 250 mm deeper. Sufficient backfill is placed in the hole around the pole to keep the butt in place but it should not be tamped at this time.

The two outside faces of the corner poles are plumbed, using a straightedge and spirit level and the poles braced temporarily (see Fig. 3-64). The remainder of the outside poles are erected and aligned to that all those on the perimeter are in line and vertical on the outside face. Interior poles, if any, can now be erected and plumbed.

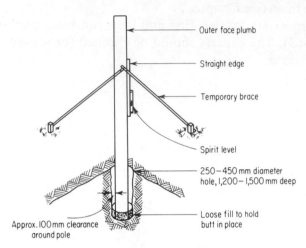

Outer face plumb

Straight edge

Temporary brace

Spirit level

250–450 mm diameter hole, 1,200–1,500 mm deep

Loose fill to hold butt in place

Approx. 100 mm clearance around pole

FIGURE 3-64:   *Corner pole in place.*

Rafter Supports and Rafters

Before any roof construction begins, a level grade line must be run along the bottom of the perimeter poles, from which to measure the rafter support height. Starting at the highest corner, a level line is run around the bottom of the poles, with a nail driven into each one where the level line crosses it.

Roof construction can now proceed as follows:

1. Measure up on each outside pole the designated distance to the outside *rafter support* and below that mark, nail a 38 × 140 mm block, 600 mm long, to the outside face, with 125 mm nails (see Fig. 3-65).

2. Set the outside rafter supports on top of the blocks and nail them to the poles with 125 mm nails. Check to see that the support is level for the length of the building. Supports must project beyond the corner posts for at least 38 mm. The size of the support material will depend on the spacing of poles and the roof load and will range from 38 × 140 to 38 × 235 mm.

3. Where conventional rafters are being used, attach the top end rafter supports to the interior row of poles which is to carry them, at the height designated.

4. Nail knee braces in place from pole to outside rafter support (see Fig. 3-66).

5. Set the rafters in place, starting at one end of the building and nailing the *end rafters* to the outer face of the end poles,

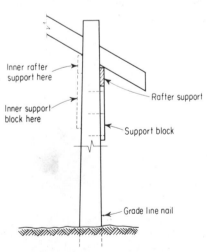

Inner rafter support here

Inner support block here

Rafter support

Support block

Grade line nail

FIGURE 3-65:   *Support blocks in place.*

as they rest on the projecting rafter support. Rafter spacing will usually be 400 or 600 mm and rafters can be secured temporarily by toenailing to the rafter support.

6. After all the rafters are in place, nail the *inside* rafter supports to the poles, keeping them up tight to the bottom edge of the rafters. Use 125 mm nails.

7. Nail on the inside support blocks under the inside supports (see Fig. 3-65).

8. Cut off the tops of the poles in line with the slope of the roof (see Fig. 3-66). Fill and tamp all holes.

9. Nail *rafter ties* (see Fig. 3-66) which fit snugly between inner and outer rafter supports against the sides of rafters.

10. Nail 38 × 140 mm *girts* or *nailers* at 600 mm intervals to the outside of the poles to support the plywood sheathing.

11. Apply plywood roof sheathing and roofing as specified. For a clear span building, trussed rafters will normally be used, prefabricated and raised into position with the aid of some type of mechanical equipment (see Fig. 3-67).

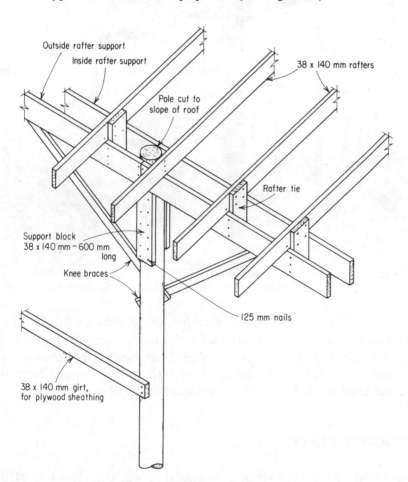

FIGURE 3-66: *Rafter supports and rafters.*

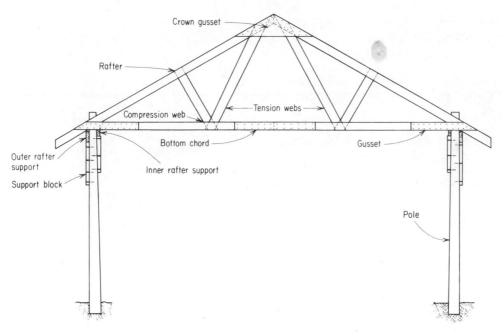

FIGURE 3-67: *Clear span poles with trussed rafters.*

Labels on figure: Crown gusset, Rafter, Compression web, Tension webs, Bottom chord, Gusset, Outer rafter support, Inner rafter support, Support block, Pole

FIGURE 3-68: *Pressure-treated pole building frame (Courtesy, Canadian Inst. of Timber Construction).*

Other styles of roof frame, with less slope, may be used in place of conventional or trussed rafters. One of those alternative systems in illustrated in Fig. 3-68, in which slightly arched roof beams are set on top of the poles and tied in place with *strap anchors*. Note the method used to allow workmen to reach the top of poles.

CONCRETE PLACING

Regardless of the care spent in building forms, the final test of the strength and durability of the foundation being built will lie in the quality of the concrete used. That quality will depend on a number of factors, all of major importance. They include:

1. Clean and well-graded aggregate and properly proportioned fine and coarse aggregate.

2. Clean water; water fit for human consumption is the best test.

3. The amount of water used in the mix per unit of cement—a matter of primary importance. This ratio to a large extent controls the strength of the concerete. The less water used, within limits, the stronger the concrete will be and, conversely, the more water used, the less strength will be achieved. The ratio, expressed in ml of water per kg of cement, will ordinarily vary from 400 to 825 ml per kg.

4. Whether or not *entrained air* is included in the mix. Entrained air consists of thousands of tiny, stable, bubbles of air which are introduced into the fresh concrete to improve the *flowability* of the mix. Air entrainment does, however, result in some reduction in compressive strength.

Table 3-7 indicates the probable compressive strength which will be achieved, using a number of different water/cement ratios, both with and without entrained air.

TABLE 3-7: *Compressive strengths of concrete for various water/cement ratios*

Water/cement ratio (ml per kg of cement)	Probable compressive strength after 28 days (MPa)	
	Nonair-entrained concrete	*Air-entrained concrete*
827	13.8	11.0
752	17.25	13.8
681	20.65	16.5
626	24.0	19.3
571	27.5	22.0
527	31.0	24.8
480	34.5	27.5
445	38.0	30.3
410	41.4	33.0

The concrete may be mixed on the job, delivered ready-mixed from a concrete mixing plant, or delivered from a batching plant, mixed in transit. No matter which method is used, great care must be taken in placing the concrete in the forms.

1. Concrete should not be allowed to drop freely more than 1200 mm. If the height of the form is greater than that, some type of chute is required so that the concrete may be conducted to at least within 1200 mm of the bottom.

2. Concrete should be placed in such a way that it will drop straight down, not bounce from one form face to the other.

3. Place in even layers around the form—don't try to place all in one spot and allow the concrete to flow to its final position.

4. Start placing at the corners and work toward the center of the form. All of these precautions will help to prevent *segregation,* the separation of the aggregates from the water-cement paste.

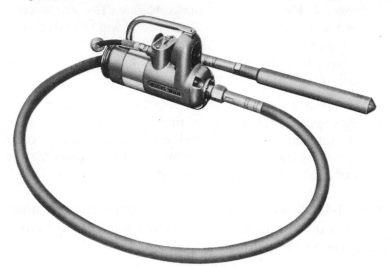

FIGURE 3-69:   *Electric internal vibrator.*

Concrete can best be consolidated in the form by vibration. This may be done either internally or externally. An internal vibrator (see Fig. 3-69) is inserted into the concrete and operated until consolidation has taken place. An external vibrator is operated against the outside of the form. Care must be taken not to over-vibrate, because excess paste will be brought to the top or out to the face of the forms.

Proper curing of the concrete, that is, allowing it to gain its rated strength, is very important. Temperature and moisture conditions control the curing. Concrete cures best at a temperature of about 21 °C and cures very slowly below 5 °C. Moist conditions are required for good curing. If the concrete is allowed to dry out soon after it is placed, it cannot be expected to gain the strength required of it. Keep the concrete warm and moist for as long as possible.

One means of keeping the concrete moist is to leave the forms in place. However, if it is necessary to remove the forms early in the curing process, care must be taken not to damage the green concrete. Remove the braces, take off the wedges from the rod ends, and remove the walers. Take out all the nails or bolts holding the sections of form together and remove panels carefully.

There are occasions when it is necessary to have the concrete made with other than normal cement. If the land on which the foundation will rest contains alkali salts, concrete made with normal cement will set and cure poorly. In such cases, it is wise to specify alkali-resistant cement, which will produce concrete that will set and cure under alkaline conditions. Sometimes it may be necessary to have the concrete set and cure more quickly than is normally the case. If this is so, a special cement, called high-early-strengh cement, should be used in making the concrete. Concrete so made will cure much more rapidly in its early stages than that made with normal cement.

BASEMENT FLOOR

The concrete basement floor may be placed in either one or two layers. In the first case, the complete thickness is placed in one operation; in the second, a base slab is placed first, over which a topping slab, perhaps slightly different in character, is laid later.

In either case, proper preparations for the floor are important. First, there should be a well-packed gravel base provided, at least 150 mm deep.

A 6 mil polyethylene membrane should then be laid over the gravel, initially to prevent the loss of water from the concrete to the base and eventually, to prevent the migration of moisture upward through the concrete slab.

Screeds are then laid to the proper level. A screed is simply a *guide strip,* the top of which represents the level of the finished floor. They should be so spaced that a straightedge, 2 to 3 m in length, can span from one to the next to *strike off* the concrete to the right level (see Fig. 3-70). Straight 38 × 89 or 38 × 140 mm members, set on edge on some type of support which rests on the covered gravel base, or 25 mm pipe, carried on adjustable *chairs* (see Fig. 3-70) are commonly used as screeds. In either case, they must be set to provide for a minimum depth of floor of 90 mm.

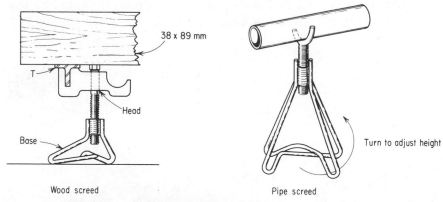

Wood screed   Pipe screed

FIGURE 3-70: *Floor screeds.*

Concrete Joints and Reinforcement

The joint between floor and wall may require some special consideration. Since the floor is probably placed after the wall concrete has hardened, there is little bond between them, and eventually shrinkage will produce a crack around the perimeter. This crack may be a source of trouble if moisture collects under the footings, because the water will find its way up through the joint. Such an occurrence may be prevented by sealing the joint with an asphalt caulking compound.

An oiled, wedge-shaped strip should be placed against the wall, outside the outer screed (see Fig. 3-71) and left there when the screed is removed. After the concrete has hardened, the strip is removed and the space packed with caulking compound (see Fig. 3-71).

The need for reinforcement will depend on the size of the floor and its use. Residential floors do not usually require reinforcing, but larger ones may. Reinforcing may be done for two reasons, one being to give the concrete greater strength in bending, the other to control contraction and expansion of the top surface due to temperature changes. In the first case, the reinforcement will be rod or heavy wire mesh placed near the bottom of the slab. In the second, it will be light wire mesh placed close to the top surface.

Check the plans for any slope that may be required in the floor. If a plumbing drain is present, the floor will be sloped to it and the screeds must be set so that the slope will appear.

The final step in placing the floor is producing its surface finish, which may be done either by hand or with a power trowel. Whichever method is used, it is important that the job be done at just the right time. The concrete should be partially set, hard enough to bear the workman's weight, but with the surface still workable. It is first worked smooth with a float and then given a final treatment with a steel trowel.

The final step in the construction of a foundation is to *backfill* around the outside and shape the grade so that it *slopes away* from the building on a minimum slope of 1 in 12. The backfill material should be deposited and compacted in layers of not more than 300 mm, preferably using mechanical compaction equipment, similar to that illustrated in Fig. 3-72 and at least the top layer should be low porosity material, resistant to water penetration.

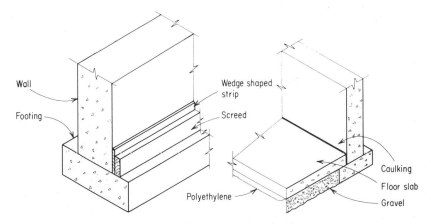

FIGURE 3-71: *Floor-to-wall joint.*

FIGURE 3-72: *Compacting backfill.*

Now the foundation is complete, and the job is ready for the erection of the superstructure. If it has been carefully planned and carried out, the completion of the remainder of the building will be made easier, with fewer chances of errors as work continues.

Approximate imperial equivalents to metric quantities

6 mils	— 0.006 in.	0.4 m²	— 4.3 ft²	38 × 89	— 2 × 4
12 mm	— ½ in.	0.75 m²	— 8.0 ft²	38 × 140	— 2 × 6
15 mm	— ⅝ in.	1.0 m²	— 10.7 ft²	38 × 184	— 2 × 8
19 mm	— ¾ in.	1 kPa	— 20.8 lbs/ft²	38 × 235	— 2 × 10
25 mm	— 1 in.	1 MPa	— 145 lbs/in²	38 × 286	— 2 × 12
95 mm	— 3¾ in.	1 ml	— 0.035 fl. oz.	64 × 89	— 3 × 4
300 mm	— 1 ft	1 kg	— 2.2 lb		
1200 mm	— 4 ft	5 °C	— 40 °F		
2400 mm	— 8 ft	21 °C	— 70 °F		

REVIEW QUESTIONS

3-1. What is the general purpose of a building foundation?

3-2. Outline the essential difference between a full basement foundation and a surface foundation.

3-3. Explain the reason for placing foundation footings below the level of frost penetration.

3-4. How does a gravel pad under a slab foundation compensate for the fact that the foundation is not below the frost line?

3-5. Why is it necessary, in many cases, to make the excavation larger than the size of the foundation?

3-6. Why is cribbing used in excavating?

3-7. Explain the reason for coating a footing keyway with asphalt before a wall is placed on it.

3-8. What is the reason for placing a layer of mortar under a sill plate before bolting it down?

3-9. Explain what is meant by "cast-in" joists.

3-10. According to Table 3-4, what size and spacing of studs for a preserved wood foundation are required under each of the following sets of conditions:

(a) One-story house with conventional siding, Douglas fir, No. 1 lumber, with backfill 2 m deep.

(b) One-story house with brick veneer, W. Hemlock, No. 2 lumber, with backfill 1700 mm deep.

(c) Two-story house with brick veneer and conventional siding, E. Hemlock, No. 1 lumber, with backfill 1800 mm deep.

3-11. What is the purpose of using screeds when placing a basement floor?

3-12. Explain the reason for using a bearing wall, rather than a center girder, to support interior floor loads.

COMPONENT PARTS

After the foundation has been completed, the next logical step in the construction of a building is the erection of the floor frame. This, as the name implies, is the part of the structure which carries the floor and interior walls, along with its supporting members. This floor frame consists of *bearing posts,* the *girder* which they support, the *floor joists* carried by the girder and foundation walls, the *bridging* between the joists and the *subfloor;* sometimes a *bearing wall* will replace posts and girder. When the box sill type of construction is used, a sill plate becomes one of the components of the floor frame.

POSTS AND GIRDERS

Posts and girders are fundamental structural components of the floor frame which support approximately half the total load of the building and transmit it to end foundation walls and footings (see Fig. 3-8).

Posts

The bearing posts may be made of either steel, wood, or concrete. Wooden ones are sometimes one solid piece of timber, but more often are built up of three or four pieces of 38 mm material laminated together. The cross-sectional area depends on the load to be carried, but usually 140 × 140 mm will prove ample. One factor governing the size will be the width of the girder. One dimension of the post should be equal to that width in order to provide full bearing.

A steel post, usually round, will be smaller in cross section than a wooden one. It must be capped by a steel plate to provide a suitable bearing area. Steel posts are manufactured which have a thread on the inside of the top end so that a short, heavy stem may be turned into them (see Fig. 4-1). Consequently, the post becomes adjustable in length. This is a decided advantage, because the post can be adjusted to the exact length required on installation, and later, if the girder shrinks in its depth, the post can be lengthened to take up the shrinkage.

Concrete posts are cast at the same time as the girder (girder and posts are monolithic) so that forms for the two must be integrated (see Fig. 4-2).

Post forms are made from four pieces of material—board or plywood—two of which will be the same width as one dimension of the post (see Fig. 4-3). The use of sufficient form ties is very important, to prevent concrete pressure from spreading or bulging the forms. The number of ties required will vary depending on the cross-sectional

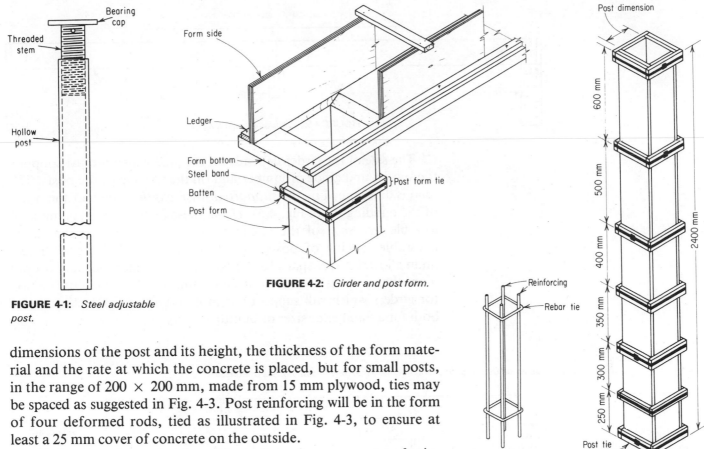

FIGURE 4-1:   *Steel adjustable post.*

FIGURE 4-2:   *Girder and post form.*

FIGURE 4-3:   *Post form and reinforcing bars.*

dimensions of the post and its height, the thickness of the form material and the rate at which the concrete is placed, but for small posts, in the range of 200 × 200 mm, made from 15 mm plywood, ties may be spaced as suggested in Fig. 4-3. Post reinforcing will be in the form of four deformed rods, tied as illustrated in Fig. 4-3, to ensure at least a 25 mm cover of concrete on the outside.

Girders may be made of wood, steel, or, in some cases, of reinforced concrete. A wooden girder has been most popular for light construction. It is often built up of a number of pieces of 38 mm material laminated together, although it may be one solid piece of timber. When the girder is laminated, care must be taken in its construction. Pieces may be nailed, bolted, or glued and nailed together, the latter method providing the most rigid unit. A glue must be chosen that will stand up under the atmospheric conditions to which the girder will be subjected. Rarely will it be possible to find pieces long enough to reach from one end of the girder to the other, and consequently pieces must be end jointed, usually with butt joints. Select or cut pieces of such a length that the joints will come directly over posts (see Fig. 4-4). If only nails are used in laminating, they should be spaced not over 300 mm apart and staggered, one at the top and the next at the bottom of the girder, as illustrated in Fig. 4-4.

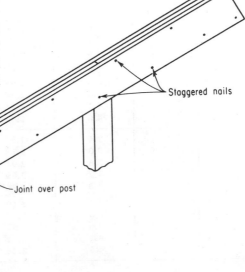

FIGURE 4-4:   *Laminated girder and posts.*

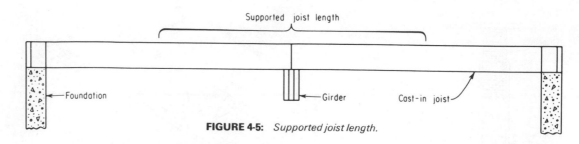

FIGURE 4-5: *Supported joist length.*

The size of the girder depends on the load which it must support, the species and grade of lumber and on the spacing of the posts. The load is determined by the *supported joist length*—one-half the width of the building—(see Fig. 4-5). Using these factors, the maximum allowable *free span* of the girder or, in other words, the maximum allowable spacing of posts, is determined. Table 4-1 gives maximum allowable free spans for wooden girders which will support not more than one residential floor and Table 4-2 the same information for girders which will support not more than two residential floors, both for a number of sizes of builtup girders.

TABLE 4-1: *Maximum spans for built-up wood beams supporting not more than one floor in houses (meters)*

Lumber Species	Grade	Supported joist length (m)	SIZE OF BUILT-UP BEAM (MM)					
			3-38x184	4-38x184	3-38x235	4-38x235	3-38x286	4-38x286
			m	m	m	m	m	m
Douglas Fir, Larch	No. 1	2.4	3.70	4.27	4.72	5.45	5.74	6.63
		3.0	3.31	3.82	4.22	4.87	5.13	5.93
		3.6	3.02	3.49	3.85	4.45	4.69	5.41
		4.2	2.76	3.23	3.53	4.12	4.29	5.01
		4.8	2.46	3.02	3.14	3.85	3.82	4.69
	No. 2	2.4	3.33	3.84	4.24	4.90	5.16	5.96
		3.0	2.97	3.44	3.80	4.38	4.62	5.33
		3.6	2.71	3.14	3.47	4.00	4.22	4.87
		4.2	2.51	2.90	3.21	3.70	3.90	4.51
		4.8	2.35	2.71	3.00	3.46	3.65	4.22
Hem-Fir	No. 1	2.4	3.19	3.69	4.07	4.71	4.96	5.72
		3.0	2.85	3.30	3.64	4.21	4.43	5.12
		3.6	2.61	3.01	3.33	3.84	4.05	4.67
		4.2	2.30	2.79	2.93	3.56	3.87	4.33
		4.8	2.06	2.61	2.92	3.33	3.69	4.05
	No. 2	2.4	2.86	3.31	3.65	4.22	4.45	5.13
		3.0	2.56	2.96	3.27	3.77	3.98	4.59
		3.6	2.34	2.70	2.98	3.45	3.63	4.19
		4.2	2.16	2.50	2.76	3.19	3.36	3.88
		4.8	2.02	2.34	2.58	2.98	3.14	3.63
Eastern Hemlock Tamarack	No. 1	2.4	3.56	4.11	4.54	5.25	5.53	6.38
		3.0	3.18	3.68	4.06	4.69	4.94	5.71
		3.6	2.91	3.36	3.71	4.28	4.51	5.21
		4.2	2.69	3.11	3.43	3.97	4.18	4.82
		4.8	2.46	2.91	3.14	3.71	3.82	4.51
	No. 2	2.4	3.19	3.69	4.07	4.71	4.96	5.72
		3.0	2.85	3.30	3.64	4.21	4.43	5.12
		3.6	2.61	3.01	3.33	3.84	4.05	4.67
		4.2	2.42	2.79	3.08	3.56	3.75	4.33
		4.8	2.26	2.61	2.88	3.33	3.50	4.05

Table 4-1: *(Cont.)*

Lumber Species	Grade	Supported joist length (m)	SIZE OF BUILT-UP BEAM (MM)					
			3-38x184	4-38x184	3-38x235	4-38x235	3-38x286	4-38x286
			m	m	m	m	m	m
Coast Species	No. 1	2.4	3.15	3.64	4.02	4.65	4.90	5.65
		3.0	2.64	3.26	3.37	4.16	4.56	5.06
		3.6	2.26	2.89	2.88	3.69	3.51	4.49
		4.2	1.99	2.53	2.54	3.23	3.09	3.93
		4.8	1.79	2.26	2.28	2.88	2.77	3.51
	No. 2	2.4	2.82	3.26	3.60	4.16	4.38	5.06
		3.0	2.52	2.91	3.22	3.72	3.92	4.52
		3.6	2.26	2.66	2.88	3.39	3.51	4.13
		4.2	1.99	2.46	2.54	3.14	3.09	3.82
		4.8	1.79	2.26	2.28	2.88	2.77	3.51
Spruce-Pine-Fir	No. 1	2.4	3.09	3.57	3.95	4.56	4.80	5.55
		3.0	2.77	3.19	3.53	4.08	4.30	4.96
		3.6	2.44	2.92	3.11	3.72	3.79	4.53
		4.2	2.14	2.70	2.74	3.45	3.33	4.19
		4.8	1.92	2.44	2.45	3.11	2.98	3.79
	No. 2	2.4	2.78	3.21	3.54	4.09	4.21	4.98
		3.0	2.48	2.87	3.17	3.66	3.85	4.45
		3.6	2.26	2.62	2.89	3.34	3.52	4.06
		4.2	2.10	2.42	2.68	3.09	3.26	3.76
		4.8	1.92	2.26	2.45	2.89	2.98	3.52
Western Cedar	No. 1	2.4	3.13	3.62	4.00	4.62	4.86	5.62
		3.0	2.80	3.24	3.58	4.13	4.35	5.02
		3.6	2.56	2.95	3.26	3.77	3.97	4.59
		4.2	2.26	2.73	2.88	3.49	3.51	4.24
		4.8	2.02	2.56	2.58	3.26	3.14	3.97
	No. 2	2.4	2.80	3.23	3.57	4.12	4.34	5.02
		3.0	2.50	2.89	3.19	3.69	3.88	4.49
		3.6	2.28	2.64	2.91	3.37	3.55	4.10
		4.2	2.11	2.44	2.70	3.12	3.28	3.79
		4.8	1.98	2.28	2.52	2.91	3.07	3.55
Northern Species	No. 1	2.4	2.99	3.45	3.82	4.41	4.64	5.36
		3.0	2.64	3.09	3.37	3.94	3.51	4.38
		3.6	2.26	2.82	2.88	3.60	3.51	4.38
		4.2	1.99	2.53	2.54	3.23	3.09	3.93
		4.8	1.79	2.26	2.28	2.88	2.77	3.51
	No. 2	2.4	2.68	3.10	3.43	3.96	4.17	4.81
		3.0	2.40	2.77	3.06	3.54	3.73	4.30
		3.6	2.19	2.53	2.80	3.23	3.40	3.93
		4.2	1.99	2.34	2.54	2.99	3.09	3.64
		4.8	1.79	2.19	2.28	2.80	2.77	3.40
Northern Aspen	No. 1	2.4	3.09	3.57	3.95	4.56	4.80	5.55
		3.0	2.69	3.19	3.44	4.08	4.18	4.96
		3.6	2.30	2.92	2.94	3.72	3.58	4.53
		4.2	2.03	2.58	2.59	3.29	3.15	4.01
		4.8	1.82	2.30	2.32	2.94	2.83	3.58
	No. 2	2.4	2.78	3.21	3.54	4.09	4.31	4.98
		3.0	2.48	2.87	3.17	3.66	3.85	4.45
		3.6	2.26	2.62	2.89	3.34	3.52	4.06
		4.2	2.03	2.42	2.59	3.09	3.15	3.76
		4.8	1.82	2.26	2.32	2.89	2.83	3.52

Note: These tables provide maximum allowable spans for main beams or girders which are built up from 38 mm members in the species, sizes and grades indicated. Allowable spans for solid wood beams, glue-laminated wood beams or built-up beams is sizes or grades other than the ones shown must be determined from standard engineering formulae.

Supported joist length means one-half the sum of the joist spans on both sides of the beam.

Table 4-2: *Maximum spans for built-up wood beams supporting not more than two floors in houses (meters).*

Lumber Species	Grade	Supported joist length, (m)	SIZE OF BUILT-UP BEAM (MM)					
			3-38x184	4-38x184	3-38x235	4-38x235	3-38x286	4-38x286
			m	m	m	m	m	m
Douglas Fir - Larch	No. 1	2.4	2.78	3.24	3.55	4.13	4.32	5.03
		3.0	2.30	2.90	2.93	3.70	3.57	4.50
		3.6	1.97	2.51	2.52	3.21	3.07	3.90
		4.2	1.74	2.20	2.23	2.81	2.44	3.07
		4.8	1.57	1.97	2.01	2.52	2.44	3.07
	No. 2	2.4	2.52	2.91	3.22	3.72	3.92	4.52
		3.0	2.26	2.61	2.88	3.33	3.50	4.05
		3.6	1.97	2.38	2.52	3.04	3.07	3.69
		4.2	1.74	2.20	2.23	2.81	2.71	3.42
		4.8	1.57	1.97	2.01	2.52	2.44	3.07
Hem-Fir	No. 1	2.4	2.31	2.80	2.95	3.57	3.59	4.34
		3.0	1.92	2.44	2.45	3.12	2.99	3.79
		3.6	1.66	2.10	2.12	2.68	2.58	3.25
		4.2	1.48	1.85	1.89	2.36	2.29	2.87
		4.8	1.34	1.66	1.71	2.12	2.08	2.58
	No. 2	2.4	2.17	2.51	2.77	3.20	3.37	3.89
		3.0	1.92	2.24	2.45	2.86	2.99	3.48
		3.6	1.66	2.05	2.12	2.61	2.58	3.18
		4.2	1.48	1.85	1.89	2.36	2.29	2.87
		4.8	1.34	1.66	1.71	2.12	2.08	2.58
Eastern Hemlock-Tamarack	No. 1	2.4	2.70	3.12	3.45	3.98	4.19	4.84
		3.0	2.30	2.79	2.93	3.56	3.57	4.33
		3.6	1.97	2.51	2.52	3.21	3.07	3.90
		4.2	1.74	2.20	2.23	2.81	2.71	3.42
		4.8	1.57	1.97	2.01	2.52	2.44	3.07
	No. 2	2.4	2.42	2.80	3.09	3.57	3.76	4.34
		3.0	2.16	2.50	2.76	3.19	3.36	3.88
		3.6	1.97	2.28	2.52	2.91	3.07	3.54
		4.2	1.74	2.11	2.23	2.70	2.71	3.28
		4.8	1.57	1.97	2.01	2.52	2.44	3.07
Coast Species	No. 1	2.4	2.00	2.55	2.55	3.25	3.11	3.95
		3.0	1.67	2.11	2.14	2.69	2.60	3.28
		3.6	1.45	1.82	1.86	2.32	2.26	2.82
		4.2	1.30	1.61	1.66	2.06	2.02	2.50
		4.8	1.18	1.45	1.51	1.86	1.84	2.26
	No. 2	2.4	2.00	2.47	2.55	3.15	3.11	3.84
		3.0	1.67	2.11	2.14	2.69	2.60	3.28
		3.6	1.45	1.82	1.86	2.32	2.26	2.82
		4.2	1.30	1.61	1.66	2.06	2.02	2.50
		4.8	1.18	1.45	1.51	1.86	1.84	2.26
Spruce, Pine, Fir	No. 1	2.4	2.16	2.71	2.75	3.46	3.35	4.21
		3.0	1.80	2.28	2.30	2.91	2.79	3.53
		3.6	1.56	1.96	1.99	2.50	2.42	3.04
		4.2	1.39	1.73	1.77	2.21	2.16	2.69
		4.8	1.26	1.56	1.61	1.99	1.96	2.42
	No. 2	2.4	2.10	2.43	2.69	3.10	3.27	3.77
		3.0	1.80	2.17	2.30	2.77	2.79	3.38
		3.6	1.56	1.96	1.99	2.50	2.43	3.04
		4.2	1.39	1.73	1.77	2.21	2.16	2.69
		4.8	1.26	1.56	1.61	1.99	1.96	2.42

TABLE 4-2: *(Cont.)*

Lumber Species	Grade	Supported joist length, (m)	SIZE OF BUILT-UP BEAM (MM)					
			3-38x184	4-38x184	3-38x235	4-38x235	3-38x286	4-38x286
			m	m	m	m	m	m
Western Cedar	No. 1	2.4	2.27	2.74	2.90	3.50	3.53	4.26
		3.0	1.89	2.40	2.41	3.06	2.94	3.73
		3.6	1.64	2.06	2.09	2.63	2.54	3.20
		4.2	1.45	1.82	1.86	2.32	2.26	2.82
		4.8	1.32	1.64	1.68	2.09	2.05	2.54
	No. 2	2.4	2.12	2.45	2.71	3.13	3.29	3.81
		3.0	1.89	2.19	2.41	2.80	2.94	3.40
		3.6	1.64	2.00	2.09	2.55	2.54	3.11
		4.2	1.45	1.82	1.86	2.32	2.26	2.82
		4.8	1.32	1.64	1.68	2.09	2.05	2.54
Northern Species	No. 1	2.4	2.00	2.55	2.55	3.25	3.11	3.95
		3.0	1.67	2.11	2.14	2.69	2.60	3.28
		3.6	1.45	1.82	1.86	2.32	2.26	2.82
		4.2	1.30	1.61	1.66	2.06	2.02	2.50
		4.8	1.18	1.45	1.51	1.86	1.84	2.26
	No. 2	2.4	2.00	2.35	2.55	3.00	3.11	3.65
		3.0	1.67	2.10	2.14	2.68	2.60	3.26
		3.6	1.45	1.82	1.86	2.32	2.26	2.82
		4.2	1.30	1.61	1.66	2.06	2.02	2.50
		4.8	1.18	1.45	1.51	1.86	1.84	2.26
Northern Aspen	No. 1	2.4	2.04	2.60	2.60	3.32	3.17	4.03
		3.0	1.70	2.15	2.18	2.75	2.65	3.34
		3.6	1.48	1.85	1.89	2.37	2.30	2.88
		4.2	1.32	1.64	1.69	2.09	2.05	2.55
		4.8	1.20	1.48	1.53	1.89	1.87	2.30
	No. 2	2.4	2.04	2.43	2.60	3.10	3.17	3.77
		3.0	1.70	2.15	2.18	2.75	2.65	3.34
		3.6	1.48	1.85	1.89	2.37	2.30	2.88
		4.2	1.32	1.64	1.69	2.09	2.05	2.55
		4.8	1.20	1.48	1.53	1.89	1.87	2.30

Notes: These tables provide maximum allowable spans for main beams or girders which are built up from 38 mm members in the species, sizes and grades indicated. Allowable spans for solid wood beams, glue-laiminated wood beams or built-up beams in sizes or grades other than those shown must be determined from standard engineering formulae.

Supported joist length means one-half the sum of the joist spans on both sides of the beam.

The method for setting the bottom of the bearing post has already been discussed in Chapter 3. At the top end some provision must be made for adjustment, so that the girder will be held exactly level and also so that shrinkage in the depth of the girder can be taken up at a later date. This provision is made by placing two wedge-shaped pieces between the top of the post and the girder (see Fig. 4-6). By driving them both inward, the girder is raised to its correct level; later, further compensation may be made for girder shrinkage in the same way.

How to Construct and Set a Wooden Girder

1. Obtain the length of the girder and the position of the bearing posts from the plans.

2. Select and cut the material so that all end joints will come over posts.

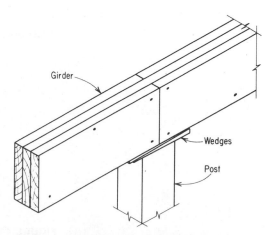

FIGURE 4-6: *Wedged post.*

3. Lay out the material for one lamination, crown up, and place the second on top, making sure that the joints are staggered. Fasten these two together.

4. Apply the third lamination in the same way, still keeping the joints staggered. Do likewise with any further laminations.

5. Cut the fire cuts on both ends of the girder (see Fig. 4-4), and apply two coats of wood preservative to each end.

6. Determine the spacing and position of joists from the plan and lay off the top face of the girder for joists.

7. Set the girder in place and adjust until it is perfectly level.

Steel Girder

A steel girder for light construction may be a *standard* or *wide flange rolled shape* (see Fig. 4-7) or it may be made up of *two cold-formed steel joist sections* welded or bolted together, as shown in Fig. 4-8.

Several depths of rolled shapes are commonly used, the number of supports (posts) required being determined by the supported joist length (see Table 4-3). If the joists rest on top of the girder, a wooden pad is generally used to facilitate fastening the joist ends and the height of the girder must be regulated accordingly (see Fig. 4-7). If the top of joists and girder are to be flush, the joist ends must be carried by the bottom flange of the girder, as illustrated in Fig. 4-7.

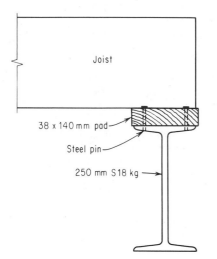

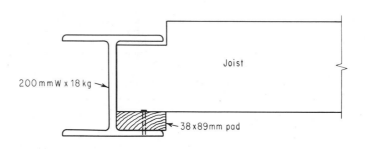

FIGURE 4-7: *Steel girders supporting joist ends.*

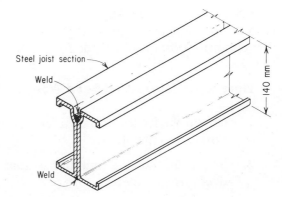

FIGURE 4-8: *Girder made from two steel joist sections.*

TABLE 4-3: *Maximum spans for steel girders in residential construction (meters)*

No. of floors supported	Min. depth (mm)	Min. mass (kg/m)	Supported Joist Length (m)				
			2.4	3.0	3.6	4.2	4.8
1	101	S 11.46	4.06	3.63	3.33	3.07	2.90
	127	S 14.88	5.11	4.57	4.19	3.89	3.63
	152	S 18.60	6.25	5.61	5.16	4.77	4.47
	152	W 23.07	7.01	6.30	5.77	5.38	5.03
	203	W 25.30	8.28	7.47	6.81	6.33	5.87
	203	S 27.38	8.66	7.80	7.01	6.63	6.20
2	101	S 11.46	3.08	2.74	2.52	2.34	2.18
	127	S 14.88	3.89	3.48	3.18	2.94	2.72
	152	S 18.60	4.77	4.27	3.91	3.61	3.38
	152	W 23.07	5.38	4.80	4.39	4.06	3.81
	203	W 25.30	6.33	5.66	5.18	4.80	4.50
	203	S 27.38	6.63	5.96	5.44	5.03	4.72

NOTES: 1. S—standard rolled section.
  3. W—wide flange rolled section.
  3. For supported joist lengths intermediate between those shown in the table, straightline interpolation may be used to determine the maximum girder span.

Cold-formed joist sections normally have a standard depth of 140 mm and the number of supports required for a girder made from two such sections is also determined from the supported joist length.

Concrete Girder

When a reinforced concrete girder is specified, forms must be built for posts and girder (see Fig. 4-9). The form should be built in such a way that the sides may be removed first without disturbing the bottom (see Fig. 4-2). This may be done by setting the form sides *on* the form bottom and holding them in place with ledgers. The form bottom must be amply supported with *T-head shores* (see Fig. 4-9) and should be set with a slight *crown* (upward curvature) since the weight of the concrete will tend to bend the girder downward.

FIGURE 4-9: *Reinforced concrete girder and beam forms.*

BEARING WALLS

In a good many cases, posts and girder are replaced by a *bearing wall* as the primary support for a building. Such a wall will carry the load quite adequately and has the advantage of providing a wall framework if the basement space is to be divided into rooms.

As was illustrated in Chapter 3, the bearing wall is supported by a continuous footing having a raised center portion to which the wall is anchored (see Fig. 3-18). The material must be 38 × 140 mm, minimum, with top and bottom plates and studs spaced not more than 400 mm o.c. (see Fig. 4-10). At the midpoint between top and bottom, blocks must be fitted snugly between the studs, staggered if required, to facilitate nailing, as illustrated in Fig. 4-10. The double top plate will be level with the top of the sill plate or with the bottom edge of the joists, depending on whether box sill or cast-in construction is used.

When an opening occurs in the bearing wall it must be framed with a lintel across the top (see Fig. 4-10) made with two 38 × 140 mm members, if the opening is not more than 1200 mm wide.

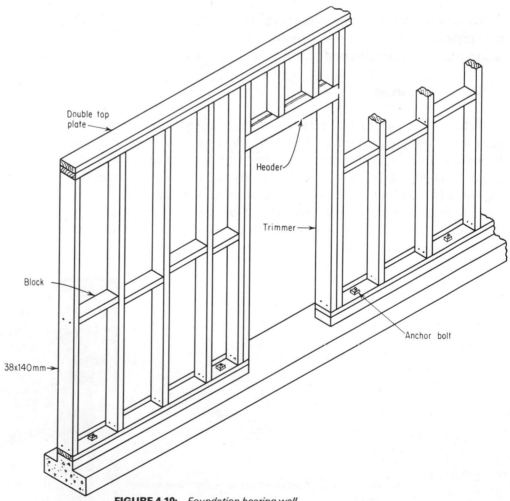

FIGURE 4-10: *Foundation bearing wall.*

SILL PLATE (WOOD FLOOR JOISTS)

The sill plate, sometimes called a *mud sill,* is set on the wall in a bed of mortar in order to provide full bearing between the bottom of the plate and the wall on which it rests (see Fig. 4-11). The sill is set in this mortar, with the anchor bolts projecting through previously drilled bolt holes. The sill is tapped down so that is bedded in the mortar, firm and level. Mortar will squeeze out from under the sill as the anchor nuts are tightened to bring it to its correct position. After the mortar has set, the nuts may be tightened slightly more.

The anchor bolts should be 19 mm in diameter, about 350 mm long, with either a head or a bend at one end. They should be suspended from the top of the form (see Fig. 4-12) so as to provide about 300 mm of anchorage. Care must be taken in their location so that they will not interfere with the position of the floor joists.

SILL PLATE (STEEL FLOOR JOISTS)

The location of sill plates for a steel joist floor frame has been described in Chapter 3 (see Figs. 3-35, 3-36 and 3-37).

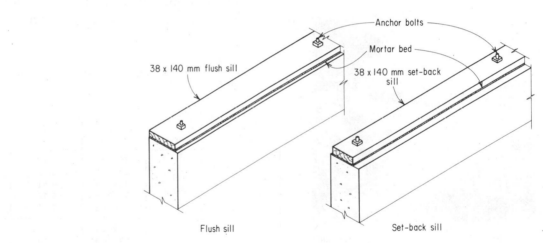

FIGURE 4-11: *Sill plates.*

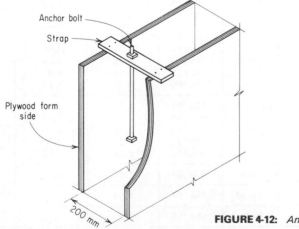

FIGURE 4-12: *Anchor bolt suspended in form.*

115

JOISTS

Floor joists, the members which span from foundation wall to girder or from wall to wall, in some cases, and transfer the individual building loads to those members, may be of wood, steel or reinforced concrete. Wooden joists have been widely used, particularly in residential construction (see Fig. 4-13) but steel joists are gaining in popularity, particularly for long spans (see Fig. 4-14). Reinforced concrete joists are normally reserved for heavier construction.

Wood Joists

Wood joists consist of 38 mm material, in widths varying from 140 to 286 mm, depending on their *load, length, spacing,* and the *species and grade* of lumber. Common spacings are 300, 400, and 600 mm o.c. Table 4-4 gives maximum spans for floor joists for residential construction living quarters and Table 4-5 the same information for residential construction bedrooms and attics which are accessible by a stairway, based on *lumber species* and *grade, joist size, spacing,* and, in the case of bedrooms and attics, also on the *type of ceiling.*

For buildings other than residential, with heavier loads, the size of joists should be calculated by a competent authority.

FIGURE 4-13: *Wood joists in residential construction.*

FIGURE 4-14: *Steel joists in residential construction.*

TABLE 4-4: *Maximum spans for floor joists living quarters (meters) (all ceilings)— (live load 1.9k N/m^2)*

Lumber Species	Grade	Size (mm)	JOIST SPACING		
			300 mm	400 mm	600 mm
Douglas Fir, Larch (N)	Sel. Str.	38x 89	2.17	1.98	1.72
		38x140	3.42	3.11	2.71
		38x184	4.51	4.10	3.58
		38x235	5.76	5.23	4.57
		38x286	7.00	6.36	5.56
	No. 1	38x 89	2.17	1.98	1.72
		38x140	3.42	3.11	2.71
		38x184	4.51	4.10	3.58
		38x235	5.76	5.23	4.57
		38x286	7.00	6.36	5.56
	No. 2	38x 89	2.10	1.91	1.67
		38x140	3.31	3.00	2.59
		38x184	4.36	3.96	3.42
		38x235	5.56	5.05	4.36
		38x286	6.77	6.15	5.31
	No. 3	38x 89	1.88	1.63	1.33
		38x140	2.77	2.40	1.96
		38x184	3.66	3.17	2.59
		38x235	4.67	4.04	3.30
		38x286	5.68	4.92	4.01
	Const	38x 89	2.02	1.83	1.52
	Stand	38x 89	1.62	1.40	1.14
	Util	38x 89	1.10	0.95	0.78

TABLE 4-4: *(Cont.)*

Lumber Species	Grade	Size (mm)	JOIST SPACING		
			300 mm	400 mm	600 mm
Hem-Fir (N)	Sel Str.	38x 89	2.10	1.90	1.66
		38x140	3.30	2.99	2.61
		38x184	4.35	3.95	3.45
		38x235	5.55	5.04	4.40
		38x286	6.75	6.13	5.35
	No. 1	38x 89	2.10	1.90	1.66
		38x140	3.30	2.99	2.49
		38x184	4.35	3.95	3.28
		38x235	5.55	5.04	4.19
		38x286	6.75	6.14	5.09
	No. 2	38x 89	2.02	1.84	1.54
		38x140	3.16	2.73	2.23
		38x184	4.16	3.60	2.94
		38x235	5.31	4.60	3.76
		38x286	6.46	5.60	4.57
	No. 3	38x 89	1.62	1.40	1.14
		38x140	2.39	2.07	1.69
		38x184	3.16	2.73	2.23
		38x235	4.03	4.39	2.85
		38x286	4.90	4.24	3.46
	Const	38x 89	1.86	1.61	1.32
	Stand	38x 89	1.40	1.21	0.99
	Util	38x 89	0.95	0.83	0.67
Eastern Hemlock-Tamarack (N)	Sel. Str.	38x 89	2.00	1.81	1.58
		38x140	3.14	2.85	2.49
		38x184	4.14	3.76	3.29
		38x235	5.28	4.80	4.19
		38x286	6.43	5.84	5.10
	No. 1	38x 89	2.00	1.81	1.58
		38x140	3.14	2.85	2.49
		38x184	4.14	3.76	3.29
		38x235	5.28	4.80	4.19
		38x286	6.43	5.84	5.10
Eastern Hemlock-Tamarack (N)	No. 2	38x 89	1.92	1.75	1.53
		38x140	3.03	2.75	2.40
		38x184	3.99	3.63	3.17
		38x235	5.09	4.63	4.04
		38x286	6.20	5.63	4.92
	No. 3	38x 89	1.81	1.57	1.28
		38x140	2.66	2.31	1.88
		38x184	3.51	3.04	2.48
		38x235	4.48	3.88	3.17
		38x286	5.45	4.72	3.85
	Const	38x 89	1.85	1.68	1.47
	Stand	38x 89	1.54	1.33	1.09
	Util	38x 89	1.07	0.93	0.76
Coast Species	Sel. Str.	38x 89	2.10	1.90	1.66
		38x140	3.30	2.99	2.61
		38x184	4.35	3.95	3.45
		38x235	5.55	5.04	4.40
		38x286	6.75	6.13	5.35

TABLE 4-4: *(Cont.)*

Lumber Species	Grade	Size (mm)	JOIST SPACING		
			300 mm	400 mm	600 mm
Coast Species	No. 1	38x 89	2.10	1.90	1.66
		38x140	3.30	2.99	2.46
		38x184	4.35	3.95	3.24
		38x235	5.55	5.04	4.13
		38x286	6.75	6.13	5.03
	No. 2	38x 89	2.02	1.84	1.52
		38x140	3.11	2.69	2.20
		38x184	4.10	3.55	2.90
		38x235	5.23	4.53	3.70
		38x286	6.36	5.51	4.50
	No. 3	38x 89	1.60	1.39	1.13
		38x140	2.36	2.05	1.67
		38x184	3.12	2.70	2.20
		38x235	3.98	3.44	2.81
		38x285	4.84	4.19	3.42
	Const	38x 89	1.83	1.59	1.29
	Stand	38x 89	1.37	1.19	0.97
	Util	38x 89	0.95	0.83	0.67
Spruce-Pine-Fir	Sel. Str.	38x 89	1.98	1.79	1.57
		38x140	3.11	2.82	2.46
		38x184	4.10	3.72	3.25
		38x235	5.23	4.75	4.15
		38x286	6.36	5.78	5.05
	No. 1	38x 89	1.98	1.79	1.57
		38x140	3.11	2.82	2.41
		38x184	4.10	3.72	3.18
		38x235	5.23	4.75	4.06
		38x286	6.36	5.78	4.93
	No. 2	38x 89	1.91	1.73	1.49
		38x140	3.00	2.65	2.16
		38x184	3.96	3.49	2.85
		38x235	5.05	4.46	3.64
		38x286	6.15	5.42	4.43
	No. 3	38x 89	1.58	1.37	1.12
		38x140	2.33	2.02	1.65
		38x184	3.07	2.66	2.17
		38x235	3.92	3.40	2.77
		38x286	4.77	4.13	3.37
	Const	38x 89	1.80	1.56	1.27
	Stand	38x 89	1.35	1.17	0.95
	Util	38x 89	0.92	0.80	0.65
Western Cedar (N)	Sel. Str.	38x 89	1.90	1.73	1.51
		38x140	2.99	2.73	2.37
		38x184	3.94	3.58	3.13
		38x235	5.02	4.57	3.99
		38x286	6.12	5.56	4.86
	No. 1	38x 89	1.90	1.83	1.51
		38x140	2.99	2.72	2.37
		38x184	3.94	3.58	3.13
		38x235	5.03	4.57	3.99
		38x286	6.12	5.56	4.86
	No. 2	38x 89	1.84	1.67	1.46
		38x140	2.89	2.63	2.18
		38x184	3.81	3.46	2.87
		38x235	4.87	4.42	3.67
		38x286	5.92	5.38	4.46

TABLE 4-4: *(Cont.)*

Lumber Species	Grade	Size (mm)	JOIST SPACING		
			300 mm	400 mm	600 mm
Western Cedar (N)	No. 3	38x 89	1.58	1.37	1.12
		38x140	2.33	2.02	1.65
		38x184	3.07	2.66	2.17
		38x235	3.92	3.40	2.77
		38x286	4.77	4.13	3.37
	Const	38x 89	1.77	1.57	1.28
	Stand	38x 89	1.35	1.17	0.95
	Util	38x 89	0.92	0.80	0.65
Northern Species	Sel. Str.	38x 89	1.90	1.73	1.51
		38x140	2.99	2.72	2.37
		38x184	3.94	3.57	3.13
		38x235	5.03	4.57	3.99
		38x286	6.12	5.56	4.86
	No. 1	38x 89	1.90	1.73	1.51
		38x140	2.99	2.72	2.33
		38x184	3.94	3.58	3.07
		38x235	5.03	4.57	3.92
		38x286	6.12	5.56	4.77
	No. 2	38x 89	1.84	1.67	1.45
		38x140	2.89	2.56	2.09
		38x184	3.81	3.38	2.76
		38x235	4.87	4.31	3.52
		38x286	5.92	5.25	4.28
	No. 3	38x 89	1.52	1.32	1.07
		38x140	2.23	1.93	1.58
		38x184	2.94	2.55	2.08
		38x235	3.76	3.25	2.65
		38x286	4.57	3.96	3.23
	Const	38x 89	1.75	1.51	1.23
	Stand	38x 89	1.31	1.13	0.92
	Util	38x 89	0.89	0.77	0.63
Northern Aspen	Sel. Str.	38x 89	1.93	1.75	1.53
		38x140	3.04	2.76	2.41
		38x184	4.01	3.64	3.18
		38x235	5.11	4.65	4.06
		38x286	6.22	5.65	4.94
	No. 1	38x 89	1.93	1.75	1.53
		38x140	3.04	2.76	2.41
		38x184	4.01	3.64	3.18
		38x235	5.11	4.65	4.06
		38x286	6.22	5.65	4.93
	No. 2	38x 89	1.86	1.69	1.48
		38x140	2.93	2.65	2.16
		38x184	3.86	3.49	2.85
		38x235	4.93	4.46	3.64
		38x286	6.00	5.42	4.43
Northern Aspen	No. 3	38x 89	1.58	1.37	1.12
		38x140	2.33	2.02	1.65
		38x184	3.07	2.66	2.17
		38x235	3.92	3.40	2.77
		38x286	4.77	4.13	3.77
	Const	38x 89	1.79	1.56	1.27
	Stand	38x 89	1.35	1.17	0.95
	Util	38x 89	0.92	0.80	0.65

Courtesy Canadian Wood Council

TABLE 4-5: *Maximum spans for floor joists — bedrooms and attics accessible by a stairway (meters) (live load — 1.4 KN/m²).*

Lumber Species	Grade	Size (mm)	GYPSUM BOARD OR PLASTERED CEILING			OTHER CEILINGS		
			Joist Spacing			Joist Spacing		
			300 mm	400 mm	600 mm	300 mm	400 mm	600 mm
Douglas Fir - Larch (N)	Sel. Str.	38x 89	2.41	2.19	1.91	2.76	2.50	2.19
		38x140	3.79	3.44	3.00	4.34	3.94	3.44
		38x184	4.99	4.54	3.96	5.72	5.19	4.54
		38x235	6.37	5.79	5.06	7.30	6.63	5.79
		38x286	7.75	7.04	6.15	8.87	8.06	7.04
	No. 1	38x 89	2.41	2.19	1.91	2.76	2.50	2.19
		38x140	3.79	3.44	3.00	4.34	3.94	3.28
		38x184	4.99	4.54	3.96	5.72	5.19	4.33
		38x235	6.37	5.79	5.06	7.30	6.63	5.52
		38x286	7.75	7.04	6.15	8.87	8.06	6.72
	No. 2	38x 89	2.33	2.11	1.85	2.67	2.42	2.05
		38x140	3.66	3.33	2.90	4.18	3.62	2.95
		38x184	4.83	4.38	3.83	5.51	4.77	3.89
		38x235	6.16	5.60	4.89	7.03	6.09	4.97
		38x286	7.49	6.81	5.95	8.55	7.40	6.04
	No. 3	38x 89	2.14	1.86	1.51	2.14	1.86	1.51
		38x140	3.16	2.74	2.23	3.16	2.74	2.23
		38x184	4.17	3.61	2.95	4.17	3.61	2.95
		38x235	5.32	4.61	3.76	5.32	4.61	3.76
		38x286	6.47	5.60	4.57	6.47	5.60	4.57
	Const	38x 89	2.23	2.03	1.73	2.45	2.12	1.73
	Stand	38x 89	1.84	1.60	1.30	1.84	1.60	1.30
	Util	38x 89	1.26	1.09	0.89	1.26	1.09	0.89
Hem-Fir (N)	Sel. Str.	38x 89	2.32	2.11	1.84	2.66	2.41	2.11
		38x140	3.65	3.32	2.90	4.18	3.74	3.05
		38x184	4.81	4.37	3.82	5.51	4.93	4.02
		38x235	6.14	5.58	4.87	7.03	6.29	5.13
		38x286	7.47	6.79	5.93	8.55	7.65	6.24
	No. 1	38x 89	2.32	2.11	1.84	2.66	2.38	1.94
		38x140	3.65	3.32	2.83	5.29	4.58	3.74
		38x184	4.81	4.37	3.74	5.29	4.58	3.74
		38x235	6.14	5.58	4.77	6.75	5.84	4.77
		38x286	7.47	6.79	5.80	8.21	7.11	5.80
	No. 2	38x 89	2.24	2.04	1.76	2.49	2.15	1.76
		38x140	3.52	3.11	2.54	3.60	3.11	2.54
		38x184	4.65	4.11	3.35	4.74	4.11	3.35
		38x235	5.93	5.24	4.28	6.05	5.24	4.28
		38x286	7.21	6.37	5.20	7.36	6.37	5.20
	No. 3	38x 89	1.84	1.60	1.30	1.84	1.60	1.30
		38x140	2.73	2.36	1.93	2.73	2.36	1.93
		38x184	3.60	3.11	2.54	3.60	3.11	2.54
		38x235	4.59	3.97	3.24	4.59	3.97	3.24
		38x286	5.58	4.84	3.95	5.58	4.84	3.95
	Const	38x 89	2.12	1.84	1.50	2.12	1.84	1.50
	Stand	38x 89	1.59	1.38	1.12	1.59	1.38	1.12
	Util	38x 89	1.09	0.94	0.77	1.09	0.94	0.77
Eastern Hemlock- Tamarack (N)	Sel. Str.	38x 89	2.21	2.01	1.75	2.53	2.30	2.01
		38x140	3.48	3.16	2.76	3.98	3.62	3.16
		38x184	4.58	4.16	3.64	5.25	4.77	4.16
		38x235	5.85	5.32	4.64	6.70	6.09	5.32
		38x286	7.12	6.47	5.65	8.15	7.40	6.47

TABLE 4-5: *(Cont.)*

Lumber Species	Grade	Size (mm)	GYPSUM BOARD OR PLASTERED CEILING			OTHER CEILINGS		
			Joist Spacing			Joist Spacing		
			300 mm	400 mm	600 mm	300 mm	400 mm	600 mm
Eastern Hemlock-Tamarack (N)	No. 1	38x 89	2.21	2.01	1.75	2.53	2.30	2.01
		38x140	3.48	3.16	2.76	3.98	3.62	3.16
		38x184	4.58	4.16	3.64	5.25	4.77	4.16
		38x235	5.85	5.32	4.64	6.70	6.09	5.32
		38x286	7.12	6.47	5.65	8.15	7.40	6.47
	No. 2	38x 89	2.13	1.94	1.69	2.44	2.22	1.94
		38x140	3.35	3.04	2.66	3.84	3.47	2.83
		38x184	4.42	4.01	3.51	5.05	4.58	3.74
		38x235	5.64	5.12	4.48	6.46	5.84	4.77
		38x286	6.86	6.23	5.44	7.85	7.11	5.80
	No. 3	38x 89	2.05	1.79	1.46	2.07	1.79	1.46
		38x140	3.03	2.63	2.14	3.03	2.63	2.14
		38x184	4.00	3.46	2.83	4.00	3.46	2.83
		38x235	5.11	4.42	3.61	5.11	4.42	3.61
		38x286	6.21	5.38	4.39	6.21	5.38	4.39
	Const	38x 89	2.05	1.87	1.63	2.35	2.05	1.68
	Stand	38x 89	1.76	1.52	1.24	1.76	1.52	1.24
	Util	38x 89	1.22	1.06	0.86	1.22	1.06	0.86
Coast Species	Sel. Str.	38x 89	2.32	2.11	1.84	2.66	2.41	2.08
		38x140	3.65	3.32	2.90	4.18	3.70	3.02
		38x184	4.81	4.37	3.82	5.51	4.88	3.98
		38x235	6.14	5.58	4.87	7.03	6.22	5.08
		38x286	7.47	6.79	5.93	8.55	7.57	6.18
	No. 1	38x 89	2.32	2.11	1.84	2.66	2.35	1.92
		38x140	3.65	3.32	2.80	3.96	3.43	2.80
		38x184	4.81	4.37	3.69	5.22	4.52	3.69
		38x235	6.14	5.58	4.71	6.66	5.77	4.71
		38x286	7.47	6.79	5.73	8.10	7.02	5.73
	No. 2	38x 89	2.24	2.04	1.73	2.45	2.12	1.73
		38x140	3.52	3.07	2.50	3.54	3.07	2.50
		38x184	4.65	4.04	3.30	4.67	4.04	3.30
		38x235	5.93	5.16	4.21	5.96	5.16	4.21
		38x286	7.21	6.28	5.12	7.25	6.28	5.12
	No. 3	38x 89	1.82	1.58	1.29	1.82	1.58	1.29
		38x140	2.69	2.33	1.90	2.69	2.33	1.90
		38x184	3.55	3.07	2.51	3.55	3.07	2.51
		38x235	4.53	3.92	3.20	4.53	4.77	3.20
		38x286	5.51	4.77	3.89	5.51	4.77	3.89
	Const	38x 89	2.09	1.81	1.47	2.09	1.81	1.47
	Stand	38x 89	1.57	1.36	1.11	1.57	1.36	1.11
	Util	38x 89	1.09	0.94	0.77	1.09	0.94	0.77
Spruce-Pine-Fir	Sel. Str.	38x 89	2.19	1.99	1.74	2.50	2.28	1.99
		38x140	3.44	3.13	2.73	3.94	3.58	2.95
		38x184	4.54	4.12	3.60	5.19	4.72	1.89
		38x235	5.79	5.26	4.59	5.63	6.02	4.97
		38x286	7.04	6.40	5.59	8.06	7.32	6.04
	No. 1	38x 89	2.19	1.99	1.74	2.50	2.28	1.88
		38x140	3.44	3.13	2.73	3.88	3.36	2.75
		38x184	4.54	4.12	3.60	5.12	4.44	3.62
		38x235	5.79	5.26	4.59	6.54	5.66	4.62
		38x286	7.04	6.40	5.59	7.95	6.89	5.62

TABLE 4-5: *(Cont.)*

Lumber Species	Grade	Size (mm)	GYPSUM BOARD OR PLASTERED CEILING			OTHER CEILINGS		
			Joist Spacing			Joist Spacing		
			300 mm	400 mm	600 mm	300 mm	400 mm	600 mm
Spruce Pine-Fir	No. 2	38x 89	2.11	1.92	1.68	2.41	2.08	1.70
		38x140	3.33	3.02	2.46	3.49	3.02	2.46
		38x184	4.38	3.98	3.25	4.60	3.98	3.25
		38x235	5.60	5.08	4.15	5.87	5.08	4.15
		38x286	6.81	6.18	5.04	7.13	6.18	5.04
	No. 3	38x 89	1.80	1.56	1.27	1.80	1.56	1.27
		38x140	2.65	2.30	1.88	2.65	2.30	1.88
		38x184	3.50	3.03	2.47	3.50	3.03	2.47
		38x235	4.47	3.87	3.16	4.47	3.87	3.16
		38x286	5.44	4.71	3.84	5.44	4.71	3.84
	Const	38x 89	2.04	1.77	1.45	2.05	1.77	1.45
	Stand	38x 89	1.54	1.33	1.09	1.54	1.33	1.09
	Util	38x 89	1.05	0.91	0.74	1.05	0.91	0.74
Western Cedar (N)	Sel. Str.	38x 89	2.11	1.91	1.67	2.41	2.19	1.91
		38x140	3.31	3.01	2.63	3.79	3.44	2.99
		38x184	4.37	3.97	3.47	5.00	4.54	3.94
		38x235	5.57	5.06	4.42	6.38	5.80	5.02
		38x286	6.78	6.16	5.38	7.76	7.05	6.11
	No. 1	38x 89	2.11	1.91	1.67	2.41	2.19	1.90
		38x140	3.31	3.01	2.63	3.79	3.41	2.78
		38x184	4.37	3.97	3.47	5.00	4.49	3.67
		38x235	5.57	5.06	4.42	6.38	5.73	4.68
		38x286	6.78	6.16	5.18	7.78	6.97	5.69
	No. 2	38x 89	2.04	1.85	1.61	2.33	2.11	1.72
		38x140	3.20	2.91	2.48	3.51	3.04	2.48
		38x184	4.22	3.84	3.27	4.63	4.01	3.27
		38x235	5.39	4.90	4.18	5.91	5.12	4.18
		38x286	6.55	5.95	5.08	7.19	6.23	5.08
	No. 3	38x 89	1.80	1.56	1.27	1.80	1.56	1.27
		38x140	2.65	2.30	1.88	2.65	2.30	1.88
		38x184	3.50	3.03	2.47	3.50	3.03	2.47
		38x235	4.47	3.87	3.16	4.47	3.87	3.16
		38x286	5.44	4.71	3.84	5.44	4.71	3.84
	Const	38x 89	1.96	1.78	1.46	2.07	1.79	1.46
	Stand	38x 89	1.54	1.33	1.09	1.54	1.33	1.09
	Util	38x 89	1.05	0.91	0.74	1.05	0.91	0.74
Northern Species	Sel. Str.	38x 89	2.11	1.91	1.67	2.41	2.19	1.91
		38x140	3.31	3.01	2.63	3.79	3.44	2.87
		38x184	4.37	3.97	3.47	5.00	4.54	3.78
		38x235	5.57	5.06	4.42	6.38	5.80	4.83
		38x286	6.78	6.16	5.38	7.76	7.05	5.87
	No. 1	38x 89	2.11	1.91	1.67	2.41	2.19	1.82
		38x140	3.31	3.01	2.63	3.76	3.25	2.65
		38x184	4.37	3.97	3.47	4.95	4.29	3.50
		38x235	5.57	5.06	4.42	6.32	5.47	4.47
		38x286	6.78	6.16	5.38	7.69	6.66	5.44
	No. 2	38x 89	2.04	1.85	1.61	2.33	2.02	1.65
		38x140	3.20	2.91	2.38	3.37	2.92	2.38
		38x184	4.22	3.84	3.14	4.45	2.85	3.14
		38x235	5.39	4.90	4.01	5.67	4.91	4.01
		38x286	6.55	5.95	4.88	6.90	5.98	4.88

TABLE 4-5: *(Cont.)*

Lumber Species	Grade	Size (mm)	GYPSUM BOARD OR PLASTERED CEILING			OTHER CEILINGS		
			Joist Spacing			Joist Spacing		
			300 mm	400 mm	600 mm	300 mm	400 mm	600 mm
Northern Species (cont'd)	No.3	38x 89	1.73	1.50	1.22	1.73	1.50	1.22
		38x140	2.54	2.20	1.80	2.54	2.20	1.80
		38x184	3.35	2.90	2.37	3.35	2.90	2.37
		38x235	4.28	3.70	3.02	4.28	3.70	3.02
		38x286	5.20	4.51	3.86	5.20	4.51	3.68
	Const	38x 89	1.96	1.72	1.41	1.99	1.72	1.41
	Stand	38x 89	1.49	1.29	1.05	1.49	1.29	1.05
	Util	38x 89	1.01	0.88	0.71	1.01	0.88	0.71
Northern Aspen	Sel. Str.	38x 89	2.14	1.94	1.70	2.45	2.23	1.94
		38x140	3.36	3.06	2.67	3.85	3.50	2.95
		38x184	4.44	4.03	3.52	5.08	4.61	3.89
		38x235	5.66	5.14	4.49	6.48	5.89	4.97
		38x286	6.89	6.26	5.47	7.88	7.16	6.04
	No. 1	38x 89	2.14	1.94	1.70	2.45	2.23	1.88
		38x140	3.36	3.06	2.67	3.85	3.36	2.75
		38x184	4.44	4.03	3.52	5.08	4.44	3.62
		38x235	5.66	5.14	4.49	6.48	5.66	4.62
		38x286	6.89	6.26	5.47	7.88	6.89	5.62
	No. 2	38x 89	2.06	1.87	1.64	2.36	2.10	1.71
		38x140	3.24	2.95	2.46	3.49	3.02	2.46
		38x184	4.28	3.89	3.25	4.60	3.98	3.25
		38x235	5.46	4.96	4.15	5.87	5.08	4.15
		38x286	6.64	6.03	5.04	7.13	6.18	5.04
	No. 3	38x 89	1.80	1.56	1.27	1.80	1.56	1.27
		38x140	2.65	2.30	1.88	2.65	2.30	1.88
		38x184	3.50	3.03	2.47	3.50	3.03	2.47
		38x235	4.47	3.87	3.16	4.47	3.87	3.16
		38x286	5.44	4.71	3.84	5.44	4.71	3.84
	Const	38x 89	1.98	1.77	1.45	2.05	1.77	1.45
	Stand	38x 89	1.54	1.33	1.09	1.54	1.33	1.09
	Util	38x 89	1.05	0.91	0.74	1.05	0.91	0.74

Courtesy Canadian Wood Council

Joist Framing

Two systems are used for assembling joists—the *"cast-in"* system previously described in Chapter 3 and the *box sill* system, in which the whole assembly is mounted on top of the foundation wall, secured to a sill plate.

In the box system, joists are held in position at the foundation wall by the *header joists,* running at right angles to the regular joists and bearing on the sill plate (see Fig. 4-15). At the inner end, the joists may be carried *on top* of the girder, rest *on ledgers* nailed to the sides of the girder or be suspended in *joist hangers,* secured against the sides of the girder (see Fig. 4-16). In cases where the joists are butted over the beam, rest on ledgers or are carried in joist hangers, they will have to be cut to length before assembly.

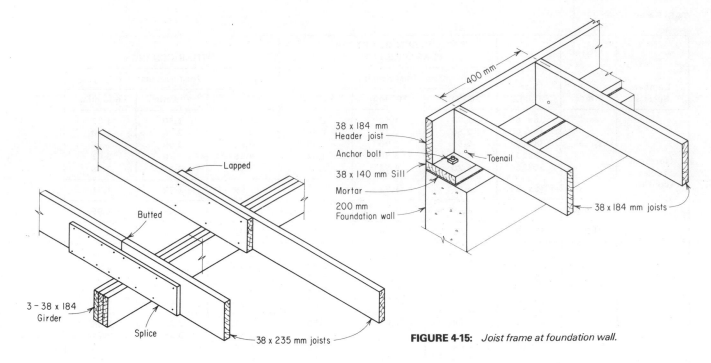

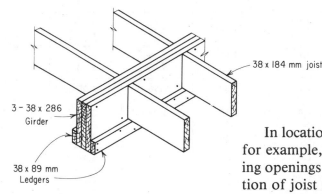

FIGURE 4-15: *Joist frame at foundation wall.*

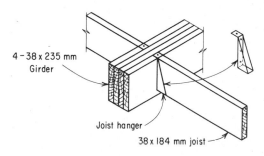

FIGURE 4-16: *Joist supports at girder.*

In locations where an extra load is imposed on the floor frame, as, for example, where a partition over 1800 mm in length and containing openings that are not full ceiling height, runs parallel to the direction of joist run, joists have to be *doubled*. This may be done either by placing two joists side by side or by using two which are separated by not more than 200 mm by blocking (see Fig. 4-17). The blocking must be at least 38 × 89 mm material and blocks should be spaced not more than 1200 mm o.c.

Openings in the floor frame for a stair well or where a chimney or fireplace comes through the floor, must be framed in the proper size. Most codes require that a chimney opening be at least 50 mm larger on all sides than the dimensions of the chimney and that framing be kept back 100 mm from the back of a fireplace. See Chapter 9 for calculations of length and width of a stair well.

Openings are framed on two sides by means of *headers,* which run at right angles to the regular joists and on the other two by *trimmers.* Headers in openings must be doubled if they exceed 1200 mm in length and, if they exceed 3200 mm, their size must be calculated. Trimmers must be doubled when the length of the header joist exceeds 800 mm and, if the header joist exceeds 2000 mm in length, the size of the trimmer joist must be determined by calculation (see Fig. 4-18).

124

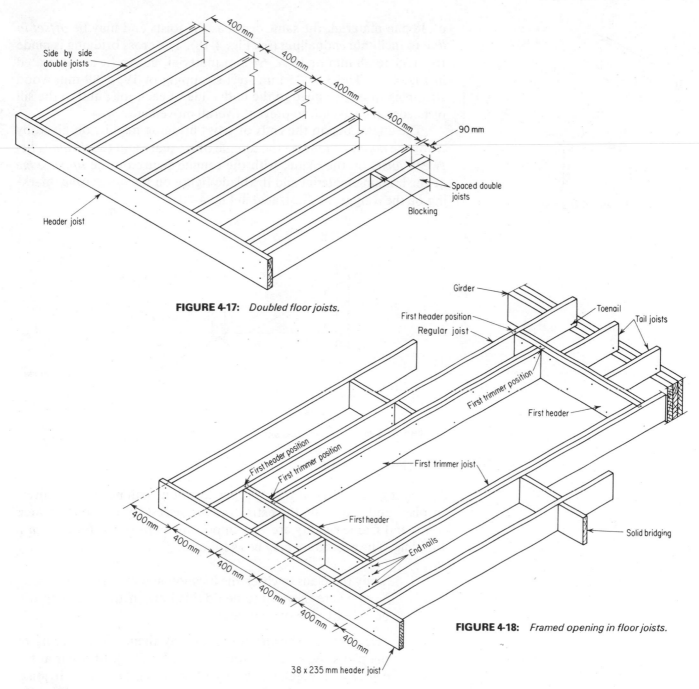

FIGURE 4-17: *Doubled floor joists.*

FIGURE 4-18: *Framed opening in floor joists.*

Bridging

It is important that joists be prevented from twisting after they are in place and, unless *ceiling furring* or *plywood cladding* is installed on the underside, restraint must be provided, both at end supports and at intervals not exceeding 2100 mm between supports. At the end supports, the restraint is provided by toenailing the joists to the supports and by endnailing through the header joist.

The intermediate restraint is provided by *bridging*, which may be in the form of *solid blocking* between joists (see Fig. 4-18), *cross-bridging* or *wood or steel strapping*. The solid blocking will be pieces

125

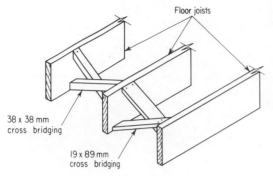

FIGURE 4-19:   *Cross bridging.*

of 38 mm material, the same depth as the joists and may be *offset in line* to facilitate endnailing (see Fig. 4-18). The cross bridging is made from 38 × 38 mm or 19 × 64 mm material, cut to fit as illustrated in Fig. 4-19. The 3 × 25 mm steel strapping or 19 × 89 mm wood strapping must be nailed to the underside of each joist and to the sill or header at each end, to prevent overall movement.

The angle cuts on the ends of cross bridging may be obtained by using the *depth of joist* on the tongue of a square and the *distance between joists* on the blade, with the tongue figure on the *upper edge* of the bridging material and the blade figure on the *lower edge,* marking on the tongue, as illustrated in Fig. 4-20.

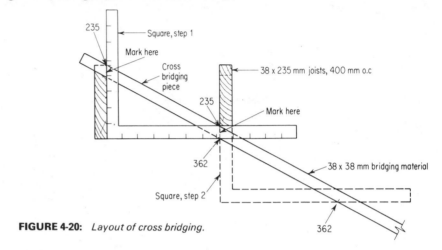

FIGURE 4-20:   *Layout of cross bridging.*

Joist Assembly

Setting the joists in their proper location, nailing them securely in place and providing the extra framing necessary for concentrated loads and frame rigidity are very important steps in the framing of a building. The procedure may be as follows:

1. Study the plans to check the location and centers of the joists. Note where they are to be doubled and if the doubling will be side by side or separated.

2. Select straight header joists and lay them off according to the plans. Be sure that joints in the header joist occur at the center of a regular joist. (see Fig. 4-21). Note that if joists are to be *lapped* at the girder, the header joist lay-off on the two opposite sides of the building will have to be offset from one another by the thickness of the joists.

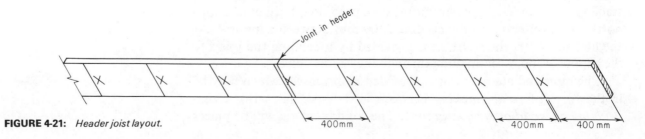

FIGURE 4-21:   *Header joist layout.*

3. Check for the number of full-length regular joists required and cut them to length, unless they are to be lapped.

4. For box sill construction, toenail the header joists in place on the sill plate (see Chapter 3 for procedure in "cast-in" construction).

5. Where joist hangers are to be used, nail them in place on the girder, in line with the header joist layout.

6. Lay out all the regular joists on one side of the building, set them up in position *with the crown up,* toenail them to the sill and to the girder if they rest on top or on ledgers and *endnail* into them through the header joist.

7. Repeat with the regular joists on the opposite side and if joists butt at the girder, nail a board 1 m long across the butt joint (see Fig. 4-16). If they lap, nail the two together through the lap joint.

8. Check the plans for location of floor openings, mark the regular joists for the first header positions (see Fig. 4-18), cut the headers to the exact length required and endnail them in place.

9. Mark on the headers the location of the first trimmer joists, cut to exact length and endnail in place (see Fig. 4-18).

10. Add the second trimmer, if doubling is required.

11. Add the second header, if doubling is required.

12. Cut tail joists to exact length and nail them in place *on regular centers.*

13. Space the top edges of the joists properly over the girder, using a 19 × 89 mm nailing strip to hold them in place (see Fig. 4-13).

14. Mark the location for bridging (not more than 2100 mm from end supports), run a tight line across the joists from end to end and nail in the bridging to the line.

Steel Joists

Steel joists of various kinds are available for use in place of wood joists and are particularly useful where relatively long spans are required. They are all prefabricated units, some made in various depths to suit span requirements.

One type, known as *truss joists,* have 38 × 89 mm top and bottom chords of wood, with 18 mm rod webs (see Fig. 4-22). A similar type, called *open web joists,* are made entirely of steel, as illustrated in Fig. 4-23. These require a wooden pad to be attached to the top chord, to which the subfloor can be fastened.

A third type, *cold-formed steel joists,* are made from sheet steel

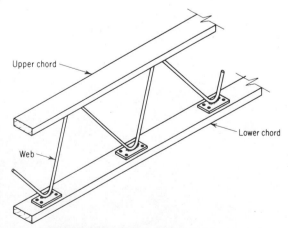

FIGURE 4-22: *Section of truss joist.*

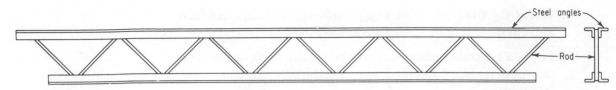

FIGURE 4-23: *Open web steel joist.*

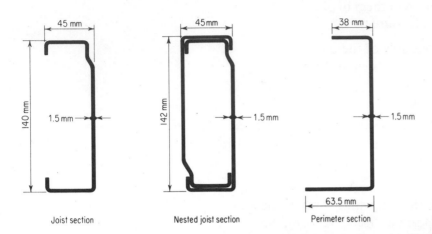

45 mm

140 mm

1.5 mm

Joist section

45mm

142 mm

1.5mm

Nested joist section

38 mm

1.5 mm

63.5 mm

Perimeter section

FIGURE 4-24: *Cold-formed steel joist shapes (Courtesy, Steel Co. of Canada).*

FIGURE 4-25: *Steel joists with wood header joist (Courtesy, U.S. Steel Corp.).*

in several standard depths, one of which is shown in Fig. 4-24. The single joist, 140 mm deep, has a greater load-bearing capacity than a 38 × 235 mm wood joist, conventionally used. The nested joist section is used as a trimmer joist at floor openings and the perimeter section as a header joist, in an all-steel floor frame.

Cold-formed steel joists may be used with a conventional wooden header joist in box sill construction, as illustrated in Fig. 4-25. The joist ends may be fitted with end clips (see Fig. 4-26) and nailed to the header through the clips or wooden blocks may be fitted into the ends (see Fig. 4-26), in which case the joists are secured by endnailing through the header into the blocks.

128

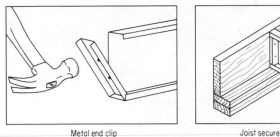
Metal end clip

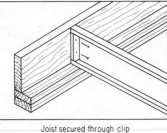
Joist secured through clip

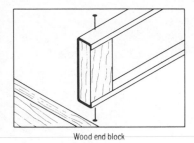
Wood end block

FIGURE 4-26: *End anchors for steel joists.*

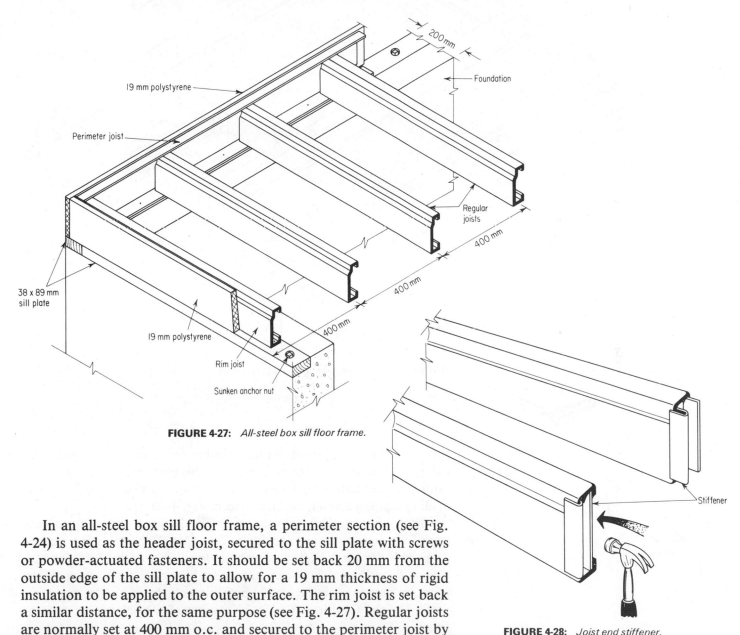

FIGURE 4-27: *All-steel box sill floor frame.*

FIGURE 4-28: *Joist end stiffener.*

In an all-steel box sill floor frame, a perimeter section (see Fig. 4-24) is used as the header joist, secured to the sill plate with screws or powder-actuated fasteners. It should be set back 20 mm from the outside edge of the sill plate to allow for a 19 mm thickness of rigid insulation to be applied to the outer surface. The rim joist is set back a similar distance, for the same purpose (see Fig. 4-27). Regular joists are normally set at 400 mm o.c. and secured to the perimeter joist by spot welding. The inner ends of joists resting on a girder, ledger, or hanger should be provided with end clips, blocks, or *stiffeners* (see Fig. 4-28) in order to develop the required strength.

Floor openings in steel frame construction are framed in much

129

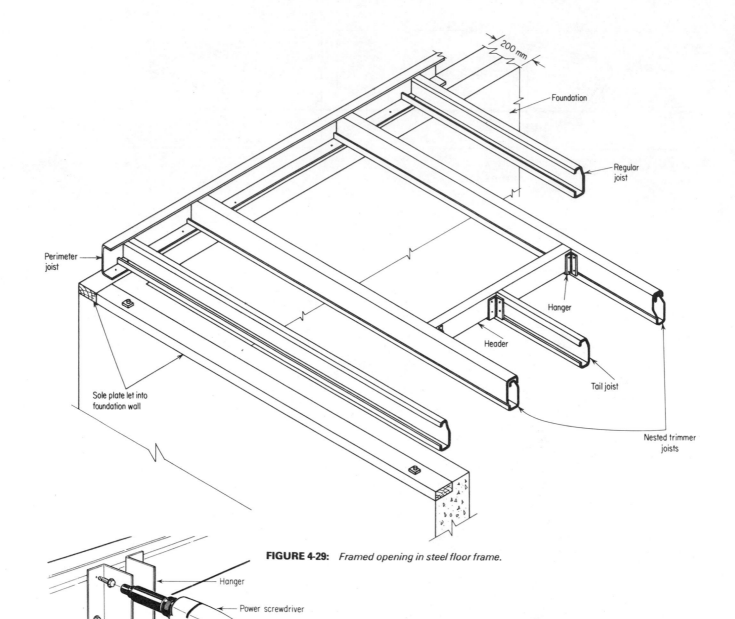

FIGURE 4-29: *Framed opening in steel floor frame.*

FIGURE 4-30: *Hanger secured with self-drilling tapping screws.*

the same way as a wood frame. Double trimmers are provided by using the *nested joist section* (see Fig. 4-24) and opening headers and tail joists are secured by *hangers* (see Fig. 4-29), held in place by self-drilling tapping screws, as illustrated in Fig. 4-30.

Steel joists may be "cast-in" (see Fig. 3-41) or *recessed* onto the top of the foundation to provide a *flush floor.* The recessing may be done by lowering the sill plate into the top, inner edge of the foundation wall (see Fig. 4-31) or by providing joist pockets for ends of the joists, as illustrated in Fig. 4-32. Both methods leave part of the upper surface of the foundation exposed as a base for brick veneer exterior finish.

When the lowered sill plate method is used, joists are provided with end clips or stiffeners and secured to the sill plate by screws through their bottom edge. When the ends of joists rest in pockets, the joist ends are blocked and *grouted* into the pockets.

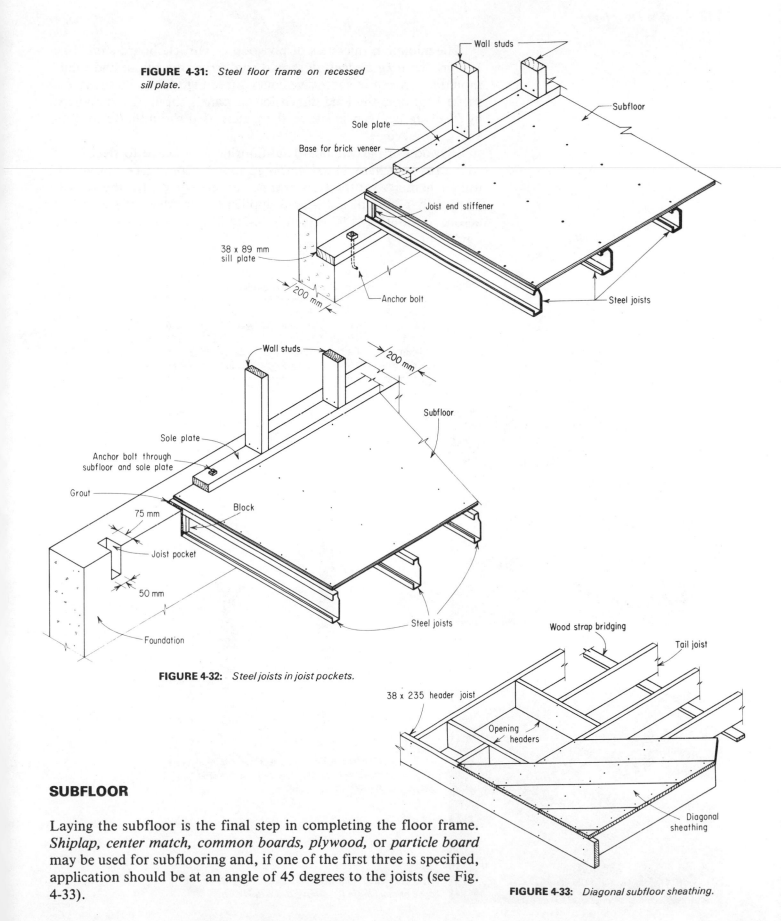

FIGURE 4-31: *Steel floor frame on recessed sill plate.*

Wall studs

Subfloor

Sole plate

Base for brick veneer

Joist end stiffener

38 x 89 mm sill plate

200 mm

Anchor bolt

Steel joists

Wall studs

200 mm

Subfloor

Sole plate

Anchor bolt through subfloor and sole plate

Grout

Block

75 mm

Joist pocket

50 mm

Foundation

Steel joists

FIGURE 4-32: *Steel joists in joist pockets.*

Wood strap bridging

Tail joist

38 x 235 header joist

Opening headers

Diagonal sheathing

SUBFLOOR

Laying the subfloor is the final step in completing the floor frame. *Shiplap, center match, common boards, plywood,* or *particle board* may be used for subflooring and, if one of the first three is specified, application should be at an angle of 45 degrees to the joists (see Fig. 4-33).

FIGURE 4-33: *Diagonal subfloor sheathing.*

131

The minimum thickness of plywood or particle board should be 15 mm, the *long dimension* should run *across* the joists, and joints should be broken in successive courses (see Fig. 4-34). To provide a stiffer subfloor, the long dimension of panels should be supported by *blocking* between joists, or the panels used should have tongue-and-grooved edges.

Plywood or particle board subflooring is attached to steel joists with *steel joist nails* or *self-drilling* tapping screws (see Fig. 4-35), using a hammer for the nails or a power screwdriver for the screws. Frequently a coat of adhesive is applied to the edges of steel joists before subflooring is laid (see Fig. 4-36) in order to provide a more rigid floor.

Approximate Imperial Equivalents to Metric Quantities

3 mm — ⅛ in.	140 mm — 5½ in.	38 × 89 — 2 × 4
15 mm — ⅝ in.	1200 mm — 4 ft	38 × 140 — 2 × 6
19 mm — ¾ in.	2100 mm — 7 ft	38 × 184 — 2 × 8
25 mm — 1 in.	1 m — 3.28 ft	38 × 235 — 2 × 10
38 mm — 1½ in.	1 kg — 2.2 lb	38 × 286 — 2 × 12

FIGURE 4-34: *Plywood subfloor.*

FIGURE 4-35: *Fasteners for subfloor-to-steel joists: (a) Steel joist nail; (b) Self-drilling tapping screw.*

FIGURE 4-36: *Adhesive for subfloor applied to edges of steel joists (Courtesy, U.S. Steel Corp.).*

REVIEW QUESTIONS

4-1. A one-story building 9.6 m wide by 12 m long is to have a center supporting girder made up of three 38 × 235 mm members of No.1 Douglas fir. How many evenly spaced posts are required to support it?

4-2. Define the "clear span" of a girder.

4-3. If the floor load in the building mentioned in No. 1 is 1.68 kg per m², how much load is carried by one post?

4-4. Outline two primary reasons for using bridging.

4-5. What figures would you use on the square to lay out the end cuts for 38 × 38 cross bridging, to fit between 38 × 235 mm joists, spaced 500 mm o.c.?

4-6. A building 10.8 m wide, with a center supporting girder, is to have Western Hemlock, No. 1 Girder joists, spaced 400 mm o.c. What size of joist is required?

4-7. An opening 1050 mm wide by 1950 mm long is to be framed in the floor of the building described in No. 6 above, 900 mm from one side and 3300 mm from one end. What length would you cut:

(a) the opening headers?

(b) the trimmer joists?

(c) the tail joists on the outside?

4-8. Carefully draw two sketches to illustrate the differences between a box sill floor frame and a cast-in joist floor frame.

4-9. Fill in the blanks with the word or phrase which makes the sentence correct.

(a) Material for bearing wall studs must be at least _____ mm in width.

(b) Joists spanning 4.8 m should have _____ rows of bridging.

(c) Strap bridging is usually made from _____ .

(d) Common spacing for anchor bolts in sill plates is _____ .

(e) Joists may be carried on the side of a girder by a _____ or by _____ .

(f) A three-piece, laminated girder, 7.2 m long, supported by end walls and two posts, could be made up of _____ pc. _____ mm long and _____ pc. _____ mm long.

(g) _____ bridging is usually used when the space between joists is no greater than the width of joists.

There are two basic systems used for framing walls, namely the *western* or *platform* frame (see Fig. 5-1) and the *balloon* frame, shown in Fig. 5-2. Many of the members are the same in both and the main differences lie in the method of starting the frame at the ground floor level, the length of the wall framing members and the method of framing in the floor for the second story.

COMPONENT PARTS, WESTERN FRAME

As illustrated in Fig. 5-1, a western frame begins on the subfloor. The bottom member is the *sole plate* to which are attached *regular studs* one story in length, special arrangements of studs at corners, one of which is called a *western corner,* extra studs to which partitions are attached—*partition junctions*—and other shorter members. On top of these vertical members is a *top plate* and on top of that a *cap plate.* Between studs, halfway up their length, are horizontal blocks called *firestops.* Over door and window openings are *headers* or *lintels,* and, supporting the ends of these, *trimmer studs.* The bottom of a window opening is framed by a *rough sill,* and the spaces between rough sill and sole plate and between header and top plate are framed with *cripple studs. Wall backing* is placed where sinks, drapes, etc. are to be attached to interior walls, and *sheathing* covers the exterior of the frame. Where platform frame buildings are more than one story high or where the exterior sheathing is to be such material as gypsum board or some type of insulative material (see Fig. 5-2) *"let-in"* wind bracing is usually required.

COMPONENT PARTS, BALLOON FRAME

A balloon frame begins down at the sill plate (see Fig. 5-3). Full-length *regular studs* and *corner posts* rest on the sill and are capped at the top by *top plate* and *cap plate.* At the first floor level, a 19 mm *ribbon* is let into the studs, and the ends of the *first-floor joists* rest on it. 19 × 89 mm *let-in bracing* is nailed to the outside of the studs at an angle to brace the frame. *Partition junctions* are set in only one story high. *Firestops, window and door headers, trimmers, rough sills, cripple studs,* and *wall backing* are similar to those in platform frame. *Sheathing* completes the frame.

PLATFORM FRAME WALL CONSTRUCTION

Plate Layout

The first step in the construction of a wall is to *lay out* on the sole plate—the base for a platform frame—the exact location of each member required in that wall. They will include *corner posts, regular*

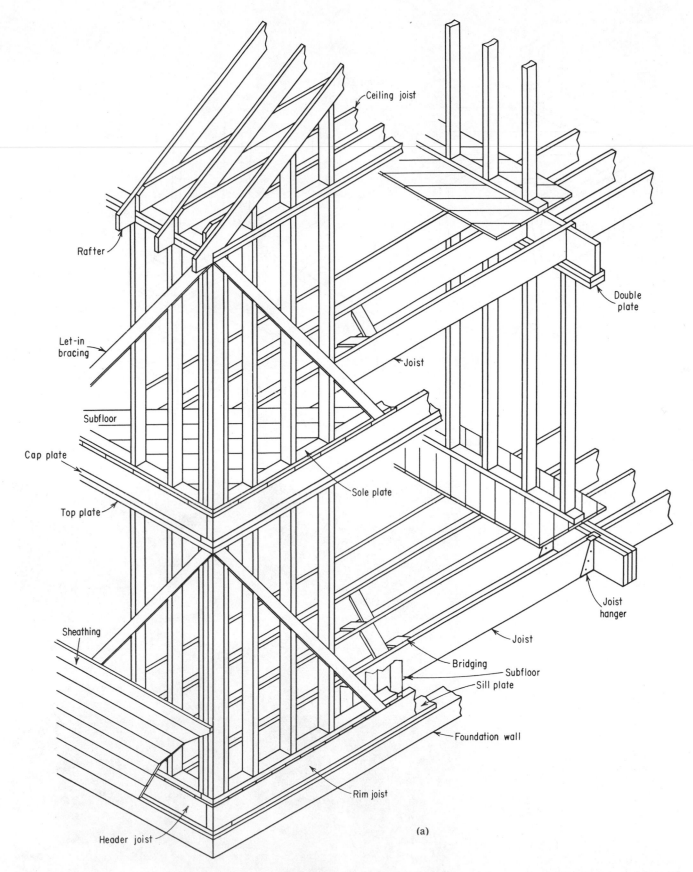

Ceiling joist

Rafter

Let-in
bracing

Subfloor

Cap plate

Top plate

Sheathing

Header joist

Double
plate

Joist

Sole plate

Joist
hanger

Joist

Bridging

Subfloor

Sill plate

Foundation wall

Rim joist

(a)

FIGURE 5-1: *Platform frame.*

135

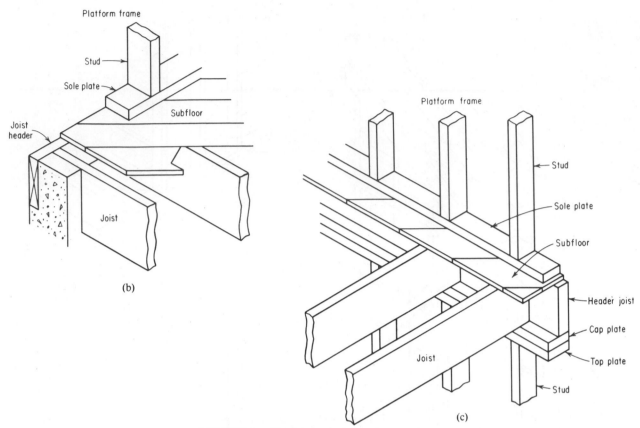

FIGURE 5-1: *(Cont.).*

FIGURE 5-2: *Let-in wind bracing.*

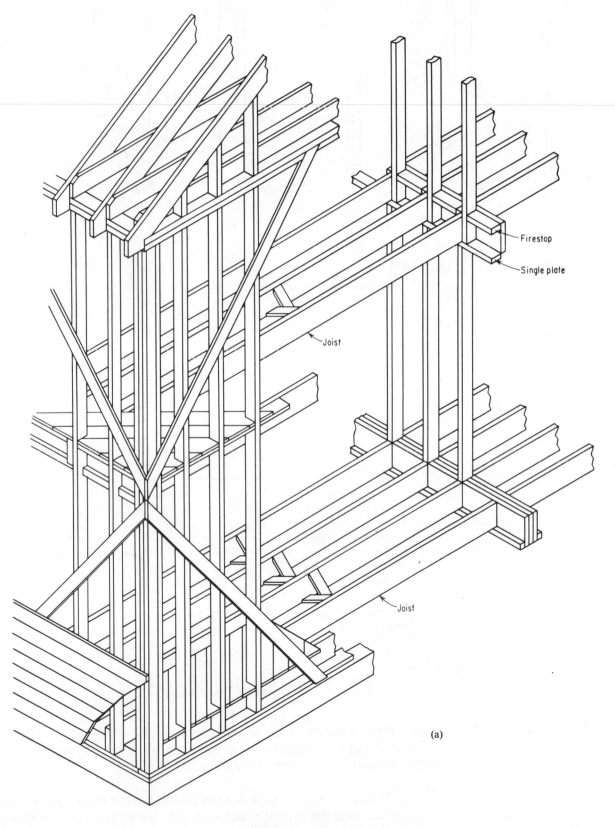

Firestop

Single plate

Joist

Joist

(a)

FIGURE 5-3: *Balloon frame.*

137

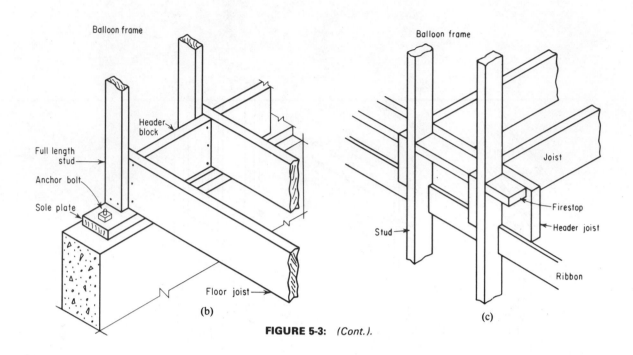

FIGURE 5-3: *(Cont.).*

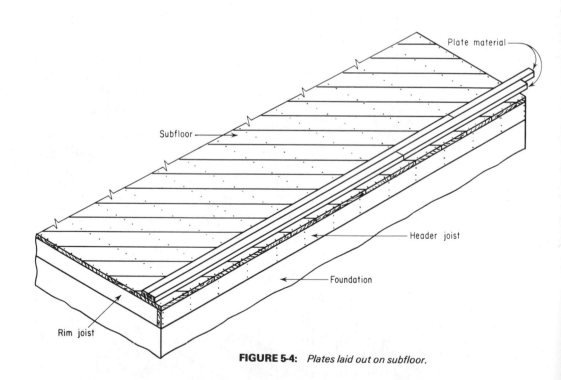

FIGURE 5-4: *Plates laid out on subfloor.*

studs, opening trimmers, partition junctions, and *cripple studs.* Since the location of the members on the top plate will be identical, the two plates are laid out together. Proceed as follows:

1. Pick out straight stock for the plates; two or more pieces are probably required for each one. Set them out across the subfloor, side by side (see Fig. 5-4).

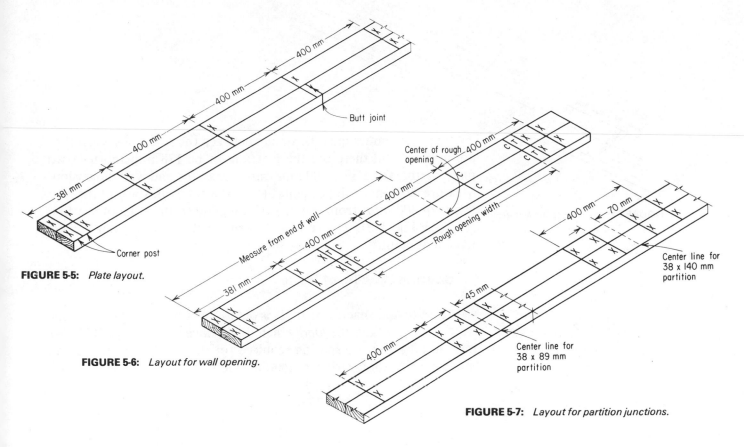

FIGURE 5-5: *Plate layout.*

FIGURE 5-6: *Layout for wall opening.*

FIGURE 5-7: *Layout for partition junctions.*

2. Square off one end of each, mark the position of the corner post at the end, and lay off the entire length on the required centers. Be sure that end joints in either plate come in the center of a stud position and that the joint in the top and bottom plate does not come on the same stud (see Fig. 5-5).

3. Check the plans for the locations of the centers of door and window openings. Mark these on the plates by a center line, as illustrated in Fig. 5-6.

4. Measure on each side of the center line one half the width of the opening, and mark for trimmer studs outside these points (see Fig. 5-6). Use a "T" to indicate trimmer.

5. Outside the trimmer lay off the position of a full-length stud (see Fig. 5-6). Use an "X" to indicate full-length stud.

6. Mark all the original layout positions between the trimmers for cripple studs. In addition, cripple studs may be laid out immediately inside the trimmers. Use a "C" to indicate cripples.

7. Check the plans for positions of partition centers and mark them on the plates. Measure 45 mm (for a 38 × 89 mm partition) or 70 mm (for a 38 × 140 mm partition) on each side of the center line and mark the position of a full-length stud outside these points (see Fig. 5-7).

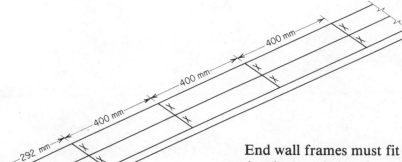

FIGURE 5-8: *End wall plate layout.*

End wall frames must fit snugly between the side walls when they are in place and therefore the plates must be 178 mm shorter (two plate widths, for a 38 × 89 mm frame) than the end wall dimension. Measure 292 mm (width of plate + one-half the thickness of the stud less than 400 mm) from the end of the plate to the edge of the first stud (see Fig. 5-8). The rest of the studs will be on regular centers from that point.

Size and Spacing of Studs

The size and spacing of studs is determined by the *location* of the wall, its *height,* and the *load* which it will have to support. Table 5-1 indicates the size and spacing required for studs in both exterior and interior walls, for a variety of loading conditions.

TABLE 5-1: *Size and spacing of studs*

Type of wall	Supported loads (including dead loads)	Min. stud size (mm)	Max. stud spacing (mm)	Max. unsupported height (m)
Interior	No load	38 × 38	400	2.4
		38 × 89 flat	400	3.6
	Limited attic storage (1)	38 × 64	600	3.0
		38 × 89	600	3.6
	Full attic storage (2) plus 1 floor, or roof load plus 1 floor, or limited attic storage (1) plus 2 floors	38 × 89	400	3.6
	Full attic storage (2) or roof load, or roof load plus 2 floors	38 × 89	300	3.6
		64 × 89	400	3.6
		38 × 140	400	4.2
	Full attic storage (2) plus 3 floors, or roof load plus 3 floors	38 × 140	300	4.2
Exterior	Roof with or without attic storage	38 × 64	400	2.4
		38 × 89	600	3.0
	Roof with or without attic storage plus 1 floor	38 × 89	400	3.0
		38 × 140	600	3.0
	Roof with or without attic storage plus 2 floors	38 × 89	300	3.0
		64 × 89	400	3.0
		38 × 140	400	3.6
	Roof with or without attic storage plus 3 floors	38 × 140	300	1.8

NOTES: 1. Applies to attics not accessible by a stairway.
2. Applies to attics accessible by a stairway.

140

CUTTING THE FRAME

The assembly of the frame will be made much simpler if all the pieces have been cut accurately first. Read the drawings carefully and find the length of studs. Check sole and top plate layouts for the number of full-length studs required, taking into account the extras needed at corners, partition junctions, wall openings, etc. Check the plans for the width and height of all exterior openings and for the height of the top of the openings above the subfloor. See Chapter 11 for details of window frame sizes. For standard wood-sash windows, the rough opening should be 20 mm larger in height and width than the frame. For other types of windows, be sure to determine the proper rough opening sizes required. Rough openings for wooden door frames should also be 20 mm larger than the frame. See Chapter 11 for details on door-frame sizes.

Count the number of trimmers, lintels, rough sills, and cripples required from the layout. With rough opening sizes and heights above floor, it is not difficult to calculate the length and cut these ready for assembly.

Stud Lengths

Regular: The length of regular studs, corner post members and partition junction studs will be the finished wall height plus clearance (usually 25 mm) less the thickness of *three* plates. For example, if the finished wall height is to be 2400 mm, the regular stud length will be $2400 + 25 - (3 \times 38) = 2311$ mm.

Trimmers: The length of a trimmer stud will be the height of the top of the opening above the floor less the thickness of *one* plate.

Lower cripple studs: The length of the lower cripple stud will be the height of the bottom of the opening above the floor less the thickness of *two* plates.

Upper cripple studs: Although it is possible to calculate the length of the upper cripple studs, it is usually more satisfactory, from a practical standpoint, to measure the distance between lintel and top plate after the remainder of the members in the wall have been assembled (see Fig. 5-9).

Rough sill length

The length of the rough sill (see Fig. 5-9) will be equal to the width of the rough opening.

Lintel

The length of the lintel will be the width of the rough opening (see Fig. 5-9) plus the thickness of two trimmers (76 mm), while its

141

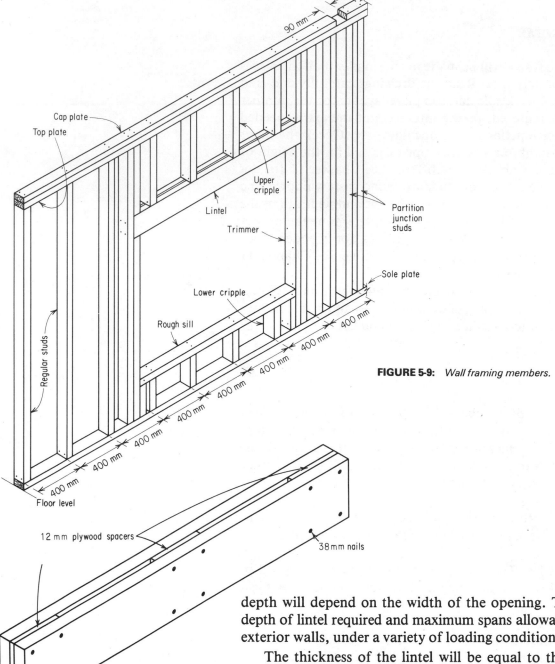

FIGURE 5-9: *Wall framing members.*

FIGURE 5-10: *Double lintel for 89 mm wall frame.*

depth will depend on the width of the opening. Table 5-2 gives the depth of lintel required and maximum spans allowable for interior and exterior walls, under a variety of loading conditions.

The thickness of the lintel will be equal to the thickness of the wall frame and must be made up accordingly. For a 89 mm frame, it is usually made of two pieces of 38 mm material nailed together, with the proper thickness of spacer between them, as illustrated in Fig. 5-10. For a 140 mm frame, 3 pieces of material could be used, spaced with the same thickness of plywood.

ASSEMBLING THE FRAME

When the pieces have all been cut, the process of assembly can begin, with the first step being to make up the corner posts and lintels. A number of types of corner posts are used, two of which are illustrated in Fig. 5-11, but for assembly on a flat surface, a partial corner, made

TABLE 5-2: *Maximum spans for wood lintels (meters)*

Location of lintels	Supported loads including dead loads and ceiling	Nominal depth of lintel (mm)	Maximum allowable span
Interior walls	Limited attic storage	100	1.22
		150	1.83
		200	2.44
		250	3.05
		300	3.81
	Full attic storage or roof load or limited attic storage plus 1 floor	100	0.61
		150	0.91
		200	1.22
		250	1.52
		300	1.83
	Full attic storage plus 1 floor or roof load plus 1 floor or limited attic storage plus 2 or 3 floors	100	—
		150	0.76
		200	0.91
		250	1.22
		300	1.52
	Full attic storage plus 2 or 3 floors or roof load plus 2 or 3 floors	100	—
		150	0.61
		200	0.91
		250	1.10
		300	1.22
Exterior walls	Roof with or without attic storage	100	1.12
		150	1.68
		200	2.23
		250	2.75
		300	3.35
	Roof with or without attic storage plus 1 floor	100	0.33
		150	1.23
		200	1.84
		250	2.23
		300	2.52
	Roof with or without attic storage plus 2 or 3 floors	100	0.33
		150	1.12
		200	1.68
		250	1.84
		300	2.23

(Courtesy National Research Council)

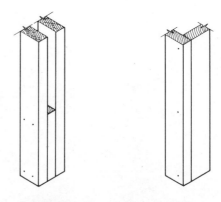

FIGURE 5-11: *Corner posts.*

Western corner   Three-stud corner

Block

by omitting the unit which is part of the end wall frame, is the most practical arrangement. The third member of the corner will be supplied by the end wall frame (see Fig. 5-12). Lintels are normally constructed as illustrated in Fig. 5-10.

The assembly of the wall frames can now begin, starting with one of the side walls. If the project is a platform frame, the wall will be assembled on the subfloor and raised into position in one or more units, depending on the length. Proceed as follows:

1. Lay out the sole and top plates on edge, spaced stud length apart, with the laid-out faces toward each other. The sole plate should be near the edge of the floor frame on which it will rest.

FIGURE 5-12: *Partial corner posts.*

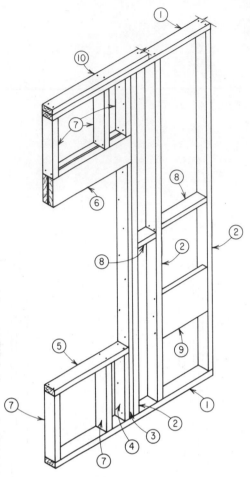

1. Sole and top plates
2. Regular studs
3. Trimmer
4. Lower end cripple
5. Rough sill
6. Lintel
7. Upper and lower cripples
8. Firestops
9. Wall backing
10. Cap plate

FIGURE 5-13: *Order of wall member assembly.*

2. Place a full-length stud at each position indicated on the layout and a corner post at each end.

3. Nail the sole and top plates to the ends of these with two 75 mm nails in each end.

4. Nail the trimmers to the full-length studs on each side of openings.

5. Nail the two end lower cripple studs to the inside of the trimmers, as shown in Fig. 5-13.

6. Lay the rough sill on the ends of the two lower cripples and nail.

7. Set the lintels on the ends of the trimmers and endnail through the full length studs.

8. Set the remainder of the cripple studs, upper and lower, in position and nail. The upper cripples must be toenailed to the top edge of the lintel.

9. Run a line across the frame at the specified height, set in and nail the firestops, either in line or offset (see Fig. 5-14).

10. Set the wall backing in place and nail (inside face of the wall is *down*).

11. Nail on the cap plate. It must be kept back 89 mm from the ends of the wall and a gap left open at partition junctions (see Fig. 5-14).

WALL SHEATHING

In the case of a platform frame, it is usually advantageous to sheathe the frame before standing it in place. Begin by making sure that the frame is square. Check the diagonal distances from the bottom corners to the opposite top ones. They should be exactly the same. Nail a long board diagonally across the frame to keep it square until some sheathing is applied.

There are a number of materials available which may be used as sheathing. They include *shiplap, common boards, plywood, exterior fiber board, exterior gypsum board* and *styrofoam insulating sheathing.* Sheathing grade plywood is probably the most widely used but all the others do a satisfactory job and, in an age of energy conservation, styrofoam sheathing is particularly attractive because of its high insulation value.

Shiplap or common boards must be applied diagonally for best results. Although this method of application uses more material, it gives much greater rigidity than horizontal application. Boards should be applied at an angle of 45 degrees (see Fig. 5-15).

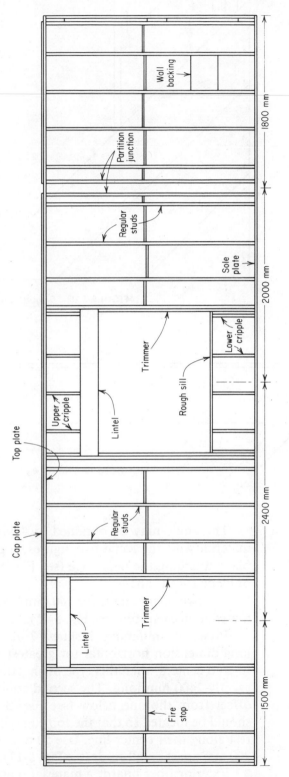

FIGURE 5-14: *Wall frame assembled.*

Cap plate

Top plate

Upper cripple

Lintel

Trimmer

Regular studs

Partition junction

Wall backing

Sole plate

Lower cripple

Rough sill

Regular studs

Trimmer

Lintel

Fire stop

1800 mm

2000 mm

2400 mm

1500 mm

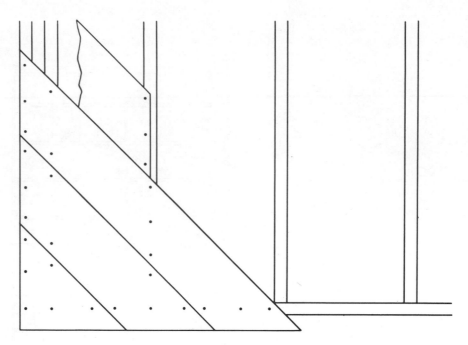

FIGURE 5-15: *Diagonal board sheathing.*

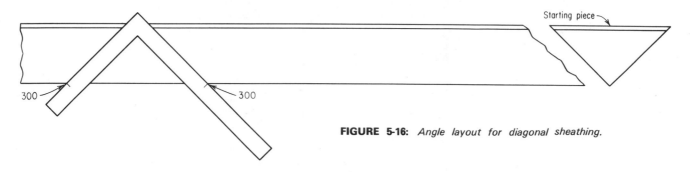

FIGURE 5-16: *Angle layout for diagonal sheathing.*

The angle may be obtained by laying the square on a piece of material with the same two figures, e.g., 300, on both tongue and blade touching the near edge (see Fig. 5-16). Mark on either tongue or blade for the angle.

Use two 60 mm nails for 140 mm boards and three nails for wider material on each stud (see Fig. 5-15).

Plywood, minimum thickness 7 mm, should be applied with the long dimension horizontal for greatest rigidity. Check the accuracy of stud centers when this type of sheathing is used, for the sheets are exactly 2400 mm long. The second course should have the end joint offset from the one below (see Fig. 5-17). The firestops or girths should be located so that the top edge of the 1200 mm wide sheet will rest along their center line. Use 50 mm coated or spiral nails, spaced 200 mm apart on all studs (see Fig. 5-17).

Exterior fiber board, a material made from shredded wood fiber impregnated with asphalt, is commonly made in 1200 × 2400 mm sheets, 12 mm thick. It should be applied with the long dimension horizontal and it is essential that the top edge rest on the girths. Nail

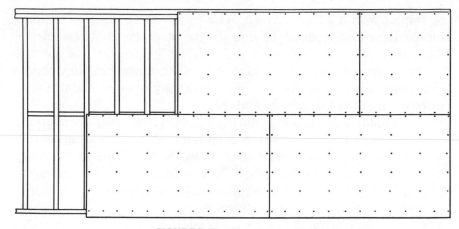

FIGURE 5-17: *Plywood sheathing.*

with 60 mm broad-head nails or 50 mm staples, spaced 150 mm apart on all studs. Vertical joints should be offset, as with plywood.

Exterior gypsum board is made from a core of gypsum encased in asphalt-impregnated paper. The sheet is 600 × 2400 × 12 mm, with the long edges having a tongue and groove for a tight horizontal joint. It is applied with the long dimension horizontal. Fifty mm coated or spiral nails, spaced 150 mm apart on all studs, are used. All vertical joints must be staggered (see Fig. 5-18). Some building codes require let-in diagonal bracing with this type of sheathing.

Styrofoam insulating sheathing is a synthetic material made from expanded polystyrene in rigid sheets with a smooth, high density skin. It has a thermal resistance (r-value) of 5.0 per 25 mm. The sheets are 600 × 2400 mm, 25 or 38 mm thick, with sliplapped edges for a tight closure and are applied horizontally.

Fasteners may be broad headed (roofing) nails, staples, screws, or clips, with spacing of 150 mm for nails with a 12 mm diameter head

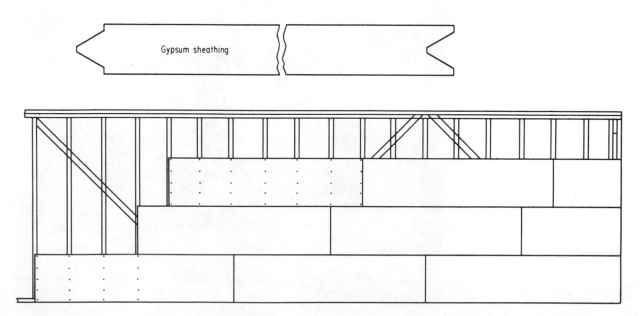

FIGURE 5-18: *Gypsum board exterior sheathing.*

147

or staples with a 12 mm crown. The length of the nails or staples should be a minimum of 12 mm longer than the thickness of the sheathing.

The styrofoam should be covered with exterior building paper, over which any type of exterior finish, including wood or metal siding, stucco or brick veneer may be applied.

Styrofoam will burn and during shipping, storage, installation, and use it must not be exposed to open flame or other ignition source.

It is generally a good practice to allow the sheathing to overhang the bottom of the sole plate about 50 mm (see Fig. 5-17). This overhang helps to line the wall up with the edge of the floor frame as it is erected and it also allows the wall and floor frames to be tied together. At the top of the wall, the sheathing is often stopped at the top of the top plate so that the rafter birdsmouth can fit over the cap plate without any extra cutting.

It is also sometimes desirable to apply the outside paper and stucco wire—where specified—before the wall is raised.

ERECTING THE FRAME

Usually a one-story wall frame can be raised by hand unless it is particularly long or heavy, in which case a crane of some sort must be used. Be sure that the bottom of the frame is close to the edge of the subfloor so that as the wall is raised the sheathing overhang does not catch on the floor (see Fig. 5-19).

FIGURE 5-19: *Raising a section of wall by hand.*

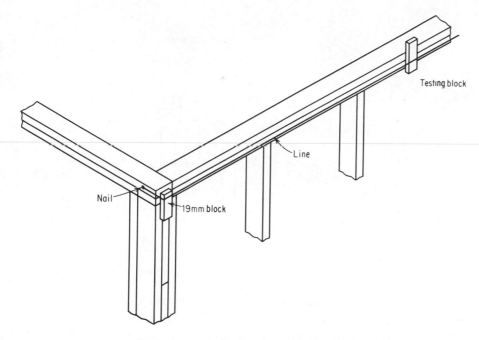

FIGURE 5-20: *Straightening top plate with line.*

When the wall is in a vertical position, it must be tied in at the bottom and straightened and braced at the top. Adjust at the bottom until the overhang of the wall sheathing is snug against the face of the floor frame. Nail the sole plate down with two 85 mm nails between each pair of studs. Be sure the nails reach a joist or the joist header. Plumb the corner studs and tie them in place with diagonal bracing.

To straighten the top, run a line very tightly along the top plate, tying it around the ends. Block the line out at the ends with a small piece of 19 mm material (see Fig. 5-20). Take another piece of 19 mm material and check at various points to see if the line is the correct distance from the plate. Push the top of the wall in or out, where necessary, to correct any points not in line. Brace by nailing one end of a board to the face of a stud at the top and the other end to a block fastened to the subfloor.

When one side wall has been erected and plumbed, the opposite one may be assembled and erected in the same manner, followed by the end walls, one by one. It is impractical to sheathe the end wall frames completely on the subfloor because the end wall sheathing should extend over the corner posts, but the majority of it may be applied at this time. With the end wall erect and the sole plate nailed in position, the end studs can be nailed to the side wall partial corner posts, to make the post complete.

The remainder of the sheathing can now be applied, the wall plumbed and braced and the end wall cap plate set in place. It will overlap the sidewall top plates to tie side and end walls securely together (see Fig. 5-21).

When a balloon frame is being erected, special problems are involved. Since the studs rest on the sill plate there is no sole plate, and they must be held properly spaced by some other means until the

149

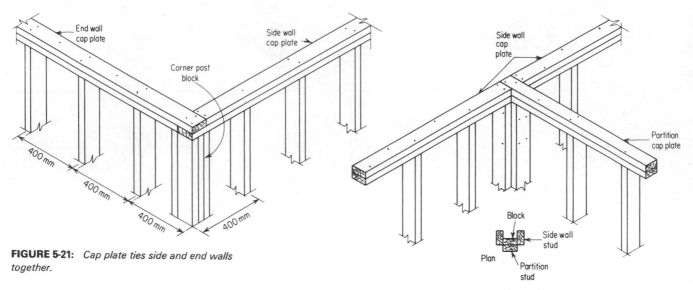

FIGURE 5-21: *Cap plate ties side and end walls together.*

FIGURE 5-22: *Partition tied to outside wall.*

frame is erected or until the sheathing is applied. Because of its height, it is usually impractical to try to raise a balloon frame wall, assembled on the floor, by hand. A crane is required to do the job efficiently, and if one is available, assembly on the floor is the best method. Otherwise, the studs have to be placed in position one at a time. If the wall is sheathed on the floor, the ribbon must be put in after the wall is erected. In nearly every case, scaffolding will have to be erected during the building of balloon frame walls.

PARTITIONS

Partitions may be *bearing* or *non-bearing*. Bearing partitions carry part of the roof load, bear one end of the ceiling joists, or both, whereas nonbearing partitions simply enclose space and carry the finishing materials.

Partitions may be laid out, assembled, and erected in the same way as outside walls. The position of the sole plate on the subfloor is first marked by *snapping a chalk line.* This is done by driving a nail at each end of the partition position and stringing a chalked line tightly between them. Pull the line up in the center and let it snap against the floor. This will mark a straight line to which the partition sole plate can be set.

Plates are laid out, studs and other members cut and assembled. Nail three blocks about 300 mm in length between the side wall partition junction studs, one at the top and bottom and one in the center (see Fig. 5-22), after which the partition can be raised into place. Plumb the end studs and nail them to the partition blocks. Finally, add the cap plate, with its ends overlapping the side wall top plate (see Fig. 5-22). Erect the longest partition first, then the cross partitions and finally, the partitions forming clothes closets, hallways, etc.

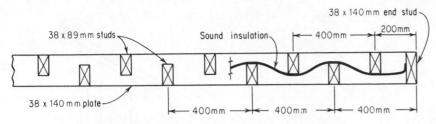

FIGURE 5-23: *Staggered studs in wide partition.*

One partition requiring special attention will be the one for the bathroom in which the main plumbing vent stack is located. In some cases, this one will have to be made 140 mm wide to accommodate the size of the stack. 38 × 89 mm studs staggered on 38 × 140 mm plates (see Fig. 5-23) will provide the width, and by weaving an insulation blanket between the studs, some sound control in that wall is also possible. Of course, 38 × 140 mm studding may be used, if desired.

Broom and clothes closet partitions may sometimes be framed with 38 × 38 material in order to save space, but only if the partition is short or in a protected location.

Sliding Door Opening

Framing to provide for doors which slide into the wall also requires special consideration. The thickness of the door must first be determined. this portion of the partition frame must be wide enough to accommodate the thickness of the door plus clearance and at least 38 mm framing on each side (see Fig. 5-24). In some cases, the track may be wider than the thickness of the door.

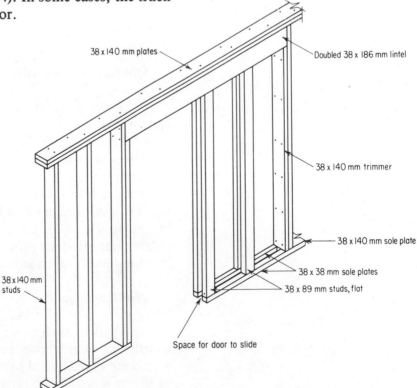

FIGURE 5-24: *Framing for sliding door.*

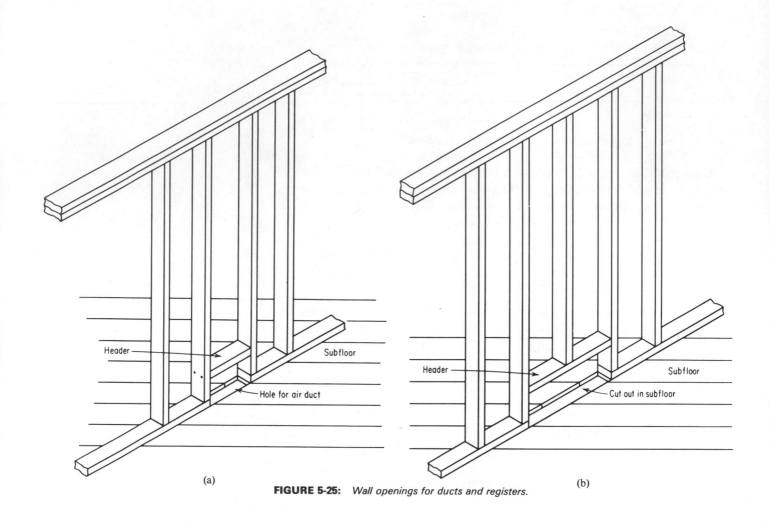

Header   Subfloor

Hole for air duct

(a)

Header   Subfloor

Cut out in subfloor

(b)

FIGURE 5-25: *Wall openings for ducts and registers.*

Openings for Heating and Ventilating

Openings must be made in the frame to accommodate heating system stacks leading to registers, if the registers are of the wall type, as well as openings for air-conditioning and ventilating systems, where they are specified.

If the register stack will fit between a pair of regular studs, all that is necessary is to cut the sole plate out between the studs, cut a hole in the subfloor, and put in a header between the studs at the required height (see Fig. 5-25a). If a wider space is needed, one or more studs must be cut off at the proper height to install a header. The sole plate is cut out and a hole made in the subfloor, as above (see Fig. 5-25b).

Wall Backing

Installations such as wall-type wash basins, wall telephones, cupboards, etc. which must be fastened to the wall, must be provided with some type of solid backing. This may be done by letting a piece of 38 mm material into the studs, as illustrated in Fig. 5-26.

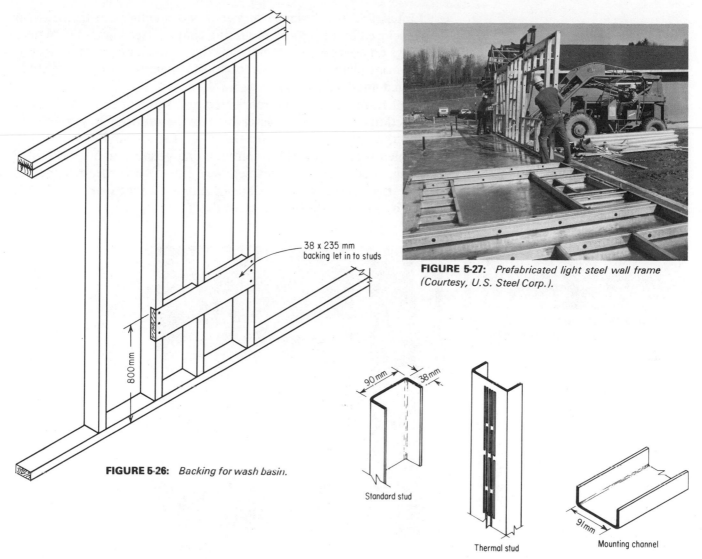

FIGURE 5-26: *Backing for wash basin.*

38 x 235 mm
backing let in to studs

800 mm

FIGURE 5-27: *Prefabricated light steel wall frame (Courtesy, U.S. Steel Corp.).*

90 mm

38 mm

Standard stud

Thermal stud

91 mm

Mounting channel

FIGURE 5-28: *Light steel framing members.*

LIGHT STEEL WALL FRAMING

Light steel wall framing members in several styles, depending on the manufacturer, are made from sheet steel, cold-formed, and consist basically of *studs* and *mounting channels* (see Fig. 5-27).

Studs are made in the form of channels, in two types, *load-bearing* and *nonload-bearing*. Load-bearing studs are made from approximately 1.5 mm material, with a 90 mm web and a 38 mm flange (see Fig. 5-28). Nonload-bearing studs are made from lighter gauge steel and in narrower widths. A special load-bearing *thermal stud* is also produced, which has five rows of alternately spaced slots in the web to reduce the heat flow.

Mounting channels are made slightly wider, to receive the ends of studs (see Fig. 5-27) and are used for top and bottom plates and rough sill. No cap plate is required, (see Fig. 5-27) since all members are spot-welded together.

FIGURE 5-29:   *Steel wall frame raised into position (Courtesy, Steel Co. of Canada).*

Lintels are usually made of two wood members, with their top edge enclosed by a length of mounting channel (see Fig. 5-29). Where openings do not reach to the bottom edge of the lintel, another length of mounting channel forms the top of the opening, with cripple studs between it and the lintel (see Fig. 5-27).

Wall frames may be prefabricated and brought to the site ready for erection (see Fig. 5-27), assembled on the subfloor and raised into position, as in Fig. 5-29 or, in the case of most interior partitions, assembled piece by piece in their standing position and spot-welded (see Fig. 5-30). Usually preassembled frames are sheathed before being raised with 9 mm plywood sheathing, fastened with steel nails driven by a pneumatic hammer (see Fig. 5-31).

FIGURE 5-30:   *Erecting interior wall frame (Courtesy, Steel Co. of Canada).*

FIGURE 5-31:   *Nailing with pneumatic hammer.*

FIGURE 5-32: *U-clips for roof members (Courtesy, U.S. Steel Corp.).*

FIGURE 5-33: *Interior steel partitions.*

Wall frames are anchored to the subfloor by powder-actuated pins, placed every 600 mm and rafters or trusses are anchored to the top plate with *U-clips* which are welded to the frame and bolted to the roof member (see Fig. 5-32).

The lighter, narrower, nonload-bearing framing material used for interior partitions allows for a considerable saving of floor space (see Fig. 5-33). They also provide a means of reducing sound transmission through the walls. Horizontal *furring channels* sound transmission punched-out openings in the studs to support *nailing channels* or *half-studs*. Furring channels and nailing channels are isolated from one another by neoprene blocks (see Fig. 5-34). The sheathing on one side of the wall is carried by the regular studs and on the other by the nailing channels.

Approximate imperial equivalents to metric quantities		
19 mm — ¾ in.	60 mm — 2⅜ in.	19 × 89 mm — 1 × 4 in.
20 mm — 0.8 in.	75 mm — 3 in.	38 × 38 mm — 2 × 2 in.
25 mm — 1 in.	400 mm — 16 in.	
38 mm — 1½ in.	2400 mm — 8 ft	
45 mm — 1.8 in.		

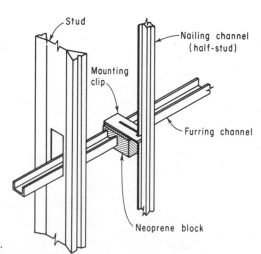

FIGURE 5-34: *Framing for sound transmission reduction.*

REVIEW QUESTIONS

5-1. There are three basic differences between balloon frame and platform frame. Outline these differences briefly.

5-2. What is the purpose of firestops in a wall frame?

5-3. Explain why it is important to have wall backing at some locations in the wall frame.

5-4. Give two reasons for the use of cap plates in wood wall frames.

5-5. The frame for a given window is 900 mm wide and 1050 mm high. If the bottom of the opening is to be 600 mm above the subfloor, calculate the length of each of the following members:

    (a) window header.

    (b) rough sill.

    (c) trimmer.

    (d) bottom cripple stud.

5-6. If board sheathing is used on the exterior of a wall frame, why should it be applied diagonally?

5-7. Explain why let-in diagonal bracing may be required when fiber board or gypsum board exterior sheathing is being used.

5-8. Using the following information, lay out a sole plate for an end wall 4.95 m in length:

    (a) western corners used.

    (b) studs 400 mm o.c.

    (c) exterior door 800 × 2000 mm, centered 1500 mm from left end.

    (d) window frame 800 × 1200 mm, centered 3300 mm from left end.

The ceiling frame consists of those members which will carry the materials forming the ceiling immediately below an attic which is not accessible by a stairway. On other levels, the ceiling materials are carried by floor joists.

JOIST SIZES

The size of members used for ceiling joists depends on (a) the span and spacing of the members, (b) the type of material used for the ceiling, and (c) the species and grade of lumber used (see Table 6-1).

CUTTING JOISTS

The length of the joists will depend on how they meet over the bearing partition. If two joists butt together over the partition (see Fig. 6-1), they must be cut to exact length from outside of frame to the center of the partition. If they lap one another over the partition, exact lengths are not required (see Fig. 6-2).

At its outer end, the joist must be cut to conform to the rise of the rafters (see Fig. 6-3). To make this cut properly, two things must be known: (a) the *rise* of the rafters (see Fig. 7-3, page 175) and (b) the height of the back of the rafter above the plate (see Fig. 6-4). Having determined these, proceed as follows:

1. Check to see which is the crown edge of the stock and make sure that it becomes the *upper* edge.
2. Measure up from the bottom edge of the joist, at the end, a distance equal to the height of the back of the rafter (see Fig. 6-5) and mark point A.
3. Lay the square on the stock with the unit rise on the tongue and 250 (unit run) on the blade touching the top edge and the edge of the blade passing through A.
4. Mark on the blade and cut the joist end to that line.

When a hip roof is involved, ceiling joists cannot be set close to the end walls, because they would interfere with the end wall rafters. In such a case, the regular ceiling joists must be stopped back far enough for the rafters to clear them (normally one or two joist spacings, depending on the rise of the rafters) and *stub* joists are run at right angles to the end wall plate (see Fig. 6-6), with the end cut exactly the same as for the regular ceiling joists.

6

THE CEILING FRAME

TABLE 6-1: *Maximum spans for ceiling joists — attic or access by stairway (meters) (live load — 0.5kn/m²)*

Lumber Species	Grade	Size (mm)	GYPSUM BOARD OR PLASTERED CEILING			OTHER CEILINGS		
			Joist Spacing			Joist Spacing		
			300 mm	400 mm	600 mm	300 mm	400 mm	600 mm
Douglas Fir - Larch (N)	Sel. Str.	38x 89	3.40	3.09	2.69	3.89	3.53	3.09
		38x140	5.34	4.85	4.24	6.11	5.55	4.85
		38x184	7.04	6.40	5.59	8.06	7.32	6.40
		38x235	8.98	8.16	7.13	10.28	9.34	8.16
		38x286	10.93	9.93	8.67	12.51	11.36	9.93
	No. 1	38x 89	3.40	3.09	2.69	3.89	3.53	3.09
		38x140	5.34	4.85	4.24	6.11	5.55	4.85
		38x184	7.04	6.40	5.59	8.06	7.32	6.40
		38x235	8.98	8.16	7.13	10.28	9.34	8.16
		38x286	10.93	9.93	8.67	12.51	11.36	9.93
	No. 2	38x 89	3.28	2.98	2.60	3.76	3.41	2.98
		38x140	5.16	4.69	4.10	5.91	5.37	4.49
		38x184	6.81	6.18	5.40	7.79	7.08	5.92
		38x235	8.68	7.89	6.89	9.94	9.03	7.56
		38x286	10.56	9.60	8.38	12.09	10.99	9.19
	No. 3	38x 89	3.15	2.82	2.31	3.26	2.82	2.31
		38x140	4.81	4.16	3.40	4.81	4.16	3.40
		38x184	6.34	5.49	4.48	6.34	5.49	4.48
		38x235	8.09	7.01	5.72	8.09	7.01	5.72
		38x286	9.84	8.52	6.96	9.84	8.52	6.96
	Const	38x 89	3.15	2.86	2.50	3.61	3.23	2.64
	Stand	38x 89	2.81	2.43	1.98	2.81	2.43	1.98
	Util	38x 89	1.91	1.66	1.35	1.91	1.66	1.35
Hem-Fir (N)	Sel. Str.	38x 89	3.27	2.97	2.60	3.75	3.40	2.97
		38x140	5.15	4.67	4.08	5.89	5.35	4.64
		38x184	6.78	6.16	5.38	7.77	7.06	6.12
		38x235	8.66	7.87	6.87	9.91	9.00	7.81
		38x286	10.53	9.57	8.36	12.06	10.95	9.50
	No. 1	38x 89	3.27	2.97	2.60	3.75	3.40	2.95
		38x140	5.15	4.67	4.08	5.89	5.35	4.64
		38x184	6.78	6.16	5.38	7.77	6.96	5.68
		38x235	8.66	7.87	6.87	9.91	8.89	7.25
		38x286	10.53	9.57	8.36	12.06	10.81	8.82
	No. 2	38x 89	3.16	2.87	2.51	3.62	3.28	2.67
		38x140	4.97	4.51	3.87	5.47	4.74	3.87
		38x184	6.55	5.95	5.10	7.21	6.25	5.10
		38x235	8.36	7.60	6.51	9.21	7.97	6.51
		38x286	10.17	9.24	7.92	11.20	9.70	7.92
	No. 3	38x 89	2.81	2.43	1.98	2.81	2.43	1.98
		38x140	4.15	3.59	2.93	4.15	3.59	2.93
		38x184	5.47	4.74	3.87	5.47	4.74	3.87
		38x235	6.98	6.05	4.94	6.98	6.05	4.94
		38x286	8.49	7.36	6.01	8.49	7.36	6.01
	Const	38x 89	3.04	2.76	2.29	3.23	2.80	2.29
	Stand	38x 89	2.42	2.10	1.71	2.42	2.10	1.71
	Util	38x 89	1.66	1.43	1.17	1.66	1.43	1.17
Eastern Hemlock- Tamarack (N)	Sel. Str.	38x 89	3.12	2.83	2.47	3.57	3.24	2.83
		38x140	4.90	4.45	3.89	5.61	5.10	4.45
		38x184	6.46	5.87	5.13	7.40	6.72	5.87
		38x235	8.25	7.49	6.55	9.44	8.58	7.49
		38x286	10.03	9.12	9.96	11.49	10.43	9.12

Lumber Species	Grade	Size (mm)	GYPSUM BOARD OR PLASTERED CEILING			OTHER CEILINGS		
			Joist Spacing			Joist Spacing		
			300 mm	400 mm	600 mm	300 mm	400 mm	600 mm
Eastern Hemlock Tamarack (N) (cont'd)	No. 1	38x 89	3.12	2.38	2.47	3.57	3.24	2.83
		38x140	4.90	4.45	3.89	5.61	5.10	4.45
		38x184	6.46	5.87	5.13	7.40	6.72	5.87
		38x235	8.25	7.49	6.55	9.44	8.58	7.49
		38x286	10.03	9.12	7.96	11.49	10.43	9.12
	No. 2	38x 89	3.01	2.73	2.38	3.44	3.13	2.73
		38x140	4.73	4.29	3.75	5.41	4.92	4.29
		38x184	6.23	5.66	4.94	7.13	6.48	5.66
		38x235	7.95	7.22	6.31	9.10	8.27	7.22
		38x286	9.67	8.79	7.68	11.07	10.06	8.79
	No. 3	38x 89	2.90	2.63	2.22	3.15	2.72	2.22
		38x140	4.55	4.00	3.26	4.62	4.00	3.26
		38x184	6.01	5.27	4.30	6.09	5.27	4.30
		38x235	7.66	6.73	5.49	7.77	6.73	5.49
		38x286	9.32	8.18	6.68	9.45	8.18	6.68
	Const	38x 89	2.90	2.63	2.30	3.32	3.01	2.55
	Stand	38x 89	2.67	2.31	1.89	2.67	2.31	1.89
	Util	38x 89	1.86	1.61	1.32	1.86	1.61	1.32
Coast Species	Sel. Str.	38x 89	3.27	2.97	2.60	3.75	3.40	2.97
		38x140	5.15	4.67	4.08	5.89	5.35	4.59
		38x184	6.78	6.16	5.38	7.77	7.05	6.05
		38x235	9.66	7.87	6.87	9.91	9.00	7.73
		38x286	10.53	9.57	8.36	12.06	10.95	9.40
	No. 1	38x 89	3.27	2.97	2.60	3.75	3.40	2.92
		38x140	5.15	4.67	4.08	5.89	5.22	4.26
		38x184	6.78	6.16	5.38	7.77	6.88	5.61
		38x235	8.66	7.87	6.87	9.91	8.78	7.17
		38x286	10.53	9.57	8.36	12.06	10.68	8.72
	No. 2	38x 89	3.16	2.87	2.51	3.62	3.23	2.64
		38x140	4.97	4.51	3.81	5.39	4.67	3.81
		38x184	6.55	5.95	5.02	7.10	6.15	5.02
		38x235	8.36	7.60	6.41	9.06	7.85	6.41
		38x286	10.17	9.24	7.79	11.03	9.55	7.79
	No. 3	38x 89	2.78	2.40	1.96	2.78	2.40	1.96
		38x140	4.10	3.55	2.89	4.10	3.55	2.89
		38x184	5.40	4.68	3.82	5.40	4.68	3.82
		38x235	6.89	5.97	4.87	6.89	5.97	4.87
		38x286	8.38	7.26	5.93	8.38	7.26	5.93
	Const	38x 89	3.04	2.75	2.24	3.18	2.75	2.24
	Stand	38x 89	2.38	2.06	1.68	2.38	2.06	1.68
	Util	38x 89	1.66	1.43	1.17	1.66	1.43	1.17
Spruce-Pine-Fir	Sel. Str.	38x 89	3.09	2.80	2.45	3.53	3.21	2.80
		38x140	4.85	4.41	3.85	5.55	5.05	4.41
		38x184	6.40	5.81	5.08	7.32	6.65	5.81
		38x235	8.16	7.41	6.48	9.34	8.49	7.41
		38x286	9.93	9.02	7.88	11.36	10.33	9.02
	No. 1	38x 89	3.09	2.80	2.45	3.53	3.21	2.80
		38x140	4.85	4.41	3.85	5.55	5.05	4.18
		38x184	6.40	5.81	5.08	7.32	6.65	5.51
		38x235	8.16	7.41	6.48	9.34	8.49	7.03
		38x286	9.93	9.02	7.88	11.36	10.33	8.55

Lumber Species	Grade	Size (mm)	GYPSUM BOARD OR PLASTERED CEILING			OTHER CEILINGS		
			Joist Spacing			Joist Spacing		
			300 mm	400 mm	600 mm	300 mm	400 mm	600 mm
Spruce - Pine - Fir	No. 2	38x 89	2.98	2.71	2.37	3.41	3.10	2.59
		38x140	4.69	4.26	3.72	5.30	4.59	3.75
		38x184	6.18	5.62	4.91	6.99	6.05	4.94
		38x235	7.89	7.17	6.26	8.92	7.73	6.31
		38x286	9.60	8.72	7.62	10.85	9.40	7.67
	No. 3	38x 89	2.74	2.37	1.94	2.74	2.37	1.94
		38x140	4.04	3.50	2.85	4.04	3.50	2.85
		38x184	5.33	4.61	3.76	5.33	4.61	3.76
		38x235	6.80	5.89	4.80	6.80	5.89	4.80
		38x286	8.27	7.16	5.84	8.27	7.16	5.84
	Const	38x 89	2.87	2.61	2.20	3.12	2.70	2.20
	Stand	38x 89	2.34	2.03	1.66	2.34	2.03	1.66
	Util	38x 89	1.60	1.39	1.13	1.60	1.39	1.13
Western Cedar (N)	Sel. Str.	38x 89	2.97	2.70	2.36	3.40	3.09	2.70
		38x140	4.67	4.24	3.71	5.35	4.86	4.24
		38x184	6.16	5.59	4.89	7.05	6.40	5.59
		38x235	7.86	7.14	6.24	9.00	8.17	7.14
		38x286	9.56	8.68	7.58	10.94	9.94	8.68
	No. 1	38x 89	2.97	2.70	2.36	3.40	3.09	2.70
		38x140	4.67	4.24	3.71	5.35	4.86	4.23
		38x184	6.16	5.59	4.89	7.05	6.40	5.58
		38x235	7.86	7.14	6.24	9.00	8.17	7.12
		38x286	9.56	8.68	7.58	10.94	9.94	8.66
	No. 2	38x 89	2.87	2.61	2.28	3.29	2.99	2.61
		38x140	4.51	4.10	3.58	5.17	4.63	3.78
		38x184	5.95	5.41	4.72	6.82	6.10	4.98
		38x235	7.60	6.90	6.03	8.70	7.79	6.36
		38x286	9.24	8.39	7.33	10.58	9.47	7.73
	No. 3	38x 89	2.74	2.37	1.94	2.74	2.37	1.94
		38x140	4.04	3.50	2.85	4.04	3.50	2.85
		38x184	5.33	4.61	3.76	5.33	4.61	3.76
		38x235	6.80	5.89	4.80	6.80	5.89	4.80
		38x286	8.27	7.16	5.84	8.27	7.16	5.84
	Const	38x 89	2.77	2.51	2.19	3.15	2.72	2.22
	Stand	38x 89	2.34	2.03	1.66	2.34	2.03	1.66
	Util	38x 89	1.60	1.39	1.13	1.60	1.39	1.13
Northern Species	Sel. Str.	38x 89	2.97	2.70	2.36	3.40	3.09	2.70
		38x140	4.67	4.24	3.71	5.35	4.86	4.24
		38x184	6.16	5.59	4.89	7.05	6.40	5.59
		38x235	7.86	7.14	6.24	9.00	8.17	7.14
		38x286	9.56	8.68	7.58	10.94	9.94	8.68
	No. 1	38x 89	2.97	2.70	2.36	3.40	3.09	2.70
		38x140	4.67	4.24	3.71	5.35	4.86	4.04
		38x184	6.16	5.59	4.89	7.05	6.40	5.33
		38x235	7.86	7.14	6.24	9.00	8.17	6.80
		38x286	9.56	8.68	7.58	10.94	9.94	8.27
	No. 2	38x 89	2.87	2.61	2.28	3.29	2.99	2.51
		38x140	4.51	4.10	3.58	5.13	4.44	2.63
		38x184	5.95	5.41	4.72	6.76	5.86	4.78
		38x235	7.60	6.90	6.03	8.63	7.47	6.10
		38x286	9.24	8.39	7.33	10.50	9.09	7.42

Lumber Species	Grade	Size (mm)	GYPSUM BOARD OR PLASTERED CEILING			OTHER CEILINGS		
			Joist Spacing			Joist Spacing		
			300 mm	400 mm	600 mm	300 mm	400 mm	600 mm
Northern Species	No. 3	38x 89	2.64	2.29	1.86	2.63	2.29	1.86
		38x140	3.87	3.35	2.73	3.87	3.35	2.73
		38x184	5.10	4.42	3.60	5.10	4.42	3.60
		38x235	6.51	5.64	4.60	6.51	5.64	4.60
		38x286	7.92	6.85	5.60	7.92	6.85	5.60
	Const	38x 89	2.77	2.51	2.14	3.03	2.62	2.14
	Stand	38x 89	2.26	1.96	1.60	2.26	1.96	1.60
	Util	38x 89	1.54	1.33	1.09	1.54	1.33	1.09
Northern Aspen	Sel. Str.	38x 89	3.02	2.74	2.39	3.45	3.14	2.74
		38x140	4.74	4.31	3.76	5.43	4.91	4.31
		38x184	6.26	5.68	4.96	7.16	6.51	5.68
		38x235	7.98	7.25	6.33	9.14	8.30	7.25
		38x286	9.71	8.82	7.70	11.11	10.10	8.82
	No. 1	38x 89	3.02	2.74	2.39	3.45	3.14	2.74
		38x140	4.74	4.31	3.76	5.43	4.93	4.18
		38x184	6.26	5.68	4.96	7.16	6.51	5.51
		38x235	7.98	7.25	6.33	9.14	8.30	7.03
		38x286	9.71	8.82	7.70	11.11	10.10	8.55
	No. 2	38x 89	2.91	2.64	2.31	3.33	3.03	2.60
		38x140	4.57	4.16	3.63	5.24	4.59	3.75
		38x184	6.03	5.48	4.79	6.90	6.05	4.94
		38x235	7.70	6.99	6.11	8.81	7.71	6.31
		38x286	9.36	8.51	7.43	10.72	9.40	7.67
	No. 3	38x 89	2.74	2.37	1.94	2.74	2.37	1.94
		38x140	4.04	3.50	2.85	4.04	3.50	2.85
		38x184	5.33	4.61	3.76	5.33	4.61	3.76
		38x235	6.80	5.89	4.80	6.80	5.89	4.80
		38x286	8.27	7.16	5.84	8.27	7.16	5.84
	Const	38x 89	2.79	2.54	2.20	3.12	2.70	2.20
	Stand	38x 89	2.34	2.03	1.66	2.34	2.03	1.66
	Util	38x 89	1.60	1.39	1.13	1.60	1.39	1.13

Courtesy Canadian Wood Council

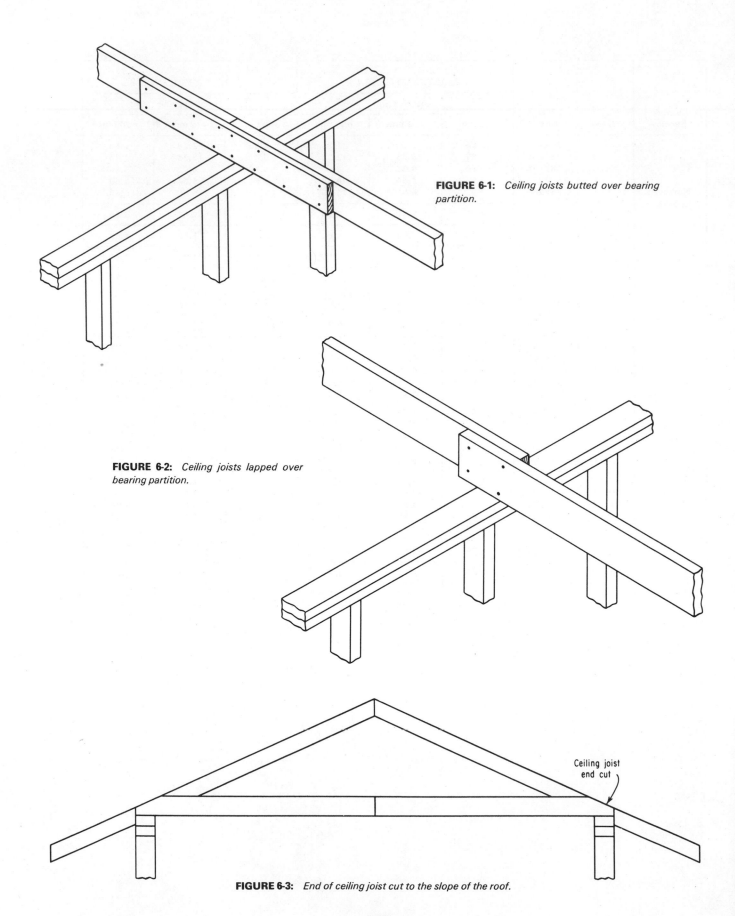

FIGURE 6-1: *Ceiling joists butted over bearing partition.*

FIGURE 6-2: *Ceiling joists lapped over bearing partition.*

Ceiling joist
end cut

FIGURE 6-3: *End of ceiling joist cut to the slope of the roof.*

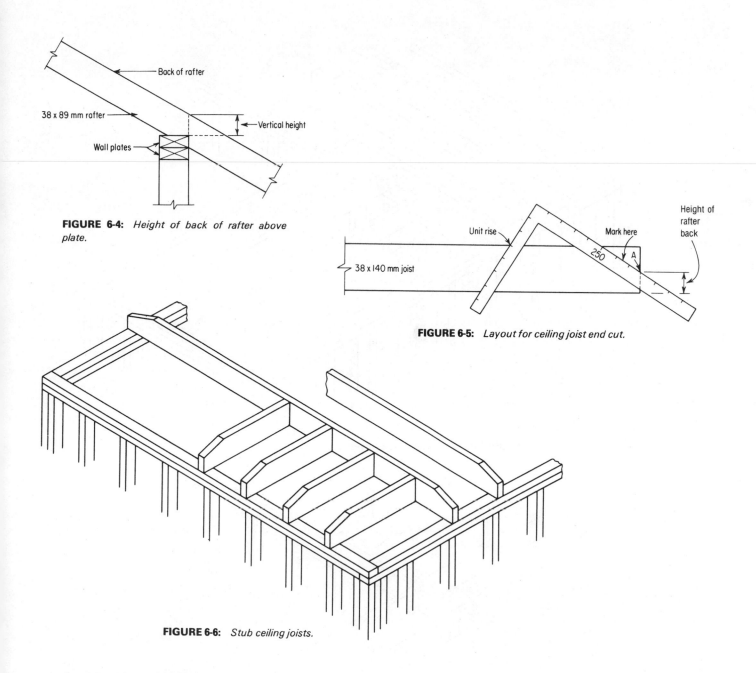

FIGURE 6-4: *Height of back of rafter above plate.*

FIGURE 6-5: *Layout for ceiling joist end cut.*

FIGURE 6-6: *Stub ceiling joists.*

ASSEMBLING JOISTS

Normally, ceiling joists run across the narrow dimension of the building, but this need not always be the case. Some joists may run in one direction and others at right angles to them. The main consideration is that there be adequate bearing and support at the ends (see Fig. 6-7).

Sometimes it is desired to have a *clear span ceiling* in some part of the building—a ceiling that runs unbroken from one outside wall to the other. Some means of supporting the inner ends of the joists is required and this is done by means of a *flush beam*. A flush beam is one which has its bottom edge flush with the bottom of the ceiling joists and is supported at its ends by a bearing wall or bearing partition (see Fig. 6-8).

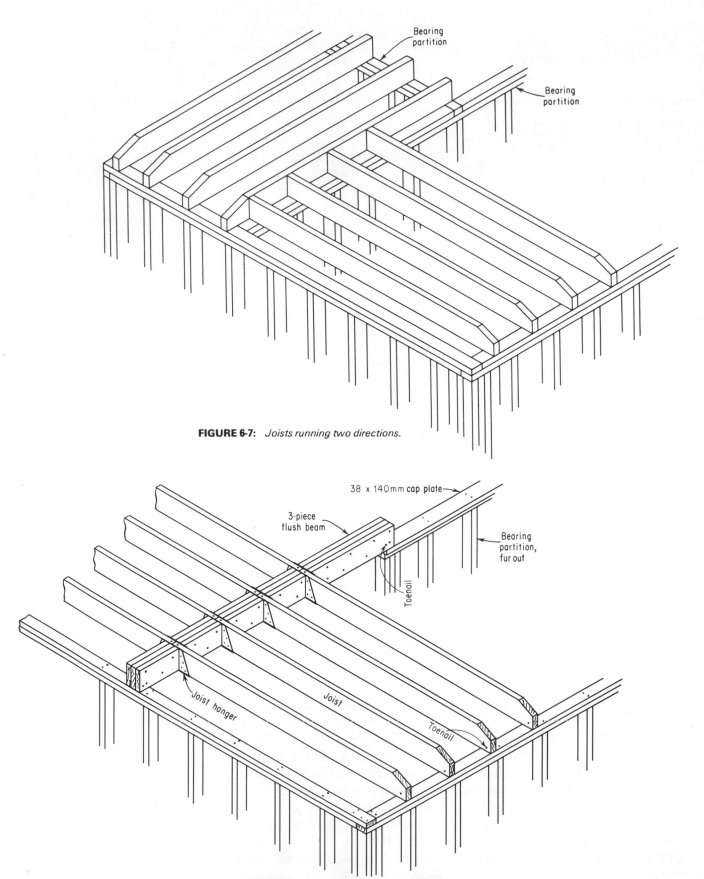

FIGURE 6-7: *Joists running two directions.*

FIGURE 6-8: *Flush beam with joist hangers.*

Ceiling joists are carried by a flush beam on *joist hangers* (see Fig. 6-8), by *end-nailing* to the two outer sections of the beam (see Fig. 6-9) or on *ledger strips* nailed to the bottom edges of the beam (see Fig. 6-10).

Layout for Ceiling Joists

The first step in the placing of ceiling joists is the layout of their positions on the wall plate. Ceiling joists are normally spaced at 300, 400, or 600 mm o.c. and, wherever possible, should be located to conform to the spacing of the rafters. This procedure not only facilitates the locating of the rafters but also makes it possible for ceiling joists and rafters to be nailed together.

Layout may begin either from the corners, from the center of the wall or from some point along it, depending on the type of roof and the dimensions of the building. For a gable roof, the two side wall plates must be laid out, while in the case of a hip roof, all four plates must be marked. For example, for a gable roof on a building 8000 mm long, in which the ceiling joists and rafters are spaced at 400 mm o.c., proceed as follows:

1. Check the building length to see whether it may be divided evenly by the specified spacing. In this case the length divides evenly into 20 spaces, so layout may begin at a corner.

2. From one, measure along the plate 400 mm to a point A, which will be the *center of the first rafter*.

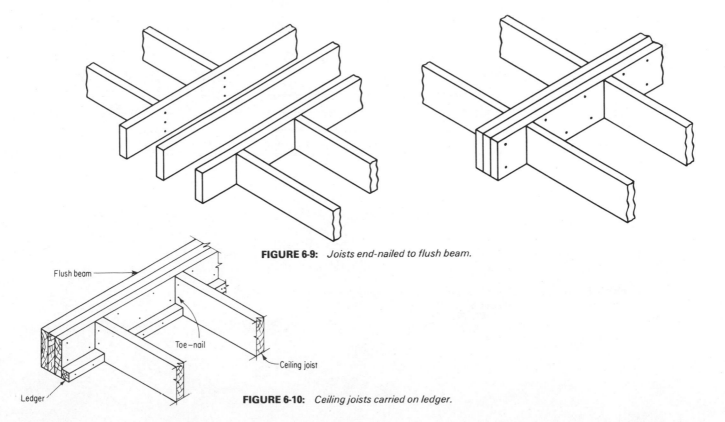

FIGURE 6-9: *Joists end-nailed to flush beam.*

Flush beam

Toe–nail

Ceiling joist

Ledger

FIGURE 6-10: *Ceiling joists carried on ledger.*

3. Measure back 19 mm (one-half the rafter thickness) and square across the plate at that point. That line will represent the *outside edge* of both the *rafter* and the ceiling joist, each sitting on opposite sides of the line. Mark with an X the position of the joist on the plate (see Fig. 6-11a).

4. Lay the square on the plate with the inner edge of the tongue against the edge of the plate and the *end of the tongue* touching the joist position line just drawn. Mark on the blade and mark an X on the same side of the line as above (see Fig. 6-11b). since the tongue of the square is 400 mm long, the position of the second ceiling joist has been established.

5. Step off as many times as necessary to lay out the entire wall plate. The line marking the last joist position should be 419 mm from the end of the plate.

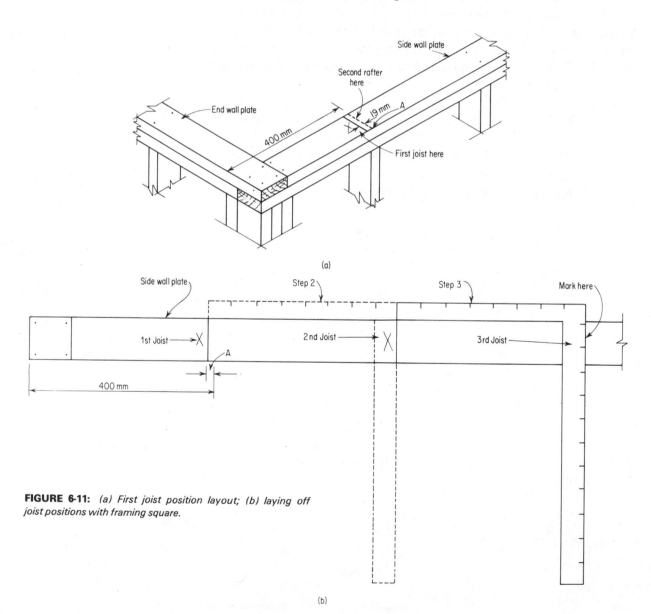

FIGURE 6-11: *(a) First joist position layout; (b) laying off joist positions with framing square.*

If the spacing is 600 mm o.c., use the blade of the square for measuring, rather than the tongue, while, if the spacing is 300 mm o.c. lay the 300 mm mark on the tongue to the position line (see Fig. 6-12).

If the length is not evenly divisible by the joist spacing, it may be preferable to begin layout at the center of the wall and lay out both ways towards the corners (see Fig. 6-13).

In a hip roof, there will normally be an end common rafter (see Fig. 7-2), which will be located in the center of the end wall. There should be a stub joist position next to it and the remainder of the stub joist positions may be laid out from it with the square as illustrated in Fig. 6-13.

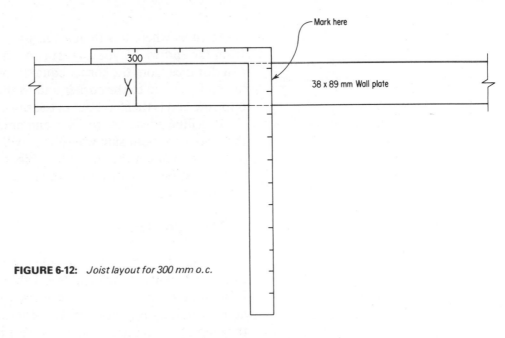

FIGURE 6-12: *Joist layout for 300 mm o.c.*

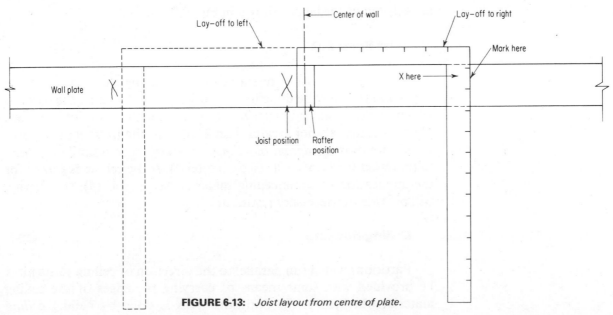

FIGURE 6-13: *Joist layout from centre of plate.*

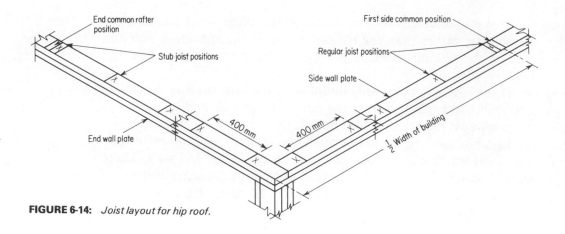

FIGURE 6-14: *Joist layout for hip roof.*

In cases where less than a full joist spacing remains at the corner from the end wall layout, layout for the side wall joists should begin at a distance from the corner equal to one half the width of the building and proceed to the corner and to the center of the wall plate. The opposite end is then laid out in the same manner (see Fig. 6-14).

If ceiling joists are to *butt* one another over the center bearing, the layout on both side wall plates will be identical. However, if the joists are to *lap* at the center (see Fig. 6-2), then the positions on one plate must be *offset* by the thickness of the joist from those on the opposite plate.

Nailing of Joists

Ceiling joists must be toenailed to the plates with a minimum of two 82 mm nails at each end (see Table 7-1, page 198). In addition, if joists butt together at the center, a 19 mm board, joist width and about 1 m long is nailed across the joint, as illustrated in Fig. 6-1. If they lap at the center, there must be a minimum of two 76 mm nails at each end of the lap, as shown in Fig. 6-2.

Joist Restraint

Ceiling joists must be restrained from twisting along their bottom edges and this may be done in several ways. At the ends, the toenails which tie the joists and plates together provide the restraint. Between plates, at intervals not greater than 2100 mm, the joists must be provided with *cross-bridging, blocking,* or *strapping* in a similar manner to that used for floor joists (see Chapter 4). If the ceiling is *furred* for the application of some ceiling material (see Fig. 6-15), the furring will provide the necessary restraint.

Ceiling Backing

Partitions which run parallel to the direction of ceiling joists must be provided with some means of carrying the edges of the ceiling material which meet the partition. This is done by nailing *ceiling*

168

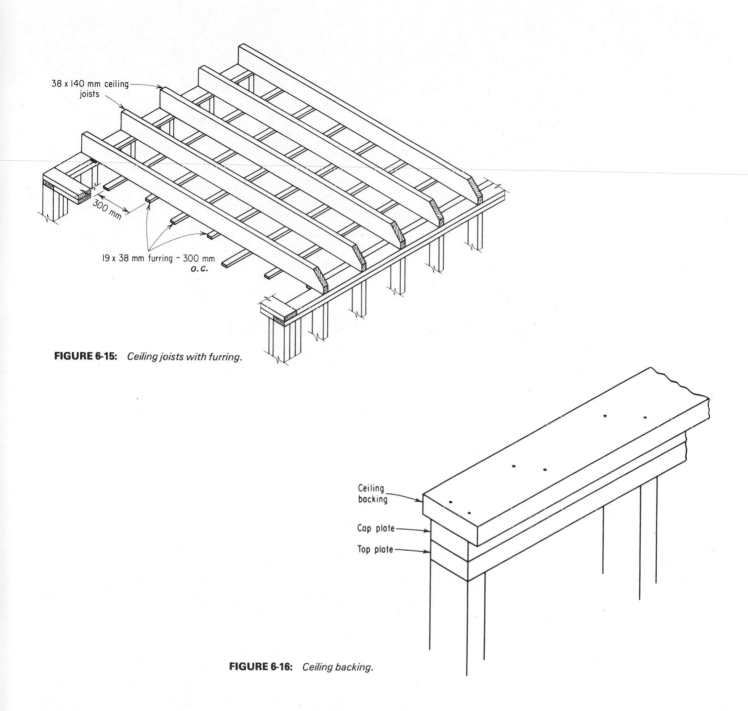

FIGURE 6-15: *Ceiling joists with furring.*

38 x 140 mm ceiling joists

300 mm

19 x 38 mm furring – 300 mm *o.c.*

Ceiling backing

Cap plate

Top plate

FIGURE 6-16: *Ceiling backing.*

backing to the cap plate (see Fig. 6-16). A piece of 38 mm material, at least 50 mm wider than the cap plate is used, allowing it to project the same amount on both sides.

Attic Access

Building codes and fire regulations demand that there be access to the attic and it is provided by a framed opening or *hatchway* at least 500 × 700 mm (see Fig. 6-17). For appearance sake, it is usually placed in a relatively inconspicuous location and provided with a trap door or other type of cover which opens upward.

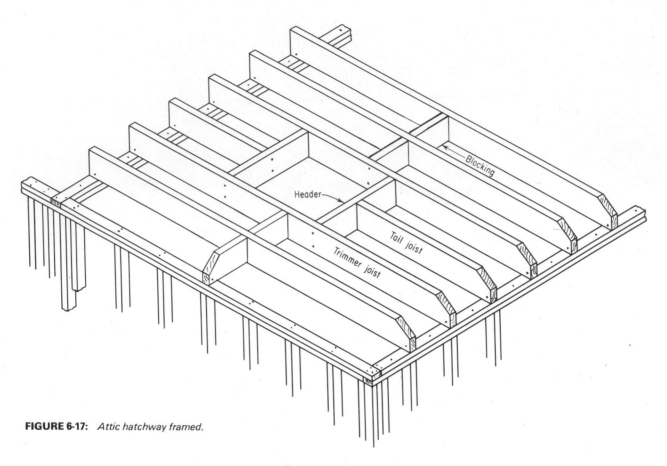

FIGURE 6-17: *Attic hatchway framed.*

Sound Reduction Through Ceilings

In buildings such as apartments of more than one story, a sound transmission problem arises where the floor joists at one level also carry the ceiling material for the rooms below, because sound is transmitted through the floor frame from one level to another.

One method of overcoming the problem is to provide a separate frame to carry the ceiling materials (see Fig. 6-18). The ends of the regular floor joists will not rest directly on the plates but will have some type of resilient pad, such as rubber, neoprene or fiberboard under each end. Thus the bottom edges of the joists will be above the level of the top of the plate. Then smaller members, acting as ceiling joists, are set between each pair of floor joists, directly on the plates. They carry the ceiling material, which, in this way, will not be in contact with the floor joists.

Approximate imperial equivalents to metric quantities

19 mm	—	¾ in.	500 mm — 20 in.	38 × 89 mm	— 2 × 4 in.
50 mm	—	2 in.	600 mm — 24 in.	38 × 140 mm	— 2 × 6 in.
76 mm	—	3 in.	700 mm — 2 ft 4 in.	38 × 184 mm	— 2 × 8 in.
82 mm	—	3¼ in.	2100 mm — 7 ft	38 × 235 mm	— 2 × 10 in.
300 mm	—	12 in.	8000 mm — 26 ft 3 in.	38 × 286 mm	— 2 × 12 in.
500 mm	—	16 in.	1 m — 3 ft 3 in.		
419 mm	—	16¾ in.			

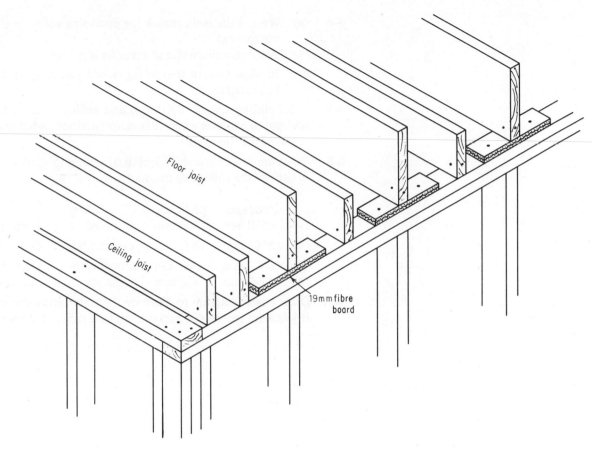

FIGURE 6-18: *Separated floor and ceiling joists.*

REVIEW QUESTIONS

6-1. List three main factors that influence the size of ceiling joists to be used in any particular situation.

6-2. What figures would you use on the framing square to lay out the cut on the outer end of ceiling joists used in conjunction with a 175 mm rise roof. Mark on_____ .

6-3. When is it necessary to use "stub" ceiling joists?

6-4. What is the minimum ceiling height, according to national Housing Standards, in each of the following areas?

(a) living room.

(b) bedroom.

(c) laundry area above grade.

6-5. (a) What is the purpose of ceiling backing?

(b) What width of ceiling backing should be used on a 38 × 89 mm partition?

171

6-6. (a) What is the main reason for providing access to the attic through the ceiling?

    (b) What minimum size of opening is required?

    (c) In what area of the ceiling would you suggest that the opening be placed?

6-7. If a building span is 8780 mm and ceiling joists must have at least 600 mm of lap over a center bearing partition, what standard length is required for the joists?

6-8. What depth and standard length of ceiling joist material are required in each of the following situations:

	Joist span	Joist spacing	Ceiling	Material
(a)	4570 mm	400 mm	plastered	Hem–Fir, No. 1
(b)	5560 mm	600 mm	gypsum board	Douglas Fir, No. 1
(c)	6020 mm	300 mm	acoustic tile	Hem–Fir, No. 2
(d)	4390 mm	400 mm	6 mm plywood	Spruce–Pine–Fir, No. 1

6-9. Draw a neat diagram to illustrate the plate layout for joists and rafters if joists are spaced 400 mm o.c. and the rafters are spaced 600 mm o.c.

The final step in completing the skeleton of a building is the framing of the roof. The work involved depends on the type of roof to be used, and the student must first become familiar with the types of roof in common use. Each has some special problems involved in its construction.

ROOF SHAPES

The shape of the roof may be one of several common designs, which include *shed* roof, *gable roof, hip* roof, *gambrel* roof, and *intersecting* roof (see Fig. 7-1).

The shed roof slopes in only one direction. The gable roof has two slopes, and the continuation of the end walls up to meet the roof is known as a *gable end*. The hip roof has four slopes, which terminate at a point if the plan is square or in a ridge if the plan is rectangular (see Fig. 7-1). A gambrel roof is a modification of a gable, each side having two slopes instead of one. An intersecting roof is formed by the meeting of two sloped roofs of one type or another.

ROOF PLAN

By examining a plan view of a roof frame, the different types of rafters involved in forming roofs can be easily distinguished. Figure 7-2 is a plan view of the frame of an intersecting hip roof. Here all types of rafters are involved.

The *common* rafters are those which run at right angles to the wall plate and meet the *ridge* at their top end. In a gable roof, all the rafters are *commons,* while in a hip roof, the two center end rafters and those side rafters which meet the ridge are *commons.* Hip rafters run from the corners of the wall plates to the ridge at an angle of 45 degrees to the plates and form the intersection of two adjacent roof surfaces. *Valley* rafters occur where two roofs intersect. Jack rafters run parallel to the commons but are shorter and are named according to their position. *Hip jacks* run from plate to hip, usually meeting at the hip in pairs. *Valley jacks* run from the valley rafter to the ridge or plate. *Cripple jacks* run from hip to valley or from valley to valley, touching neither plate nor ridge. The part of any rafter that projects beyond the wall plate is known as the *rafter tail*.

RAFTER TERMS

In order to be able to understand and solve the problems involved in laying out and cutting a set of rafters, it is necessary to know the terms used in discussing the subject.

7

ROOF, GABLE, AND DORMER FRAME

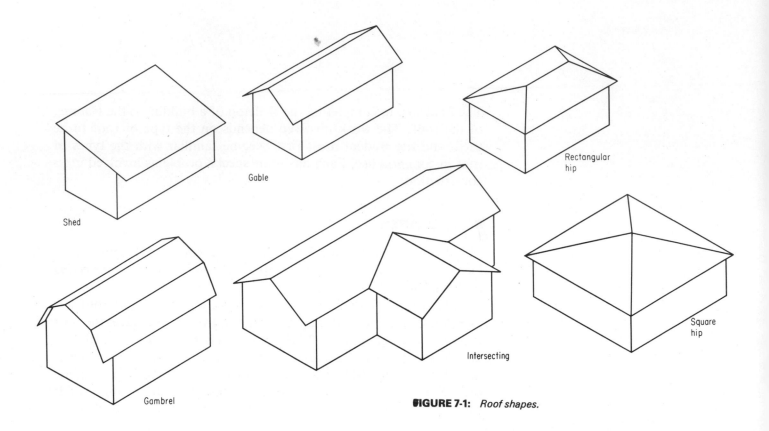

Shed

Gable

Rectangular hip

Gambrel

Intersecting

Square hip

FIGURE 7-1: *Roof shapes.*

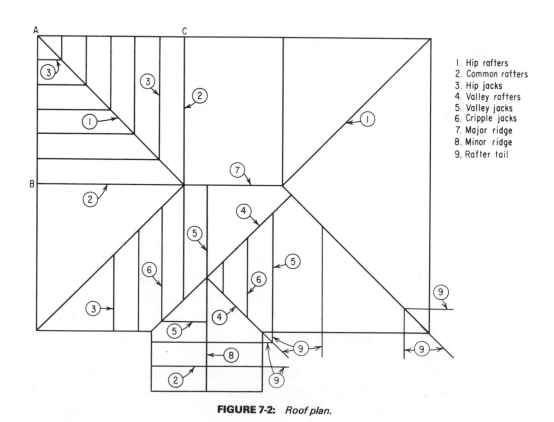

1. Hip rafters
2. Common rafters
3. Hip jacks
4. Valley rafters
5. Valley jacks
6. Cripple jacks
7. Major ridge
8. Minor ridge
9. Rafter tail

FIGURE 7-2: *Roof plan.*

174

Common Rafter

One of the basic terms, which applies to all rafters, is the *span,* the dimension of a building bridged by a pair of common rafters, while that part of the span traversed by one of the pair is called the *run* of the rafter. The length of the rafter, measured on a line through the outside edge of the building frame, is the *line length* of the rafter (see Fig. 7-3). The vertical distance from the level of the wall plates to the line length meeting point of a pair of rafters is the *total rise* of the rafter (see Fig. 7-3).

In order to make rafter layout simpler, run, rise and line length are broken down into *units.* The basic one is the *unit run*—a standard length of 250 mm (see Fig. 7-4a). The *unit rise* is the vertical distance which a rafter rises for one unit of run, while the length of rafter resulting from one unit of run is the *unit line length* (see Fig. 7-4a).

If a framing square is applied to a common rafter in position, as in Fig. 7-4a, with the 250 mm mark on the blade coinciding with the outside edge of the wall plate, a figure on the tongue will indicate the *unit rise* of the rafter. In this case, the figure is 150 mm and the diagonal distance between 150 on the tongue and 250 on the blade is the *unit line length* for that rafter (see Fig. 7-4b).

The inclination of a rafter has often been called the *pitch,* expressed as a fraction, or the *slope,* expressed in degrees but, for the

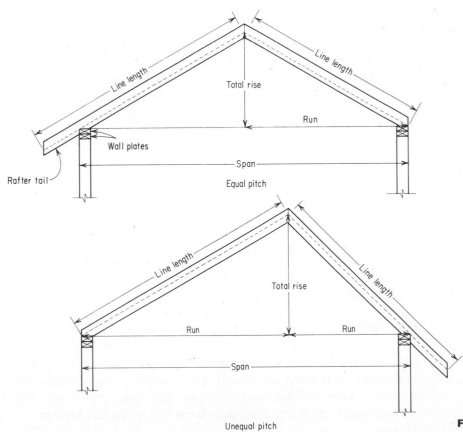

FIGURE 7-3: *Span, run, rise and line length of a rafter.*

175

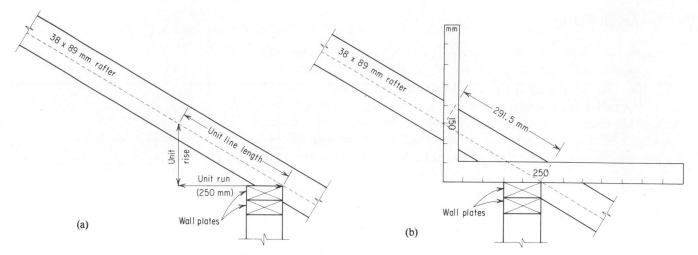

FIGURE 7-4: *(a) unit run, rise and line length; (b) unit run, rise and line length on the framing square.*

sake of simplicity, the inclination—pitch or slope—may well be called just the *rise of the rafter,* expressed in millimeters of unit rise per unit of run. For example, in Fig. 7-4b, the unit rise of that rafter is 150 mm.

In order that rafters may seat securely on the wall plate, it is common practice to cut a triangular section from the bottom edge, at the point at which it meets the wall plate, as shown in Fig. 7-5. This notch is called a *birdsmouth,* which is made by making a *seat cut*—horizontal when the rafter is in position—and a *plumb cut*—vertical when the rafter is in position (see Fig. 7-5). Common rafters are made to fit together at the top or fit to a ridgeboard (see Fig. 7-6) by making a *plumb cut* at the upper end of each and the rafter tail may have a single *plumb cut* or a plumb cut and a *seat cut* at the bottom end (see Fig. 7-5). The horizontal distance from that bottom plumb cut to outside of the wall frame is known as the *overhang* (see Fig. 7-4).

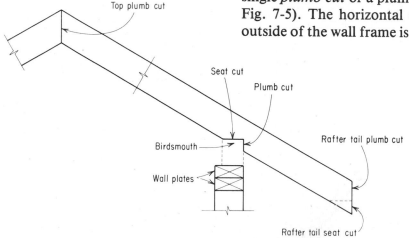

FIGURE 7-5 *Plumb and seat cuts and birdsmouth.*

Jack Rafter

Jack rafters run parallel to common rafters and therefore have the same unit run, rise and line length. They have the same birdsmouth at the plate and must have a top plumb cut. But, since they meet a hip rafter at an angle, each one must also have a *side cut* or *cheek cut* at the top end.

176

Hip Rafter

Hip rafters also have a birdsmouth at the plate but, since they run at an angle to the plate and the ridge, they must also have a *side cut* at the top end, as well as a plumb cut. That side cut may be *single* or *double* (see Fig. 7-6), depending on how the rafter meets the ridge.

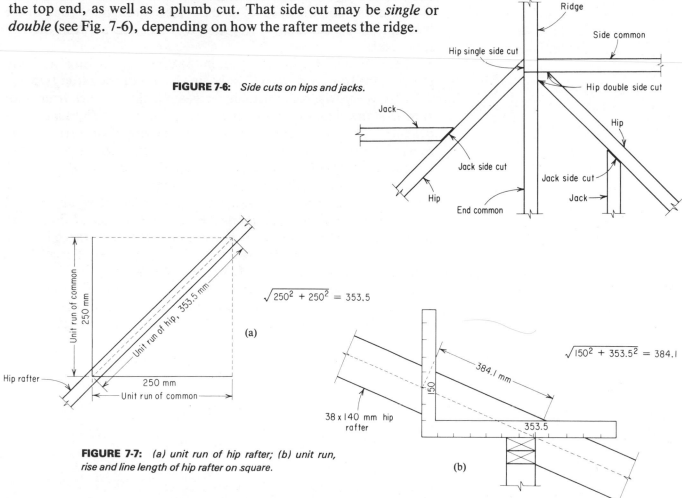

FIGURE 7-6: *Side cuts on hips and jacks.*

$$\sqrt{250^2 + 250^2} = 353.5$$

$$\sqrt{150^2 + 353.5^2} = 384.1$$

FIGURE 7-7: *(a) unit run of hip rafter; (b) unit run, rise and line length of hip rafter on square.*

Hip rafters run at an angle of 45 degrees to the wall plate (see Fig. 7-2) and, as a result, their unit run is different from that of a common rafter. As illustrated in Fig. 7-7a, a hip rafter must traverse the diagonal of a square in order to span one unit of common run. Thus the unit run of a hip rafter will be the length of the diagonal of a square with sides of 250 mm—namely, 353.5 mm.

If the framing square is applied to a hip rafter in position, as shown in Fig. 7-7b, the 353.5 mm mark on the blade must coincide with the outside edge of the wall plate to represent the *unit run* and a figure on the tongue will indicate the *unit rise*. If the rafter has the same rise as the one shown in Fig. 7-4, then that figure will be 150. Again, the diagonal distance between 150 on the tongue and 353.5 on the blade is the *unit line length* for the hip rafter.

Since hip rafters occur at the intersection of two surfaces of a hip roof, the *roof sheathing* on each surface must meet on a hip. To provide a flat surface on which the sheathing ends may rest, the top edges of hips are *backed* (beveled), as shown in Fig. 7-8.

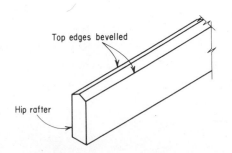

FIGURE 7-8: *Hip rafter backing.*

Shortening

In Fig. 7-9, two common rafters have first been represented by two lines *AC* and *BC*. Then full-width rafters have been superimposed in such a way that the lines *AC* and *BC* pass through the peak of the birdsmouth. In addition, a ridgeboard is inserted between the two rafter ends.

The two lines *AC* and *BC* meet in the center of the ridge at *C* and the distance from *A* or *B* to *C* is the line length of the rafter (see Fig. 7-3). However, the rafter actually ends at *D*; the distance from *A* or *B* to *D* is the actual length of the rafter; it has been *shortened* by a distance *CD*, which varies, depending on the rise of the rafter. However, if the *shortening* is measured at *right angles to the plumb cut*, its length will remain constant—*one-half the thickness of the ridge.* For a 38 mm ridge, that distance will be 19 mm.

With regard to a hip rafter, it meets the ridge at an angle of 45 degrees (see Fig. 7-9b) and therefore must be *shortened,* in a horizontal direction (at right angles to a plumb cut) by a distance *CD* (see Fig. 7-9b), *one-half the diagonal thickness of the ridge.* For a 38 mm ridge, that will amount to approximately 27 mm.

A jack rafter meets the hip at an angle of 45 degrees in plan (see Fig. 7-9b) and must be *shortened* by a distance equal to *EF,* taken at right angles to the plumb cut. For a 38 mm hip, that distance will also be 27 mm.

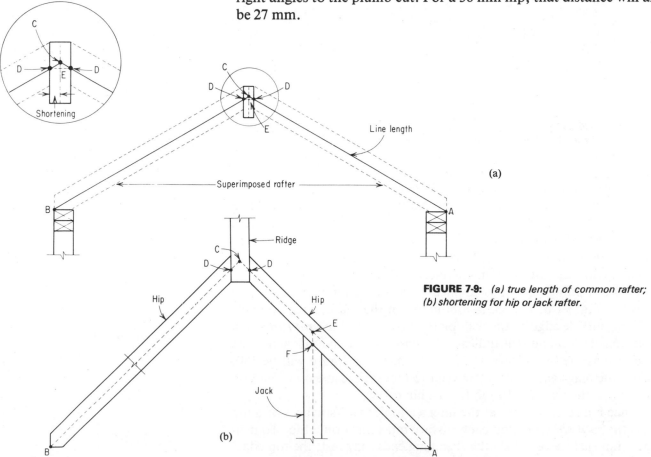

FIGURE 7-9: *(a) true length of common rafter; (b) shortening for hip or jack rafter.*

RIDGE

Rather than have a pair of rafters meet together at their top end, it is customary to introduce a ridgeboard between them. This ridgeboard makes it easier to keep the top line of the roof straight and provides support for the roof sheathing between rafters.

The ridge of a gable roof will have the same length as the length of the building plus roof overhang at the gable ends, if any. The length of a hip roof ridge, however, takes a little more consideration.

Turn back to Fig. 7-2 and study it a moment. In plan, the hip rafter is the diagonal of a square, the sides of which are *AB* and *AC*, *AB* being equal to half the width of the building. The top end of the hip is at a point half the width of the building *along* the length. The hip at the opposite end covers a like distance. The distance between the top ends of the two hips, then, is equal to the length of the building minus the width. In other words, the line length of the ridge is the length of building minus the width.

When a ridgeboard is introduced into the frame, the common rafters are shortened by half the ridge thickness. Consequently, the end commons would not reach the ends of the ridge if they were cut to true length. So the ridge length is increased by half its own thickness at each end. In other words, the *true length of the hip roof ridge is the length of building minus the width plus the thickness of the ridge.*

An intersecting roof contains two ridges. The ridge of the main roof is called the *major* ridge, whereas the ridge in the projection is known as the *minor* ridge.

HOW TO USE THE RAFTER TABLE

Having considered rafter framing terminology, it is now necessary to examine the methods used to determine the lengths of various types of rafters and how to lay out and cut them.

Calculation of lengths may be done in several ways, including the use of the *rafter table and mathematics,* by *scaling on the framing square* and by *scale drawings.* The layout of lengths may be done by *tape measurement* or by *framing square step-off.* For most situations, the combination of rafter table and math, with tape measurement of lengths, is the simplest and most accurate.

Rafter Table

Figure 7-10 illustrates a framing square, with a *rafter table* on the face of the blade. The numbers along the top edge of the blade represent *unit rises,* with calculations for 10 rises ranging from 50 to 500 mm, in increments of 50 mm. The first step in using the rafter table, then, is to locate the number which corresponds to the unit rise of the roof in question.

To find the *unit line length* of a common rafter, look on the first

179

LENGTH OF COM. PER UNIT RUN (250)		559.0
" " HIP	(353.5)	612.4
DIFF. IN JACKS AT 400 – O.C.		894
SIDE CUT HIP OR VALLEY		144
" " JACKS		112
ANGLE OF COM. AT PLATE		63.44°

8.05	15.79	22.99	29.50	35.27	40.32	44.71	48.53
10.70	20.70	29.54	37.08	43.37	48.58	52.91	56.51
275.4	288.7	309.6	336.6	368.6	404.2	442.5	483.1
979	1034	1120	1229	1358	1500	1652	1811
246	235	219	201	184	168	153	140
102	97	89	81	74	67	61	55

line of the table under the unit rise concerned; the figure found there is the line length for one unit (250 mm) of common run. Multiply that figure by the number of units of run for that rafter to obtain the line length of the common rafter in mm. The number of units of run for the rafter may be calculated by dividing the *total run* of the rafter in mm by 250.

The second line gives the *unit line length* of a hip or valley rafter per unit of common run. The line length of the hip or valley rafter will be that figure, multiplied by the number of units of common run in the building.

The third line gives the difference in length of successive jack rafters spaced 400 mm o.c. and is also the line length of the first jack rafter from the corner, spaced 400 mm o.c. Thus, having found the *true* (shortened) length of the first jack rafter from the corner, the length of the next one is found by adding that "difference in length" figure to the shortened length.

The fourth line indicates the figure to use on the tongue of the square in laying out the side cuts for hip or valley rafters. The blade figure is always 250 and the cut is always marked on the blade.

The fifth line indicates the figure to use on the tongue for the side cut of jack rafters. Again, 250 is the blade figure and the cut is marked on the blade.

The sixth line indicates the size of the angle formed by a common rafter at the point at which it meets the plate.

The center line on the face of the tongue provides alternative figures to use on the square to obtain side cuts of hips, valleys and jack rafters, indicating the side on which to mark. The same line also provides figures to use to obtain face angles for sheathing meeting a hip or valley rafter.

The back of the blade contains a table providing figures to be used when framing an octagon roof and also the size of angles formed by a hip and an octagon hip at the point at which they meet the wall plate.

Framing Calculations and Layout

Figure 7-11 is a plan view of a hip roof with an intersecting gable roof, with dimensions as indicated. On it are marked a number of typical roof framing members, whose length and layout will be demonstrated.

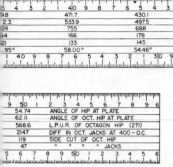

54.74	ANGLE OF HIP AT PLATE
62.11	ANGLE OF OCT. HIP AT PLATE
568.6	L.P.U.R. OF OCTAGON HIP (271)
2147	DIFF. IN OCT. JACKS AT 400 - O.C.
119	SIDE CUT OF OCT. HIP
47	" " " JACKS

FIGURE 7-10: *Metric framing square (Courtesy, Fredrickson's Metric Systems Ltd.).*

Length of Major Ridge (A)

The length of the ridge for a hip roof is the length of the building minus the width plus the thickness of the ridge (see section on Ridge, page 179)—in this case 10,000 mm − 8000 mm + 38 mm = 2038 mm. The size of the material for the ridge will normally be 38 × 89 mm or 38 × 140 mm.

Length of Minor Ridge (B)

The length of the minor ridge will be the length of the projection (see Fig. 7-11) plus one-half of its width plus the overhang minus one-half the diagonal thickness of the supporting valley rafter. In this case the length will be 2000 mm + 1400 mm + 400 mm − 27 mm = 3773 mm.

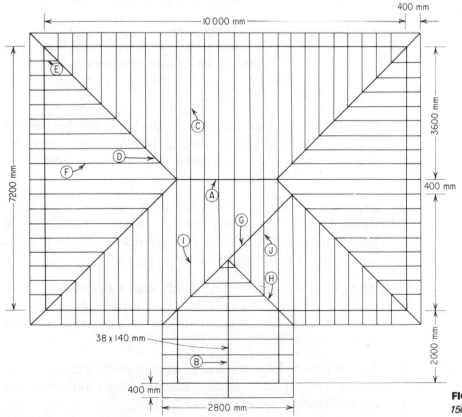

FIGURE 7-11: *Plan view, intersecting roof, 150 mm rise.*

Length and Layout of Common Rafter (C)

The unit line length for a common rafter with a 150 mm rise shown under "15," (Fig. 7-10) is 291.5 mm. The number of units of common run for a rafter with a run of 3600 mm $\frac{span}{2}$ and an overhang of 400 mm will be $\frac{3600 + 400}{250} = \frac{4000}{250} = 16$. The line length of the entire rafter then will be 291.5 × 16 = 4664 mm (4.664 m). The line length of the rafter tail is $^{400}/_{250}$ × 291.5 = 466.4 mm.

A typical common rafter (C) may now be laid out, cut and used as a pattern for all the common rafters. Proceed as follows:

1. Pick out a piece of straight 38 × 89 mm stock of sufficient length—4.8 m in this case—and mark on the face the depth to which the birdsmouth is to be cut (see Fig. 7-12a). Through that point draw a line parallel to the *top edge,* from end to end. This is the measuring line.

2. As near one end of the piece as possible draw a plumb cut. This is done by laying the square on the stock with the rise (150) on the tongue and the unit run (250) on the blade touching the measuring line (see Fig. 7-12b). Mark along the tongue. This will be the rafter tail plumb line.

3. From the intersection of this plumb line and the measuring line (point S, Fig. 7-12c) measure 466.4 mm along the measure line to point T. This is the *peak of the birdsmouth.*

4. Lay the square on the stock again, using 150 and 250 as before, with the 150 mm mark coinciding with point T (see Fig. 7-12c). Draw a line along the tongue from measuring line to bottom edge. This is the plumb cut line of the birdsmouth (see Fig. 7-5).

5. Slide the square *back* until 250 on the blade touches point T (see Fig. 7-12d). Draw a line along the blade from measuring line to bottom edge. This is the seat cut line for the birdsmouth (see Fig. 7-5).

6. From the peak of the birdsmouth measure along the measuring line 4664 mm and through that point, U, draw a plumb line (see Fig. 7-13a). The distance from S to U is the line length of the common ₌after.

7. At right angles to the top plumb line, measure *back* one-half the thickness of the ridge (19 mm) and draw another plumb line parallel to the first. The rafter is now properly *shortened* for the ridge (see Fig. 7-13b).

8. Square across the bottom edge at each cutting line (see Fig. 7-13c), cut carefully along the lines drawn and mark the rafter "Pattern" (see Fig. 7-13d).

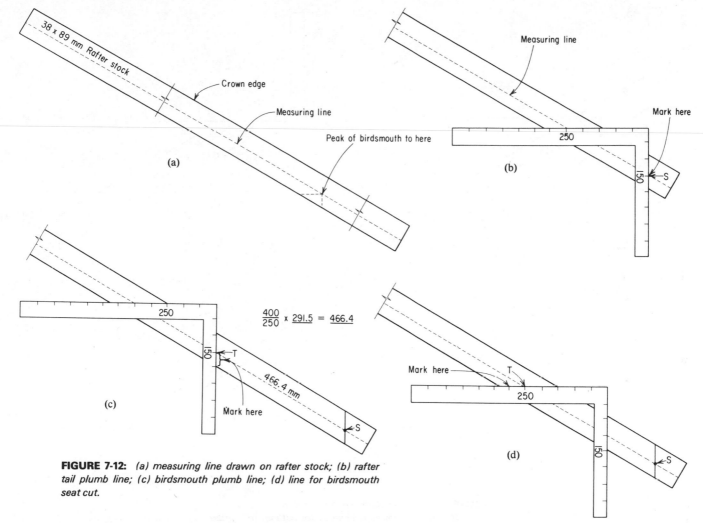

FIGURE 7-12: *(a) measuring line drawn on rafter stock; (b) rafter tail plumb line; (c) birdsmouth plumb line; (d) line for birdsmouth seat cut.*

9. Use that pattern to lay out all the common rafters required, placing the pattern *face down* on all those pieces to be marked (see Fig. 7-14). Make sure that any bow—*crown*—in the pieces being marked is to the top edge.

Length and Layout of Hip Rafter (D)

The unit line length of a hip rafter with a 150 mm rise is 384.1 mm (shown under "15," Fig. 7-10). Since the number of units of common run is 16, the line length of the entire rafter will be 384.1 × 16 = 6145.6 mm (6.1456 m). The line length of the rafter tail will be $^{400}/_{250}$ × 384.1 = 614.5 mm.

A typical hip rafter (D) may now be laid out, cut and used as a pattern for the other hip rafters. Proceed as follows:

1. Pick out a straight piece of 38 × 140 mm stock of sufficient length—6.3 m in this case—and draw the measuring line *the same distance from the top edge* as for the common rafter (see Fig. 7-15a).

183

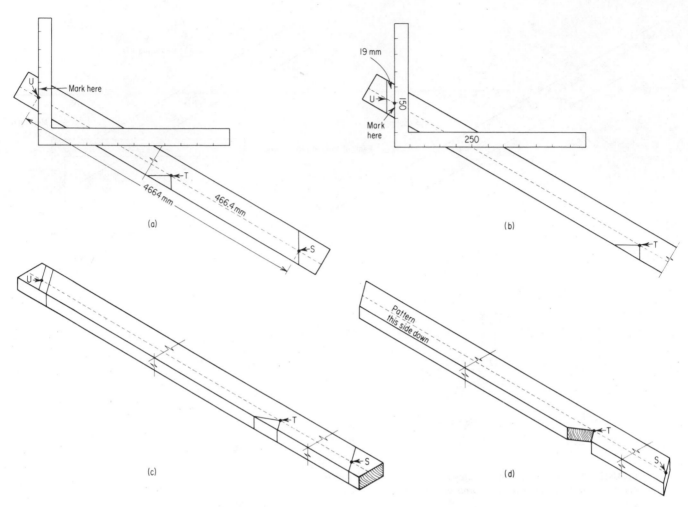

FIGURE 7-13: *(a) top plumb cut line; (b) shortening for common rafter; (c) bottom edge squared for cutting; (d) pattern ready for use.*

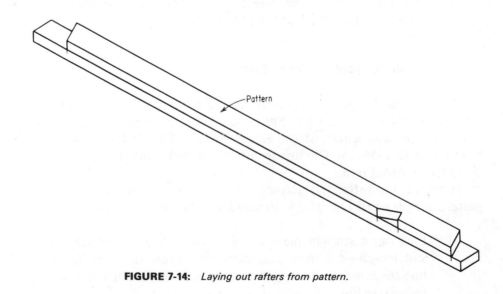

FIGURE 7-14: *Laying out rafters from pattern.*

2. As close to one end as possible, lay the square on the stock with 150 on the tongue and 353.5 on the blade touching the measuring line. Mark the tongue for the rafter tail plumb cut (see Fig. 7-15 a).

3. Measure 614.5 mm along the measuring line from point *S* (see Fig. 7-15b) to establish point *T,* the peak of the birdsmouth. Lay out the birdsmouth from that point, using 150 and 353.5 mm on the square.

4. From point *S,* measure 6145.6 mm along the measuring line to point *U* and through that point draw a plumb cut line (see Fig. 7-15c). The distance from *S* to *U* is the line length of the hip rafter.

5. From the top plumb cut line, measure *back* at right angles a distance equal to one-half the diagonal thickness of the ridge (27 mm) to point *V* and through it, draw a second plumb line. The hip rafter is now properly *shortened* for the ridge (see Fig. 7-15d).

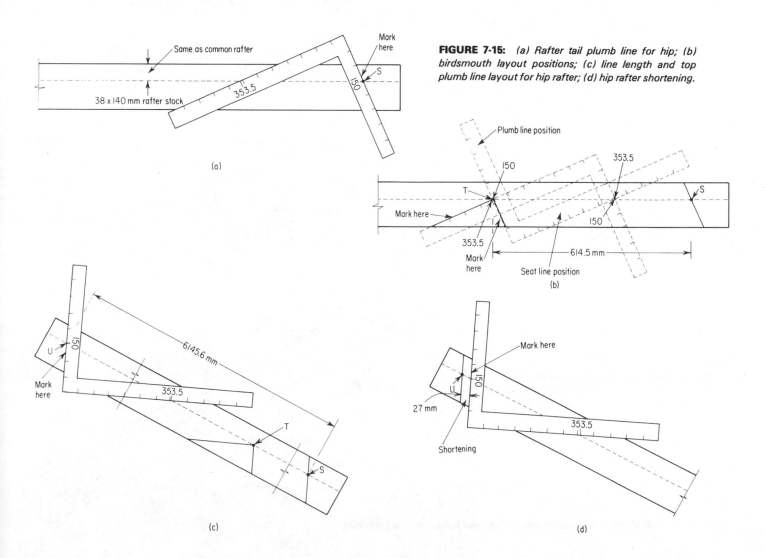

FIGURE 7-15: *(a) Rafter tail plumb line for hip; (b) birdsmouth layout positions; (c) line length and top plumb line layout for hip rafter; (d) hip rafter shortening.*

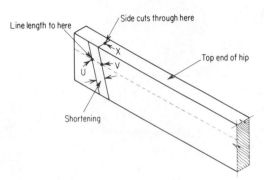

FIGURE 7-16: *Hip rafter shortened and marked for side cuts.*

6. Square across the top edge of the rafter from this line and mark the center point *X*. Single or double side cuts will be drawn through this point (see Fig. 7-16).

7. The fourth line of the rafter table indicates that, for a 150 mm rise, side cuts for hip or valley are laid out using 230 on the tongue of the square. The 250 value will be used on the blade, with the line drawn on the blade. Lay the square on the top edge of the rafter with 250 on the blade and 230 on the tongue touching one top edge, with the blade edge passing through *X*. Mark the side cut (see Fig. 7-17a). If a double side cut is required, mark the second from the opposite edge (see Fig. 7-17b).

8. Draw a new plumb line on one or both sides as required (see Fig. 7-17b).

9. The end of a hip rafter tail must fit into the apex of an external angle and therefore must have a *double cut* at the end (see Fig. 7-18a). Lay out two side cuts, using the square in the same way as at the top end (see Fig. 7-18b).

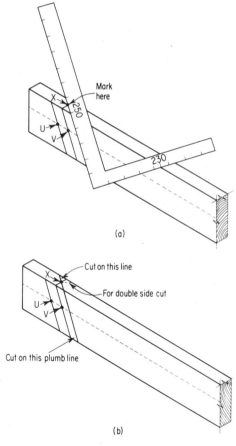

FIGURE 7-17: *(a) square in place for hip rafter side cut; (b) top of hip laid out for single or double side cuts.*

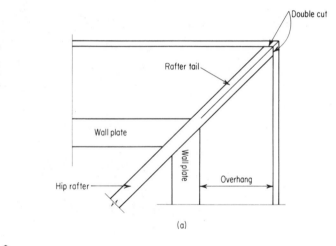

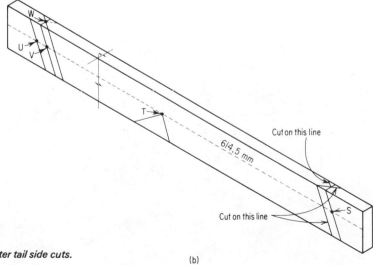

FIGURE 7-18: *(a) plan view of hip rafter tail; (b) rafter tail side cuts.*

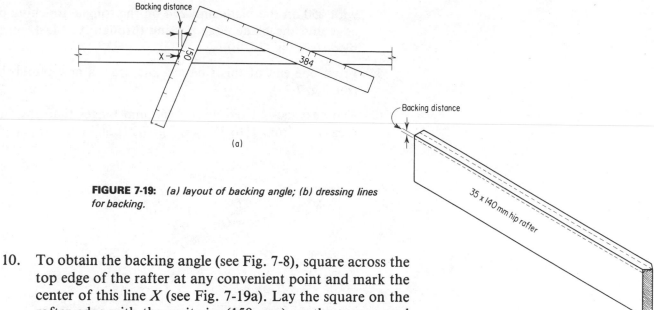

FIGURE 7-19: *(a) layout of backing angle; (b) dressing lines for backing.*

10. To obtain the backing angle (see Fig. 7-8), square across the top edge of the rafter at any convenient point and mark the center of this line X (see Fig. 7-19a). Lay the square on the rafter edge with the *unit rise* (150 mm) on the tongue and the *unit line length* of the hip (384 mm) on the blade touching one edge and the tongue passing through X (see Fig. 7-19a).

11. Take the distance indicated in Fig. 7-19(a) and measure it off from the top edge of the rafter on both faces (see Fig. 7-19b). Draw lines through these points from end to end of the rafter and one down the center of the top edge (see Fig. 7-19b).

12. Plane off both top corners to these lines (see Fig. 7-8).

Length and Layout of Jack Rafter (E)

The rafter tail and birdsmouth of this rafter are exactly the same as for the common rafter. The third line of the rafter table indicates that, for a 150 mm rise, the difference in length of jack rafters 400 mm o.c. is 466 mm. That is also the length of the first jack from the corner To lay out this rafter, proceed as follows:

1. On a piece of stock, lay out a rafter tail and birdsmouth as for a common rafter (see Fig. 7-20a).

2. From point T measure 466 mm and draw a plumb line as for a common rafter and mark point U (see Fig. 7-20a).

3. Measure back the *shortening,* 27mm, (one-half the diagonal thickness of the hip) and draw a second plumb line (see Fig. 7-20b). Square across the top edge of the stock and mark the center at X.

4. The fifth line of the rafter table indicates that 214 is the figure to use on the tongue of the square for the side cut of a jack rafter with a 150 mm rise. Lay the square on the stock

with 250 on the blade and 214 on the tongue touching one edge and the blade edge passing through *X*. Mark on the blade (see Fig. 7-20b).

5. From one end of this side cut line draw a new plumb line (see Fig. 7-21).

6. The next jack rafter will be 466 mm longer than the first, measured from *V* to *W* (see Fig. 7-21) and every other jack

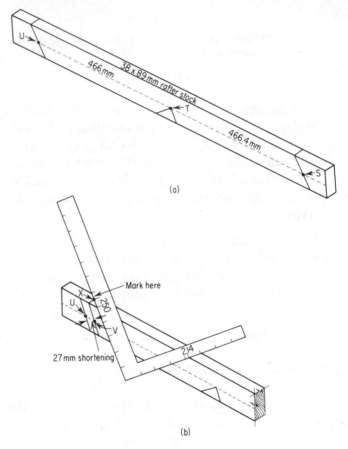

(a)

(b)

FIGURE 7-20: *(a) first jack rafter, line length; (b) first jack, shortened and marked for side cut.*

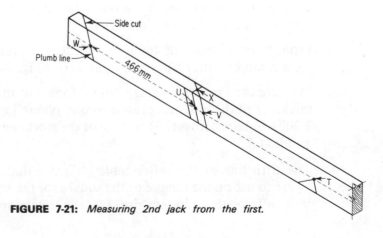

FIGURE 7-21: *Measuring 2nd jack from the first.*

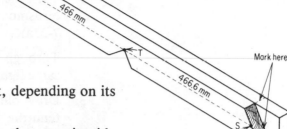

FIGURE 7-22: *Laying out the second of a pair of jacks.*

will be *n* × 466 mm longer than the first, depending on its position in the series.

7. The *mate* to each jack rafter, occurring on the opposite side of the hip, may be laid out as illustrated in Fig. 7-22, with the side cut being marked *back* from the peak of the one used as a pattern.

Line Length and Layout of Jack Rafter (F)

Jack rafter (F) is the seventh rafter in the series and therefore its length will be 7 times as long as jack rafter (E), measured from point V (see Fig 7-21).

Length and Layout of Valley Rafter (G)

The total common run of valley rafter (G) is 400 mm less than that of a common rafter, namely 3600 mm. Its line length will be $^{3600}\!/_{250}$ × 384.1 = 5531 mm.

The layout for rafter tail plumb line, birdsmouth and top plumb line is the same as for a hip of the same rise and, in this case, is made using 150 and 353.5 mm on the square.

The valley meets the hip at right angles in the plan view and therefore the *shortening* will be one-half the thickness of the hip (19 mm), measured at right angles to the plumb line (see Fig. 7-23b)

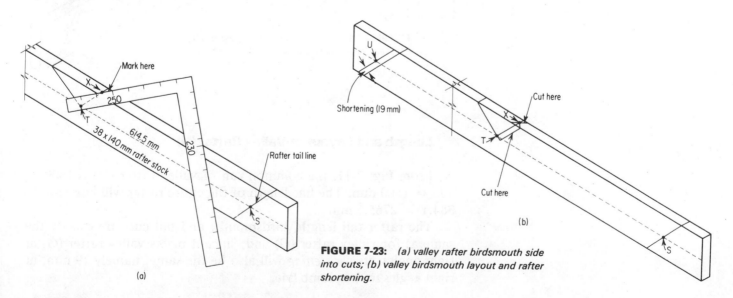

FIGURE 7-23: *(a) valley rafter birdsmouth side into cuts; (b) valley birdsmouth layout and rafter shortening.*

189

A valley rafter birdsmouth fits into an internal angle (see Fig. 7-24a) and must be cut accordingly. Proceed as follows:

1. Turn the rafter upside down, square across the edge at the birdsmouth plumb line and mark the center point *X* (see Fig. 7-23a).

2. Through this center point, draw two side cuts, using the same figures as for hip rafter side cuts.

3. Draw plumb lines from the ends of both side cut lines, extend the seat cut line to meet them and cut the birdsmouth along these lines (see Fig. 7-23b).

The end of the valley rafter tail must also fit into an internal angle, as illustrated in Fig. 7-24a. To obtain that double cut, proceed as follows:

1. Square across the top of the rafter tail at the plumb line and mark the center point *X* (see Fig. 7-24b).

2. Through this point draw two side cuts, using the same figures as for the birdsmouth side cuts. From the ends draw new plumb lines and cut as indicated in Fig. 7-24b.

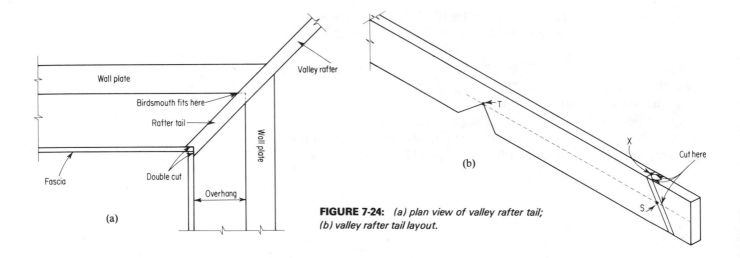

FIGURE 7-24: *(a) plan view of valley rafter tail; (b) valley rafter tail layout.*

Length and Layout of Valley Rafter (H)

From Fig. 7-11, the common run of valley rafter (H) is 1400 + 400 = 1800 mm. The line length of the entire rafter will be $^{1800}/_{250} \times 384.1 = 2765.5$ mm.

The rafter tail length, birdsmouth, and tail cuts are exactly the same as for valley rafter (G) and, since it meets valley rafter (G) at right angles, its *shortening* will also be the same, namely 19 mm, at right angles to the plumb line.

Length and Layout of Valley Jack (I)

From Fig. 7-11, the run of valley jack (I) is 400 mm less than the run of a common rafter without rafter tail—3200 mm. The line length of the rafter will be $^{3200}/_{250} \times 291.5 = 3731$ mm.

The plumb line and shortening at the top end are the same as for a common rafter, while the plumb line, shortening (one-half the diagonal thickness of the valley rafter) and the side cut at the bottom end are identical to the top end of a hip jack.

Line Length and Layout of Cripple Jack (J)

From Fig. 7-11, the common run of cripple jack (J) is $5 \times 400 = 2000$ mm. The line length of the rafter will be $^{2000}/_{250} \times 291.5 = 2332$ mm. Shortening and side cuts, top and bottom, are the same as for other jack rafters.

SPECIAL RAFTERS

Rafters for two of the roof shapes illustrated in Fig. 7-1 require special attention, namely those for a *shed* and for a *gambrel* roof.

Shed Roof Rafter

Figure 7-25 illustrates the position of a shed-roof rafter on the wall plates. At the lower end, the birdsmouth fits over the plate in the same way as any other common rafter. But at the top end, the birdsmouth fits over the *inner edge* of the wall plate. The run of the shed rafter, then from one birdsmouth peak to the other, will be the width of the building *minus the width of the upper plate.*

For a building 3000 mm wide, the number of units of common run will be $^{3000}/_{250} = 12$. With a total rise of 600 mm, the unit rise will be $^{600}/_{12} = 50$ mm.

From the rafter table on the framing square, for a 50 mm unit rise, the unit line length of a common rafter will be 255 mm (see Fig. 7-10). The line length of the lower rafter tail then will be $^{400}/_{250} \times 255 = 408$ mm.

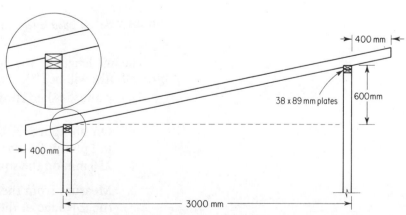

FIGURE 7-25: *Shed roof rafter.*

191

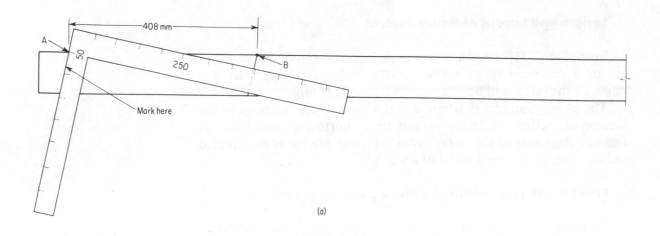

(a)

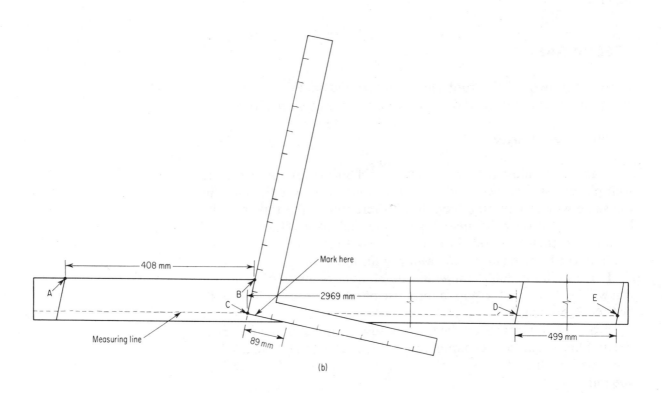

(b)

FIGURE 7-26: *(a) shed rafter plumb line layouts; (b) shed rafter line lengths and layout.*

The line length of the upper rafter tail, from the peak of the upper birdsmouth, will be (^{400} + $^{89}/_{250}$) × 255 = 499 mm.

To lay out the shed roof rafter, proceed as follows:

1. On an appropriate piece of stock, lay out the lower rafter tail plumb line, as close to one end as possible, using 50 and 250 mm on the square (see Fig. 7-26a).

2. Measure from the top end of the plumb line (point *A*) along the top edge of the rafter 408 mm to point *B*.

3. From point *B* draw another plumb line (see Fig. 7-26a). With the framing square laid to that plumb line, as illustrated in Fig. 7-26b, locate a point *C*, on the plumb line, which is 89 mm from the bottom edge of the rafter. Draw the seat cut line through that point. A birdsmouth has been laid out with a seat cut the same length as the width of the wall plate.

4. Through the peak of the birdsmouth (point *C*) draw a measuring line the length of the rafter (see Fig. 7-26b).

5. The line length of the rafter, from the lower birdsmouth peak to the upper one, will be $(^{3000} - {}^{89}\!/_{250}) \times 255 = 2969$ mm. From *C,* measure 2969 mm along the measuring line to point *D* and, from that point, lay out another birdsmouth, exactly the same as the first.

6. From *D,* measure 499 mm to *E* and, through that point, draw a plumb line. The rafter layout is complete.

Gambrel Roof Rafters

Figure 7-27 illustrates the shape of a gambrel roof frame and one method of supporting the rafters at the break in the slope, namely by bringing the upper and lower rafters together at an interior wall plate. Notice that the measuring line can be the upper edge of the rafters.

Line Length and Layout of Lower Rafter

The lower rafter has a total run of 1800 mm and a total rise of 2700 mm (see Fig. 7-27a).

The number of units of common run is $^{1800}\!/_{250} = 7.2$. The unit rise then will be $^{2700}\!/_{7.2} = 375$ mm.

Measure across from 250 on the blade of the square to 375 on the tongue to find the unit line length of the lower rafter. That distance will be found to be 450.5 mm.

The line length of the lower rafter will be $450.5 \times 7.2 = 3244$ mm. To lay out the lower rafter, proceed as follows:

1. Pick out a straight piece of stock of sufficient length and, as close as possible to one end, lay out a plumb line, using 250 on the blade and 375 on the tongue (see Fig. 7-27b).

2. From the end of the plumb line, measure 3244 mm along the top edge to point *A.*

3. At point *A,* draw a seat cut line across the face of the stock (see Fig. 7-27b). The layout is complete.

Line Length and Layout of Upper Rafter

The upper rafter has a total run of $^{9000 - 3600}\!/_{2} = 2700$ mm and a total rise of 900 mm (see Fig. 7-27a).

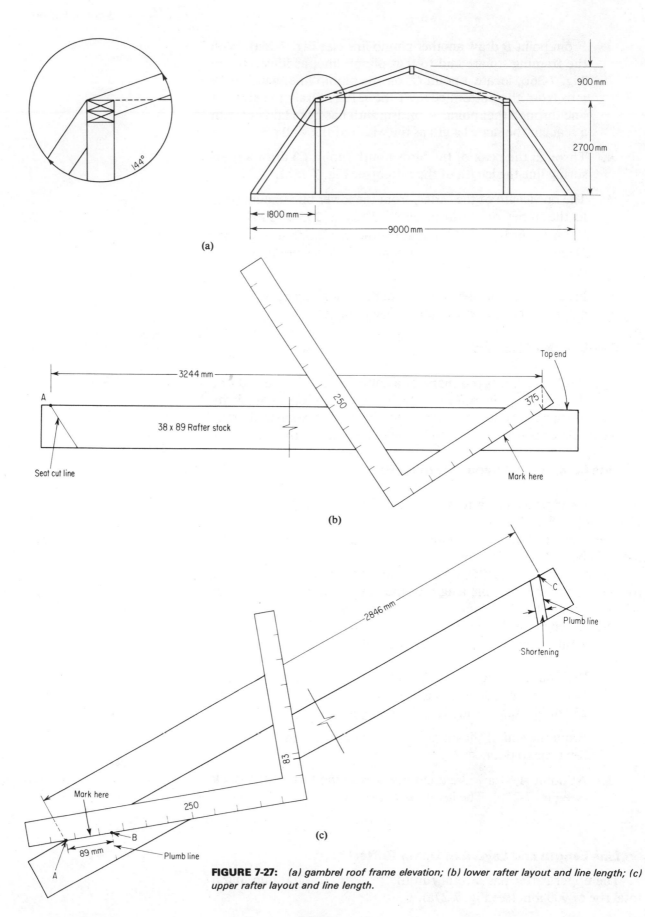

FIGURE 7-27: *(a) gambrel roof frame elevation; (b) lower rafter layout and line length; (c) upper rafter layout and line length.*

194

The number of units of common run is $^{2700}/_{250}$ = 10.8. The unit rise will be $^{900}/_{10.8}$ = 83 mm (approx.).

Measure across the square from 250 on the blade to 83 on the tongue to find the unit line length. The distance will be 263.5 mm (approx.).

Line length of the upper rafter is 263.5 $\times$ 10.8 = 2846 mm.

To lay out the upper rafter, proceed as follows:

1. Pick out a piece of straight stock of sufficient length and, as close to one end as possible, lay out a *seat cut,* using 250 on the blade and 83 on the tongue (see Fig. 7-27c).

2. From the outer end of that seat cut (point *A*) measure 89 mm to point *B* and from there draw a plumb line to the bottom edge of the rafter (see Fig. 7-27c).

3. From *A,* measure 2846 mm along the top edge of the rafter to point *C.* At *C,* draw a plumb line and shorten the rafter one-half the thickness of the ridge. The layout is now complete.

Gambrel Roof Gusseted Rafter

Another method of framing a gambrel roof is to butt the ends of the upper and lower rafters together at the break in the slope and reinforce the joint with a *gusset plate* (see Fig. 7-28).

It is necessary to know the size of the angle formed at the junction of the upper and lower rafters; measurement on a scale drawing with a *protractor* indicates that, in this case, the angle is 144 degrees (see Fig. 7-27a, inset).

The angle of cut at the meeting ends of both rafters will be 72 degrees, which may be laid off with a protractor, set on a sliding T-bevel square and transferred to the rafter ends. The seat cut at the bottom and the plumb cut at the top will remain as in the previous method.

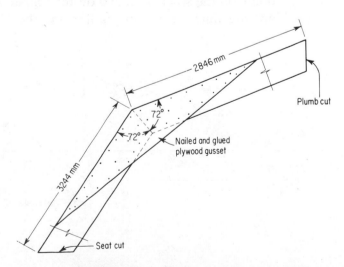

FIGURE 7-28: *Gusseted gambrel rafters.*

Unit Line Length by Calculation

The unit line length of a rafter may be found by calculation, based on a right-angle triangle. In such a triangle, the square of the *hypotenuse*—representing the unit line length—is equal to the sum of the squares of the *base*—representing the unit run—and the *perpendicular*—representing the unit rise.

For example, for a rafter with a unit rise of 200 mm, the calculation will be as follows:

$$\text{Base}^2 = 250^2 = 62,500$$

$$\text{Perpendicular}^2 = 200^2 = 40,000$$

$$\text{Hypotenuse}^2 = 62,500 + 40,000 = 102,500$$

$$\text{Hypotenuse (unit line length)} = \sqrt{102,500} = 320.15 \text{ mm}$$

(see Fig. 7-29).

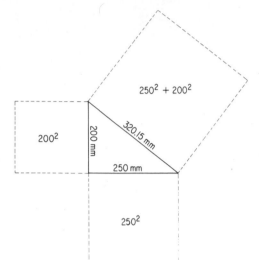

FIGURE 7-29: *Calculation of unit line length.*

Alternative Layout of Rafter Length

Instead of *calculating* the line length of a rafter and measuring it by tape, the length may be *stepped off*, using the framing square. Since the *unit line length* of a rafter is represented on the square as the distance between the *unit run figure* (250) on the blade and the *unit rise figure* on the tongue, that distance may be laid off along a rafter *as many times as there are units of run,* to produce the line length.

For example, for a rafter with a unit rise of 200 mm, a run of 1500 mm and an overhang of 400 mm, proceed as follows:

1. On a piece of stock, draw the measuring line and lay out a birdsmouth, leaving sufficient length at the end for a rafter tail (see Fig. 7-30).

2. Lay the square on the stock with 200 on the tongue and 250 on the blade touching the measuring line and the 250 mark

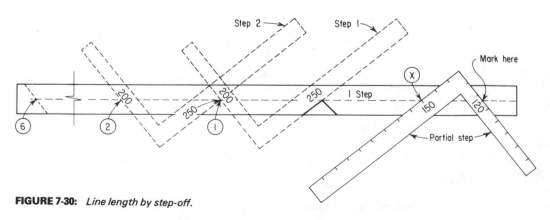

FIGURE 7-30: *Line length by step-off.*

196

coinciding with the peak of the birdsmouth (see Fig. 7-30). Carefully mark point 1 on the tongue at the measuring line (Step 1).

3. Move the square up until the 250 mark coincides with point 1 and mark point 2 (Step 2).

4. Repeat as many times as there are units of run—in this case 6 —to produce the line length.

5. A rafter tail with an overhang of 400 mm requires $\frac{400}{250} = 1.6$ steps to lay out the line length.

6. Lay out one step from the birdsmouth, as above and mark point X (see Fig. 7-30).

7. For 0.6 step, use *0.6 of the unit run* (150 mm) on the blade and *0.6 of the unit rise* (120 mm) on the tongue and lay off that partial step from point X, as illustrated in Fig. 7-30, to obtain the rafter tail line length.

ROOF FRAME ASSEMBLY

When all the rafters have been cut, they can then be assembled into a roof frame. In a gable roof, the end rafters are positioned first, at the ends of the wall plates (see Fig. 7-31) and nailed to the plate and to the ridge according to the nailing schedule in Table 7-1, page 198. The remainder of the rafters are then raised and positioned against ceiling joists (see Chapter 6, layout of ceiling joists), properly spaced at the top end and nailed to the plate and the ridge according to the nailing schedule. Rafters are also nailed to the ceiling joists, according to the nailing schedule if the ridge is supported or as specified in Table 7-1, if the ridge is unsupported. One rafter of each pair may be *endnailed* through the ridge, while the other will be *toenailed* to the ridge.

In a hip roof, the common rafters at the ends of the ridge (see Fig. 7-2) will be erected first, with their bottom end against a ceiling joist and nailed, bottom and top, as above. The end commons are raised next, followed by the hip rafters and finally, the jacks, in pairs. End commons and all jacks will be located against a regular or stub joist (see Fig. 6-6) and nailed, top and bottom according to the schedule or to Table 7-1.

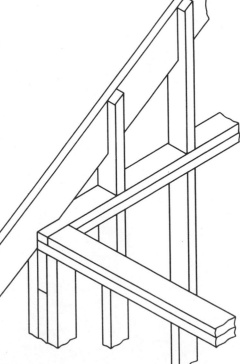

FIGURE 7-31: *Gable studs.*

TABLE 7-1: *Minimum rafter-to-joist nailing (unsupported ridge)* (Courtesy National Research Council)

Rise of Roof (mm)	Rafter Spacing (mm)	Rafter tied to every joist						Rafter tied to joist every 1200 mm					
		Building width up to 8 m			Building width up to 9.8 m			Building width up to 8 m			Building width up to 9.8 m		
		Roof snow load (kN)											
		1 or less	1.5	2 or more	1 or less	1.5	2 or more	1 or less	1.5	2 or more	1 or less	1.5	2 or more
80	400	4	5	6	5	7	8	11	—	—	—	—	—
	600	6	8	9	8	—	—	11	—	—	—	—	—
100	400	4	4	5	5	6	7	7	10	—	9	—	—
	600	5	7	8	7	9	11	7	10	—	—	—	—
125	400	4	4	4	4	4	5	6	8	9	8	—	—
	600	4	5	6	5	7	8	6	8	9	8	—	—
145	400	4	4	4	4	4	4	5	6	8	7	9	11
	600	4	4	5	5	6	7	5	6	8	7	9	11
185	400	4	4	4	4	4	4	4	5	6	5	6	7
	600	4	4	4	4	4	5	4	5	6	5	6	7
250	400	4	4	4	4	4	4	4	4	4	4	4	5
	600	4	4	4	4	4	4	4	4	4	4	4	5

GABLE FRAME

In a building with a gable roof, that triangular portion of the end wall which extends from the top of the wall plate to the rafters is known as the *gable*.

The method used to frame the gables will depend on the type of framing system employed. If a *balloon frame* is being used, the end wall studs extend from sill plate to rafters. If *platform framing* is used, the gable is framed separately; those short studs extending from top plate to rafters are *gable studs* (see Fig. 7-31). In either case, the cuts at the top ends of the studs will be the same.

Layout for a Gable Stud

Figure 7-32a illustrates a part of a gable frame, in which the rise of the rafter is 150 mm and the gable studs are spaced 400 mm o.c.

The line length of the first gable stud from the corner will be the rise of the rafter at that point, namely $\frac{400}{250} \times 150 = 240$ mm, while the line length of the second stud will be $\frac{800}{250} \times 150 = 480$ mm.

However, the stud must be cut to fit *under* the rafter and therefore must be *shortened* by a distance equal to *AB* (see Fig. 7-32a). Notice that the distance *AB* is equal to the plumb cut of the birdsmouth.

To lay out the first gable stud, proceed as follows:

1. Square one end of a piece of 38 × 89 mm stock and draw a center line along one edge (see Fig. 7-32b).

2. Measure 240 mm from the squared end to point *A* and then measure *back* a distance *AB* to point *B*.

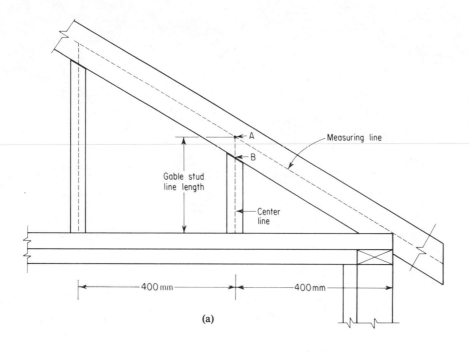

(a)

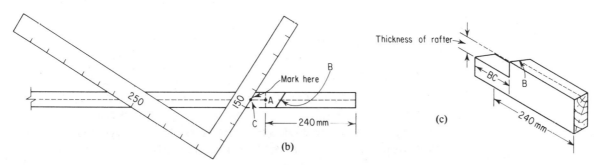

(b)   (c)

FIGURE 7-32: *(a) section of gable frame; (b) layout of gable stud; (c) finished gable stud.*

3. Lay the square on the stock with 150 on the tongue and 250 on the blade touching one edge and the tongue passing through *B*. Mark on the tongue (see Fig. 7-32b).

4. From *B*, measure a distance *BC,* equal to the width of the rafter along a plumb line, along the stud and mark through *C* as above (see Fig. 7-32b).

5. Cut out a section at the top end of the stud, as illustrated in Fig. 7-32c, as deep as the thickness of the rafter.

Each gable stud will be laid out in exactly the same way and each will be longer than the preceding one by the line length of the first. Those on the opposite side of center will be marked and cut with the opposite slope. A center gable stud will be square cut at the top end to fit under the ridgeboard (see Fig. 7-33a).

Openings for ventilating louvres are framed as illustrated in Fig. 7-33(b) and should be as near the ridge as possible.

199

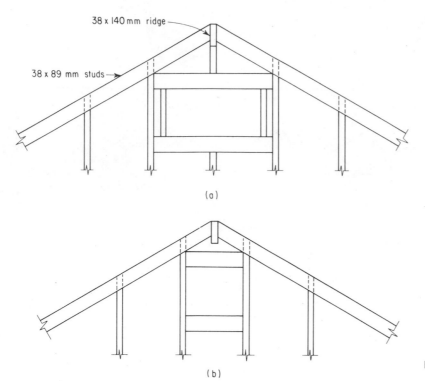

38 x 140 mm ridge

38 x 89 mm studs

(a)

(b)

FIGURE 7-33: *Openings for ventilating louvres.*

RAFTER BRACING

As is the case with other load-bearing members, the free span of rafters is limited, depending on width of rafter, spacing, and species of timber used. Table 7-2 gives maximum free spans for a number of species, with varying widths and spacings. The free span is expressed in terms of the horizontal projection of the rafter.

TABLE 7-2

Lumber Species	Grade	Size (mm)	LIVE LOAD 2.5 kN/m² Rafter spacing			LIVE LOAD 2.0 kN/m² Rafter spacing			LIVE LOAD 1.5 kN/m² Rafter spacing			LIVE LOAD 1.5 kN/m² Rafter spacing		
			300 mm	400 mm	600 mm	300 mm	400 mm	600 mm	300 mm	400 mm	600 mm	300 mm	400 mm	600 mm
Douglas Fir, Larch (N)	Sel. Str.	38x 89	2.50	2.27	1.98	2.69	2.45	2.14	2.97	2.69	2.35	3.40	3.09	2.69
		38x140	3.93	3.57	3.09	4.24	3.85	3.36	4.66	4.24	3.70	5.34	4.85	4.24
		38x184	5.19	4.71	4.07	5.59	5.08	4.43	6.15	5.59	4.88	7.04	6.40	5.59
		38x235	6.62	6.01	5.19	7.13	6.48	5.66	7.13	6.48	5.40	8.16	7.41	6.36
		38x286	8.05	7.31	6.32	8.67	7.88	6.88	8.67	7.88	6.57	9.93	9.02	7.73
	No. 1	38x 89	2.50	2.27	1.98	2.69	2.45	2.14	2.97	2.69	2.35	3.40	3.09	2.69
		38x140	3.93	3.50	2.86	4.24	3.85	3.16	4.66	4.24	3.57	5.34	4.85	4.20
		38x184	5.19	4.62	3.77	5.59	5.08	4.16	6.15	5.59	4.71	7.04	6.40	5.54
		38x235	6.62	5.90	4.81	7.13	6.48	5.31	7.85	7.13	6.01	8.98	8.16	7.07
		38x286	8.05	7.17	5.86	8.76	7.88	6.46	9.54	8.67	7.31	10.93	9.93	8.60
	No. 2	38x 89	2.42	2.19	1.79	2.60	2.37	1.97	2.87	2.60	2.23	3.28	2.98	2.60
		38x140	3.64	3.15	2.57	4.02	3.48	2.88	4.51	3.93	3.21	5.16	4.63	3.78
		38x184	4.80	4.16	3.39	5.30	4.59	3.74	5.94	5.19	4.23	6.81	6.10	4.98
		38x235	6.13	5.30	4.33	6.76	5.85	4.78	7.59	6.62	5.40	8.68	7.79	6.36
		38x286	7.45	6.45	5.27	8.22	7.12	5.81	9.23	8.05	6.57	10.56	9.47	7.73
	No. 3	38x 89	1.87	1.62	1.32	2.06	1.78	1.46	2.33	2.02	1.65	2.74	2.38	1.94
		38x140	2.75	2.38	1.95	3.04	2.63	2.15	3.44	2.98	2.43	4.04	3.50	2.86
		38x184	3.63	3.15	2.57	4.01	3.47	2.83	4.53	3.92	3.20	5.33	4.62	3.77
		38x235	4.64	4.01	3.28	5.12	4.43	3.62	5.78	5.01	4.09	6.81	5.89	4.81
		38x286	5.64	4.88	3.99	6.22	5.39	4.40	7.03	6.09	4.97	8.28	7.17	5.85
	Const	38x 89	2.14	1.85	1.51	2.36	2.04	1.67	2.67	2.31	1.89	3.14	2.72	2.22
	Stand	38x 89	1.61	1.39	1.14	1.77	1.54	1.25	2.01	1.74	1.42	2.36	2.04	1.67
	Util	38x 89	1.09	0.95	0.77	1.21	1.05	0.85	1.37	1.18	0.96	1.61	1.39	1.14

TABLE 7-2 *(cont.)*

Lumber Species	Grade	Size (mm)	LIVE LOAD 2.5 kN/m² Rafter spacing			LIVE LOAD 2.0 kN/m² Rafter spacing			LIVE LOAD 1.5 kN/m² Rafter spacing			LIVE LOAD 1.5 kN/m² Rafter spacing		
			300 mm	400 mm	600 mm	300 mm	400 mm	600 mm	300 mm	400 mm	600 mm	300 mm	400 mm	600 mm
Hem-Fir (N)	Sel. Str.	38x 89	2.41	2.19	1.84	2.60	2.36	2.03	2.86	2.60	2.27	3.27	2.97	2.60
		38x140	3.76	3.26	2.66	4.08	3.59	2.93	4.49	4.06	3.32	5.15	4.67	3.90
		38x184	4.96	4.29	3.51	5.38	4.74	3.87	5.93	5.36	4.37	6.78	6.16	5.15
		38x235	6.33	5.48	4.47	6.87	6.05	4.94	7.56	6.84	5.58	8.66	7.87	6.57
		38x286	7.70	6.67	5.44	8.36	7.36	6.01	9.20	8.32	6.79	10.53	9.57	7.99
	No. 1	38x 89	2.39	2.07	1.69	2.60	2.29	1.86	2.86	2.58	2.11	3.27	2.97	2.60
		38x140	3.49	3.03	2.47	3.85	3.34	2.72	4.36	3.77	3.08	5.13	4.44	3.63
		38x184	4.61	3.99	3.26	5.08	4.40	3.59	5.75	4.98	4.06	6.76	5.86	4.78
		38x235	5.88	5.09	4.16	6.49	5.62	4.59	7.33	6.35	5.18	8.63	7.47	6.10
		38x286	7.15	6.19	5.06	7.89	6.81	5.58	8.92	7.73	6.31	10.50	9.09	7.42
	No. 2	38x 89	2.17	1.88	1.53	2.39	2.07	1.69	2.70	2.34	1.91	3.16	2.76	2.25
		38x140	3.13	2.71	2.21	3.46	2.99	2.44	3.91	3.39	2.76	4.60	3.98	3.25
		38x184	4.13	3.58	2.92	4.56	3.95	3.22	5.15	4.46	3.64	6.07	5.25	4.29
		38x235	5.27	4.57	3.73	5.82	5.04	4.11	6.58	5.70	4.65	7.74	6.71	5.47
		38x286	6.42	5.56	4.54	7.08	6.13	5.00	8.00	6.93	5.66	9.42	8.16	6.66
	No. 3	38x 89	1.61	1.39	1.14	1.77	1.54	1.25	2.01	1.74	1.42	2.36	2.04	1.67
		38x140	2.38	2.06	1.68	2.62	2.27	1.85	2.97	2.57	2.10	3.49	3.02	2.47
		38x184	3.13	2.71	2.22	3.46	3.00	2.44	3.91	3.39	2.76	4.60	3.99	3.25
		38x235	4.00	3.46	2.83	4.41	3.82	3.12	4.99	4.32	3.53	5.87	5.09	4.15
		38x286	4.87	4.21	3.44	5.37	4.65	3.80	6.07	5.26	4.29	7.15	6.19	5.05
	Const	38x 89	1.85	1.60	1.31	2.04	1.77	1.44	2.31	2.00	1.63	2.72	2.35	1.92
	Stand	38x 89	1.39	1.20	0.98	1.53	1.32	1.08	1.73	1.50	1.22	2.04	1.76	1.44
	Util	38x 89	0.95	0.82	0.67	1.05	0.90	0.74	1.18	1.02	0.83	1.39	1.21	0.98
Eastern Hemlock Tamarack (N)	Sel. Str.	38x 89	2.30	2.09	1.82	2.47	2.25	1.96	2.72	2.47	2.16	3.12	2.83	2.47
		38x140	3.61	3.28	2.86	3.89	3.53	3.09	4.28	3.89	3.40	4.90	4.45	3.89
		38x184	4.76	4.33	3.78	5.13	4.66	4.07	5.65	5.13	4.48	6.46	5.87	5.13
		38x235	6.08	5.52	4.82	6.55	5.95	5.19	7.21	6.55	5.72	8.25	7.49	6.55
		38x286	7.39	6.71	5.87	7.96	7.23	6.32	8.76	7.96	6.95	10.03	9.12	7.96
	No. 1	38x 89	2.30	2.09	1.82	2.47	2.25	1.96	2.72	2.47	2.16	3.12	2.83	2.47
		38x140	3.61	3.28	2.75	3.89	3.53	3.04	4.28	3.89	3.40	4.90	4.45	3.89
		38x184	4.76	4.33	3.63	5.13	4.66	4.01	5.65	5.13	4.48	6.46	5.87	5.13
		38x235	6.08	5.52	4.64	6.55	5.95	5.12	7.21	6.55	5.72	8.25	7.49	6.55
		38x286	7.39	6.71	5.64	7.96	7.23	6.22	8.76	7.96	6.95	10.03	9.12	7.79
	No. 2	38x 89	2.21	2.01	1.72	2.38	2.17	1.89	2.62	2.38	2.08	3.01	2.73	2.38
		38x140	3.48	3.03	2.47	3.75	3.34	2.72	4.13	3.75	3.08	4.73	4.29	3.63
		38x184	4.59	3.99	3.26	4.94	4.40	3.59	5.44	4.94	4.06	6.23	5.66	4.78
		38x235	5.86	5.09	4.16	6.31	5.62	4.59	6.59	6.31	5.18	7.59	7.22	6.10
		38x286	7.12	6.19	5.06	7.68	6.83	5.58	8.45	7.68	6.31	9.67	8.79	7.42
	No. 3	38x 89	1.80	1.56	1.27	1.99	1.72	1.40	2.25	1.95	1.59	2.65	2.29	1.87
		38x140	2.64	2.29	1.87	2.92	2.53	2.06	3.30	2.86	2.33	3.88	3.36	2.74
		38x184	3.49	3.02	2.46	3.85	3.33	2.72	4.35	3.77	3.07	5.12	4.43	3.62
		38x235	4.45	3.85	3.15	4.91	4.25	3.47	5.55	4.81	3.93	6.53	5.66	4.62
		38x286	5.41	4.69	3.83	5.97	5.17	4.22	6.57	5.85	4.77	7.95	6.88	5.62
	Const	38x 89	2.07	1.79	1.46	2.28	1.97	1.61	2.53	2.23	1.82	2.90	2.63	2.15
	Stand	38x 89	1.53	1.32	1.08	1.69	1.46	1.19	1.91	1.65	1.35	2.25	1.95	1.59
	Util	38x 89	1.07	0.92	0.75	1.18	1.02	0.83	1.33	1.15	0.94	1.57	1.36	1.11
Coast Species	Sel. Str.	38x 89	2.41	2.19	1.81	2.60	2.36	2.00	2.86	2.60	2.26	3.27	2.97	2.60
		38x140	3.72	3.22	2.63	4.08	3.56	2.90	4.49	4.02	3.28	5.15	4.67	3.86
		38x184	4.91	4.25	3.47	5.38	4.69	3.83	5.93	5.30	4.33	6.78	6.16	5.09
		38x235	6.26	5.42	4.43	6.87	5.98	4.88	7.56	6.76	5.52	8.66	7.87	6.50
		38x286	7.62	6.60	5.38	8.36	7.28	5.94	9.20	8.23	6.72	10.53	9.57	7.90
	No. 1	38x 89	2.37	2.05	1.67	2.60	2.36	2.00	2.86	2.56	2.26	3.27	2.97	2.60
		38x140	3.45	2.99	2.44	3.81	3.30	2.69	4.31	3.73	3.04	5.07	3.39	3.58
		38x184	4.55	3.94	3.22	5.02	4.35	3.55	5.68	4.92	4.01	6.68	5.79	4.72
		38x235	5.81	5.03	4.11	6.41	5.55	4.53	7.27	6.27	5.12	8.53	7.38	6.03
		38x286	7.06	6.21	4.99	7.79	6.75	5.51	8.81	7.63	6.23	10.37	8.98	7.33
	No. 2	38x 89	2.14	1.85	1.51	2.36	2.04	1.67	2.67	2.31	1.89	3.14	2.72	2.22
		38x140	3.09	2.67	2.18	3.41	2.95	2.41	3.85	3.33	2.72	4.53	3.92	3.20
		38x184	4.07	3.52	2.88	4.49	3.89	3.17	5.08	4.40	3.59	5.98	5.17	4.22
		38x235	5.19	4.50	3.67	5.73	4.96	4.05	6.48	5.61	4.58	7.62	6.60	5.39
		38x286	6.32	5.47	4.47	6.97	6.04	4.93	7.88	6.82	5.57	9.27	8.03	6.56
	No. 3	38x 89	1.59	1.38	1.12	1.75	1.52	1.24	1.98	1.72	1.40	2.33	2.02	1.65
		38x140	2.35	2.03	1.66	2.59	2.24	1.83	2.93	2.53	2.07	3.44	2.98	2.43
		38x184	3.09	2.68	2.19	3.41	2.96	2.41	3.86	3.34	2.73	4.54	3.93	3.21
		38x235	3.95	3.42	2.79	4.36	3.77	3.08	4.93	4.26	3.48	5.80	5.02	4.10
		38x286	4.80	4.16	3.39	5.30	4.59	3.75	5.99	5.19	4.23	7.05	6.11	4.98
	Const	38x 89	1.82	1.57	1.28	2.01	1.74	1.42	2.27	1.96	1.60	2.67	2.31	1.89
	Stand	38x 89	1.36	1.18	0.96	1.51	1.30	1.06	1.70	1.47	1.20	2.00	1.74	1.42
	Util	38x 89	0.95	0.82	0.67	1.05	0.90	0.74	1.18	1.02	0.83	1.39	1.21	0.98

TABLE 7-2 (cont.)

Lumber Species	Grade	Size (mm)	LIVE LOAD 2.5 kN/m² Rafter spacing			LIVE LOAD 2.0 kN/m² Rafter spacing			LIVE LOAD 1.5 kN/m² Rafter spacing			LIVE LOAD 1.5 kN/m² Rafter spacing		
			300 mm	400 mm	600 mm	300 mm	400 mm	600 mm	300 mm	400 mm	600 mm	300 mm	400 mm	600 mm
Spruce-Pine-Fir	Sel. Str.	38x 89	2.27	2.06	1.78	2.45	2.22	1.94	2.69	2.45	2.14	3.09	2.80	2.45
		38x140	3.57	3.15	2.57	3.85	3.48	2.84	4.24	3.85	3.21	4.85	4.41	3.78
		38x184	4.71	4.16	3.39	5.08	4.59	3.74	5.59	5.08	4.23	6.40	5.81	4.98
		38x235	6.01	5.30	4.33	6.48	5.85	4.78	7.13	6.48	5.40	8.16	7.41	6.36
		38x286	7.31	6.45	5.27	7.88	7.12	5.81	8.67	7.88	6.57	9.93	9.02	7.73
	No. 1	38x 89	2.27	2.00	1.64	2.45	2.21	1.80	2.69	2.45	2.04	3.09	2.80	2.40
		38x140	3.39	2.93	2.39	3.74	3.23	2.64	4.22	3.66	2.99	4.85	4.30	3.51
		38x184	4.46	3.87	3.16	4.93	4.27	3.48	5.57	4.82	3.94	6.40	5.68	4.63
		38x235	5.70	4.93	4.03	6.29	5.44	4.44	7.11	6.15	5.02	8.16	7.24	5.91
		38x286	6.93	6.00	4.90	7.65	6.62	5.41	8.64	7.49	6.11	9.93	8.81	7.19
	No. 2	38x 89	2.10	1.81	1.48	2.31	2.00	1.63	2.60	2.26	1.85	2.98	2.67	2.18
		38x140	3.04	2.63	2.15	3.35	2.90	2.37	3.79	3.28	2.68	4.46	3.86	3.15
		38x184	4.01	3.47	2.83	4.42	3.83	3.12	5.00	4.33	3.53	5.88	5.09	4.16
		38x235	5.11	4.43	3.61	5.64	4.88	3.99	6.38	5.52	4.51	7.50	6.50	5.31
		38x286	6.22	5.38	4.40	6.86	5.94	4.85	7.76	6.72	5.48	9.13	7.90	6.45
	No. 3	38x 89	1.57	1.36	1.11	1.73	1.50	1.22	1.96	1.70	1.38	2.31	2.00	1.63
		38x140	2.31	2.00	1.63	2.55	2.21	1.80	2.89	2.50	2.04	3.40	2.94	2.40
		38x184	3.05	2.64	2.16	3.37	2.92	2.38	3.81	3.30	2.69	4.46	3.88	3.17
		38x235	3.89	3.37	2.75	4.30	3.72	3.04	4.86	4.21	3.43	5.72	4.95	4.04
		38x286	4.74	4.10	3.35	5.23	4.53	3.69	5.91	5.12	4.18	6.95	6.02	4.92
	Const	38x 89	1.79	1.55	1.26	1.97	1.71	1.39	2.23	1.93	1.57	2.62	2.27	1.85
	Stand	38x 89	1.34	1.16	0.95	1.48	1.28	1.05	1.67	1.45	1.18	1.97	1.71	1.39
	Util	38x 89	0.92	0.79	0.65	1.01	0.87	0.71	1.14	0.99	0.81	1.35	1.16	0.95
Western Cedars (N)	Sel. Str.	38x 89	2.19	1.99	1.73	2.36	2.14	1.87	2.59	2.36	2.06	2.97	2.70	2.36
		38x140	3.44	3.12	2.60	3.71	3.37	2.87	4.08	3.71	3.24	4.67	4.24	3.71
		38x184	4.54	4.12	3.43	4.89	4.44	3.79	5.38	4.89	4.27	6.16	5.59	4.89
		38x235	5.79	5.26	4.38	6.24	5.66	4.83	6.86	6.24	5.45	7.86	7.14	6.24
		38x286	7.04	6.40	5.13	7.58	6.89	5.88	8.35	7.58	6.63	9.56	8.68	7.58
	No. 1	38x 89	2.19	1.99	1.65	2.36	2.14	1.83	2.59	2.36	2.06	2.97	2.70	2.36
		38x140	3.43	2.97	2.42	3.71	3.28	2.67	4.08	3.70	3.02	4.67	4.24	3.56
		38x184	5.42	3.92	3.20	4.89	4.32	3.53	5.38	4.88	3.99	6.16	5.59	4.69
		38x235	5.77	5.00	4.08	6.24	5.51	4.50	6.86	6.23	5.09	7.86	7.14	5.99
		38x286	7.02	6.08	4.96	7.58	6.71	5.48	8.35	7.58	6.19	9.56	8.68	7.29
	No. 2	38x 89	2.11	1.84	1.50	2.28	2.03	1.66	2.51	2.28	1.87	2.87	2.61	2.20
		38x140	3.06	2.65	2.16	3.38	2.93	2.39	3.82	3.31	2.70	4.50	3.89	3.18
		38x184	4.04	3.50	2.85	4.46	3.86	3.15	5.04	4.36	3.56	5.93	5.13	4.19
		38x235	5.15	4.46	3.64	5.69	4.92	4.02	6.43	5.57	4.54	7.56	6.55	5.35
		38x286	6.27	5.43	4.43	6.92	5.99	4.89	7.82	6.77	5.53	9.20	7.97	6.51
	No. 3	38x 89	1.57	1.36	1.11	1.73	1.50	1.22	1.96	1.70	1.38	2.31	2.00	1.63
		38x140	2.31	2.00	1.63	2.55	2.21	1.80	2.89	2.50	2.04	3.40	2.94	2.40
		38x184	3.05	2.64	2.16	3.37	2.92	2.38	3.81	3.30	2.69	4.48	3.88	3.17
		38x235	3.89	3.37	2.75	4.30	3.72	3.04	4.86	4.21	3.43	5.72	4.95	4.04
		38x286	4.74	4.10	3.35	5.23	4.53	3.69	5.91	5.12	4.18	6.95	6.02	4.92
	Const	38x 89	1.80	1.56	1.27	1.99	1.72	1.40	2.25	1.95	1.59	2.65	2.29	1.87
	Stand	38x 89	1.34	1.16	0.95	1.48	1.28	1.05	1.67	1.45	1.18	1.97	1.71	1.39
	Util	38x 89	0.92	0.79	0.65	1.01	0.87	0.71	1.14	0.99	0.81	1.35	1.16	0.95
Northern Species	Sel. Str.	38x 89	2.19	1.99	1.72	2.36	2.14	1.87	2.58	2.36	2.06	2.97	2.70	2.36
		38x140	3.44	3.06	2.50	3.71	3.37	2.76	4.08	3.71	3.12	4.67	4.24	3.67
		38x184	4.54	4.04	3.30	4.89	4.44	3.64	5.38	4.89	4.11	6.16	5.59	4.84
		38x235	5.79	5.15	4.21	6.24	5.66	4.64	6.86	6.24	5.25	7.86	7.14	6.18
		38x286	7.04	6.27	5.12	7.58	6.89	5.65	8.35	7.58	6.38	9.56	8.68	7.51
	No. 1	38x 89	2.19	1.95	1.59	2.36	2.14	1.75	2.59	2.36	1.98	2.97	2.70	2.33
		38x140	3.27	2.83	2.31	3.61	3.13	2.55	4.08	3.54	2.89	4.67	4.16	3.40
		38x184	4.32	3.74	3.05	4.76	4.12	3.37	5.38	4.66	3.81	6.16	5.49	4.48
		38x235	5.51	4.77	3.89	6.08	5.26	4.30	6.86	5.95	4.86	7.86	7.00	5.72
		38x286	6.70	5.80	4.74	7.39	6.40	5.23	8.35	7.24	5.91	9.56	8.57	6.95
	No. 2	38x 89	2.04	1.76	1.44	2.25	1.95	1.59	2.51	2.20	1.80	2.87	2.59	2.11
		38x140	2.94	2.54	2.08	3.24	2.81	2.29	3.67	3.17	2.59	4.31	3.74	3.05
		38x184	3.87	3.35	2.78	4.27	3.70	3.02	4.83	4.18	3.42	5.69	4.93	4.02
		38x235	4.94	4.28	3.49	5.46	4.72	3.86	6.17	5.34	4.25	7.26	6.29	5.13
		38x286	6.01	5.21	4.25	6.64	5.75	4.69	7.50	6.50	5.30	8.83	7.65	6.24
	No. 3	38x 89	1.51	1.31	1.07	1.67	1.44	1.18	1.89	1.63	1.33	2.22	1.92	1.57
		38x140	2.21	1.92	1.56	2.44	2.12	1.73	2.76	2.39	1.95	3.25	2.82	2.30
		38x184	2.92	2.53	2.06	3.22	2.79	2.28	3.64	3.16	2.58	4.29	3.71	3.03
		38x235	3.73	3.23	2.63	4.11	3.56	2.91	4.65	4.03	3.29	5.47	4.74	3.87
		38x286	4.54	3.93	3.21	5.00	4.33	3.54	5.66	4.90	4.00	6.66	5.77	4.71
	Const	38x 89	1.73	1.50	1.22	1.91	1.66	1.35	2.16	1.87	1.53	2.55	2.20	1.80
	Stand	38x 89	1.30	1.12	0.92	1.43	1.24	1.01	1.62	1.40	1.14	1.90	1.65	1.35
	Util	38x 89	0.88	0.76	0.62	0.97	0.84	0.69	1.10	0.95	0.78	1.30	1.12	0.92

TABLE 7-2 *(cont.)*

Lumber Species	Grade	Size (mm)	LIVE LOAD 2.5 kN/m² Rafter spacing			LIVE LOAD 2.0 kN/m² Rafter spacing			LIVE LOAD 1.5 kN/m² Rafter spacing			LIVE LOAD 1.5 kN/m² Rafter spacing		
			300 mm	400 mm	600 mm	300 mm	400 mm	600 mm	300 mm	400 mm	600 mm	300 mm	400 mm	600 mm
Northern Aspen	Sel. Str.	38x 89	2.22	2.02	1.76	2.39	2.17	1.90	2.64	2.39	2.09	3.02	2.74	2.39
		38x140	3.49	3.15	2.57	3.76	3.42	2.84	4.14	3.76	3.21	4.74	4.31	3.76
		38x184	4.61	4.16	3.39	4.96	4.51	3.74	5.46	4.96	4.23	6.26	5.68	4.96
		38x235	5.88	5.30	4.33	6.33	5.75	4.78	6.97	6.33	5.40	7.98	7.25	6.33
		38x286	7.15	6.45	5.27	7.70	7.00	5.81	8.48	7.70	6.57	9.71	8.82	7.70
	No. 1	38x 89	2.22	2.00	1.64	2.39	2.17	1.80	2.64	2.39	2.04	3.02	2.74	2.39
		38x140	3.39	2.93	2.39	3.74	3.23	2.64	4.14	3.66	2.99	4.74	4.30	3.51
		38x184	4.46	3.87	3.16	4.93	4.27	3.48	5.46	4.82	3.94	6.26	5.68	4.63
		38x235	5.70	4.93	4.03	6.29	5.44	4.44	6.97	6.15	5.02	7.98	7.24	5.91
		38x286	6.93	6.00	4.90	7.65	6.62	5.41	8.48	7.49	6.11	9.71	8.81	7.19
	No. 2	38x 89	2.11	1.83	1.49	2.31	2.02	1.65	2.54	2.28	1.76	2.91	2.64	2.19
		38x140	3.04	2.63	2.15	3.35	2.90	2.37	3.79	3.28	2.68	4.46	3.86	3.15
		38x184	4.01	3.47	2.83	4.42	3.83	3.21	5.00	4.33	3.53	5.88	5.09	4.16
		38x235	5.11	4.43	3.61	5.64	4.88	3.99	6.38	5.52	4.51	7.50	6.50	5.31
		38x286	6.22	5.18	4.40	6.86	5.94	4.85	7.76	6.72	5.48	9.13	7.90	6.45
	No. 3	38x 89	1.57	1.36	1.11	1.73	1.50	1.22	1.96	1.70	1.38	2.31	2.00	1.63
		38x140	2.31	2.00	1.63	2.55	2.21	1.80	2.89	2.50	2.04	3.40	2.94	2.40
		38x184	3.03	2.64	2.16	3.37	2.92	2.39	3.81	3.30	2.69	4.48	3.88	3.17
		38x235	3.89	3.37	2.75	4.30	3.72	3.04	4.86	4.21	3.43	5.72	4.95	4.04
		38x286	4.74	4.10	3.35	5.23	4.53	3.69	5.91	5.12	4.18	6.95	6.02	4.92
	Const	38x 89	1.79	1.55	1.26	1.97	1.71	1.39	2.23	1.93	1.57	2.62	2.27	1.85
	Stand	38x 89	1.34	1.16	0.95	1.48	1.28	1.05	1.67	1.45	1.18	1.97	1.71	1.39
	Util	38x 89	0.92	0.79	0.65	1.01	0.87	0.71	1.14	0.99	0.81	1.35	1.16	0.95

Courtesy Canadian Wood Council

When the free span of rafters exceeds the maximum allowable, they must be provided with a support. The support is given, where possible, by braces resting on a bearing partition (see Fig. 7-34). First, a *purlin* is nailed to the underside of the rafters, as shown in Fig. 7-34, and a purlin plate to the ceiling joists over the partition. Purlin studs are cut to fit between these, preferably at right angles to the rafters. If they are so placed, the cut at the bottom of the stud will be the same as that on gable studs. If the purlin studs are vertical, this same cut will apply to the top end (see Fig. 7-35).

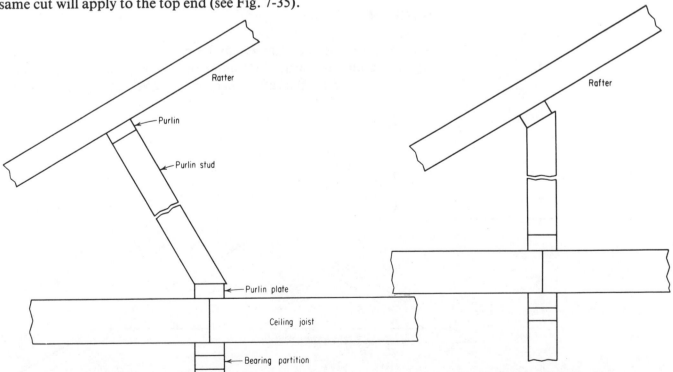

FIGURE 7-34: *Rafters supported on bearing partition.*

FIGURE 7-35: *Vertical purlin stud.*

203

When no bearing partition is available to carry the load, a strong-back must be used (see Fig. 7-36). A strongback is a straight timber, either solid or laminated, rigid enough to carry the imposed roof load. It can be made by glue-laminating two 38 × 235 mm or 38 × 286 mm pieces (depending on the rafter span). This member runs over the ceiling joists, blocked up at its ends and at other points, if possible, so that it will clear the joists by 19 mm.

Collar Ties

Rafters are tied together and stiffened by means of *collar ties*. These are horizontal supports nailed to the rafters, as illustrated in Fig. 7-37, and should be located in the middle third of the rafter length. 19 × 140 mm material may be used, unless the collar ties are to support a ceiling, in which case 38 × 89 mm or 38 × 140 mm material must be used.

The collar tie length will depend on its vertical distance below the rafter peaks and will be 500 mm for every unit of rise. For example, with rafters having a 200 mm rise, if the bottom edge of the collar tie is to be 1000 mm below the peak, the length of the collar tie, along its bottom edge will be $^{1000}/_{200}$ × 500 = 2500 mm. The cut on the ends will be obtained by using 250 and the rise—in this case 200—on the square, marking on the blade.

The 19 mm collar ties may be further stiffened by nailing a 19 × 100 mm member across the center of their span, from end to end of the roof.

ROOF SHEATHING

Sheathing for the roof frame may be plywood, particleboard, ship-lap, or common boards. Minimum thicknesses for roof sheathing materials, based on the rafter spacing, are given in Table 7-3.

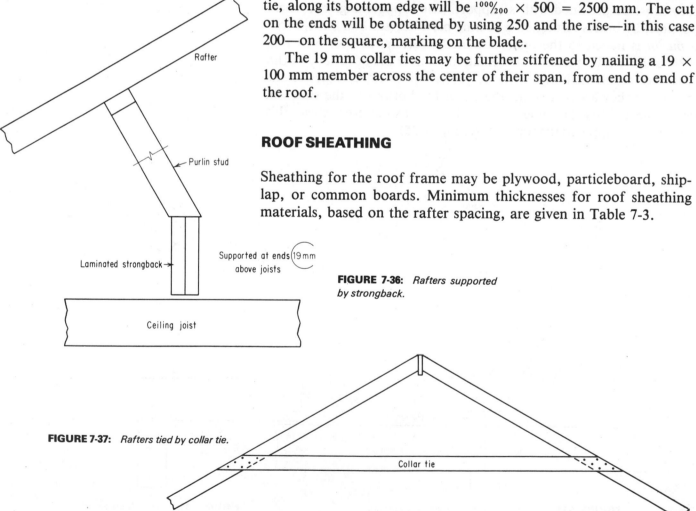

FIGURE 7-36: *Rafters supported by strongback.*

FIGURE 7-37: *Rafters tied by collar tie.*

TABLE 7-3 *Minimum thicknesses of roof sheathing (mm)* (Courtesy National Research Council)

Joist or rafter spacing (mm)	Minimum plywood thickness		Minimum particle board thickness, edges supported	Minimum lumber thickness
	Edges supported	Edges unsupported		
300	8	8	9.5	17.5
400	8	9.5	9.5	17.5
500	9.5	12.7	11	19
600	9.5	12.7	11	19

NOTE: Lumber shall not be wider than 300 mm

Shiplap or common boards must be applied solid if composition roofing is to be used, but the boards may be spaced if wood shingles or tile roofing is specified (see Fig. 7-38).

Layout for Hip Roof Sheathing Cuts

Ends of sheathing on a hip roof must be cut at an angle across the face of the material in order that the ends will follow the line of the center of the hip. In addition, the end cuts should also be *beveled* in order that two meeting pieces from adjoining surfaces can form a tight joint over the hip.

The table on the face of the tongue of the square (see Fig. 7-10) indicates that the face angle is obtained by using the side cut figures for jack rafters but marking on the tongue, rather than the blade. It also indicates that the edge bevel cut is obtained by using the unit line length on the blade and the rise on the tongue and marking on the tongue. For example, for a hip roof with a 150 mm rise, proceed as follows:

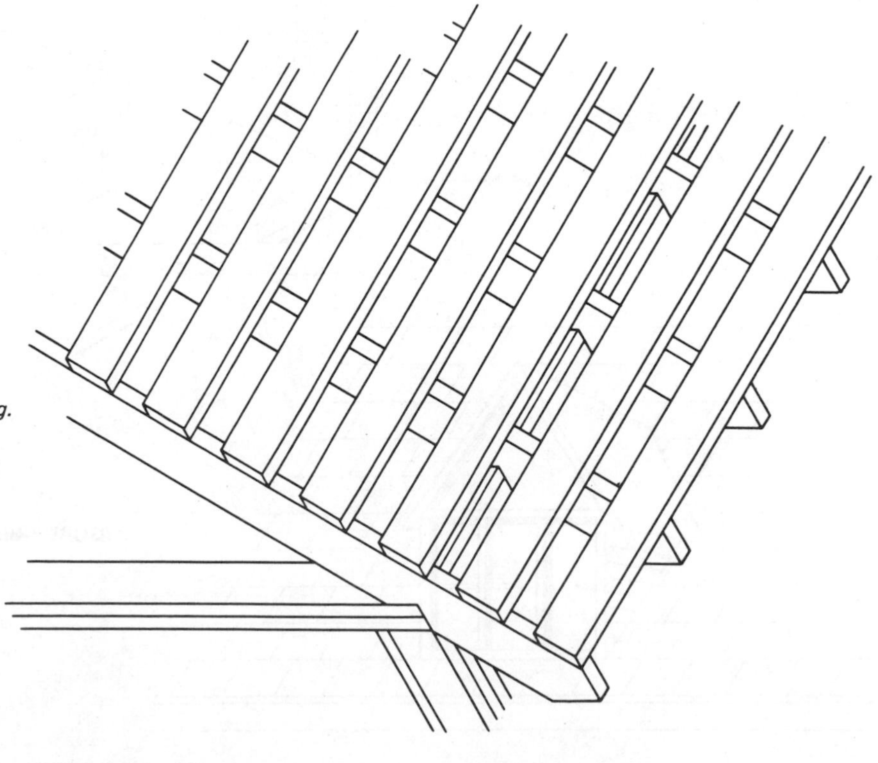

FIGURE 7-38:   *Spaced roof sheathing.*

205

1. From the rafter table, the unit line length of a common or jack rafter with a 150 mm rise is 291.5 mm. Also, from the table, the side cut figures for a jack rafter are 214 and 250 mm.

2. Apply the square to the *face* of the sheathing, with 250 on the blade and 214 on the tongue touching one edge. Mark on the tongue (see Fig. 7-39).

3. Apply the square to the *edge* of the sheathing with 291.5 on the blade and 150 on the tongue touching the edge, with the 150 mark coinciding with the end of the face angle line (see Fig. 7-39). Mark on the tongue.

DORMER FRAME

Sometimes it is desirable to let light into the building through the roof, and this may be done by means of vertical windows. The house-like structure containing such windows is called a *dormer* (see Fig. 7-40). In addition to letting in light, a dormer may increase the usable floor space in the attic.

The roof frame must be reinforced to support the dormer. This is done by doubling the rafters on which the sides of the dormer rest and by putting in double headers at the upper and lower ends of the opening (see Fig. 7-41). On this reinforced frame the dormer is built, as illustrated in Fig. 7-42. Framing procedure is the same as for any

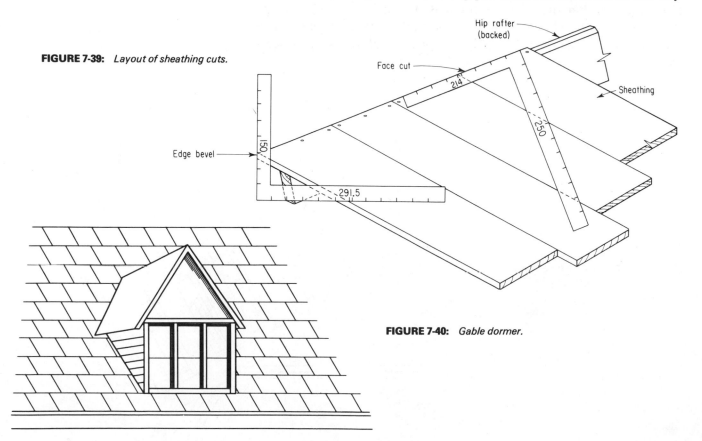

FIGURE 7-39: *Layout of sheathing cuts.*

FIGURE 7-40: *Gable dormer.*

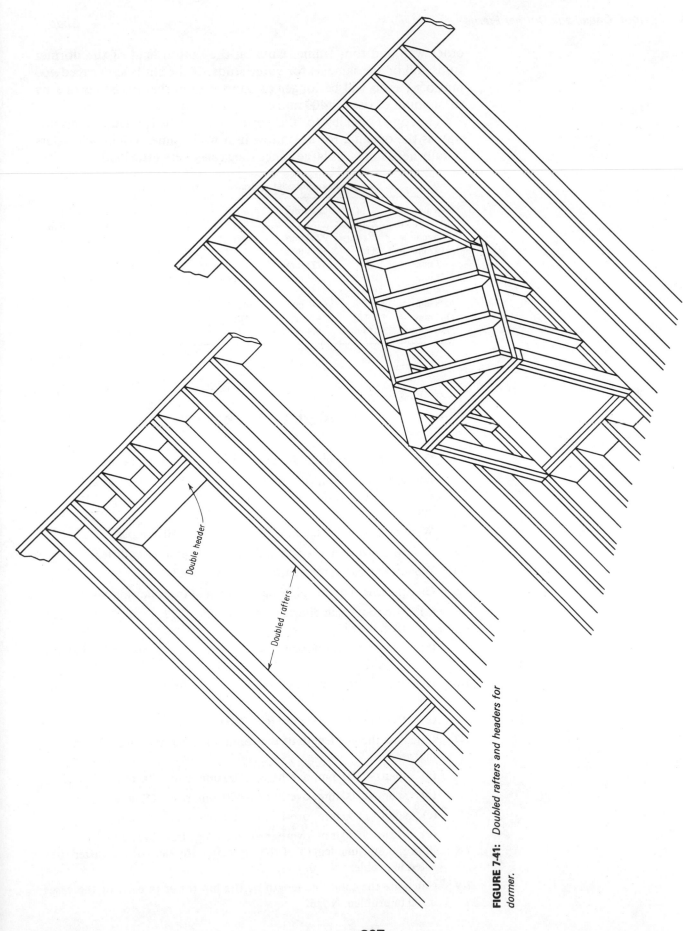

FIGURE 7-41: Doubled rafters and headers for dormer.

Double header

Doubled rafters

FIGURE 7-42: Dormer frame.

207

other wall and roof frame. Cuts on the bottom end of the dormer studs will be the same as for gable studs. If the studs are spaced 400 mm o.c., each will be longer or shorter than the preceding one by the amount of rise for 400 mm of common run.

The rough opening for the dormer window is framed in the same way as the opening for a window in a wall frame. Window headers usually need not be as large, since they carry very little load.

Approximate imperial equivalents to metric quantities

8 mm	—	5⁄16 in.	2846 mm	—	9 ft 4 in.	19 × 100 mm — 1 × 4 in.
9.5 mm	—	3⁄8 in.	2969 mm	—	9 ft 9 in.	19 × 150 mm — 1 × 6 in.
17.5 mm	—	11⁄16 in.	3244 mm	—	10 ft 3 in.	38 × 89 mm — 2 × 4 in.
19 mm	—	3⁄4 in.	3731 mm	—	12 ft 3 in.	38 × 140 mm — 2 × 6 in.
25 mm	—	1 in.	3773 mm	—	12 ft 4 in.	38 × 184 mm — 2 × 8 in.
27 mm	—	1⁄8 in.	4664 mm	—	15 ft 4 in.	38 × 235 mm — 2 × 10 in.
400 mm	—	16 in.	5531 mm	—	18 ft 2 in.	38 × 286 mm — 2 × 12 in.
2038 mm	—	6 ft 8 in.	6146 mm	—	20 ft 2 in.	
2332 mm	—	7 ft 7 in.	4.8 m	—	16 ft	
2766 mm	—	9 ft 1 in.	6.3 m	—	21 ft	

REVIEW QUESTIONS

7-1. On a simple diagram, illustrate each of the following rafter terms:

(a) span; **(b)** run; **(c)** unit run; **(d)** unit rise; **(e)** total rise; **(f)** overhang: **(g)** rafter tail; **(h)** line length; **(i)** plumb cut; **(j)** seat cut.

7-2. What do you understand by "a rafter with a 250 mm rise"?

7-3. By how much do line length and true length of a rafter differ?

7-4. What is the reason for "backing" a hip rafter?

7-5. Give the length of the ridgeboard in each of the following cases:

(a) Hip roof, plan dimensions 6600 mm × 7800 mm, 38 × 89 mm ridgeboard.

(b) Hip roof, plan dimensions 7850 mm × 9675 mm, 19 × 140 mm ridgeboard.

7-6. Give the unit length of the common rafter for each of the following rises:

(a) 160 mm; **(b)** 200 mm; **(c)** 240 mm.

7-7. Calculate the line length of the common rafter in each of the following:

(a) span—7500 mm; overhang—500 mm; rise—200 mm.

(b) span—8000 mm; overhang—400 mm; rise—150 mm.

(c) span—6400 mm; overhang—600 mm; rise—175 mm.

(d) span—9600 mm; overhang—700 mm; rise—100 mm.

7-8. Find the unit line length of the hip rafter for each of the rafter rises listed in problem No. 6.

7-9. Calculate the total line length of the hip rafter in each of the cases listed in problem No. 6.

8

ALTERNATIVE
ROOF
SYSTEMS

When one thinks of a roof on a building in the category of light construction, particularly a house roof, the same picture usually appears. It is the picture of a sloped roof, either gable or hip, made with the conventional roof-framing materials. And, indeed, a great percentage of the roofs, on dwelling houses especially, are made in just that way.

There are alternatives to the conventional roof, and more and more in modern light construction so one of these alternatives is being used. Among them are (a) a *flat roof* in which the ceiling joists are also the roof joists, (b) a flat roof carried by laminated beams resting on the top of the walls, (c) a flat roof carried by box beams resting on top of the walls, (d) a *sloped roof carried by beams* with their ends resting on the wall gables, (e) a *pitched roof with the rafters resting on the ends of ceiling joists* which project beyond the walls, (f) a *sloped roof made with trussed rafters or roof trusses,* (g) a roof framed by what is known as the *rigid frame* system, (h) the *A-frame,* and (i) a *stressed-skin panel roof.*

The roof to be used in a particular situation is a matter of some architectural importance. A number of factors are involved in the choosing of a roof type, and they must all be weighed carefully before making the final choice.

One of the important factors is the over-all appearance desired. If the long, low look is being sought, the flat or low-pitched roof will probably do most to enhance it. On the other hand, flat roofs may tend to be troublesome in wet climates or where the snowfall is heavy or wet. If wide overhangs are required with a pitched roof, they are best achieved by setting the rafters on the ends of overhanging joists. In this way, the cornice never drops below the plate level, so it does not reduce the possible window height, but the walls may tend to look higher from the outside.

If wide open spaces on the inside are desired, with no obstructions in the way of partitions or posts, the answer is to make the roof with roof trusses. In this way long, free spans are achieved. Remember, however, that you are now somewhat restricted as to roof shape. Trusses lend themselves best to gable roofs.

Special effects are obtained by using roof beams with either a flat or a sloped roof, but the cost of the roof may be increased, because of the quality of roof decking usually required.

From the foregoing it is evident that there are a number of alternatives possible in the selection of a roof type. However, that choice should not be made lightly. Once the choice is made, every effort should be made to see that it is properly executed. The following pages will outline the general appearance and steps in construction of each of the roof types mentioned above.

FLAT ROOF WITH REGULAR JOISTS

We have already seen in Chapter 6 the procedure for framing a ceiling when a regular sloped roof is to be used on the building. If a flat roof is to be used instead, the same general ceiling framing scheme may be used with some important alterations.

In the first place, the size of the ceiling joists will have to be in-

Lumber Species	Grade	Size (mm)	LIVE LOAD 2.5 kN/m²						LIVE LOAD 2.0 kN/m²					
			Gypsum board or plastered ceiling			Other ceilings			Gypsum board or plastered ceiling			Other ceilings		
			300 mm	400 mm	600 mm	300 mm	400 mm	600 mm	300 mm	400 mm	600 mm	300 mm	400 mm	600 mm
Douglas Fir-Larch (N)	Sel. Str.	38x 89	1.98	1.80	1.57	2.27	2.06	1.80	2.14	1.94	1.70	2.45	2.22	1.94
		38x140	3.12	2.83	2.48	3.57	3.24	2.83	3.36	3.05	2.57	3.85	3.50	3.05
		38x184	4.11	3.74	3.27	4.71	4.28	3.74	4.43	4.03	3.52	5.08	4.61	4.03
		38x235	5.25	4.77	4.17	6.01	5.46	4.77	5.66	5.14	4.49	6.48	5.88	5.14
		38x286	6.39	5.80	5.07	7.31	6.64	5.80	6.88	6.25	5.46	7.88	7.16	6.25
	No. 1	38x 89	1.98	1.80	1.57	2.27	2.06	1.80	2.14	1.94	1.70	2.45	2.22	1.94
		38x140	3.12	2.83	2.48	3.57	3.25	2.76	3.36	3.05	2.67	3.85	3.50	3.03
		38x184	4.11	3.74	3.27	4.71	4.28	3.64	4.43	4.03	3.52	5.08	4.61	3.99
		38x235	5.25	4.77	4.17	6.01	5.46	4.65	5.66	5.14	4.49	6.48	5.88	5.10
		38x286	6.39	5.80	5.07	7.31	6.64	5.66	6.88	6.25	5.46	7.88	7.16	6.20
	No. 2	38x 89	1.92	1.74	1.52	2.20	1.99	1.72	2.07	1.88	1.64	2.37	2.15	1.88
		38x140	3.02	2.74	2.39	3.45	3.04	2.49	3.75	2.95	2.58	3.72	3.34	2.72
		38x184	3.98	3.61	3.16	4.55	4.02	3.28	4.29	3.89	3.40	4.91	4.40	3.59
		38x235	5.08	4.61	4.03	5.81	5.12	4.18	5.47	4.97	4.14	6.26	5.61	4.58
		38x286	6.17	5.61	4.90	7.07	6.23	5.09	6.65	6.04	5.28	7.62	6.81	5.57
	No. 3	38x 89	1.80	1.56	1.27	1.80	1.56	1.27	1.98	1.71	1.40	1.98	1.71	1.40
		38x140	2.66	2.30	1.88	2.66	2.30	1.88	2.92	2.52	2.06	2.92	2.52	2.06
		38x184	3.51	3.04	2.48	3.51	3.04	2.48	3.84	3.33	2.72	3.84	3.33	2.72
		38x235	4.48	3.88	3.17	4.48	3.88	3.17	4.91	4.25	3.47	4.91	4.25	3.47
		38x286	5.45	4.72	3.85	5.45	4.72	3.85	5.97	5.17	4.22	5.97	5.17	4.22
	Const	38x 89	1.84	1.67	1.46	2.07	1.79	1.46	1.98	1.80	1.57	2.26	1.96	1.60
	Stand	38x 89	1.55	1.34	1.10	1.55	1.34	1.10	1.70	1.47	1.20	1.70	1.47	1.20
	Util	38x 89	1.06	0.92	0.75	1.06	0.92	0.75	1.16	1.00	0.82	1.16	1.00	0.82
Hem-Fir (N)	Sel. Str.	38x 89	1.91	1.74	1.52	2.19	1.99	1.74	2.06	1.87	1.63	2.36	2.14	1.87
		38x140	3.01	2.73	2.19	3.44	3.13	3.57	3.57	2.94	2.57	3.71	3.37	2.81
		38x184	3.97	3.60	3.15	4.54	4.12	3.39	4.27	3.88	3.39	4.89	4.44	3.71
		38x235	5.06	4.60	4.02	5.79	5.26	4.32	5.45	4.95	4.33	6.24	5.67	4.73
		38x286	6.16	5.59	4.89	7.05	6.40	5.26	6.63	6.03	5.26	7.59	6.90	5.76
	No. 1	38x 89	1.91	1.74	1.52	2.19	1.99	1.63	2.06	1.87	1.63	2.36	2.14	1.79
		38x140	3.01	2.73	2.39	3.38	2.92	2.39	3.24	2.94	2.57	3.70	3.20	2.61
		38x184	3.97	3.60	3.15	4.45	3.85	3.15	4.27	3.88	3.39	4.88	4.22	3.45
		38x235	5.06	4.60	4.01	5.68	4.92	4.01	5.45	4.95	4.33	6.22	5.39	4.40
		38x286	6.16	5.59	4.88	6.91	5.98	4.88	6.63	6.03	5.26	7.57	6.55	5.35
	No. 2	38x 89	1.85	1.68	1.46	2.09	1.81	1.48	1.99	1.81	1.58	2.28	1.99	1.62
		38x140	2.90	2.62	2.14	3.03	2.62	2.14	3.13	2.84	2.34	3.32	2.87	2.34
		38x184	3.83	3.46	2.82	3.99	3.46	2.82	4.13	3.75	3.09	4.37	3.79	3.09
		38x235	4.89	4.41	3.60	5.10	4.41	3.60	5.27	4.78	3.95	5.58	4.83	3.95
		38x286	5.95	5.37	4.38	6.20	5.37	4.38	6.41	5.82	4.80	6.79	5.88	4.80
	No. 3	38x 89	1.55	1.34	1.10	1.55	1.34	1.10	1.70	1.47	1.20	1.70	1.47	1.30
		38x140	2.30	1.99	1.62	2.30	1.99	1.62	2.52	2.18	1.78	2.52	2.18	1.78
		38x184	3.03	2.62	2.14	3.03	2.62	2.14	3.32	2.87	2.34	3.32	2.87	2.34
		38x235	3.87	3.35	2.73	3.87	3.35	2.72	4.23	3.67	2.99	4.23	3.67	2.99
		38x286	4.70	4.07	3.32	4.70	4.07	3.32	5.15	4.46	3.64	5.15	4.46	3.64
	Const	38x 89	1.78	1.55	1.26	1.79	1.55	1.26	1.91	1.70	1.38	1.96	1.70	1.38
	Stand	38x 89	1.34	1.16	0.95	1.34	1.16	0.95	1.47	1.27	1.04	1.47	1.27	1.04
	Util	38x 89	0.92	0.79	0.65	0.92	0.79	0.65	1.00	0.87	0.71	1.00	0.87	0.71
Eastern Hemlock-Tamarack (N)	Sel. Str.	38x 89	1.82	1.65	1.44	2.09	1.89	1.65	1.96	1.78	1.56	2.25	2.04	1.78
		38x140	2.86	2.60	2.27	3.28	2.98	2.60	3.09	2.80	2.45	3.53	3.21	2.80
		38x184	3.78	3.43	3.00	4.33	3.93	3.43	4.07	3.70	3.23	4.66	4.23	3.70
		38x235	4.82	4.38	3.83	5.52	5.01	4.38	5.19	4.72	4.12	5.95	5.80	4.72
		38x286	5.87	5.33	4.65	6.71	6.10	5.33	6.32	5.74	5.01	7.23	6.57	5.74

creased. As we pointed out in Chapter 6, the size depends on the free span. In general 38 × 140 mm or 38 × 184 mm members are commonly used for ceiling joists. If the ceiling joists are also to be the roof joists, the size must be increased, because of the additional loads of roofing materials, snow, and live loads. Size 38 × 184 mm, 38 × 235 and 38 × 286 mm members are commonly used, the choice in a particular case depending on the above-mentioned factors. See Table 8-1 for sizes and spans.

TABLE 8-1 *(cont.)*

Lumber Species	Grade	Size (mm)	LIVE LOAD 1.5 kN/m²						LIVE LOAD 1.0 kN/m²					
			Gypsum board or plastered ceiling			Other ceilings			Gypsum board or plastered ceiling			Other ceilings		
			300 mm	400 mm	600 mm	300 mm	400 mm	600 mm	300 mm	400 mm	600 mm	300 mm	400 mm	600 mm
Douglas Fir-Larch (N)	Sel. Str.	38x 89	2.35	2.14	1.87	2.69	2.45	2.14	2.69	2.45	2.14	3.09	2.80	2.45
		38x140	3.70	3.36	2.94	4.24	3.85	3.36	4.24	3.85	3.36	4.85	4.41	3.85
		38x184	4.88	4.43	3.87	5.59	5.08	4.43	5.59	5.08	5.43	6.40	5.81	5.08
		38x235	6.23	5.66	4.94	7.13	6.48	5.66	7.13	6.48	5.66	8.16	7.41	6.48
		38x286	5.57	6.88	6.01	8.67	7.88	6.88	8.67	7.88	6.88	9.93	9.02	7.88
	No. 1	38x 89	2.35	2.14	1.87	2.69	2.45	2.14	2.69	2.45	2.14	3.09	2.80	2.45
		38x140	3.70	3.36	2.94	4.24	3.85	3.36	4.24	3.85	3.36	4.85	4.41	3.85
		38x184	4.88	4.43	3.87	5.59	5.08	4.43	5.59	5.08	4.43	6.40	5.81	5.08
		38x235	6.23	5.66	4.94	7.13	6.48	5.66	7.13	6.48	5.66	8.16	7.41	6.48
		38x286	7.57	6.88	6.01	8.67	7.88	6.88	8.67	7.88	6.88	9.93	9.02	7.88
	No. 2	38x 89	2.27	2.07	1.80	2.60	2.17	2.07	2.60	2.37	2.07	2.98	2.71	2.37
		38x140	3.58	3.25	2.84	4.10	3.72	3.04	4.10	3.72	3.25	4.69	4.26	3.52
		38x184	4.72	4.39	3.74	5.40	4.91	4.02	5.40	4.91	4.29	6.18	5.67	4.64
		38x235	6.02	5.47	4.78	6.89	6.26	5.12	6.89	6.26	5.47	7.89	7.17	5.92
		38x286	7.32	6.65	5.81	8.38	7.62	6.23	8.38	7.62	6.65	9.60	8.72	7.20
	No. 3	38x 89	2.18	1.91	1.56	2.21	1.91	1.56	2.50	2.21	1.80	2.55	2.21	1.80
		38x140	3.26	2.82	2.30	3.26	2.82	2.30	3.77	3.26	2.66	3.77	3.26	2.66
		38x184	4.30	3.72	3.04	4.30	3.72	3.04	4.96	4.30	3.51	4.96	4.30	3.51
		38x235	5.49	4.75	3.88	5.49	4.75	3.88	6.34	5.49	4.48	6.34	5.49	4.48
		38x286	6.67	5.78	4.72	6.67	5.78	4.72	7.71	6.67	5.45	7.71	6.67	5.45
	Const	38x 89	2.18	1.98	1.73	2.50	2.19	1.79	2.50	2.27	1.98	2.86	2.53	2.07
	Stand	38x 89	1.90	1.65	1.14	1.90	1.65	1.34	2.20	1.90	1.55	2.20	1.90	1.55
	Util	38x 89	1.30	1.12	0.92	1.30	1.12	0.92	1.50	1.30	1.06	1.50	1.30	1.06
Hem-Fir (N)	Sel. Str.	38x 89	2.27	2.06	1.80	2.60	2.36	2.06	2.60	2.36	2.06	2.97	2.70	2.36
		38x140	3.57	3.24	2.83	4.08	3.71	3.15	4.08	3.71	3.24	4.67	4.25	3.63
		38x184	4.70	4.27	3.73	5.38	4.89	4.15	5.18	4.89	4.27	6.16	5.60	4.79
		38x235	6.00	5.45	4.76	6.87	6.24	5.29	6.87	6.24	5.45	7.87	7.15	6.11
		38x286	7.30	6.63	5.79	8.36	7.59	6.44	8.36	7.59	6.63	9.57	8.69	7.44
	No. 1	38x 89	2.27	2.06	1.80	2.60	2.36	2.00	2.60	2.16	2.06	2.97	2.70	2.31
		38x140	3.51	3.24	2.83	4.08	3.58	2.92	4.08	3.71	3.24	4.67	4.14	3.18
		38x184	4.70	4.27	3.73	5.38	4.72	3.85	5.18	4.89	4.27	6.15	5.45	4.45
		38x235	6.00	5.45	4.76	6.87	6.02	4.92	6.87	6.24	5.45	7.87	6.96	5.68
		38x286	7.30	6.63	5.79	8.36	7.33	5.98	8.36	7.59	6.63	9.57	8.46	6.91
	No. 2	38x 89	2.19	1.99	1.74	2.51	2.22	1.81	2.51	2.28	1.99	2.87	2.56	2.09
		38x140	3.44	3.13	2.62	3.71	3.21	2.62	3.94	3.58	3.03	4.28	3.71	3.03
		38x184	4.54	4.13	3.46	4.89	4.24	3.46	5.20	4.72	3.99	5.65	4.89	3.99
		38x235	5.80	5.27	4.42	6.42	5.40	4.41	6.64	6.03	5.10	7.21	6.24	5.10
		38x286	7.05	6.41	5.17	7.59	6.57	5.37	8.07	7.33	6.20	8.77	7.59	6.20
	No. 3	38x 89	1.90	1.65	1.34	1.90	1.65	1.34	2.20	1.90	1.55	2.20	1.90	1.55
		38x140	2.81	2.44	1.99	2.81	2.44	1.99	3.25	2.81	2.10	3.25	2.81	2.30
		38x184	3.71	3.21	2.62	3.71	3.21	2.62	4.28	3.71	3.03	4.28	3.71	3.03
		38x235	4.73	4.10	3.35	4.73	4.10	3.35	5.47	4.73	3.87	5.47	4.73	3.87
		38x286	5.76	4.99	4.07	5.76	4.99	4.07	6.65	5.76	4.70	6.65	5.76	4.70
	Const	38x 89	2.11	1.90	1.55	2.19	1.90	1.55	2.41	2.19	1.79	2.53	2.19	1.79
	Stand	38x 89	1.64	1.42	1.16	1.64	1.42	1.16	1.90	1.64	1.34	1.90	1.64	1.54
	Util	38x 89	1.12	0.97	0.79	1.12	0.97	0.79	1.30	1.12	0.92	1.30	1.12	0.92
Eastern Hemlock-Tamarack (N)	Sel. Str.	38x 89	2.16	1.96	1.71	2.47	2.25	1.96	2.47	2.25	1.96	2.83	2.57	2.25
		38x140	3.40	3.09	2.70	3.89	3.53	3.09	3.89	3.53	3.09	4.45	4.05	3.53
		38x184	4.48	4.07	3.55	5.13	4.66	4.07	5.13	4.66	4.07	5.87	5.33	4.66
		38x235	5.72	5.19	4.54	6.55	5.95	5.19	6.55	5.95	5.19	7.49	6.81	5.95
		38x286	6.95	6.32	5.52	7.96	7.23	6.32	7.96	7.23	6.32	9.12	8.28	7.23

TABLE 8-1 *(cont.)*

Lumber Species	Grade	Size (mm)	LIVE LOAD 2.5 kN/m² Gypsum board or plastered ceiling 300 mm	400 mm	600 mm	Other ceilings 300 mm	400 mm	600 mm	LIVE LOAD 2.0 kN/m² Gypsum board or plastered ceiling 300 mm	400 mm	600 mm	Other ceilings 300 mm	400 mm	600 mm
Eastern Hemlock Tamarack (N) (cont'd)	No. 1	38x 89	1.82	1.65	1.44	2.09	1.98	1.65	1.96	1.78	1.56	2.25	2.04	1.78
		38x140	2.86	2.60	2.27	3.28	2.98	3.43	3.09	2.80	2.45	3.53	3.21	2.80
		38x184	3.78	3.43	3.00	4.33	3.93	3.43	4.07	3.70	3.23	4.66	4.23	3.70
		38x235	4.82	4.38	3.83	5.52	5.01	4.38	5.19	4.72	4.12	5.95	5.40	4.72
		38x286	5.87	5.33	4.65	6.71	6.10	5.33	6.32	5.74	5.01	7.23	6.57	5.74
	No. 2	38x 89	1.76	1.59	1.39	2.01	1.83	1.59	1.89	1.72	1.50	2.17	1.97	1.72
		38x140	2.76	2.51	2.19	3.16	2.87	2.39	2.98	2.70	2.36	3.41	3.09	2.61
		38x184	3.64	3.31	2.98	4.17	3.79	3.15	3.92	3.56	3.11	4.49	4.08	3.45
		38x235	4.65	4.22	3.69	5.32	4.83	4.01	5.01	4.55	3.97	5.73	5.21	4.40
		38x286	5.65	5.14	4.49	6.47	5.88	4.88	6.09	5.53	4.83	6.97	6.33	5.35
	No. 3	38x 89	1.69	1.51	1.23	1.74	1.51	1.23	1.82	1.65	1.35	1.91	1.65	1.35
		38x140	2.55	2.21	1.80	2.55	2.21	1.80	2.80	2.42	1.98	2.80	2.42	1.98
		38x184	3.37	2.92	2.38	3.37	2.92	2.38	3.69	3.20	2.61	3.69	3.20	2.61
		38x235	4.30	3.72	3.04	4.30	3.72	3.04	4.71	4.08	3.33	4.71	4.08	3,33
		38x286	5.32	4.53	3.70	5.23	4.53	3.70	5.75	4.96	4.05	5.73	4.96	4.05
	Const	38x 89	1.69	1.54	1.18	1.94	1.73	1.41	1.82	1.66	1.45	2.09	1.89	1.55
	Stand	38x 89	1.48	1.28	1.04	1.48	1.28	1.04	1.62	1.40	1.14	1.62	1.40	1.14
	Util	38x 89	1.03	0.89	0.73	1.03	0.89	0.73	1.13	0.98	0.80	1.13	0.98	0.80
Coast Species	Sel. Str.	38x 89	1.91	1.74	1.52	2.19	1.99	1.74	2.06	1.87	1.63	2.36	2.14	1.87
		38x140	3.01	2.73	2.39	3.44	3.11	2.54	3.24	2.94	2.57	3.71	3.37	2.78
		38x184	3.97	3.60	3.15	4.54	4.10	3.35	4.27	3.88	3.89	4.89	4.64	3.67
		38x235	5.06	4.60	4.02	5.79	5.24	4.28	5.45	4.95	4.33	6.24	5.67	4.68
		38x286	6.16	5.59	4.89	7.05	6.37	5.20	6.63	6.03	5.26	7.59	6.90	5.70
	No. 1	38x 89	1.91	1.74	1.52	2.19	1.98	1.61	2.06	1.87	1.63	2.36	2.14	1.77
		38x140	3.01	2.73	2.16	3.33	2.98	2.36	3.24	2.94	2.57	3.65	3.16	2.58
		38x184	3.97	3.60	3.11	4.40	1.81	3.11	4.27	3.88	3.39	4.82	4.17	3.40
		38x235	5.06	4.60	3.97	5.61	4.65	3.97	5.43	4.95	4.33	6.15	5.42	4.34
		38x286	6.16	5.59	4.82	6.82	5.91	4.82	6.63	6.03	5.26	7.40	6.47	5.29
	No. 2	38x 89	1.85	1.68	1.46	2.07	1.79	1.46	1.99	1.81	1.58	2.26	1.96	1.60
		38x140	2.90	2.58	2.11	2.98	2.58	2.11	3.13	2.83	2.31	3.27	2.83	2.31
		38x184	3.83	3.40	2.78	3.94	3.40	2.78	4.13	3.73	3.04	4.31	3.73	3.04
		38x235	4.89	4.34	3.55	5.02	4.34	3.55	5.27	4.76	3.89	5.50	4.76	3.89
		38x286	5.95	5.29	4.31	6.10	5.29	4.31	6.41	5.79	4.73	6.69	5.79	4.73
	No. 3	38x 89	1.53	1.33	1.08	1.53	1.33	1.08	1.68	1.46	1.19	1.68	1.46	1.19
		38x140	2.07	1.96	1.60	2.27	1.96	1.60	2.48	2.15	1.75	2.48	2.16	1.75
		38x184	2.99	2.59	2.11	2.99	2.59	2.11	3.27	2.84	2.31	3.27	2.83	2.31
		38x235	3.81	3.30	2.70	3.81	3.30	2.70	4.18	3.62	2.95	4.18	3.62	2.95
		38x286	4.64	4.02	3.28	4.64	4.02	3.28	5.08	4.40	3.59	5.08	4.40	3.59
	Const	38x 89	1.76	1.52	1.24	1.76	1.52	1.24	1.91	1.67	1.36	1.92	1.67	1.36
	Stand	38x 89	1.32	1.14	0.93	1.32	1.14	0.93	1.44	1.25	1.02	1.44	1.25	1.02
	Util	38x 89	0.92	0.79	0.65	0.92	0.79	0.65	1.00	0.87	0.71	1.00	0.87	0.71
Spruce-Pine-Fir	Sel. Str.	38x 89	1.80	1.64	1.43	2.06	1.87	1.68	1.94	1.76	1.54	2.22	2.02	1.76
		38x140	2.83	2.58	2.25	3.25	2.95	2.49	3.05	2.77	2.42	3.50	3.18	2.72
		38x184	3.74	3.40	2.97	4.28	3.89	3.28	4.03	3.66	3.20	4.61	4.19	3.59
		38x235	4.77	4.33	3.79	5.46	4.96	4.18	5.14	4.67	4.08	5.88	5.35	4.58
		38x286	5.80	5.27	4.61	6.64	6.04	5.09	6.25	5.68	4.96	7.16	6.50	5.57
	No. 1	38x 89	1.80	1.64	1.43	2.06	1.87	1.58	1.94	1.76	1.54	2.22	2.02	1.73
		38x140	2.83	2.58	2.25	3.25	2.83	2.31	3.05	2.77	2.42	3.50	3.10	2.53
		38x184	3.74	3.40	2.97	4.28	3.71	3.05	4.03	3.66	3.20	4.61	4.09	3.14
		38x235	4.77	4.33	3.79	5.46	4.77	3.89	5.14	4.67	4.08	5.88	5.22	4.26
		38x286	5.80	5.27	4.61	6.14	5.80	4.73	6.25	5.68	4.96	7.16	6.35	5.18
	No. 2	38x 89	1.74	1.58	1.38	1.99	1.75	1.43	1.88	1.70	1.49	2.15	1.92	1.57
		38x140	2.74	2.49	2.07	2.94	2.54	2.07	2.95	2.68	2.27	3.28	2.28	2.27
		38x184	3.61	3.28	2.73	3.87	3.35	2.73	3.89	3.54	3.00	4.24	3.67	3.00
		38x235	4.61	4.19	3.49	4.94	4.28	3.49	4.97	4.51	3.82	5.41	4.68	3.82
		38x286	5.61	5.10	4.25	6.01	5.20	4.25	6.04	5.49	4.65	6.58	5.70	4.65
	No. 3	38x 89	1.52	1.31	1.07	1.52	1.31	1.07	1.66	1.44	1.17	1.66	1.44	1.17
		38x140	2.23	1.93	1.58	2.23	1.93	1.58	2.45	2.12	1.73	2.45	2.12	1.73
		38x184	2.95	2.55	2.08	2.95	2.55	2.08	3.23	2.80	2.28	3.23	2.80	2.28
		38x235	3.76	3.26	2.66	3.76	3.26	2.66	4.12	3.57	2.91	4.12	3.57	2.91
		38x286	4.58	3.96	3.23	4.58	3.96	3.23	5.01	4.34	3.54	5.01	4.34	3.54
	Const	38x 89	1.68	1.49	1.22	1.72	1.49	1.22	1.81	1.64	1.33	1.89	1.64	1.33
	Stand	38x 89	1.30	1.12	0.92	1.30	1.12	0.92	1.42	1.23	1.00	1.42	1.23	1.00
	Util	38x 89	0.88	0.76	0.62	0.88	0.76	0.62	0.97	0.84	0.68	0.97	0.84	0.68

TABLE 8-1 *(cont.)*

Lumber Species	Grade	Size (mm)	LIVE LOAD 1.5 kN/m²						LIVE LOAD 1.0 kN/m²					
			Gypsum board or plastered ceiling			Other ceilings			Gypsum board or plastered ceiling			Other ceilings		
			300 mm	400 mm	600 mm	300 mm	400 mm	600 mm	300 mm	400 mm	600 mm	300 mm	400 mm	600 mm
Eastern Hemlock Tamarack (N) (cont'd)	No. 1	38x 89	2.16	1.96	1.71	2.47	2.25	1.96	2.47	2.25	1.96	2.81	2.57	2.25
		38x140	3.40	3.09	2.70	3.89	3.53	3.09	3.89	3.53	3.09	4.45	4.05	3.53
		38x184	4.48	4.07	3.55	5.13	4.66	4.07	5.13	4.66	4.07	5.87	5.33	4.66
		38x235	5.72	5.19	4.54	6.55	5.95	5.19	6.55	5.95	5.19	7.49	6.81	5.95
		38x286	6.95	6.32	5.52	7.96	7.23	6.32	7.96	7.23	6.12	9.12	8.28	7.23
	No. 2	38x 89	2.08	1.89	1.65	2.48	2.17	1.89	2.38	2.17	1.89	2.73	2.48	2.17
		38x140	3.28	2.98	2.60	3.75	3.41	2.92	3.75	3.41	2.98	4.29	3.90	3.38
		38x184	4.32	3.92	3.43	4.94	4.49	3.85	4.94	4.49	3.92	5.66	5.14	4.45
		38x235	5.51	5.01	4.37	6.31	5.73	4.92	6.31	5.73	5.01	7.22	6.56	5.68
		38x286	6.70	6.09	5.32	7.68	6.97	5.98	7.68	6.97	6.09	8.79	7.98	6.91
	No. 3	38x 89	2.01	1.82	1.51	2.13	1.85	1.51	2.30	2.09	1.74	2.46	2.13	1.74
		38x140	3.13	2.71	2.21	3.13	2.71	2.21	3.61	3.13	2.55	3.61	3.13	2.55
		38x184	4.13	3.57	2.92	4.13	3.57	2.92	4.77	4.13	3.17	4.77	4.11	3.37
		38x235	5.27	4.56	3.72	5.27	4.56	3.72	6.08	5.27	4.30	6.08	5.27	4.30
		38x286	6.42	5.55	4.53	6.41	5.55	4.53	7.40	6.41	5.23	7.40	6.41	5.23
	Const	38x 89	2.01	1.82	1.59	2.30	2.09	1.73	2.30	2.09	1.82	2.63	2.39	2.00
	Stand	38x 89	1.81	1.57	1.28	1.81	1.57	1.28	2.09	1.81	1.48	2.09	1.81	1.48
	Util	38x 89	1.26	1.09	0.89	1.26	1.09	0.89	1.46	1.26	1.03	1.46	1.26	1.03
Coast Species	Sel. Str.	38x 89	2.27	2.06	1.80	2.60	2.36	2.06	2.60	2.36	2.06	2.97	2.70	2.36
		38x140	3.57	3.24	2.83	4.08	3.71	3.11	4.08	3.71	3.24	4.67	4.25	3.59
		38x184	4.70	4.27	3.73	5.38	4.89	4.10	5.38	4.89	4.27	6.26	5.60	4.74
		38x235	6.00	5.45	4.76	6.87	6.24	5.24	6.87	6.24	5.45	7.87	7.15	6.05
		38x286	7.30	6.63	5.79	8.36	7.59	6.37	8.36	7.59	6.63	9.57	8.69	7.36
	No. 1	38x 89	2.27	2.06	1.80	2.60	2.36	1.98	2.60	2.36	2.06	2.97	2.70	2.29
		38x140	3.57	3.24	2.83	4.08	3.54	2.89	4.08	3.71	3.24	4.67	4.08	3.33
		38x184	4.70	4.27	3.73	5.38	4.66	3.81	5.38	4.89	4.27	6.16	5.39	4.40
		38x235	6.00	5.45	4.76	6.87	5.95	4.86	6.87	6.87	5.45	7.87	6.87	5.61
		38x286	7.30	6.63	5.79	8.36	7.24	5.91	8.36	7.59	6.63	9.57	8.36	6.82
	No. 2	38x 89	2.19	1.99	1.74	2.51	2.19	1.79	2.51	2.28	1.99	2.87	2.53	2.07
		38x140	3.44	3.13	2.58	3.65	3.16	2.58	3.94	3.58	2.98	4.22	3.65	2.98
		38x184	4.54	4.13	3.40	4.82	4.17	3.40	5.20	4.72	3.93	5.56	4.82	3.93
		38x235	5.80	5.27	4.34	6.15	5.32	4.34	6.64	6.03	5.02	7.10	6.15	5.02
		38x286	7.05	6.41	5.29	7.48	6.47	5.29	8.07	7.33	6.10	8.63	7.48	6.10
	No. 3	38x 89	1.88	1.63	1.33	1.88	1.63	1.33	2.17	1.88	1.53	2.17	1.88	1.53
		38x140	2.78	2.40	1.96	2.78	2.40	1.96	3.21	2.78	2.27	3.21	2.78	2.27
		38x184	3.66	3.17	2.59	3.66	3.17	2.59	4.23	3.66	2.99	4.23	3.66	2.99
		38x235	4.67	4.05	3.30	4.67	4.05	3.30	5.40	4.67	3.81	5.40	4.67	3.81
		38x286	5.68	4.92	4.02	5.68	4.92	4.02	6.56	5.68	4.64	6.56	5.68	4.64
	Const	38x 89	2.11	1.86	1.52	2.15	1.86	1.52	2.41	2.15	1.76	2.49	2.15	1.76
	Stand	38x 89	1.61	1.40	1.14	1.61	1.40	1.14	1.87	1.61	1.32	1.87	1.61	1.32
	Util	38x 89	1.12	0.97	0.79	1.12	0.97	0.79	1.30	1.12	0.92	1.30	1.12	0.92
Spruce-Pine-Fir	Sel. Str.	38x 89	2.14	1.94	1.70	2.45	2.22	1.94	2.45	2.22	1.94	2.80	2.55	2.22
		38x140	3.36	3.05	2.67	3.85	3.50	3.04	3.85	3.50	3.05	4.41	4.00	3.50
		38x184	4.43	4.03	3.52	5.08	4.61	4.02	5.08	4.61	4.03	5.81	5.28	4.61
		38x235	5.66	5.14	4.49	6.48	5.88	5.12	6.48	5.88	5.14	7.41	6.74	5.88
		38x286	6.88	6.25	5.46	7.88	7.16	6.23	7.88	7.16	6.25	9.02	8.19	7.16
	No. 1	38x 89	2.14	1.94	1.70	2.45	2.22	1.94	2.45	2.22	1.94	2.80	2.55	2.22
		38x140	3.36	3.05	2.67	3.85	3.47	2.83	3.85	3.50	3.05	4.41	4.00	3.27
		38x184	4.43	4.03	3.52	5.08	4.57	3.73	5.08	4.61	4.03	5.81	5.28	4.31
		38x235	5.66	5.14	4.49	6.48	5.84	4.77	6.48	5.88	5.14	7.41	6.74	5.50
		38x286	6.88	6.25	5.46	7.88	7.10	5.80	7.88	7.16	6.25	9.02	8.19	6.70
	No. 2	38x 89	2.07	1.88	1.64	2.37	2.15	1.75	2.37	2.15	1.88	2.71	2.46	2.02
		38x140	3.25	2.95	2.54	3.59	3.11	2.54	3.72	3.38	2.93	4.15	3.59	2.93
		38x184	4.29	3.89	3.35	4.74	4.10	3.35	4.91	4.46	3.87	5.47	4.74	3.87
		38x235	5.47	4.97	4.28	6.05	5.24	4.28	6.26	5.69	4.94	6.99	6.05	4.94
		38x286	6.65	6.04	5.20	7.36	6.35	5.20	7.62	6.92	6.01	8.50	7.36	6.01
	No. 3.	38x 89	1.86	1.61	1.31	1.86	1.61	1.31	2.15	1.86	1.52	2.15	1.86	1.52
		38x140	2.74	2.37	1.93	2.74	2.37	1.93	3.16	2.74	2.23	3.16	2.74	2.23
		38x184	3.61	3.13	2.55	3.61	3.13	2.55	4.17	3.61	2.95	4.17	3.61	2.95
		38x235	4.61	3.99	3.26	4.61	3.99	3.26	5.32	4.61	3.76	5.32	4.61	3.76
		38x286	5.61	4.85	3.96	5.61	4.85	3.96	6.47	5.61	4.58	6.47	5.61	4.58
	Const	38x 89	1.99	1.81	1.49	2.11	1.83	1.49	2.28	2.07	1.72	2.44	2.11	1.72
	Stand	38x 89	1.59	1.38	1.12	1.59	1.38	1.12	1.84	1.59	1.30	1.84	1.59	1.30
	Util	38x 89	1.08	0.94	0.76	1.08	0.94	0.76	1.25	1.08	0.88	1.25	1.08	0.88

TABLE 8-1 *(cont.)*

Lumber Species	Grade	Size (mm)	LIVE LOAD 2.5 kN/m²						LIVE LOAD 2.0 kN/m²					
			Gypsum board or plastered ceiling			Other ceilings			Gypsum board or plastered ceiling			Other ceilings		
			300 mm	400 mm	600 mm	300 mm	400 mm	600 mm	300 mm	400 mm	600 mm	300 mm	400 mm	600 mm
Western Cedars (N)	Sel. Str.	38x 89	1.73	1.58	1.38	1.99	1.80	1.58	1.87	1.70	1.48	2.14	1.94	1.70
		38x140	2.73	2.48	2.16	3.12	2.84	2.48	2.94	2.67	2.33	3.37	3.06	2.67
		38x184	3.60	3.27	2.86	4.12	3.74	3.27	3.88	3.52	3.08	4.44	4.03	3.52
		38x235	4.59	4.17	3.64	5.26	4.78	4.17	4.95	4.50	3.93	5.66	5.15	4.50
		38x286	5.59	5.08	4.43	6.40	5.81	5.08	6.02	5.47	4.78	6.89	6.26	5.47
	No. 1	38x 89	1.73	1.58	1.38	1.99	1.80	1.58	1.87	1.70	1.48	2.14	1.94	1.70
		38x140	2.73	2.48	2.16	3.12	2.84	2.34	2.94	2.67	2.33	3.37	3.06	2.57
		38x184	3.60	3.27	2.86	4.12	3.74	3.09	3.88	3.52	3.08	4.44	4.03	3.38
		38x235	4.59	4.17	3.64	5.26	4.78	3.94	4.95	4.50	3.93	5.66	5.15	4.32
		38x286	5.59	5.08	4.43	6.40	5.81	4.79	6.02	5.47	4.78	6.89	6.26	5.25
	No. 2	38x 89	1.68	1.52	1.33	1.92	1.74	1.45	1.81	1.64	1.43	2.07	1.88	1.59
		38x140	2.64	2.40	2.09	2.96	2.56	2.09	2.84	2.58	2.25	3.24	2.81	2.29
		38x184	3.48	3.16	2.76	3.90	3.38	2.76	3.75	3.41	2.97	4.27	3.70	3.02
		38x235	4.44	4.03	3.52	4.98	4.31	3.52	4.78	4.35	3.80	5.45	4.72	3.85
		38x286	5.40	4.91	4.28	6.06	5.24	4.28	5.82	5.29	4.62	6.63	5.74	4.69
	No. 3	38x 89	1.52	1.31	1.07	1.52	1.31	1.07	1.66	1.44	1.17	1.66	1.44	1.17
		38x140	2.23	1.93	1.58	2.23	1.93	1.58	2.45	2.12	1.73	2.45	2.12	1.73
		38x184	2.95	2.55	2.08	2.95	2.55	2.08	3.23	2.80	2.28	3.23	2.80	2.28
		38x235	3.76	3.26	2.66	3.76	3.26	2.66	4.12	3.57	2.91	4.12	3.57	2.91
		38x286	4.58	3.96	3.23	4.58	3.96	3.23	5.01	4.34	3.54	5.01	4.34	3.54
	Const	38x 89	1.61	1.47	1.23	1.74	1.51	1.23	1.74	1.58	1.35	1.91	1.65	1.35
	Stand	38x 89	1.30	1.12	0.92	1.30	1.12	0.93	1.42	1.23	1.00	1.42	1.23	1.00
	Util	38x 89	0.88	0.76	0.62	0.88	0.76	0.62	0.97	0.84	0.68	0.97	0.84	0.68
Northern Species	Sel. Str.	38x 89	1.73	1.58	1.38	1.99	1.89	1.58	1.87	1.70	1.48	2.14	1.94	1.70
		38x140	2.73	2.48	2.16	3.12	2.84	2.41	2.94	2.67	2.33	3.37	3.06	2.65
		38x184	3.60	3.27	2.86	4.12	3.74	3.18	3.88	3.52	3.08	4.44	4.03	3.49
		38x235	4.59	4.17	3.64	5.26	4.78	4.06	4.95	4.50	3.93	5.66	5.15	4.45
		38x286	5.59	5.08	4.43	6.40	5.81	4.94	6.02	5.47	4.78	6.89	6.26	5.42
	No. 1	38x 89	1.73	1.58	1.38	1.99	1.80	1.53	1.87	1.70	1.48	2.14	1.94	1.68
		38x140	2.73	2.38	2.16	3.12	2.74	2.23	2.94	2.67	2.33	3.37	3.00	2.45
		38x184	3.60	3.27	2.86	4.12	3.61	2.95	3.88	3.52	3.08	4.44	3.96	3.23
		38x235	4.59	4.17	3.64	5.26	4.61	3.76	4.95	4.50	3.93	5.66	5.05	4.12
		38x286	5.59	5.08	4.43	6.40	5.61	4.58	6.02	5.47	4.78	6.89	6.14	5.01
	No. 2	38x 89	1.68	1.52	1.33	1.92	1.70	1.39	1.81	1.64	1.43	2.07	1.87	1.52
		38x140	2.64	2.40	2.01	2.84	2.46	2.01	2.84	2.58	2.20	3.11	2.69	2.20
		38x284	3.58	3.16	2.64	3.74	3.24	2.64	3.75	3.41	2.90	4.10	3.55	2.90
		38x235	4.44	4.03	3.38	4.78	4.14	3.38	4.78	4.35	3.70	5.23	4.53	3.70
		38x286	5.40	4.91	4.11	5.83	5.03	4.11	5.82	5.29	4.50	6.37	5.51	4.50
	No. 3	38x 89	1.46	1.26	1.03	1.46	1.26	1.03	1.46	1.26	1.03	1.46	1.26	1.03
		38x140	2.14	1.85	1.51	2.14	1.85	1.51	2.14	1.85	1.51	2.14	1.85	1.51
		38x184	2.82	2.44	1.99	1.82	2.44	1.99	2.82	2.44	1.99	2.82	2.44	1.99
		38x235	3.60	3.12	2.55	3.60	3.12	2.55	3.60	3.12	2.55	3.60	3.12	2.55
		38x286	4.38	3.79	3.10	4.38	3.79	3.10	4.38	3.79	3.10	4.38	3.79	3.10
	Const	38x 89	1.61	1.45	1.18	1.67	1.45	1.18	1.61	1.45	1.18	1.67	1.45	1.18
	Stand	38x 89	1.25	1.08	1.25	1.25	1.08	0.88	1.25	1.08	0.88	1.35	1.08	0.88
	Util	38x 89	0.85	0.74	0.60	0.85	0.74	0.60	0.85	0.74	0.60	0.85	0.74	0.60
Northern Aspen	Sel. Str.	38x 89	1.76	1.60	1.40	2.02	1.83	1.60	1.76	1.60	1.40	2.02	1.83	1.60
		38x140	2.77	2.52	2.20	3.17	2.88	2.49	2.77	2.52	2.20	3.17	2.88	2.49
		38x184	3.66	3.32	2.90	4.19	3.80	3.28	3.66	3.32	2.90	4.19	3.80	3.28
		38x235	4.67	4.24	3.70	5.35	4.85	4.18	4.67	4.24	3.70	5.34	4.85	4.18
		38x286	5.68	5.16	4.50	6.50	5.90	5.09	5.68	5.16	4.50	6.50	5.90	5.09
	No. 1	38x 89	1.76	1.60	1.40	2.02	1.83	1.58	1.76	1.60	1.40	2.02	1.83	1.58
		38x140	2.77	2.52	2.20	3.17	2.83	2.31	2.77	2.52	2.20	3.17	2.83	2.31
		38x184	3.66	3.32	2.90	4.19	3.73	3.05	3.66	3.32	2.90	4.19	3.73	3.05
		38x235	4.67	4.24	3.70	5.34	3.77	3.89	4.67	4.24	3.70	5.34	4.77	3.89
		38x286	5.68	5.16	4.50	6.50	5.80	4.73	5.68	5.16	4.50	6.50	5.80	4.73

TABLE 8-1 *(cont.)*

Lumber Species	Grade	Size (mm)	LIVE LOAD 1.5 kN/m² Gypsum board or plastered ceiling 300 mm	400 mm	600 mm	Other ceilings 300 mm	400 mm	600 mm	LIVE LOAD 1.0 kN/m² Gypsum board or plastered ceiling 300 mm	400 mm	600 mm	Other ceilings 300 mm	400 mm	600 mm
Western Cedars (N)	Sel. Str.	38x 89	2.06	1.87	1.63	2.36	2.14	1.87	2.36	2.14	1.87	2.70	2.45	2.14
		38x140	3.24	2.94	2.57	3.71	3.37	2.94	3.71	3.37	2.94	4.24	3.85	3.37
		38x184	4.27	3.88	3.39	4.89	4.44	3.88	4.89	4.44	3.88	5.59	5.08	4.44
		38x235	5.45	4.95	4.32	6.24	5.66	4.95	6.24	5.66	4.95	7.14	6.49	5.66
		38x286	6.63	6.02	5.26	7.58	6.89	6.02	7.58	6.89	6.02	8.68	7.89	6.89
	No. 1	38x 89	2.06	1.87	1.63	2.36	2.14	1.87	2.36	2.14	1.87	2.70	2.45	2.14
		38x140	3.24	2.94	2.57	3.71	3.37	2.87	3.71	3.17	2.94	4.24	3.85	3.31
		38x184	4.27	3.88	3.39	4.89	4.44	3.78	4.89	4.44	3.88	5.59	5.08	4.37
		38x235	5.45	4.95	4.32	6.24	5.66	4.83	6.24	5.66	4.95	7.14	6.49	5.58
		38x286	6.63	6.02	5.26	7.58	6.89	5.87	7.58	6.89	6.02	8.68	7.89	6.78
	No. 2	38x 89	1.99	1.81	1.58	2.28	2.07	1.78	2.28	2.07	1.81	2.61	2.37	2.05
		38x140	3.13	2.84	2.48	3.58	3.14	2.56	3.58	3.25	2.84	4.10	3.62	2.96
		38x184	4.13	3.75	3.27	4.72	4.14	3.38	4.72	4.29	3.75	5.41	4.78	3.90
		38x235	5.27	4.78	4.18	6.03	5.28	4.31	6.03	5.48	4.78	6.90	6.10	4.98
		38x286	6.41	5.82	5.08	7.33	6.42	5.24	7.33	6.66	5.82	8.39	7.42	6.06
	No. 3	38x 89	1.86	1.61	1.31	1.86	1.61	1.31	2.15	1.86	1.52	2.15	1.86	1.52
		38x140	2.74	2.37	1.93	2.74	2.37	1.93	3.16	2.74	2.23	3.16	2.74	2.23
		38x184	3.61	3.13	2.55	3.61	3.13	2.55	4.17	3.61	2.95	4.17	3.61	2.95
		38x235	4.61	3.99	3.26	4.61	3.99	3.26	5.32	4.61	3.76	5.32	4.61	3.76
		38x286	5.61	4.85	3.96	5.61	4.85	3.96	6.47	5.61	4.58	6.47	5.61	4.58
	Const	38x 89	1.92	1.74	1.51	2.13	1.85	1.51	2.19	1.99	1.74	2.46	2.13	1.74
	Stand	38x 89	1.59	1.38	1.12	1.59	1.38	1.12	1.84	1.59	1.30	1.84	1.59	1.30
	Util	38x 89	1.08	0.94	0.76	1.08	0.94	0.76	1.25	1.08	0.88	1.25	1.08	0.88
Northern Species	Sel. Str.	38x 89	2.06	1.87	1.63	2.36	2.14	1.87	2.36	2.14	1.87	2.70	2.45	2.14
		38x140	3.24	2.94	2.57	3.71	3.37	2.94	3.71	3.37	2.94	4.24	3.85	3.37
		38x184	4.27	3.88	3.39	4.89	4.44	3.88	4.89	4.44	3.88	5.59	5.08	4.44
		38x235	5.45	4.95	4.32	6.24	5.66	4.94	6.24	5.66	4.95	7.14	6.49	5.66
		38x286	6.63	6.02	5.26	7.58	6.89	6.02	7.58	6.89	6.02	8.68	7.89	6.89
	No.1	38x 89	2.06	1.87	1.63	2.36	2.14	1.87	2.36	2.14	1.87	2.70	2.45	2.14
		38x140	3.24	2.94	2.57	3.71	3.35	2.74	3.71	3.37	2.94	4.24	3.85	3.16
		38x184	4.27	3.88	3.39	4.89	4.42	3.61	4.89	4.44	3.88	5.59	5.08	4.17
		38x235	5.45	4.95	4.32	6.24	5.65	4.61	6.24	5.66	4.95	7.14	6.49	5.32
		38x286	6.63	6.02	5.26	7.58	6.87	5.61	7.58	6.89	6.02	8.68	7.89	6.47
	No. 2	38x 89	1.99	1.81	1.58	2.28	2.07	1.90	2.28	2.07	1.81	2.61	2.37	1.97
		38x140	3.13	2.84	2.46	3.48	3.01	2.46	3.58	3.25	2.84	4.02	3.48	2.84
		38x184	4.13	3.75	3.24	4.58	3.97	3.24	4.72	4.29	3.74	5.29	4.58	3.74
		38x235	5.27	4.78	4.14	5.85	5.07	4.14	6.03	5.48	4.78	6.76	5.85	4.78
		38x286	6.41	5.82	5.03	7.12	6.16	5.03	7.33	6.66	5.81	8.22	7.12	5.81
	No. 3	38x 89	1.79	1.55	1.26	1.79	1.55	1.26	2.07	1.79	1.46	2.07	1.79	1.46
		38x140	2.62	2.27	1.85	2.62	2.27	1.85	3.03	2.62	2.14	3.03	2.62	2.14
		38x184	3.46	2.99	2.44	3.46	2.99	2.44	3.99	3.46	2.82	3.99	3.46	2.82
		38x235	4.41	3.82	3.12	4.41	3.87	3.12	5.10	4.41	3.60	5.10	4.41	3.60
		38x286	5.37	4.65	3.79	5.37	4.65	3.79	6.20	5.37	4.38	6.20	5.37	4.38
	Const	38x 89	1.92	1.74	1.45	2.05	1.78	1.45	2.19	1.99	1.67	2.37	2.05	1.67
	Stand	38x 89	1.53	1.33	1.08	1.53	1.33	1.08	1.77	1.53	1.25	1.77	1.53	1.25
	Util	38x 89	1.04	0.90	0.74	1.04	0.90	0.74	1.21	1.04	0.85	1.21	1.04	0.85
Northern Aspen	Sel. Str.	38x 89	2.09	1.90	1.66	2.49	2.17	1.90	2.39	2.17	1.90	2.74	2.49	2.17
		38x140	3.29	2.99	2.61	3.76	3.42	2.99	3.76	3.42	2.99	4.32	3.92	3.42
		38x184	4.34	3.94	3.44	4.96	4.51	3.94	4.96	4.51	3.94	5.68	5.16	4.51
		38x235	5.53	5.03	4.39	6.33	5.75	5.03	6.33	5.75	5.03	7.25	6.59	5.75
		38x286	6.73	6.11	5.34	7.70	7.00	6.11	7.70	7.00	6.11	8.82	8.01	7.00
	No. 1	38x 89	2.09	1.90	1.66	2.39	2.17	1.90	2.39	2.17	1.90	2.74	2.49	2.17
		38x140	3.29	2.99	2.61	3.76	3.42	2.83	3.76	3.41	2.99	4.31	3.92	3.27
		38x184	4.34	3.94	3.44	4.96	4.51	3.73	4.96	4.51	3.94	4.68	5.16	4.51
		38x235	5.53	5.03	4.39	6.33	5.75	4.77	6.33	5.75	5.03	7.25	6.59	5.50
		38x286	6.73	6.11	5.34	7.70	7.00	5.80	7.70	7.00	6.11	8.82	8.01	6.70

TABLE 8-1 *(cont.)*

Lumber Species	Grade	Size (mm)	LIVE LOAD 2.5 kN/m² Gypsum board or plastered ceiling			LIVE LOAD 2.5 kN/m² Other ceilings			LIVE LOAD 2.0 kN/m² Gypsum board or plastered ceiling			LIVE LOAD 2.0 kN/m² Other ceilings		
			300 mm	400 mm	600 mm	300 mm	400 mm	600 mm	300 mm	400 mm	600 mm	300 mm	400 mm	600 mm
Northern Aspen (cont'd)	No. 2	38x 89	1.70	1.54	1.35	1.95	1.76	1.44	1.70	1.54	1.35	1.95	1.76	1.44
		38x140	2.67	2.43	2.67	2.93	2.54	2.07	2.67	2.43	2.07	2.93	2.54	2.07
		38x184	3.53	3.20	2.73	3.87	3.35	2.74	3.53	3.20	2.73	3.87	3.35	2.73
		38x235	4.50	4.09	3.49	4.94	4.28	3.49	4.50	4.09	3.49	4.94	4.28	3.49
		38x286	5.47	4.97	4.25	6.01	5.20	4.25	5.47	4.97	4.25	6.01	5.20	4.25
	No. 3	38x 89	1.52	1.31	1.07	1.52	1.31	1.07	1.52	1.31	1.07	1.52	1.31	1.07
		38x140	2.23	1.93	1.58	2.23	1.93	1.58	2.23	1.93	1.58	2.23	1.93	1.58
		38x184	2.95	2.55	2.08	2.95	2.55	2.08	2.95	2.55	2.08	2.95	2.55	2.08
		38x235	3.76	3.26	2.66	3.76	3.26	2.66	3.76	3.26	2.66	3.76	3.26	2.66
		38x286	4.58	3.96	3.23	4.58	3.96	3.23	4.58	3.96	3.23	4.58	3.96	3.23
	Const	38x 89	1.63	1.48	1.22	1.72	1.49	1.22	1.63	1.48	1.22	1.72	1.49	1.22
	Stand	38x 89	1.30	1.12	0.92	1.30	1.12	0.92	1.30	1.12	0.92	1.30	1.12	0.92
	Util	38x 89	0.88	0.76	0.62	0.88	0.76	0.62	0.88	0.76	0.62	0.88	0.76	0.62

Courtesy Canadian Wood Council.

Roof Cornice

It was also noted in Chapter 6 that the outer ends of ceiling joists are cut off flush with the outside of the plate and that the top edge at the end is cut in the plane of the roof. If they are acting as roof joists, the ends will be cut off square and the joist ends will extend beyond the wall plate if the building is to have a cornice (see Fig. 8-1).

The cornice on the end walls will be formed by stub joists extending over the end wall plates and anchored at their inner ends to a regular joist. Remember that these stub joists should extend at least as far inside the wall plate as they project beyond it. For example, if the joists are on 400 mm centers, the last regular joist should be kept back two spaces or 800 mm, from the end of the plate, when the cornice projection is up to 800 mm wide (see Fig. 8-2).

To frame the cornice at the corner of the building, proceed as follows:

1. Keep the first stub joist as far from the corner as is the last regular joist.

2. Run a joist diagonally from the junction of stub and regular joists across the wall plate at the corner (see Fig. 8-2). Its

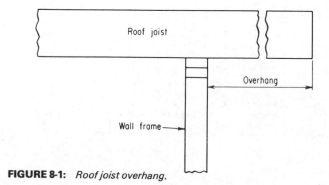

FIGURE 8-1: *Roof joist overhang.*

216

TABLE 8-1 *(cont.)*

Lumber Species	Grade	Size (mm)	LIVE LOAD 1.5 kN/m²						LIVE LOAD 1.0 kN/m²					
			Gypsum board or plastered ceiling			Other ceilings			Gypsum board or plastered ceiling			Other ceilings		
			300 mm	400 mm	600 mm	300 mm	400 mm	600 mm	300 mm	400 mm	600 mm	300 mm	400 mm	600 mm
Northern Aspen (cont'd)	No. 2	38x 89	2.02	1.83	1.60	2.31	2.10	1.76	2.31	2.10	1.83	2.64	2.40	2.04
		38x140	3.17	2.88	2.52	3.59	3.11	2.54	3.63	3.30	2.88	4.75	3.59	2.93
		38x184	4.18	3.80	3.32	4.74	4.10	3.35	4.79	4.35	3.80	5.47	4.74	3.87
		38x235	5.33	4.85	4.23	6.05	5.24	4.28	6.11	5.55	4.85	6.99	6.05	4.94
		38x286	6.49	5.90	5.15	7.36	6.37	5.20	7.43	6.75	5.90	8.50	7.36	6.01
	No. 3	38x 89	1.86	1.61	1.31	1.86	1.61	1.31	2.15	1.86	1.52	2.15	1.86	1.52
		38x140	2.74	2.37	1.93	2.74	2.37	1.93	3.16	2.74	2.23	3.16	2.74	2.23
		38x184	3.61	3.13	2.55	3.61	3.13	2.55	4.17	3.61	2.95	4.17	3.61	2.95
		38x235	4.61	3.99	3.26	4.61	3.99	3.26	5.32	4.61	3.76	5.32	4.61	3.76
		38x286	5.61	4.85	3.96	5.61	4.85	3.96	6.47	5.61	4.58	6.47	5.61	4.58
	Const	38x 89	1.93	1.76	1.49	2.11	1.83	1.49	2.22	2.01	1.72	2.44	2.11	1.72
	Stand	38x 89	1.59	1.38	1.12	1.59	1.38	1.12	1.84	1.59	1.30	1.84	1.59	1.30
	Util	38x 89	1.08	0.94	0.76	1.08	0.94	0.76	1.25	1.08	0.88	1.25	1.08	0.88

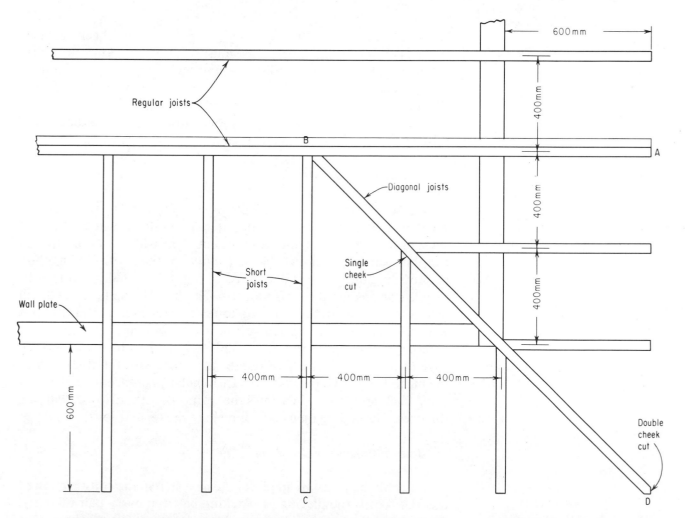

FIGURE 8-2: *Plan view of roof joists.*

length may be determined by calculating the length of the diagonal of the rectangular square *ABCD*, Fig. 8-2.

3. Cut short joists to run from the diagonal at regular 400 mm centers (see Fig. 8-2).

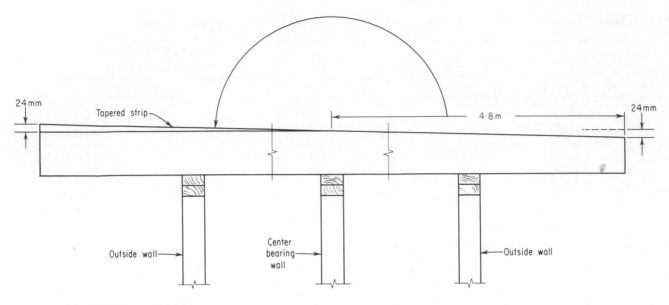

FIGURE 8-3: *Tapered roof joists.*

Note. Each end of the diagonal joist requires two cheek cuts (see Fig. 8-2) and the length of the joist must be measured down the center of the top edge. The short joists mentioned in step 3 above will have a single cheek cut, all of which may be laid out with the framing square.

Each stub joist and the diagonal joist must be nailed to the regular joist with three 75 mm nails and toenailed to the plate as well.

Sloped Roof Joists

It is sometimes desirable to have enough slope to this flat roof that water will drain in one direction. It is generally considered that a slope of 1.5 mm per 300 mm is sufficient. This will allow the water to run, but will not be noticeable as a slope on the roof. One method of providing this slope is illustrated in Fig. 8-3. Usually two lengths of joists are required to span a roof. The joist at the lower end will have a tapered strip ripped off its top edge. For example, if the joist were 4.8 mm long, the tapered strip would be 24 mm thick at one end, tapering to nothing at the other. This strip is then nailed to the top edge of the joist on the high side of the roof, with the thick end to the highest edge (see Fig. 8-3). All the regular joists are treated in this way. Each stub joist then must be stripped with strips of varying thickness, depending on its position along the regular joist.

Joist Blocking

After all the joists are in place, the next step in the construction of this flat roof is the placing of blocking between every pair of joists. There are at least two important reasons for using this blocking. One is that it provides a nailing surface for the inner edge of the plancier between joists. Another is that when loose fill insulation is used, the blocking retains the loose fill in its place.

218

In order to provide a nailing surface, the blocking must project beyond the outer edge of the top plate at least half its own thickness (see Fig. 8-4). Be sure that the blocking pieces are not as wide as the joists. There should be ample room for air circulation between each pair of joists for their entire length. For example, if the joists are 38 × 184 mm, the blocks should be not more than 38 × 140 mm.

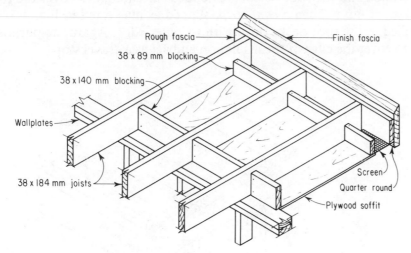

FIGURE 8-4: *Roof joist blocking and ventilation.*

Roof Ventilation

Since the spaces between the pairs of roof joists will have no connection with one another, ventilation must be provided around the entire perimeter of the roof. The best place to provide this ventilation is at the outer ends of the joists and it can be done by providing a strip of fine screen, about 125 mm wide, along the outer edge of the soffit. The 38 × 89 mm blocking is nailed between the joists, 75 mm from their ends and a rough fascia nailed to the ends of the joists. The screen is nailed across the space between the bottom edges of the rough fascia and the blocking and the soffit material cut to the proper width and nailed in place (see Fig. 8-4).

Finish Fascia

The finish fascia is the final trim on the roof overhang, made from either 19 or 38 mm material (see Fig. 8-4). It should project below the bottom edge of the rough fascia about 25 mm and far enough above the top edge to cover the thickness of the roof decking and insulation and expose a 45 degree beveled edge. This projection is to provide a gravel stop—that is, to prevent the gravel from the builtup roof from rolling off. If the roof is sloped, the gravel stop is provided on three sides only. The water drains off along the fourth side. Finally, quarter-round is nailed behind the dropped edge of the fascia to cover the outer edge of the screen and to finish off the trim.

Cant Strips

One alternative to the use of the type of finish fascia illustrated in Fig. 8-4, is shown in Fig. 8-5. A 19 mm finish fascia is nailed over the rough fascia, with its top edge level with the top of the joists, as illustrated and the roof decking extended far enough to cover the top edges of both. Then a *cant strip,* shaped as illustrated in Fig. 8-5, is nailed to the roof deck, flush with its outer edge. Again, its purpose is to cover the edge of the insulation and act as a gravel stop.

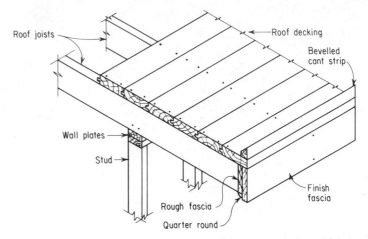

FIGURE 8-5: *Cant strip on roof deck.*

Roof Decking

The roof decking will usually be plywood, shiplap or tongue-and-grooved decking, 19 or 38 mm in thickness (see Fig. 8-5). In any case it must be well nailed to the joists and adequately supported to provide a solid base for the builtup roofing.

Flat Roof Insulation

The insulation to be used with a flat roof is a very important consideration. There are three main alternatives. One is to apply rigid insulation over the roof deck and under the builtup roof. A second is to apply insulation batts between the joists from inside the building. The third is to use loose fill insulation between the joists.

Several types of rigid insulation are available, among them wood fiberboard insulation (usually laminated), expanded foam roof insulation, and strawboard. Whichever type is used, it must be secured firmly to the roof decking, either by nailing or by cementing. Manufacturer's instructions usually explain exactly how their product should be applied.

If batt insulation is used, it is applied between the joists from the inside in the same way that batt insulation is applied to conventional ceiling joists. In this case, the builtup roof is applied directly to the roof deck.

The most effective method of introducing loose fill insulation into a flat roof system is by blowing it into place. Some type of fibrous material is used and a blower places the insulation in spaces otherwise very difficult to reach.

Roof Flashing

When the insulation is applied on top of the roof deck, the next operation is the installation of flashing. If the insulation is below, the flashing is applied next to the deck. Flashing is metal covering designed to prevent water from entering the roof structure along the edge of the roof (see Fig. 8-6). Part of the metal sheet lies flat on the deck or insulation, and the remainder is bent up over the gravel stop and down the outside face of the fascia far enough to cover all joints between cant strip and deck or between deck and joists. The open edge of the roof, the one having no gravel stop, must also be flashed (see Fig. 8-6b).

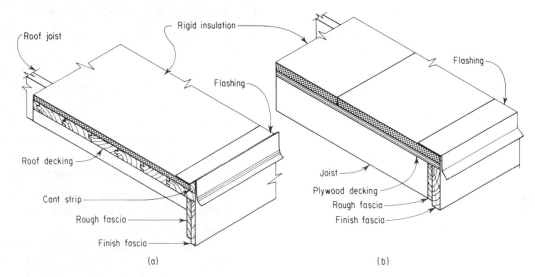

FIGURE 8-6: *Roof flashing.*

Roof Drainage

If the roof is to have cant strip all around, it is necessary to provide some means of drainage. This may be done by means of vents in the roof connected to pipes leading to the sewage disposal system. It may also be done by providing *scupper boxes* at convenient positions around the edge of the roof. These are connected to downspouts which carry away the water.

A scupper box is simply a flat metal box, open at one end, with a drainage hole at the opposite end. A section of the cant strip is cut away, and the scupper box is set into the opening, open end in. The other end projects beyond the edge of the roof far enough that a downspout may be connected to the drainage hole. The flat projecting bottom is covered by the roofing material; when water collects on the roof, it simply drains into the scupper boxes and out through the downspouts.

Builtup Roofing

The final step in the construction of a flat roof is the application of the roofing material. A builtup roof—so called because it is built up from several layers of material—is usually used on flat decks. The materials consist of heavy tarred paper, asphalt in liquid form, and pea gravel. The amount of material used determines the approximate life of the roof, usually ten, fifteen, or twenty years.

Figure 8-7 illustrates the procedure for laying a twenty-year roof over a wood deck. Here are the steps in this procedure:

1. Lay down one layer of sheathing paper, weighing at least 0.25 kg per m^2. Nail as required to hold with 25 mm roofing nails.

2. Lay down two layers of asphalt-impregnated, 0.75 kg/m^2 felt paper, lapping each sheet 475 mm over the preceding one and nailing sufficiently to hold in place. Start with a half roll, obtained simply by cutting a roll in two (see Fig. 8-7, which illustrates this half-roll starter).

3. Lay down three additional layers of the same paper as above, securing each by a layer of hot tar or asphalt, mopped full width under it. This step is begun by cutting a roll of paper into a 300 mm and a 600 mm length. Lay down the 300 mm strip first, as illustrated in Fig. 8-7, then the 600 mm strip over it, then a full-length roll. Notice that these three layers all start at the same edge, or, in other words, there are now three mopped layers of paper over the first 300 mm of roof. Start the next full roll 280 mm up from the starting edge and continue similarly with each succeeding roll. Roofing nails, driven through flat tin caps, 600 mm o.c., may be used near the back edge of each roll.

    The tar or asphalt, as hot as possible, is mopped on with a string or rag mop and the paper is laid in the mopping immediately. It should be brushed into place with a stiff-bristled push broom to make sure that no air spaces remain under the paper.

4. Cover the entire surface with a uniform coating of hot tar or asphalt at the rate of 7kg/m^2 and embed in it 19 kg of pea gravel per m^2. The gravel must be applied while the coating is hot and should be rolled to insure that it is well embedded. Of course, you must perform this operation one small section at a time, so that the tar will remain hot until the gravel is applied.

5. Check to make sure that the roofing is well up over the flashing and that there is a good seal where flashing and roofing meet, so that water cannot run under the paper.

If the roof has rigid insulation on top of the deck, the procedure must, of necessity, be somewhat different. Since paper cannot be

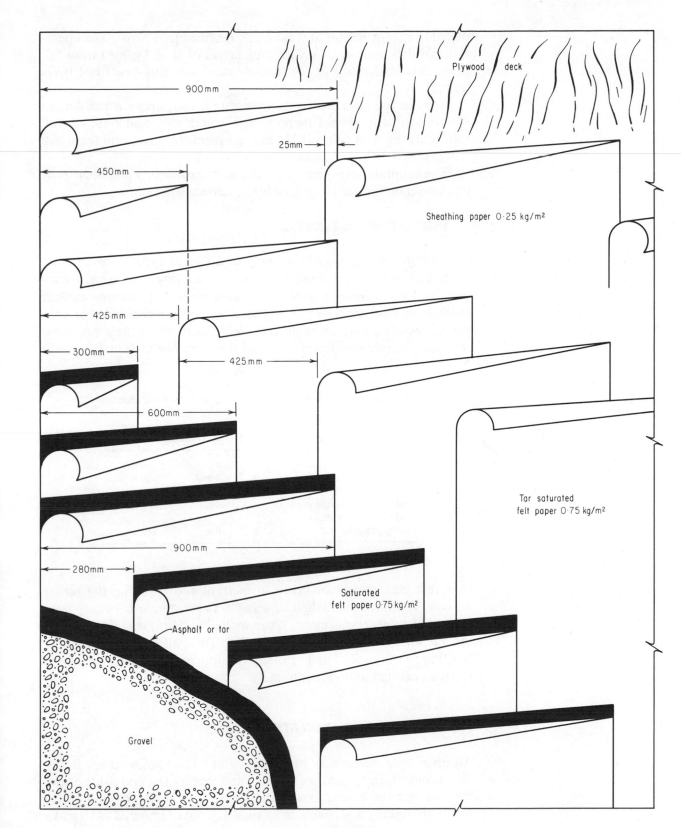

FIGURE 8-7: *Builtup roof.*

nailed to the insulation, it must all be mopped into place. The operation consists entirely of laying four layers of 0.75 kg/m² tarred felt paper directly on top of the insulation, if a twenty-year roof is required.

Start at the edge with a quarter-length roll, apply a half-length roll on top of it, then a three-quarter-length roll, and finally a full roll. Start the next full roll 210 mm up from the edge, and leave 210 mm exposed with each succeeding roll.

The mopping procedure and the application of an asphalt coat and gravel on top are done exactly the same as above.

Builtup Roofing Types

Builtup roofing may be of several different types. The one described above is a *graveled, asphalt base* roofing. An *asphalt base* may be used *without gravel* or surfaced with *wide selvage asphalt roofing*. A *coal tar* base may be used *with a gravel surface* or *cold process roofing* may be employed. With all of these there are minimum and maximum slope limits and these are outlined in Table 8-2.

TABLE 8-2: *Roofing types and slope limits (based on 250 mm run).*

Type of roofing	Minimum rise	Maximum rise
Asphalt base (graveled)	0 mm	60 mm
Asphalt base (without gravel)	10 mm	120 mm
Asphalt base (surfaced with wide selvage asphalt roofing)	40 mm	no limit
Coal tar base (graveled)	0 mm	10 mm
Cold process roofing	10 mm	185 mm

Great care should be taken in melting and handling the tar or asphalt. It should be melted in a fairly flat vat or tub by any convenient heating arrangement. When melted and hot, it is dipped from the vat with a long-handled dipper into five-gallon pails, ready for hoisting to the roof. The hoist may be simple, but make sure that it is strong enough to do the job safely.

FLAT ROOF WITH LAMINATED BEAMS

An *open style* ceiling may be produced in a flat roof by using heavy roof beams to carry the roof decking and leaving the underside of the decking and the beams exposed to view. It is necessary, therefore, that both decking and beams be of such a grade of material as to make that exposure practical.

The roof beams are normally laminated members—that is, they are made up of several pieces glued together to form a solid unit. The lamination may be of two or more pieces on edge or of several pieces laminated on the flat (see Fig. 8-8, a and b). Material to be used will usually have to be clear or nearly clear stock, since the finished beam will form part of the interior finish. In some cases, regular stock may be used and the two sides and the bottom of the beam covered with a thin veneer of the required type or texture.

The sizes of the beams to be used will depend on their span and their spacing. The size required for a particular job should never be decided arbitrarily. Consult an engineer or other building authority to determine the width and depth best suited to the case.

Laminated beams are made to order by manufacturers specializing in this type of construction. Facilities for applying great pressure are required, since the parts of the beam are glued together, no nails or other fasteners being used. In addition, suitable means of planing and sanding the beams must be available, since they represent a finished product.

If the beams are to be covered, it is possible that they may be made on the job, in most cases of two or three pieces of dry material, dressed flat and laminated to stand on edge (see Fig. 8-9). A good quality glue must be used and the manufacturer's instructions followed explicitly as to coating procedure, curing time and temperature.

The covering is usually a thin veneer of plywood on three sides, with the bottom edges mitered for best apearance (see Fig. 8-9). The end joints in the plywood must be well fitted in order that the vertical lines will be as inconspicuous as possible.

The sizes of the beams required must be calculated for each job. Size will depend, as stated previously, on span and spacing, as well as on the type of roofing used. The longer the span, of course, the greater the load imposed on the beam for any given type of roofing. And the farther apart the beams are spaced, the more of the roof must be carried by each beam. Nothing can be said, therefore, about the size of beam that should be used. Generally, however, they will be relatively narrow in width in comparison to their depth. Remember that the strength of a beam varies directly as its width. In other words, if you double the width of a beam, you double the strength. On the other hand, the strength of a beam varies as the square of its depth. That means that if you double the depth, you then increase the strength four times.

The number of beams used for the roof, or, in other words, the spacing of the beams, will depend on the span, the weight of the

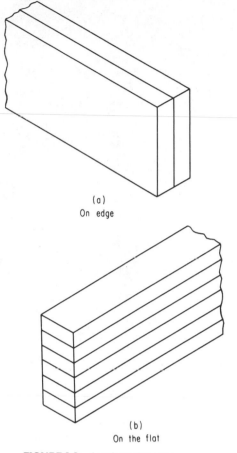

(a)
On edge

(b)
On the flat

FIGURE 8-8: *Laminated roof beams.*

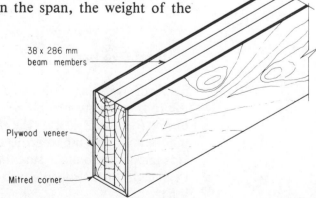

38 x 286 mm
beam members

Plywood veneer

Mitred corner

FIGURE 8-9: *Veneered beam.*

roofing material, and the type of roof decking used. The maximum spacing allowed by most codes is about 2100 mm, if 38 mm decking is to be used. Check the local building code for greater detail.

Beam Anchors

When laminated beams are used in a flat roof design, they will normally bear on the wall plates and must be anchored to them. This may be done with *steel angles,* metal *saddles,* or *wooden dowels* if visible anchors cannot be used (see Fig. 8-10).

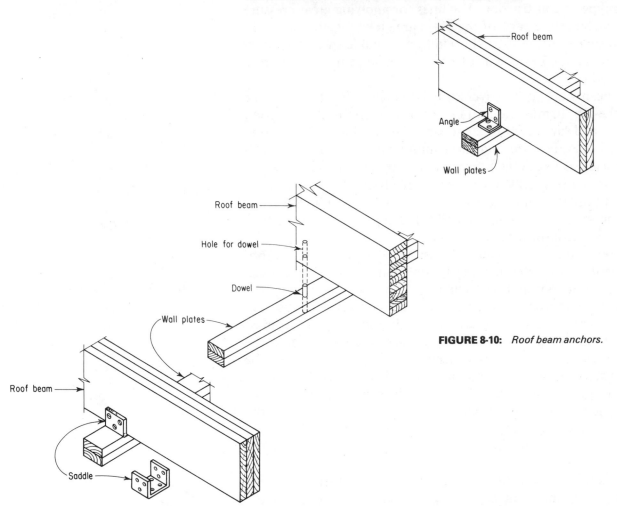

FIGURE 8-10:   *Roof beam anchors.*

Roof Overhang

Roof overhang is obtained at the *sides* of the building by allowing the roof beams to project beyond the plane of the wall as far as required (see Fig. 8-11). At the *ends,* the overhang is obtained by allowing the roof decking to project beyond the end beams (see Fig. 8-11). It is important to make sure that this end overhang is not so great that the weight of the roofing, snow, etc., will cause the projecting decking to sag.

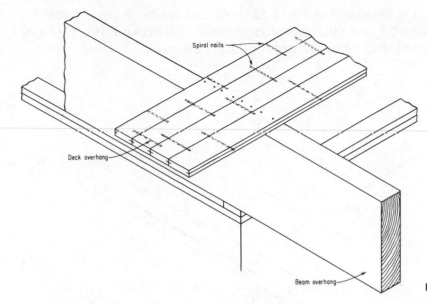

Spiral nails

Deck overhang

Beam overhang

FIGURE 8-11: *Roof overhang with laminated beams.*

Roof Decking

Roof decking over roof beams usually consists of 38 mm or 64 mm tongue-and-grooved or double tongue-and-grooved (depending on load and span) cedar, redwood, or pine decking, 140 or 184 mm wide. The underside of this decking will probably be exposed, so that certain precautions must be taken in selecting and laying it.

Firstly, the material must be dry so that shrinkage and cracking are eliminated or kept at a minimum. Secondly, the appearance of the decking must be such that it harmonizes with the rest of the interior finish. Thirdly, the pieces must be drawn tightly together by edge nailing through predrilled holes with 200 mm spiral nails, spaced about 750 mm o.c. and then face-nailed to the beams (see Fig. 8-11). In some cases, clear material may be required while in others, a knotty appearance may be specified.

The insulation for such a roof is commonly applied on top of the deck and the procedure for applying insulation, flashing, cant strips, and roofing is the same as previously described for flat roof. The fascia, which may be relatively narrow, is secured to the edge of the roof deck and may have a beveled edge extending above the roof level to serve as a cant strip.

Closures

The spaces between the roof beams, the decking and the wall plates must be closed and a number of methods may be used to accomplish this. One method is to frame the space with regular 38 × 89 mm framing and then use the same material to cover the frame, inside and out, as is used for the rest of the wall.

Another method is to use glass and one method of glazing the

227

spaces is illustrated in Fig. 8-12. Insulated *sandwich panels,* consisting of a 25 mm thickness of rigid insulation between two layers of plywood, may be substituted for the glass panels.

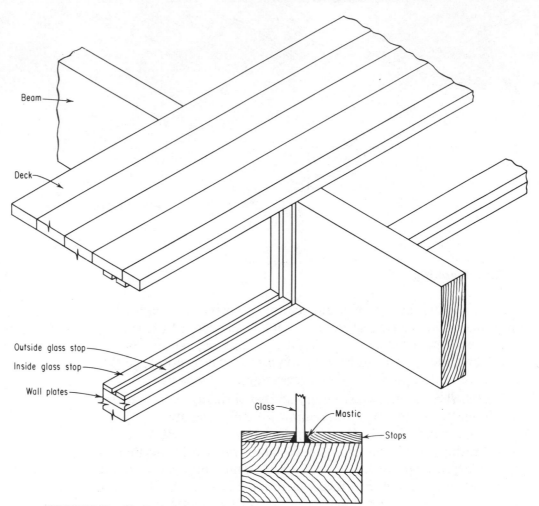

FIGURE 8-12: *Glazing between beams.*

Beam finishes

On the inside, the beams and underside of the roof deck are often treated with some transparent finish such as varnish or lacquer to preserve the natural appearance. Many other alternatives are possible, however. The underside of the deck may be covered with ceiling tile, and the beams left in their natural color. Another plan is to cover deck and beams with ceiling tile. The whole surface may be painted to match the rest of the interior decoration. Finishing is largely a matter of individual preference, and each case must be decided on its own merits.

FLAT ROOF WITH BOX BEAMS

In place of the laminated beams described in the foregoing section, *box beams* may be used for the same purpose. Such a member is called a box beam because in form it is essentially a hollow box (see Fig. 8-13). It consists of *top and bottom chords* and vertical *stiffeners* and, if it is a deep beam, *diagonal stiffeners* as well. This type of beam has certain advantages over solid beams; it is relatively light in weight and can be made on the job with no special tools or equipment.

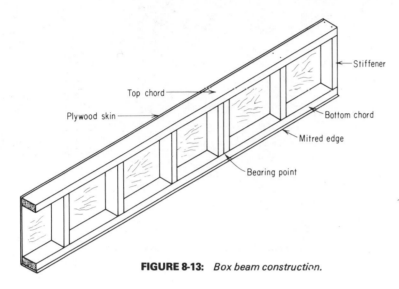

FIGURE 8-13: *Box beam construction.*

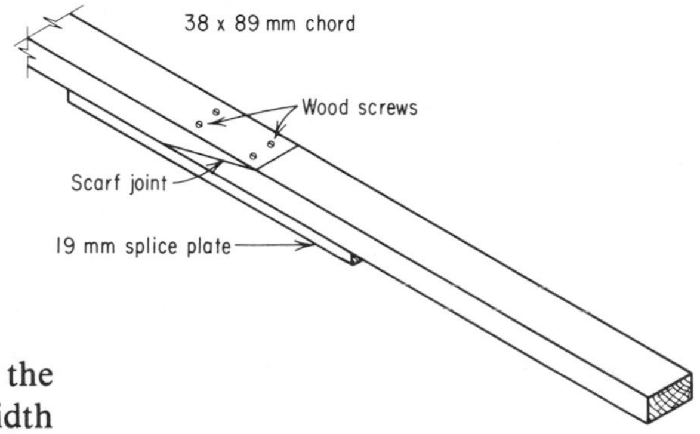

FIGURE 8-14: *Scarf joint in box beam frame.*

The procedure for making a box beam is as follows:

1. Determine the length and depth of beam required for the particular job. The thickness will nearly always be the width of 38 × 89 mm stock, although other sizes may be required in some cases.

2. Select two long, straight pieces for the top and bottom chords, the full length of the beam if possible. If available stock is not long enough, two pieces must be joined together. This is done with a long *scarf joint* (see Fig. 8-14), reinforced with a piece of 19 mm material about 800 mm in length. The two faces of the joint must fit together perfectly to ensure a good glue bond and the joint is fastened with No. 10, 38 mm wood screws (see Fig. 8-14).

3. Lay the two full length chords together and mark them off on the required centers, in the same manner as for a pair of wall plates (see Fig. 5-5, page 139). At the *bearing points* (the points at which the beam will bear on the walls or partitions, allowance should be made for two stiffeners (see Fig. 8-13).

4. Cut enough stiffeners to complete the frame. Their length will be the depth of the beam less 76 mm.

229

5. Nail the frame together, with the stiffeners exactly on the centers laid out. Where double stiffeners are required, glue and screw them together before nailing them into the frame.

6. When diagonal stiffeners are required, fit them between the vertical ones, as illustrated in Fig. 8-15. Their angle cuts may be obtained by using the length of the stiffeners and the distance between them on the framing square.

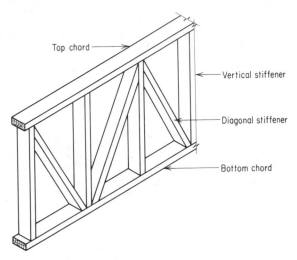

FIGURE 8-15:   *Section of deep box beam.*

7. Cut enough 2400 mm strips of plywood to cover both sides of the frame. The width will be the depth of the beam plus enough to allow a 45 degree bevel on the bottom edge. The thickness will be that specified in the particular design being used, usually 6, 8, or 11 mm sanded material.

8. Coat one side of the frame thoroughly with a coating of good glue and apply the lengths of plywood, making sure that the beveled edge projects below the bottom of the frame. Also check to see that the ends of the plywood sheet come on the center of a stiffener. If a partial length is required, place it at the end of a beam rather than in the middle. Nail every 100 mm with 35 mm finishing nails.

9. Apply the plywood skin to the opposite side in exactly the same manner.

10. Now cut 2400 mm strips of the same thickness of plywood, beveled on both edges at 45 degree and wide enough to cover the bottom of the beam. Glue and nail into place.

11. Cap the ends of the beam with plywood caps.

12. Set the nails, fill the nail holes, and sand to a smooth, clean finish.

The size of beam to use will, of course, depend on individual circumstances. The span, spacing, and roof load all have to be taken into consideration in designing the size. In addition, the ability of the beam to carry a load safely will depend on how the plywood skin is applied to the frame. There are a number of alternative methods, the results of each varying from the others. For example, the plywood may be attached by screws, nails, or glue. Combinations of two of these may also be used, namely, screws and glue or nails and glue.

The type of glue used will also affect the strength of the beam. Some glues require more pressure during their setting period than others. Some require rigid temperature controls for proper results. Some set up rigidly, whereas others are more resilient, allowing slight movement under load.

The thickness of the plywood skin is, of course, of primary importance. Other things being equal, it is the thickness of the skin that determines the ability of the beam to carry the load.

It is evident that it is difficult to compile a simple table, from which, knowing the load, one could pick the width and depth of beam to use under given conditions. The safe way is to consult an engineer or other authority about the size required for a particular job, using specified materials. Some quite extensive research has been carried on with this type of beam.

The spacing of these beams will depend to some extent on the length of the building. Usually it will be desirable to have them evenly spaced, but in any case 2100 mm will be the approximate maximum spacing when 38 mm roof decking is used.

Roof overhang will be provided in exactly the same way as described for a roof with laminated beams. Likewise, roof decking, insulation, flashing, builtup roof, and inside and outside finish are carried out the same as described above for roofs with laminated beams.

FLAT ROOF WITH OPEN WEB JOISTS

Open web joists are often used for a flat roof system in light construction, particularly in buildings with masonry walls. They may be entirely of steel (see Fig. 8-16) or they may be made with wood top and bottom chords and tubular steel web (see Fig. 8-17).

FIGURE 8-16: *Open web steel joist (Courtesy, Bethlehem Steel Co.).*

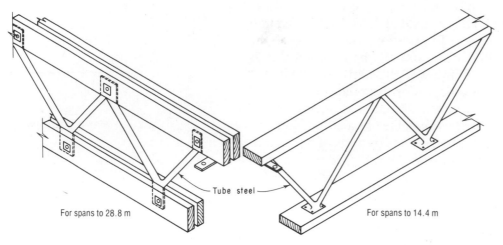

FIGURE 8-17: *Wood and steel open web joists (Courtesy, Trus-joist Western Ltd.).*

For spans to 28.8 m

Tube steel

For spans to 14.4 m

Open web steel joists are lightweight trusses which provide a light but strong structural framework for roofs and floors in a variety of modern buildings. This type of joist is made in two general types—*shortspan,* in lengths up to 14.4 m and *longspan,* in lengths up to 28.8 m. End bearing pads support the joists on a wall. They may be welded to a plate cast into a concrete or masonry wall or held in place with lag screws to a wooden plate.

Immediately after joists are placed, bridging should be installed and welded at the intersections. (see Fig. 8-18). Bridging anchors are required to secure the ends of bridging lines to walls and the type of anchor to be used will depend on the wall. Figure 8-19 illustrates the

FIGURE 8-18: *Steel joist bridging (Courtesy, Bethlehem Steel Corp.).*

FIGURE 8-19: *Steel joist bridging anchors (Courtesy, Bethlehem Steel Corp.).*

FIGURE 8-20: *Bottom chord extension (Courtesy, Bethlehem Steel Corp.).*

anchoring of a bridging line to a masonry wall. Where a ceiling is to be applied to the underside of joists, bottom chord extensions are available to provide ceiling support up to the walls (see Fig. 8-20).

Openings in the roof frame are framed with headers and tail joists (see Fig. 8-21) and roof overhangs may be provided for by top chord extensions. For short overhangs and moderate loads, the top chord itself may be extended (see Fig. 8-22). Where the overhang is long and loads heavier, joists may have a one-channel or two-channel *outrigger* welded to the top chord (see Fig. 8-23).

Wooden roof decking may be fastened to steel joists in one of two ways. Some joists have the top chord made in such a way that nails may be driven directly into a nail groove provided (see Fig. 8-24).

FIGURE 8-21: *Header and tail joist.*

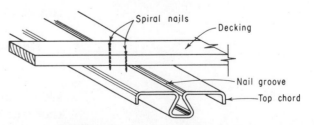

FIGURE 8-22: *Extended top (Courtesy, Bethlehem Steel Corp.).*

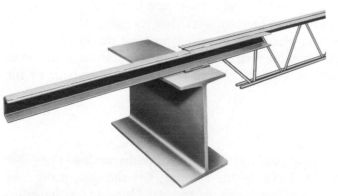

FIGURE 8-23: *One-channel outrigger (Courtesy, Bethlehem Steel Corp.).*

FIGURE 8-24: *Decking nailed to top chord.*

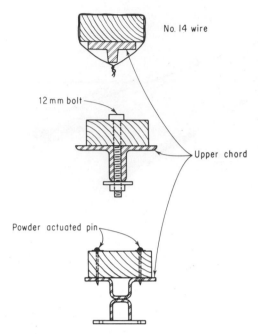

FIGURE 8-25: *Wood pads fastened to top chords of open web joists.*

Others require a wooden pad to be fastened to the top chord; this may be done in several ways, as illustrated in Figure 8-25.

Open web joists with wood top and bottom chords are used in the same way as all-steel joists except that decking can be fastened directly to the top chord and a ceiling attached directly to the bottom chord.

One of the main advantages of using open web joists is the ease with which pipes, ducts, and conduit may be installed within the system (see Fig. 8-26). Other advantages include ease of erection, permanence, rigidity, and adaptability. Either wood, concrete, or steel decks may be applied over steel joists with relative ease.

FIGURE 8-26: *Pipes and ducts installed in floor system (Courtesy, Bethlehem Steel Corp.).*

PITCHED ROOF ON PROJECTING JOISTS

This system of constructing a roof is a combination of two ideas, a cornice produced by overhanging roof joists and a sloping roof. The first step is the construction of the frame for a flat roof, as described in the section on flat roof; regular joists are used. If a hip roof is planned or if the roof is to have an overhanging gable, the joists will project over the wall plates the required amount on all four sides. However, if a regular gable roof is to be used, the joists will all run in one direction, the two end ones being flush with the outside of the end wall frames.

Hip Roof

First, consider a hip roof with this type of construction. The joists are cut and assembled exactly the same as for the flat, projecting roof (see Fig. 8-2). A rough fascia, of the same material, is nailed to the ends of the joists all around. The dimensions of this flat area are

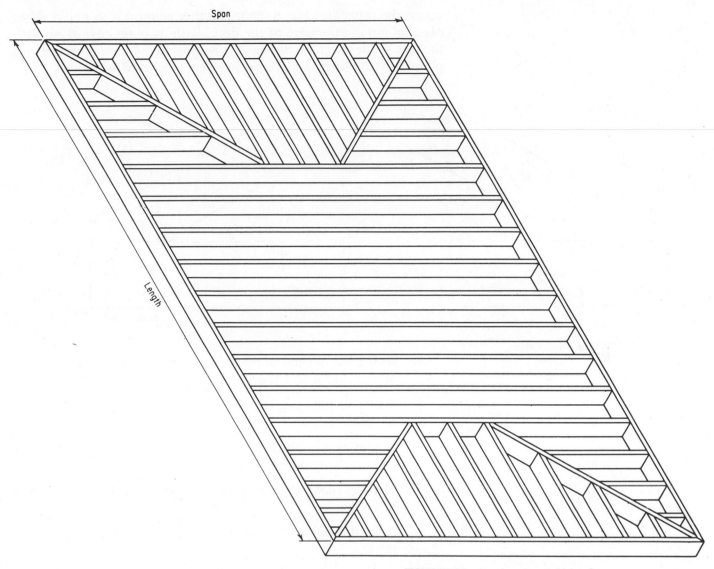

FIGURE 8-27: *Overhanging roof joist plan.*

the span and the length of the hip roof which will be constructed on
it (see Fig. 8-27).

The lengths of all the rafters—commons, hips, and jacks—and
the ridge are calculated in the same way as for a conventional roof,
except that there are no rafter tails to consider. The lengths may be
measured along the top edge of the rafter, rather than along a measuring line. Plumb cuts at the top end of the rafters, cheek cuts, and
deductions are made as described in Chapter 7.

The cut of the bottom end of the rafters will depend on the method
used to attach the rafters to the joists. One method is to set a rafter on
the top edge of a joist, with the end out flush with the outer face of
the rough fascia. In this case the bottom cut will be a seat cut right

across the rafter (see Fig. 8-28a). Another method is to nail a rafter plate all around the edge of the deck, with its outer edge flush with the face of the rough fascia (see Fig. 8-28b). In this case both seat and plumb cuts are necessary. To get these cuts, proceed as follows.

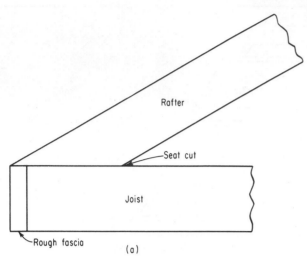

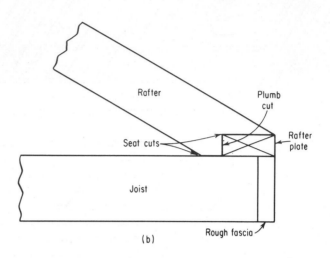

FIGURE 8-28: *Rafter seats.*

1. At the bottom end of the rafter stock, lay on the square for a seat cut, using 250 and the rise and marking on 250.

2. Measure along this seat-cut line a distance equal to the width of the rafter plate.

3. At this point, lay the square on for a plumb cut, using 250 and the rise and marking on the rise.

4. Measure along this line a distance equal to the depth of the rafter plate.

5. From this point, continue with a seat to the back edge of the rafter.

Gable Roof

When a gable roof is planned, all the rafters, of course, are commons, and the width of the deck becomes the span for the rafters. For an illustration of an overhanging gable, see Fig. 8-29. Either of the methods described above may be used to attach rafters to the joists for both types of gable roof.

There are some advantages to this system of roofing that should not be overlooked. With the conventional type of roof, the wider the cornice is made, the lower the bottom of the cornice will be, and the height of windows is restricted. With the cornice formed by overhanging joists, windows may be carried as high as desired. For conventional type roofs, the width of the cornice is restricted and is limited to a practical height for the plancier. With overhanging joists, the width of the cornice is restricted only be the ability of the joists to carry the roof loads beyond the wall plates.

There are also disadvantages to this style of roof, the main one

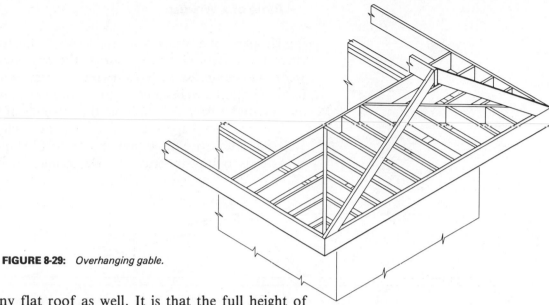

FIGURE 8-29: *Overhanging gable.*

being inherent in any flat roof as well. It is that the full height of the wall is exposed in this type of construction. In some cases the result may be that the building looks out of proportion. If the building is small with regard to area, a roof which projects at the wall plate level will probably not be appropriate. Also, the wider the overhang, the deeper the joists will have to be to carry the load. Consequently, the width of the finish fascia is increased and may be out of proportion to the rest of the building. These are things which must be taken into consideration when the building is being planned.

TRUSSED RAFTERS

Trussed rafters are rafters which have been tied together in pairs, along with a bottom chord, to form an individual unit. In addition to the two rafters and the bottom chord, compression and tension webs are incorporated into the unit, making it a *truss*—a self-supporting structure.

W-Truss

The truss illustrated in Fig. 8-30 is of the type commonly used in house construction, known as a *W-truss,* because of its conformation. It is suitable for spans from 5.4 to 10.8 m, in any of the common low-pitched roofs, such as those with unit rises of 60, 80, or 100 mm.

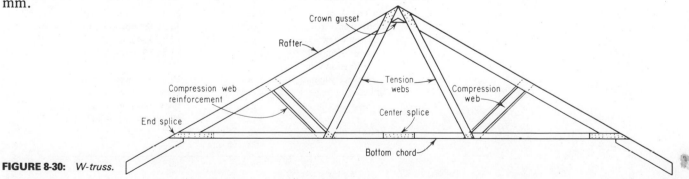

FIGURE 8-30: *W-truss.*

Parts of a W-truss

The parts of a typical W-truss, like that illustrated in Fig. 8-30, include the rafters or *upper chords,* the *bottom chord,* two *tension webs,* two *compression webs,* two *compression web reinforcements,* used to hold the webs in position, bottom *end splices,* a *center splice* and a *crown gusset,* used to hold the top ends of the rafters together.

To construct a specific W-truss, for example one with a span of 10.97 m, a unit rise of 60 mm and up to 1200 mm of rafter tail, the first step is to draw the truss to scale, as illustrated in Fig. 8-31.

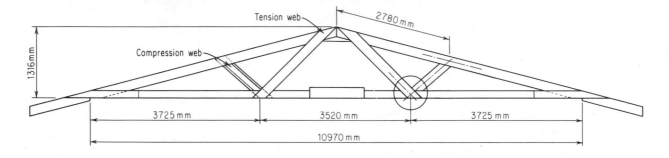

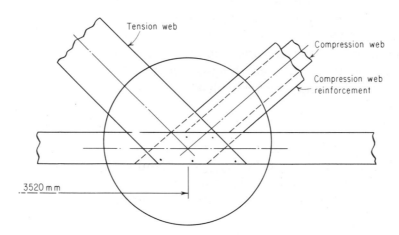

FIGURE 8-31: *W-truss plans.*

A bill of materials could then be made out as follows:

Rafters	2 pcs.	38 × 140 mm—7.0 m
Bottom chord	2 pcs.	38 × 89 mm—5.5 m
Tension webs	2 pcs.	19 × 184 mm—2.5 m
Compression webs	2 pcs.	38 × 89 mm—1.3 m
Compression web reinforcements	2 pcs.	19 × 140 mm—1.5 m
Splices	4 pcs.	19 × 89 mm—1.2 m
	2 pcs.	19 × 140 mm—1.0 m
	1 pc.	19 × 184 mm—1.0 m
Spiral nails	196—75 mm	
	50—65 mm	

Layout and Cutting of Parts

From the scale drawing, all the parts for all of the trusses required should be laid out and cut to size before any assembly begins. Figure 8-32 illustrates the layout for all the major parts of the truss, plus the splices and the crown gusset.

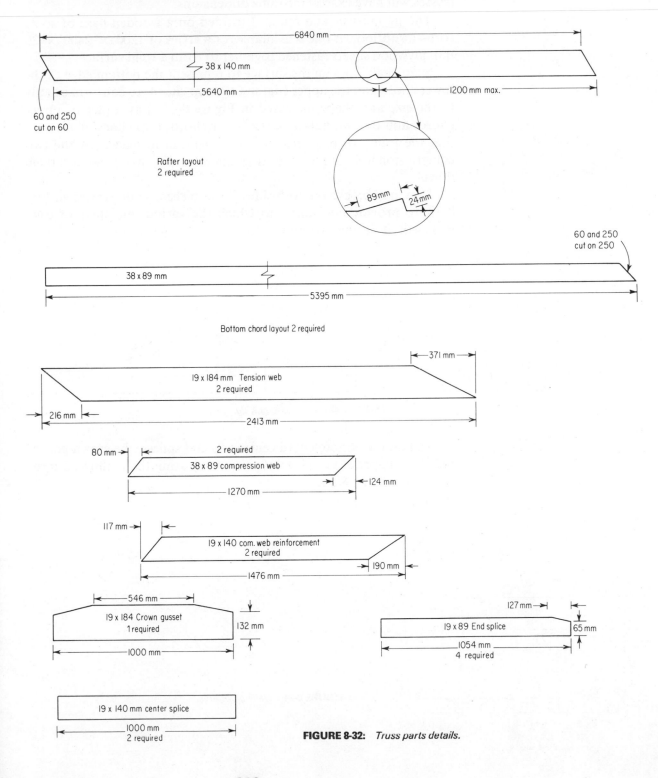

FIGURE 8-32: *Truss parts details.*

239

Truss Assembly

When a number of trusses of one size have to be assembled, it is a good plan to make use of a *jig,* which allows for the rapid positioning and nailing of all the pieces for a truss without any danger of any of them moving out of position. The use of a jig also insures that all trusses will have exactly the same dimensions.

The jig must be laid out and formed on a wooden base of some sort—a subfloor, if one is available, or a series of 1200 × 2400 × 20 mm plywood sheets fastened together to form a solid surface.

Snap chalk lines on the surface to represent the bottom edge of the lower chord and the upper edges of the top chord, to conform exactly to the size and shape indicated in Figure 8-31. Lay a pair of upper chords and the two halves of the lower chord to the lines; make sure that the joints fit properly and tack them all in place. Set the two compression webs in their proper location (see Fig. 8-31) and tack them down.

Now nail blocks on both sides of all pieces, as illustrated in Fig. 8-33, to provide positions into which the various members of each truss will fit during assembly.

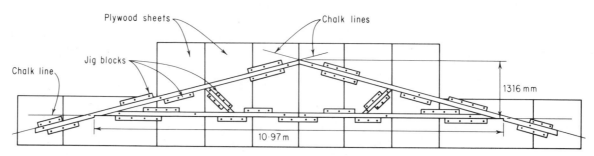

FIGURE 8-33: *Truss assembly jig.*

Nail on the bottom chord center and end splices, the crown gusset, and the compression web reinforcements, using the nailing patterns illustrated in Fig. 8-34.

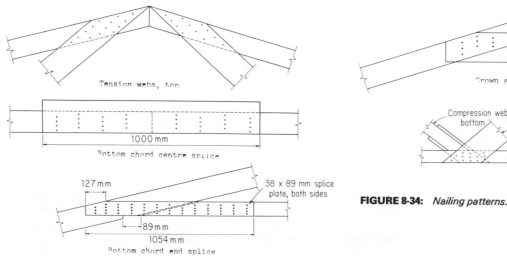

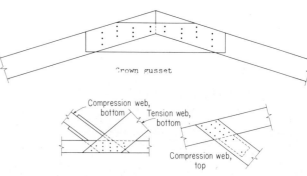

FIGURE 8-34: *Nailing patterns.*

240

Pull the nails holding the truss members down, lift the truss from the jig, turn it over, and apply the second pair of end splices and the tension webs, using the nailing pattern for the webs indicated in Fig. 8-34.

Each truss can now be assembled and nailed by placing the members in the positions outlined by blocks and nailing on the appropriate splicing pieces. Each truss will have to be turned over to complete the assembly.

Truss Types

The foregoing illustrates only one method of constructing a trussed rafter. There are a number of others equally good. Among them are the *gusseted truss,* the *skin-stressed trussed rafter,* and a *trussed rafter* connected with split rings. There are also many other styles of trusses in addition to the W-truss. These include the *scissors truss, Howe truss,* and many others. Design, construction, and allowable spans for these are dealt with in many excellent books on the subject.

Gusseted Truss

A gusseted truss may be quite simply made by using the W-truss style. However, instead of using any lapped joints, as is done in the method described above, all the web members are cut to fit between the rafters and the bottom chord. Joints are fastened by means of plywood gussets. These are glued and nailed into place, and a very strong connection is produced (see Fig. 8-35 for a diagram of a gusseted truss).

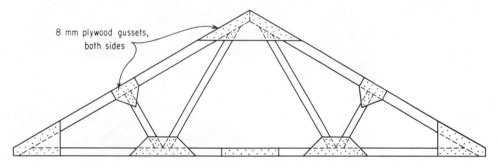

8 mm plywood gussets, both sides

FIGURE 8-35: *Gussetted truss.*

Skin-stressed Trussed Rafter

The frame for a skin-stressed trussed rafter will be made in the same way as is a gusseted truss. That is, the web members are cut to fit between the rafters and the bottom chord. In addition to the regular tension and compression webs, there will have to be vertical members on 1200 mm centers to support the ends of the plywood skin (see Fig. 8-36 for details). Then the whole frame, on either one or both sides, is covered with a plywood skin, usually 6 or 7 mm thick, glued and nailed in place. A very strong truss is produced. For longer spans and heavier loads, larger members and thicker skin may be used.

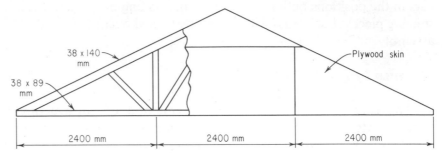

FIGURE 8-36: *Stressed-skin truss.*

Split Ring Truss Connectors

When split rings are used in connecting the members of trussed rafters, joints must be lapped. A flat metal ring is set into circular grooves cut in the meeting faces of the joint, and a bolt through the whole assembly holds it together. A special tool is used to cut the grooves (see Fig. 8-37).

FIGURE 8-37: *Split ring connection.*

Trussed Rafter Spans and Spacing

When the light type of trussed rafter being described here is used, the practical limit for span will be about 12 m. Longer spans could be accommodated by using heavier members. But before going into longer spans and heavier material, be sure to get proper specifications for the particular unit you have in mind.

The spacing of the trusses will depend on the roof load, the type of roof decking to be used, the span, and the material to be used on the ceiling. If the roof loads are large or if the roof sheathing is comparatively thin material, e.g. 9 mm plywood, trusses will probably be spaced 400 or 600 mm o.c. The same will be true if the ceiling material requires a considerable amount of support, although this may be overcome with wider spacings by strapping the underside of the bottom chord. Under other conditions, spacing may be extended to 800 or even 1200 mm o.c.

Roof Styles With Trussed Rafters

The style of roof usually produced with the use of trusses will be the gable roof, with only two slopes. Trusses have been developed, however, that will allow construction of a hip roof (see Fig. 8-38). Special truss forms are required to make the hips. In the great majority of cases, however, a simple gable roof will be the easiest when trusses are to be used in the construction of the building.

Eave overhangs may be formed with trusses in two ways. One is with the type of truss illustrated in Fig. 8-31. Here the overhang will be exactly the same as that formed by any ordinary rafter with a rafter tail. But if the truss is made so that its bottom chord extends to the ends of the rafters, then the overhang will be formed by part of the truss end extending beyond the wall plates (see Fig. 8-39).

FIGURE 8-38: *Hip trusses (Courtesy, Council of Forest Industries of B.C., Canada).*

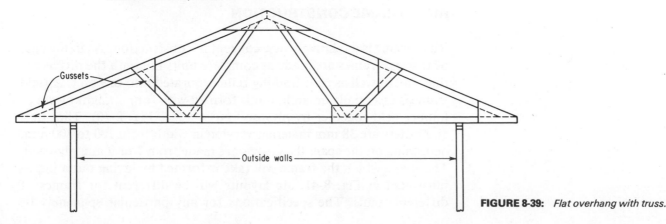

FIGURE 8-39: *Flat overhang with truss.*

Ceiling Finishes With Trussed Rafters

Application of ceiling material will depend on the spacing of the trusses and the type of material being used. Gypsum lath, gypsum board, or fiberboard may be applied directly to the underside of the bottom chords if the spacing is 400 or 600 mm o.c. The same procedure will be used as in applying a ceiling to regular joists. If the spacing is wider than this, it will be necessary to nail strapping to the underside of the trusses, at right angles to their direction and preferably 400 mm o.c. The ceiling material is then applied to the strapping. Other, heavier types of ceiling material may be applied directly to the trusses with spacings greater than 600 mm.

Advantages of Trussed Rafters

There are a number of advantages to the use of trussed rafters in roof construction. In the first place, it is an advantage to be able to assemble the whole unit on the floor or in a shop. Connections may be made more quickly and more efficiently. And when the trusses go up in place, as they do very easily, nothing remains to be done but to fasten them down at the plates and apply sheathing and finish. Second, free spans can be much greater than those which can be obtained using conventional rafters and ceiling joists. Another advantage is that the trusses may be set up, the roof sheathed, and shingles applied, before anything is done on the inside of the building. Consequently, there is a speedup in the time required to get the building closed in. When conventional joists are used, bearing partitions must be set up before the joists can be set. When trusses are used, all interior partitions may be built after the roof is in place. In fact, it may be advantageous at times to apply the ceiling before any partitions are built. Another important advantage is, of course, the reduction in cost. Very little more material is used than with the conventional roof, and the ease and speed of assembly and erection more than compensate for any additional material. Many contractors today are finding it to their advantage to use trussed rafters whenever it is possible.

RIGID FRAME CONSTRUCTION

Rigid frame is a relatively new concept in construction. As in the case of trusses, frames are made as complete units but with the difference that wall as well as roof framing is incorporated into one unit. A rigid frame is essentially an arch, but is formed with four straight pieces of lumber held together by plywood gussets (see Fig. 8-40). The studs and rafters are 38 mm material, varying in width from 100 to 300 mm, depending on the span; the gussets are made from 7 or 9 mm plywood. The shape which the frame will take is formed by laying out a jig, as illustrated in Fig. 8-41. Jig layouts will be different for frames of different spans. The specifications for any particular span may be

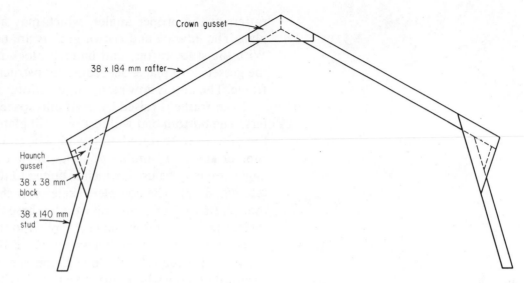

FIGURE 8-40: *Rigid frame—7-3 m span.*

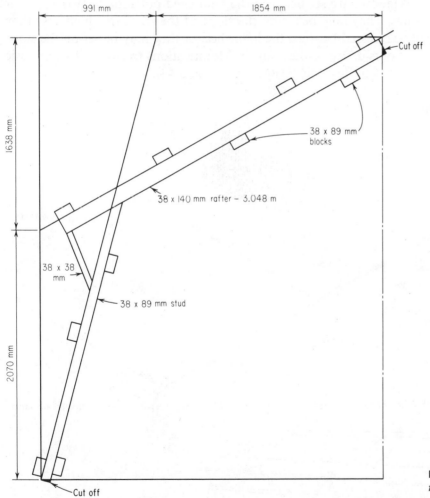

991 mm

1854 mm

Cut off

38 x 89 mm blocks

38 x 140 mm rafter – 3.048 m

1638 mm

38 x 38 mm

38 x 89 mm stud

2070 mm

Cut off

FIGURE 8-41: *Jig layout for 5.4 m span rigid frame.*

obtained by inquiring at a local lumber dealer's office or by writing to the nearest office of the Plywood Manufacturers Association.

The proper size and length of material having been obtained from the jig layout plan, the next step is to cut the ends of the studs and rafters at the proper angles, which may also be obtained from the plan. The *haunch* and *crown gussets* are next cut to size and shape. With the stud, rafter, and haunch block in position in the jig, nail the gussets into place, according to instructions, on both sides of the frame. The unit is now ready for erection.

Each frame is raised by itself and spaced usually on 600 mm centers. The bottom end will rest on a sill plate which is anchored to the top of a concrete foundation wall. The end is held in place by a metal shoe or angle. A number of styles of shoe are available, or a simple angle iron may be used, which is bolted to the sill plate and to the stud (see Fig. 8-42). The complete skeleton is sheathed with 1200 × 2400 mm sheets of 7 or 9 mm plywood. These may be butt-jointed along their long edge, or they may be applied so that each horizontal row of sheets overlaps the one below by 75 or 100 mm (see Fig. 8-43). If the latter procedure is followed, the end joints may be caulked or strapped and the whole surface painted, with no further covering.

Windows are set between the haunched portions of two adjacent frames. They may be set on the slope of the stud, in which case they will be recessed between the haunches, or they may be set on the slope of the outside leg of the haunch. Modifications to either of these basic plans may quite easily be made (see Fig. 8-44).

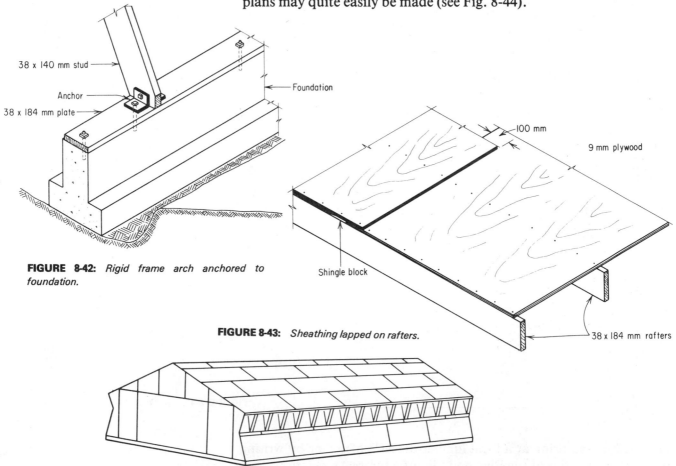

FIGURE 8-42: *Rigid frame arch anchored to foundation.*

FIGURE 8-43: *Sheathing lapped on rafters.*

FIGURE 8-44: *Windows in rigid frame building.*

Building spans will range from 5.4 to 11.4 m with the size of the material for studs and rafters increasing as the span increases. Table 8-3 shows the size and length of material required for a few basic spans.

TABLE 8-3: *Stud and rafter sizes for some rigid frame spans*

Span	Stud		Rafter	
	Size	*Length*	*Size*	*Length*
5.4 m	38 × 89　mm	2.4 m	38 × 140 mm	3.0 m
7.2 m	38 × 140 mm	2.4 m	38 × 184 mm	4.2 m
9.6 m	38 × 184 mm	2.4 m	38 × 235 mm	5.4 m
11.4 m	38 × 235 mm	3.0 m	38 × 286 mm	6.0 m

As mentioned above, jig layouts will be different for each of these spans. The 5.4 span involves a rectangle 2845 mm wide, 3708 mm high. The stud line is offset 991 mm from the perpendicular and the rafter line begins 2070 mm from the base (see Fig. 8-41). Table 8-4 gives rectangle sizes, stud offsets, and distance of rafter line ends above base, for the spans listed in Table 8-3.

TABLE 8-4: *Jig dimensions for rigid frame spans*

Span	Rectangle size	Stud offset	Rafter line above base
5.4 m	2845 × 3708 mm	991 mm	2070 mm
7.2 m	3810 × 4267 mm	1143 mm	2981 mm
9.6 m	4947 × 4953 mm	1314 mm	2095 mm
11.4 m	6045 × 5436 mm	1981 mm	2489 mm

If other spans than the ones given are required, be sure to consult an authority on the matter before selecting the size of material.

Rigid frame construction was originally designed for use in farm buildings, but today the design is being put to many other uses as well. Churches, community halls, summer cottages, garages, and warehouses are being built by this system. The whole idea is quite recent, and, no doubt, as time goes on it will be put to many more uses. Simplicity of construction, ease of erection, rigidity of the structure, and relative inexpensiveness are certainly factors in favor of its use.

GLUE-LAMINATED ARCHES

Glue-laminated arches are structural components made by gluing together thin pieces of lumber of any required width. In this way a member of any desired thickness and shape may be produced (see Fig.

8-45). Because of the wide scope in shape, size, and span, buildings using laminated arches for their frames are becoming increasingly popular. A great many are made commercially; some very large, with spans of 60 m or more. Great care is taken in the selection of lumber and the cutting of splices so that pieces fit perfectly, end to end, in the manufacture of these large arches (see Fig. 8-46). Large bandsaws and planers are used to cut and dress them to size. They are finally sanded, treated, and wrapped so that when they arrive on the job they are unmarked and, when in place, produce a finished appearance.

FIGURE 8-45: *Glue-laminated arches.*

FIGURE 8-46: *Checking cuts for scarf joints (Courtesy, Canadian Institute of Timber Construction)*

Smaller, lighter arches, in two or three standard shapes, with spans up to about 18 m, are made with less sophisticated equipment, for use in buildings such as that illustrated in Fig. 8-47.

Although many shapes are possible, probably the most often used ones are the semicircular arch, the parabolic arch, the gothic arch, and a shape, half curve, half straight line, known as the shed rafter (see Fig. 8-48). In addition, the modified shed rafter, with haunch (see Fig. 8-45) is quite widely used. The semicircular and sometimes the parabolic arch are made in one piece, but in most other cases two separate halves of the complete arch are formed. The two halves are put together on the site, being secured together at the top by bolts or with steel plates acting as gussets.

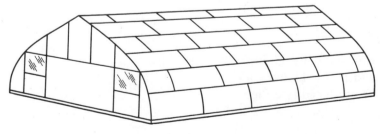

FIGURE 8-47: *Simple arched rafter building.*

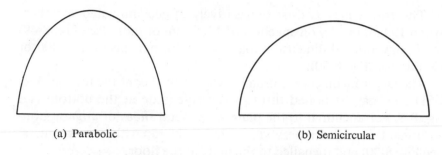

(a) Parabolic   (b) Semicircular

Spacing of the arches varies greatly, depending on the design, the span, and the type of roof deck to be applied. In some instances the roof decking will be carried on purlins running across the arches or hung in between them. With other designs, the decking will be 75 or 100 mm tongue-and-grooved material, usually cedar, spanning directly from arch to arch.

A-FRAME

In *A-frame* construction, the wall and roof are combined in a single, plane surface. Straight members are joined together at the top and anchored to a floor at the bottom, to form a tall, rigid triangle (see Fig. 8-49). The floor frame for an upper floor may be introduced at the appropriate level, to give the A-shape.

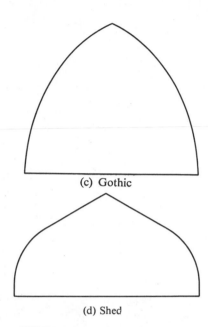

(c) Gothic

(d) Shed

FIGURE 8-48: *Common arch shapes.*

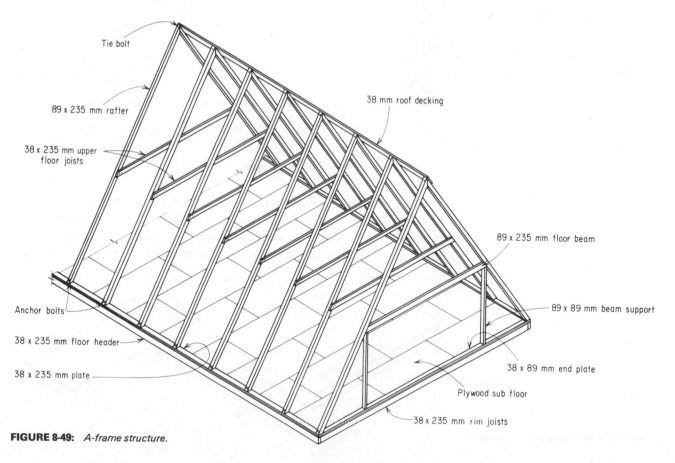

FIGURE 8-49: *A-frame structure.*

Tie bolt

89 x 235 mm rafter

38 x 235 mm upper floor joists

38 mm roof decking

Anchor bolts

38 x 235 mm floor header

38 x 235 mm plate

89 x 235 mm floor beam

89 x 89 mm beam support

38 x 89 mm end plate

Plywood sub floor

38 x 235 mm rim joists

249

The frame may consist of relatively large, laminated members (often 100 mm wide) on spacings of 1200 mm or more (see Fig. 8-49) or of conventional dimension material at normal spacings of 400 or 600 mm (see Fig. 8-50).

The larger members are usually bolted together at the top (see Fig. 8-51) and may be bolted through the sole plate at the bottom (see Fig. 8-51) or anchored to the plate with metal *shoes* or *angles*. Conventional framing members will be tied at the top with a crown gusset (see Fig. 8-30) and toenailed to the plate at the floor.

Ends may be framed with conventional, 38 × 89 mm framing or with heavier members, more widely spaced, to provide large glass areas.

Sheathing will normally be 38 mm decking over widely spaced frames or plywood over conventional framing. Wood or asphalt shingles will complete the cover.

FIGURE 8-50: *A-frame with conventional framing (Courtesy, National Research Council).*

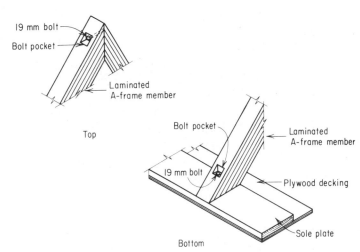

FIGURE 8-51: *Bolted connections for A-frame.*

Stressed-Skin Roof Panels

A *stressed-skin* panel consists of a frame of dimension material (usually 38 × 89 mm), covered on one or both sides with a *plywood skin* (see Fig. 8-52). The plywood skin, in addition to providing a surface covering, acts with the framing members to form a complete

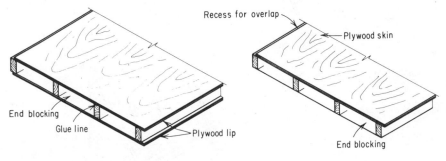

FIGURE 8-52: *Stressed-skin panels.*

structural member. In order to develop the full potential strength of the panel, the skins must be attached to the frame with glue and, in order to tie panels together effectively, the skin will project over the frame along one edge, to overlap the adjoining panel (see Fig. 8-52).

Panels may be of various shapes but are most often either *rectangular* or *triangular*. Rectangular panels are supported top and bottom, while triangular ones often fit together to form a self-supporting structure, as illustrated in Fig. 8-53.

The spacing of framing members for stressed-skin panels depends on the thickness of the plywood skin and the direction of the face grain in relation to the long dimension of the framing members. Table 8-5 gives basic spacing of framing members for various plywood grades and thicknesses.

FIGURE 8-53: *Triangular stressed-skin roof panels.*

TABLE 8-5: *Basic spacing of stressed-skin panel framing members*

Plywood thickness (mm)	Basic spacing (mm)			
	Face grain parallel to framing members		Face grain perpendicular to framing members	
	Sanded	Unsanded	Sanded	Unsanded
6 mm	256		307	
7 mm		280		396
8 mm	444		394	
9 mm		388		419
11 mm	650		643	
12 mm		584		716
14 mm	840		780	
15 mm		680		985
17 mm	1024		922	
18 mm		922		1021

Approximate imperial equivalents to metric quantities

1.5 mm	— ⅟₁₆ in.	75 mm	— 3 in.	38 × 89	— 2 × 4
6 mm	— ¼ in.	210 mm	— 8.5 in.	38 × 140	— 2 × 6
8 mm	— ⅜ in.	400 mm	— 16 in.	38 × 184	— 2 × 8
12 mm	— ½ in.	2100 mm	— 7 ft	38 × 235	— 2 × 10
19 mm	— ¾ in.	4.8 m	— 16 ft	38 × 286	— 2 × 12
24 mm	— 1 in.	12 m	— 40 ft		
38 mm	— 1½ in.	14.4 m	— 48 ft		
40 mm	— 1.6 in.	0.25 kg	— 0.55 lb		
64 mm	— 2.5 in.	m²	— 10.75 ft²		

REVIEW QUESTIONS

8-1. List two major advantages to be gained by using trusses to form the roof on a small building.

8-2. Give two reasons for using blocking between joists at the wall plates in flat roof construction. Why should the blocks not be as wide as the joists?

8-3. Give two reasons for using a cant strip around the perimeter of a flat roof.

8-4. When insulating a flat roof, what type of insulation is placed over the roof deck?

8-5. (a) List the materials used in laying a builtup roof over a wood deck.

(b) How much of each of these materials will be required for a flat roof over a building 7200 mm × 9000 mm, with a 600 mm overhang on all sides?

8-6. Outline the main difference between "laminated" beams and "box" beams.

8-7. Explain what is meant by a "sandwich" panel and draw a careful diagram to illustrate a typical sandwich panel.

8-8. What do you understand by a "skin-stressed" trussed rafter?

8-9. Explain the difference between a trussed rafter and a rigid frame unit.

8-10. List two major advantages of rigid frame and arch construction over conventional construction.

8-11. List three advantages of open web joists over conventional wood joists.

Stair building is virtually a trade in itself, and it would be impossible to cover the subject in all its facets in a single chapter. Nevertheless, a stair of one kind or another is still a necessity in many types of light construction, and we shall look into the basic elements of the subject to find out how to construct some of the most commonly required kinds of stairs.

TERMS USED IN STAIR BUILDING

Stairs lead from one floor level to another through a *stairwell opening* (see Fig. 4-34, page 132). It must be framed during the floor-framing stage of construction, so the length and width of the opening must be known. Stairs consist primarily of *risers* and *treads* carried on *stringers* (see Fig. 9-1). The height of each riser is called the *rise* and the width of the tread (exclusive of nosing) is called the *run* (see Fig. 9-2). The sum of all the individual rises gives the *total rise,* and the sum of the runs gives the *total run* (see Fig. 9-1).

Two important terms used in stair work are *line of flight* and *headroom clearance.* The line of flight is a line drawn through the extremities of the nosings (see Fig. 9-3). Headroom clearance is the vertical distance from the underside of the end of the stairwell opening to the line of flight (see Fig. 9-1).

STAIR DIMENSIONS

Most building codes provide guidelines for dimensions of stair parts. For example, interior stairs leading to unfinished basements, cellars or attics are generally allowed a maximum riser height of 225 mm, a minimum run of 200 mm and a minimum tread width of 230 mm. Other interior stairs in residences and exterior stairs serving residences are allowed a maximum riser height of 200 mm, a minimum run of 210 mm and a minimum tread width of 235 mm. Interior stairs in buildings other than residences and exterior stairs, except those serving single residences, are restricted to a maximum riser height of 195 mm, a minimum of 125 mm, a minimum run of 225 mm and a minimum tread width of 250 mm. The product of the run times the rise for such stairs must not be less than 45,000 or more than 48,500.

If the run of a stair is less than 250 mm, it is necessary to provide a *nosing* which will project at least 25 mm beyond the face of the riser (see Fig. 9-1) or to provide at least as much back slope to the risers (see Fig. 9-4).

Stairs should have a minimum width of 900 mm and a minimum

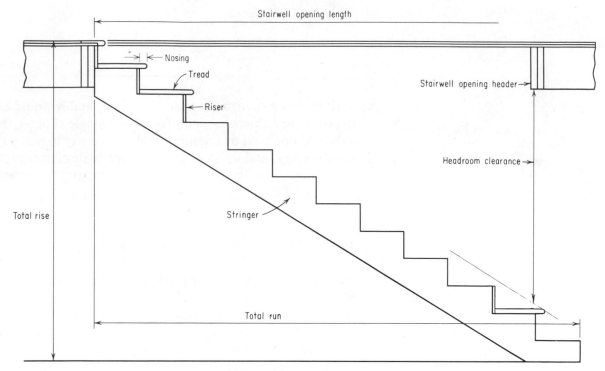

FIGURE 9-1: *Stair elevation.*

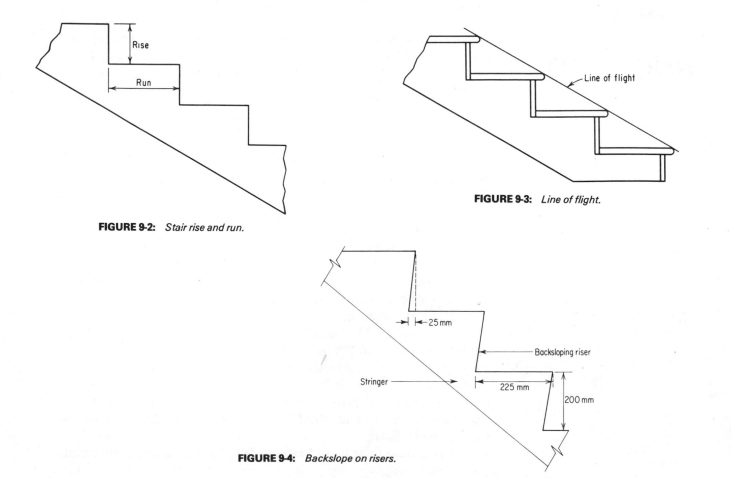

FIGURE 9-2: *Stair rise and run.*

FIGURE 9-3: *Line of flight.*

FIGURE 9-4: *Backslope on risers.*

254

headroom clearance of 1950 mm in residences (see Fig. 9-1). In other types of buildings, the minimum headroom clearance should be 2050 mm. The stairwell opening length will depend on the steepness of the stair and must be calculated accordingly.

TYPES OF STAIRS

Stairs are classified by the *kind of stringer* used in their construction, by the way the complete *stair is fitted into the building* and by the *shape* of the complete stair.

Stringer Types

One type of stringer used is the *open stringer* (see Fig. 9-5), in which pieces are cut from the stringer and risers and treads attached so that their ends are exposed. Another type is the *semi-housed stringer,* in which a piece of 19 mm material is cut out, as in Fig. 9-5 and then fastened to the face of a solid 38 mm stringer, as illustrated in Fig. 9-6. The ends of the risers and treads are thus concealed in the finished stair. A third type is the *housed stringer,* which has *dadoes,* 12 mm deep, cut on its inner face to receive the ends of the risers and treads (see Fig. 9-7). The dadoes are tapered so that wedges can be driven below the tread and behind the riser to hold each tightly in place.

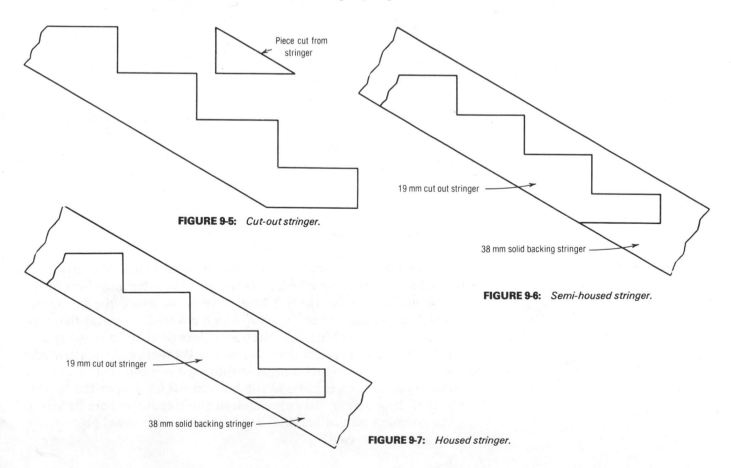

Piece cut from stringer

FIGURE 9-5: *Cut-out stringer.*

19 mm cut out stringer

38 mm solid backing stringer

FIGURE 9-6: *Semi-housed stringer.*

19 mm cut out stringer

38 mm solid backing stringer

FIGURE 9-7: *Housed stringer.*

Stair Types

A complete stair that has no wall on either side is called an *open stair*. If it has a wall on one side only, it is a *semi-housed stair;* if it is built between two walls, it is a *housed stair*.

Stair Shapes

A stair that rises with uninterrupted steps from floor to floor is known as a *straight flight;* if it has a break between top and bottom, it is a *straight flight with landing*. A stair that makes a right-angle turn by means of a landing is called a *quarter-spaced stair* and a stair that makes a right-angle turn step by step is called a *winder* (see Fig. 9-8).

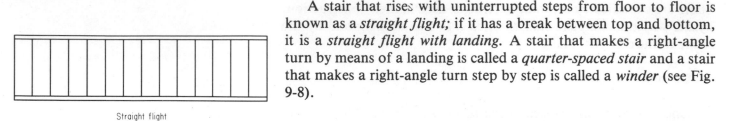

Straight flight

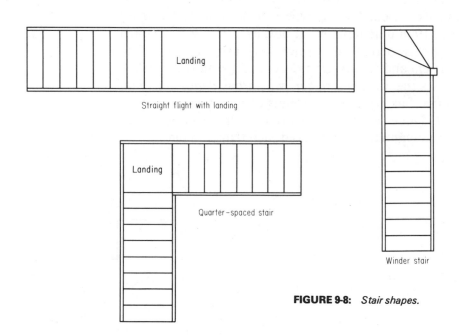

Straight flight with landing

Quarter-spaced stair

Winder stair

FIGURE 9-8: *Stair shapes.*

PARTS OF A STAIR

The parts of a stair include some already mentioned. The first is the *stringer,* the purpose of which is to carry the other members of the stair and to support the live load. Next is the *tread,* the surface on which to walk and then the *riser,* which covers the vertical spacings. A *nosing piece* is attached at the upper floor level and a *molding* may cover the joint between riser and tread. *Wedges* hold the risers and treads tight in a housed stair. A semihoused or open stair will have a *newel post* or newel posts at the bottom, which carries the bottom end of the *handrail*. Between handrail and treads there are *balusters;* the complete unit of handrail and balusters, with newel post, makes up a *balustrade* (see Fig. 9-9).

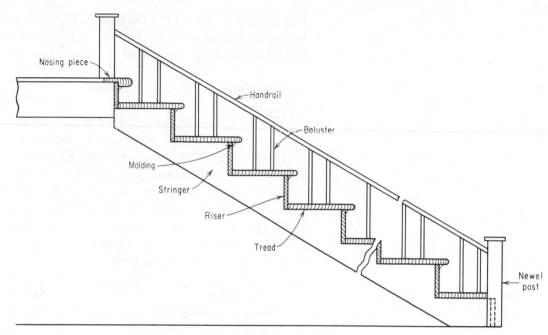

FIGURE 9-9: *Parts of a stair.*

HOW TO BUILD AN OPEN STRINGER STAIR

The first calculation necessary in connection with a stair is that of finding the length of the stairwell opening. This actually must be done during the floor framing stage, because the opening must be framed at that time.

Calculation of Stairwell Opening Length

A simple method of calculating the stairwell opening length is by comparison of two similar triangles involved in the stair layout. One contains unit rise and unit run as two sides of a triangle and the other the stairwell opening as one side and the headroom clearance plus thickness of ceiling finish, floor frame, subfloor, and finish floor as another. A portion of the line of flight is the third side of both.

As a specific example, suppose that the headroom clearance required is 1930 mm and the thickness of the ceiling, floor frame, and floors is 290 mm. The unit rise is to be 175 mm or as close to it as possible and the unit run 250 mm. What length of stairwell opening is required?

The total distance from line of flight to finish floor will be 1930 + 290 = 2220 mm. Then the similar triangle relationship will be:

$$\frac{250}{175} = \frac{\text{nominal stairwell opening length}}{2220}$$

and the opening length will be $\left(\dfrac{250 \times 2220}{175}\right) = 3171$ mm. To that

257

length must be added the *thickness of the top riser,* the *length of the nosing overhang* and the *thickness of the stairwell header finish,* in order to obtain the true length of the stairwell opening.

Calculation of Exact Unit Rise

The first step in the actual building of the stair is to calculate exactly what the unit rise of the stair will be. Stand a *story pole* (a 19 × 19 mm stick, long enough to reach from floor to floor) in the stairwell opening, as indicated in Figure 9-10. Carefully mark on the pole the height of the top of the subfloor on the upper level (see Fig. 9-10). Above this line, lay off the thickness of the finish floor above (see Fig. 9-11) and, at the bottom, deduct the thickness of the finish floor if it is not already in place. Measure on the story pole the exact distance from finish floor to finish floor.

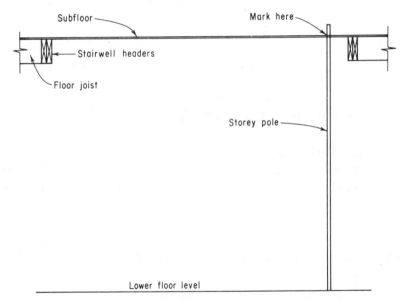

FIGURE 9-10: *Storey pole in stairwell.*

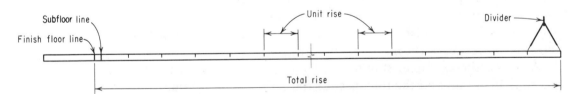

FIGURE 9-11: *Storey pole layout.*

This is the total rise of the stair and must be divided into a number of equal step rises. Divide the specified rise into the total rise. This will give the number of risers required.

As an example, suppose that the total rise is 2810 mm. If the specified rise is 175 mm, 2810 ÷ 175 = 16.06, the number of risers. Obviously, 16 must be used and the actual unit rise will be $^{2810}/_{16}$ = 175.5 mm. Set 175.5 mm on a pair of dividers and step off this distance along the pole from top to bottom (see Fig. 9-11). Theoretically, the last step should end at the bottom finish floor line. Usually, it will be a little long or a little short. Adjust the dividers and step off again, repeating until the steps work exactly into the total rise. You now have on the dividers the exact height of the riser.

Layout of Stair Stringer

Take this distance on the tongue of a framing square, the specified run on the blade, and clamp a pair of stair gauges to the square at these points (see Fig. 9-12). Lay the square on the stringer stock, close to one end, as illustrated in Fig. 9-13, and carefully draw on the stock the rise and run. Slide the square along to the end of the run line and repeat. Continue until the required number of risers and treads have been laid out. The stock will now look like the illustration in Fig. 9-14.

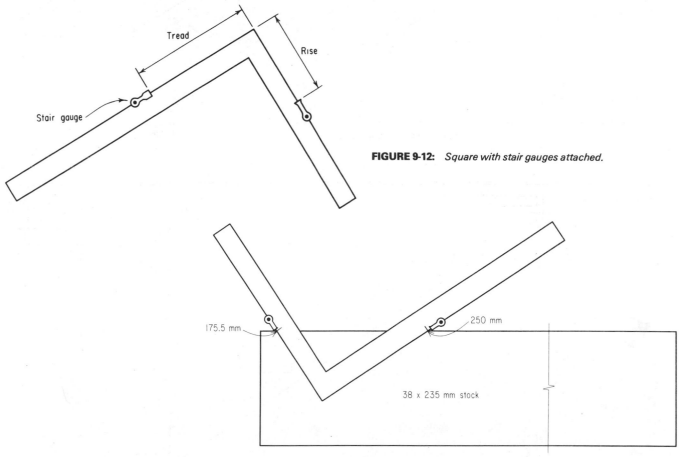

FIGURE 9-12:   *Square with stair gauges attached.*

FIGURE 9-13:   *First step in stair layout.*

FIGURE 9-14:   *Stringer laid out.*

Since the stair begins with a riser at the bottom, extend the last riser and tread lines to the back edge of the stock, as shown in Fig. 9-15. Cut the stringer off along these lines.

At the top end, extend the last riser and tread lines to the back edge of the stock, and cut as shown in Fig. 9-15. Cut very carefully along all the rise and tread lines, to produce a cut-out stringer (see Fig. 9-16).

When this stringer is set up in place (see Fig. 9-17), it is seen that the face of the header becomes the first riser. But when the treads are

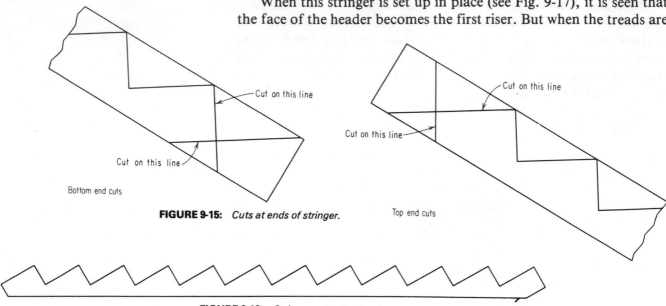

Cut on this line

Cut on this line

Bottom end cuts

Cut on this line

Cut on this line

Top end cuts

FIGURE 9-15: *Cuts at ends of stringer.*

FIGURE 9-16: *Stringer cut out.*

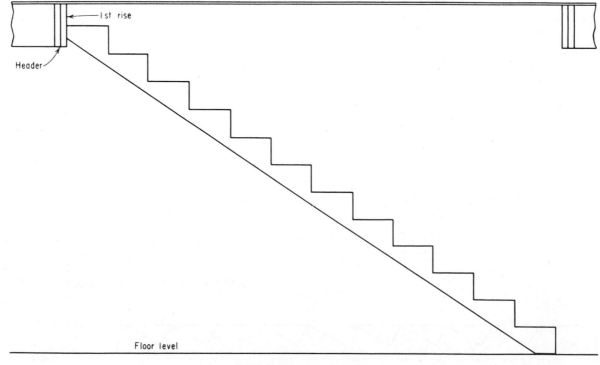

1st rise

Header

Floor level

FIGURE 9-17: *Stringer set up.*

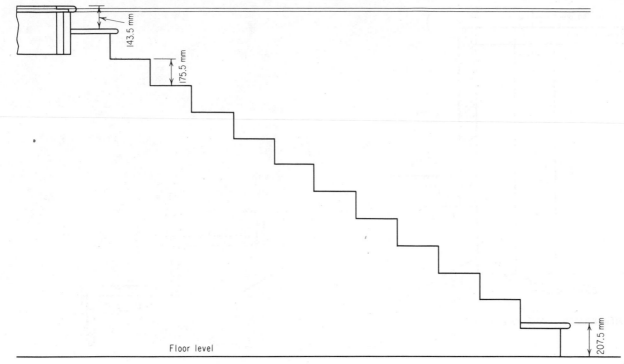

FIGURE 9-18: *Unequal risers.*

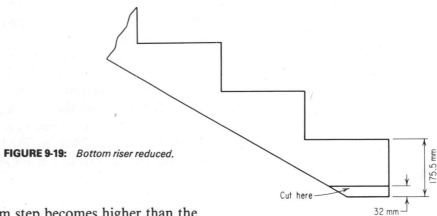

FIGURE 9-19: *Bottom riser reduced.*

set in place (see Fig. 9-18), the bottom step becomes higher than the rest, and the top step becomes shorter than the others, each by the thickness of the tread. To remedy this discrepancy, cut off from the bottom an amount equal to the thickness of the tread (see Fig. 9-19). Now when the stringer is set in place, the bottom rise is less than the rest, and the top rise is greater but when the treads are in place, all the rises will be equal.

Stair Assembly

At the top of the stair, a nosing piece is used (see Fig. 9-20). This produces the same tread overhang at the floor level as the other treads have.

Tread material should be clear, dry, edge grain (if the treads are exposed), 28 or 32 mm in thickness. The nosing is usually half-round,

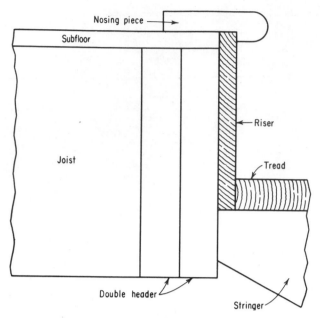

FIGURE 9-20: *Nosing piece in place.*

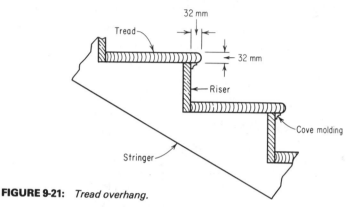

FIGURE 9-21: *Tread overhang.*

and the overhang should extend a distance equal to the thickness of the tread (see Fig. 9-21). If the tread nosing is to be capped with a metal molding, it should be shaped to fit that molding rather than being made half-round.

The risers are put in place first, nailed with 65 mm finishing nails. The treads are then put on, nailed in place, and from the back, the bottom edges of the risers are nailed to the back edge of the treads. Cove molding may then be fitted under the overhang to hide the joint between riser and tread (see Fig. 9-21).

HOW TO BUILD A SEMI-HOUSED STRINGER STAIR

When this type of stair is to be built, the 19 mm cut-out stringers are made in exactly the same way as described above. The ends of the solid, backup stringers will, however, be cut differently. At the bottom, the stringer will be allowed to run past the riser until the vertical cut is equal to the height of the baseboard, if any (see Fig. 9-22). At the top end, it will be cut as illustrated in Fig. 9-22, again so that the vertical cut will be the same height as the baseboard.

Glue and nail the 19 mm cut-out pieces to the solid stringers so that the tread nosings will come the required distance from the upper edge of the stringer. Set the stringers in place, and set in the risers and treads. Care must be taken so that the ends fit snugly against the face of the stringer.

262

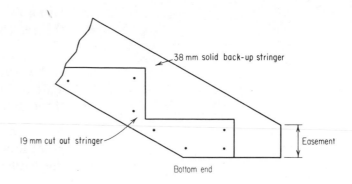

38 mm solid back-up stringer

19 mm cut out stringer

Easement

Bottom end

FIGURE 9-22: *Top and bottom ends of semi-housed stringer.*

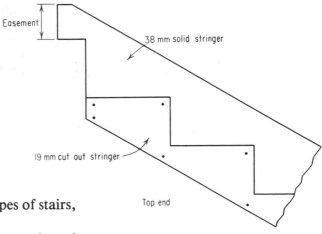

Easement

38 mm solid stringer

19 mm cut out stringer

Top end

HOW TO LAY OUT AND CUT A HOUSED STRINGER

Calculations for riser heights are the same as for other types of stairs, but the method of layout is considerably different.

Tapered dadoes are cut in the stringer to receive the treads and risers; these are drawn with the aid of templates, which can be made from 3 mm hardboard or similar material. The taper is 25 in 400 mm and, in the case of the tread template, starts at the base of the overhang. Mark the amount of overhang on the tread template and drill a small hole at the center of the circle forming the nosing. Also indicate the width of tread on the template with a notch. See Fig. 9-23 for template layout details. To lay out the stringer, proceed as follows:

1. Joint the top edge of the stringer so that it is perfectly straight.

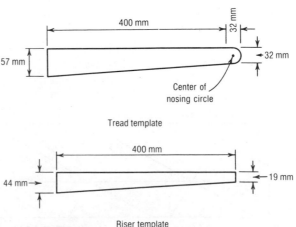

400 mm

32 mm

57 mm

32 mm

Center of nosing circle

Tread template

400 mm

44 mm

19 mm

Riser template

FIGURE 9-23: *Dado templates.*

263

2. Using the required run and rise figures, draw the slope of the tread across the face of the stringer (see Fig. 9-24).

3. Lay the tread template to this line and adjust until the nosing is the required distance from the top edge of the stringer. This is usually at least 25 mm (see Fig. 9-25). Draw a line through this point parallel to the top edge.

4. Mark on the tread line the width of tread and through this point draw a line parallel to the front edge. This is the base line from which the layout is made (see Fig. 9-26).

5. Start at one end of the stock and lay out the steps, using the specified run and rise and laying the square to the base line, rather than to the edge of the stock (see Fig. 9-27).

6. Lay the tread template to each tread line with the curve of the nosing just touching the nosing line and trace the shape of the template on the stringer. Also mark the center of the nosing circle through the hole drilled in the template (see Fig. 9-28).

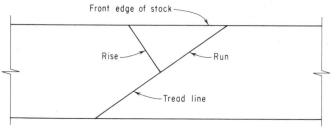

FIGURE 9-24: *Tread line drawn on stringer.*

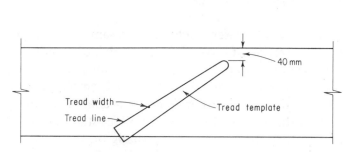

FIGURE 9-25: *Tread template in position.*

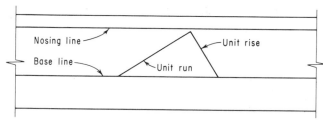

FIGURE 9-26: *Base line drawn.*

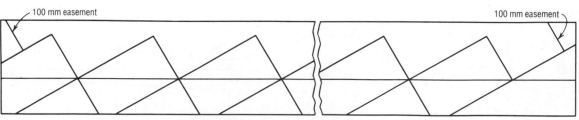

FIGURE 9-27: *Housed stringer layout.*

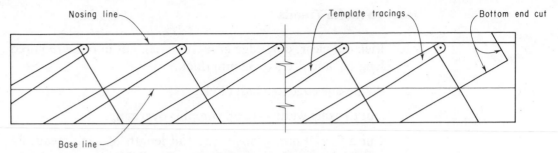

FIGURE 9-28: *Tread housings traced.*

7. Trace the riser dadoes, using the riser template, with the narrow end held up to the tread line (see Fig. 9-29).

8. Using a wood bit with a diameter equal to the thickness of the tread, bore holes 12 mm deep on the centers marked in step 6 (see Fig. 9-30).

9. Cut along the lines traced by the template and rout out the dadoes 12 mm deep.

10. At the bottom end, cut the stringer as illustrated in Fig. 9-31.

11. At the top end, cut the dado for the nosing piece, and cut stringer as shown in Fig. 9-31.

12. Chamfer the top inner edge of the stringer as required and sand the surfaces clean.

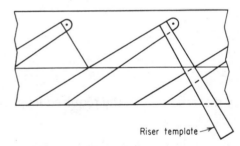

FIGURE 9-29: *Riser template in place.*

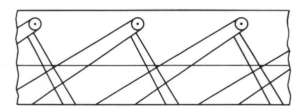

FIGURE 9-30: *Holes drilled for tread nosing.*

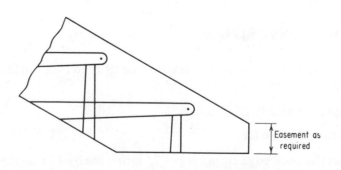

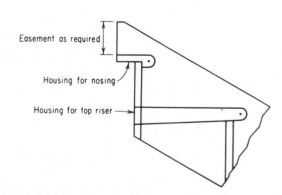

FIGURE 9-31: *Top and bottom ends of housed stringer.*

How to Make Treads

1. Pick out clear, dry, edge grain material, cut into the required lengths, and dress to 32 mm thick.

2. Shape one edge to a half circle.

3. Cut to exact width—tread run plus overhang.

4. Cut a 9 × 9 mm groove, the full length of each tread, 32 mm back from the front edge (see Fig. 9-32).

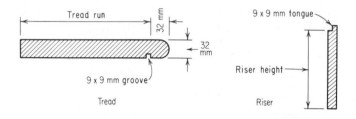

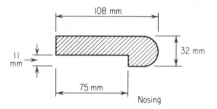

FIGURE 9-32: *Tread, riser and nosing details.*

How to Make Risers

1. Pick out clear, dry material, cut to the required lengths, and dress to 19 mm thick.

2. Rabbet one edge so as to leave a 9 × 9 mm tongue.

3. Rip to width—9 mm wider than the height of the riser + tread thickness (see Fig. 9-32). The top riser should be 19 mm wider than the rest.

How to Make a Nosing Piece

1. Pick out a clear, dry, edge grain piece of material, cut it to length, and dress it to 32 mm thick.

2. Shape one edge to a half circle.

3. Rip to 108 mm wide.

4. From the back edge cut a rabbet 75 mm wide by 11 mm deep (see Fig. 9-32).

Wedges and Cant Strips

Cut enough wedges to wedge the whole stair. They are cut from 19 mm stock, tapered 25 in 400 mm. Also cut cant strips about 150 mm long from 38 mm square stock. Three cant strips will be required for each tread (see Fig. 9-33). All the parts are now ready for assembly.

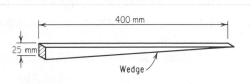
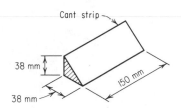

FIGURE 9-33: *Wedge and cant strip details.*

ASSEMBLING THE STAIR

Lay the stringers top edge down on the floor, far enough apart to take the treads and risers. Set all the treads in place first and hold the assembly together with bar clamps near the top and bottom. Check to see that the front edge of the groove in each tread lines up with the front edge of the riser dado. Set the nosing piece in place.

Now set all the risers in place. Check to see that the back edge of each tread fits snugly against the front face of its riser. The top riser cannot be wedged, since its dado is open at the back. Apply glue to the ends and nail it in place from the back.

The next step is to wedge the treads in place. Apply glue to the wedges, and drive each firmly into place. The tread should thus be brought into a tight fit against the upper edge of the housing. Be sure that the wedges do not project beyond the back edge of the treads.

Now wedge the risers in place. Cut off the thin end of each wedge so that, when driven, it will not interfere with the tread above. Nail the bottom of each riser to the back edge of the tread, as illustrated in Fig. 9-34.

Nail and glue three cant strips into the junctions between risers and treads, one at each end and one at the center (see Fig. 9-34). The stair is now complete and ready to install.

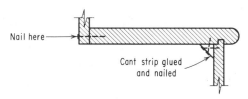

FIGURE 9-34: *Riser and tread nailed.*

Approximate imperial equivalents to metric quantities					
3 mm	—	⅛ in.	125 mm	—	5 in.	230 mm	—	9¼ in.
12 mm	—	½ in.	195 mm	—	7¾ in.	235 mm	—	9½ in.
19 mm	—	¾ in.	200 mm	—	8 in.	900 mm	—	36 in.
25 mm	—	1 in.	210 mm	—	8⅜ in.	1930 mm	—	6 ft 4 in.
38 mm	—	1½ in.	225 mm	—	9 in.	2050 mm	—	6 ft 9 in.

REVIEW QUESTIONS

9-1. Fill in the blank or blanks in each sentence with the correct word or phrase.

    (a) A stair begins at the bottom with a _____ .

    (b) A stair leads to an upper floor through a _____ .

    (c) A line drawn through the extremities of the nosings of stair treads is the _____ .

    (d) Stair risers and treads are carried on _____ .

    (e) The vertical distance from the underside of the stairwell opening header to the line of flight is the _____ .

    (f) The vertical distance from one floor level to the next is the _____ of a stair.

    (g) A stair tread is the width of the _____ wider than the run.

    (h) Stairs should have a slope of from _____ to _____ degrees.

    (i) Minimum stair width should be _____ .

    (j) Run multiplied by rise should equal approximately _____ .

9-2. Name three types of stringer used in stair building and indicate the differences between them.

9-3. Explain briefly the difference between an open, a semihoused, and a housed stair.

9-4. What is the purpose of:

    (a) wedges in a stair?

    (b) a newel post?

    (c) a baluster?

    (d) a story pole?

    (e) tread and riser templates?

9-5. If the headroom clearance is to be 1980 mm, the floor frame is 38 × 235 mm material, the subfloor 15 mm plywood, the finish floor 21 mm hardwood, the ceiling and header finish 19 mm plaster, the risers 19 mm thick and the nosing projection 32 mm:

    (a) What should the length of the stairwell opening be, if the tread run is 250 mm?

    (b) How many risers will there be in the stair, if the rise is to be kept as close to 175 mm as possible and the total rise between floors is 2858 mm?

    (c) How many treads will there be in the stair?

9-6. By means of a diagram, illustrate how a nosing piece fits at the top of an open stair stringer.

9-7. Explain why no cutoff of the stringers at the bottom is necessary when a housed stringer stair is being built.

During the course of construction, a variety of equipment is often employed, in addition to the hand and power woodworking tools used in the actual erection of the building.

SOIL TESTING EQUIPMENT

In some cases it may be desirable to determine the types and depth of soil strata to be encountered before excavation takes place. This may be done by digging a *test pit* or by the use of electronic soil testing apparatus, such as a *refraction seismograph* or an earth-resistivity meter, such as that illustrated in Fig. 10-1.

LEVELING INSTRUMENTS

See Chapter 2.

10

CON-
STRUCTION
EQUIPMENT

EARTHMOVING EQUIPMENT

Earthmoving equipment includes such machines as the *bulldozer* and the *backhoe* (see Chapter 3), used for excavating, and a *front-end loader* (see Fig. 10-2), used for moving and loading earth.

CONCRETE EQUIPMENT

Conventional foundations require the use of some type of concrete mixer, varying from the small, *portable mixer* shown in Fig. 10-3 or a large, *stationary mixer* such as that illustrated in Fig. 10-4 to a *transit-mix truck,* like that illustrated in Fig. 10-5.

At the site, concrete may have to be transported from mixer to the forms and this may be done by the use of wheelbarrows or by *power buggies* (see Fig. 10-6) and concrete in the forms may be consolidated by the use of an *internal vibrator,* such as the one shown in Fig. 3-69, page 102. A number of tools are used in finishing concrete slabs, including a *hand float,* illustrated in Fig. 10-7, *hand trowels* and *edgers* and a *power trowel,* such as that illustrated in Fig. 10-8.

FIGURE 10-1: *Earth-resistivity meter (Courtesy, Soiltest, Inc.).*

FIGURE 10-2: *Loading earth with front-end loader.*

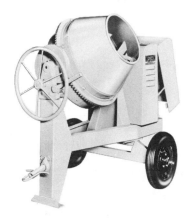

FIGURE 10-3: *Portable concrete mixer (Courtesy, Western Equipment Ltd.).*

FIGURE 10-4: *Stationary concrete mixer (Courtesy, London Concrete Machinery Co.).*

FIGURE 10-5: *Transit-mix truck (Courtesy, London Concrete Machinery Co.).*

FIGURE 10-6: *Concrete power buggy.*

FIGURE 10-7: *Concrete hand float (Courtesy, Portland Cement Association).*

FIGURE 10-8: *Concrete power trowel (Courtesy, Master Builders Co.).*

SOIL BREAKING AND COMPACTION EQUIPMENT

At some sites, it may be necessary to break up the surface to facilitate excavation and this may be done by the use of a *jack hammer,* illustrated in Fig. 10-9. A *rammer* (see Fig. 10-10) may be used to compact backfill and a *vibro-compactor* to compact a subgrade (see Fig. 10-11). Vibratory rollers may be used to compact and smooth earth and asphalt surfaces at the site (see Fig. 10-12).

FIGURE 10-9: *Jack hammer in use (Courtesy, Wacker Corp.).*

FIGURE 10-10: *Rammer compacting backfill (Courtesy, Wacker Corp.).*

FIGURE 10-11: *Vibro-compactor at work (Courtesy, Wacker Corp.).*

FIGURE 10-12: *Vibratory/static roller (Courtesy, Wacker Corp.).*

SCAFFOLDS

As construction progresses, *scaffolding* or *staging* is required to reach work areas which are beyond the normal reach of a workman standing on the ground. Scaffolding consists of elevated platforms, resting on rigid supports and strong and stiff enough to support workmen, tools and materials safely.

Scaffolding may be made of wood or metal, the wooden ones normally being made on the job, while metal scaffolds are manufactured articles, made in a variety of styles.

Pole Scaffolds

The most common wooden scaffolds are *pole scaffolds,* made in either *single-* or *double-pole* style and *half-horse* scaffolds. Double-pole scaffolds have two legs per section (see Fig. 10-13), while the single-pole scaffold has but one. In both cases, 38 × 140 mm minimum *ledgers* support the platform, usually made up of two or more planks, at least 235 mm wide. 19 × 140 mm angle braces and a ribbon under the ledger join scaffold sections together. Figure 10-13 gives recommended minimum sizes of materials used in the construction of such scaffolds. The horizontal distance between scaffold sections should not exceed 3 m and the maximum height for such scaffolds should be limited to 6 m. Bearing pads should always be placed under the bottom ends of the poles, in order to obtain maximum stability, and double-pole scaffolds should be tied to the building at intervals for greater safety.

272

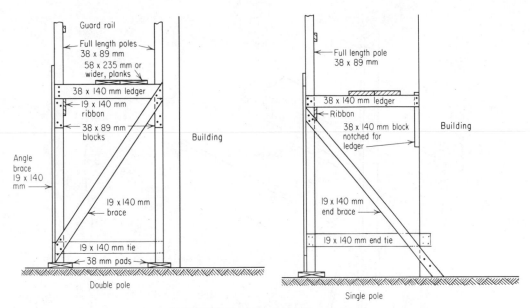

FIGURE 10-13: *Wooden pole scaffolds.*

Pole scaffolds are divided into *light trade* scaffolds, for carpenters, painters, plasterers, etc., and *heavy trades* scaffolds, for bricklayers, stone masons and concrete block workers. The main differences between them lie in the size of the members used in their construction and the fact that a "heavy trades" scaffold must have a 19 × 184 mm *toeboard* nailed along the outer edges of the platform to prevent brick or other material from being pushed over the edge, endangering workmen below. Check the local building code or safety regulations for the specified sizes of members to be used in both types of scaffold.

Half-Horse Scaffold

A *half-horse* or *lean-to* scaffold is so called because the inner end of the ledger is supported by leaning against the wall. Figure 10-14 illustrates such a scaffold and gives the recommended sizes of the materials used in its construction, recommended height of the guardrail and the maximum recommended distance between horses. The illustration also indicates three dimensions: (*h*) the distance from the ground to the ledger; (*d*) the distance from the support legs to the wall; and (*s*) the spacing between the legs at the bottom. Recommendations for those dimensions are as follows:

When $h = 1800$ mm, $d = 1000$ mm,   and $s = 550$ mm
$h = 2400$ mm, $d = 1200$ mm,   and $s = 750$ mm
$h = 3000$ mm, $d = 1500$ mm,   and $s = 1000$ mm

Although it is restricted in its uses, a half-horse scaffold has an advantage, since it may rest against a finished portion of the wall while work above continues.

273

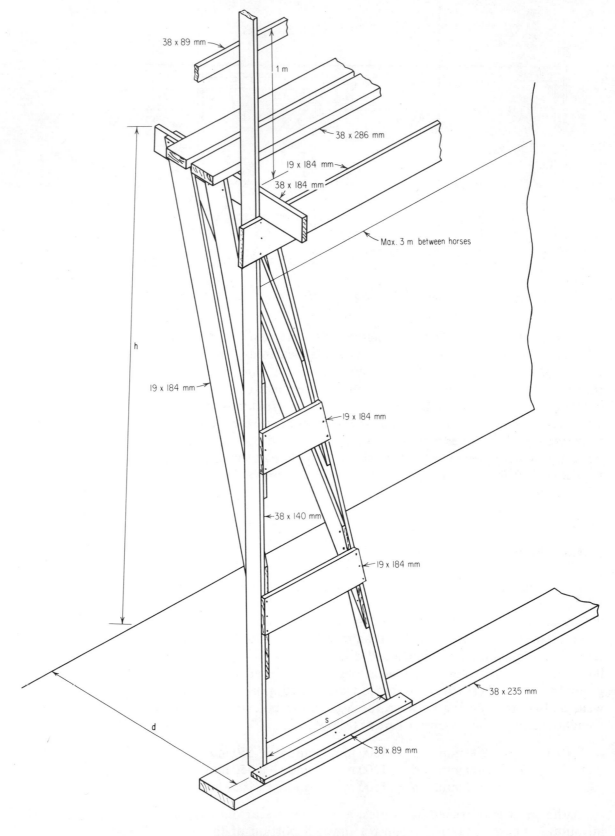

38 x 89 mm

1 m

38 x 286 mm

19 x 184 mm

38 x 184 mm

Max. 3 m between horses

h

19 x 184 mm

19 x 184 mm

38 x 140 mm

19 x 184 mm

38 x 235 mm

d

s

38 x 89 mm

FIGURE 10-14: *Half-horse scaffold.*

Metal Scaffolds

Several types of metal scaffolding are manufactured, two of the commonly used ones being *sectional* scaffolding and *tower* scaffolds.

Sectional Scaffolds

Sectional scaffolding is made up of tubular material in double-pole style, as illustrated in Fig. 10-15. A standard unit consists of two end frames and two crossed braces with holes at each end (see Fig. 10-15b). An end frame has threaded studs attached to the legs which fit into the holes in the brace ends. Braces are held in place by wing nuts so that the assembled unit appears as illustrated in Figure 10-15c. To increase the length of a scaffold, additional sets of end frames are added, using two additional crossed braces for each end frame used. To extend the height, one standard unit is mounted above another. Coupling pins (Fig. 10-15g) are inserted into the top of the tubular legs of the lower unit and the legs of additional end frames are slipped over the top half of the coupling. Additional crossed braces can be used horizontally on any unit to give it greater rigidity. By adding units as indicated, scaffolds of any length or height may be assembled (see Fig. 10-15d).

Non-skid metal planks, like that shown in Figure 10-15e, which span a standard unit, are available with this type of scaffold, or wooden planks may be used if desired.

Base plates (see Fig. 10-15j) fit into the bottom of frame legs to form the footing for a scaffold, the short one for level surfaces and the long one to compensate for uneven ground. Casters (see Fig. 10-15i), fitted with safety brakes, may be used in place of base plates on hard surfaces, when it is necessary to move the assembled scaffold from one position to another. *Screw jacks* (see Fig. 10-15h) are available for use with base plates or casters where floors are uneven or where a fine adjustment in height is required.

Steel scaffolding of this type is made with the utmost consideration for safety but of course care must be exercised in its erection and use. The following rules should be observed by erectors and workmen.

1. Provide sufficient sills or underpinning in addition to standard base plates on all scaffolds to be erected on fill or otherwise soft ground.

2. Compensate for unevenness of ground by using adjusting screws rather than blocking.

3. Be sure that all scaffolds are plumb and level at all times.

4. Anchor running scaffold to the wall approximately every 8.5 m of length and 6 m of height.

5. Adjust scaffold until braces fit into place with ease.

6. Use guard rails on all scaffolds, regardless of height.

7. Use ladders—not the cross braces—to climb scaffolds.

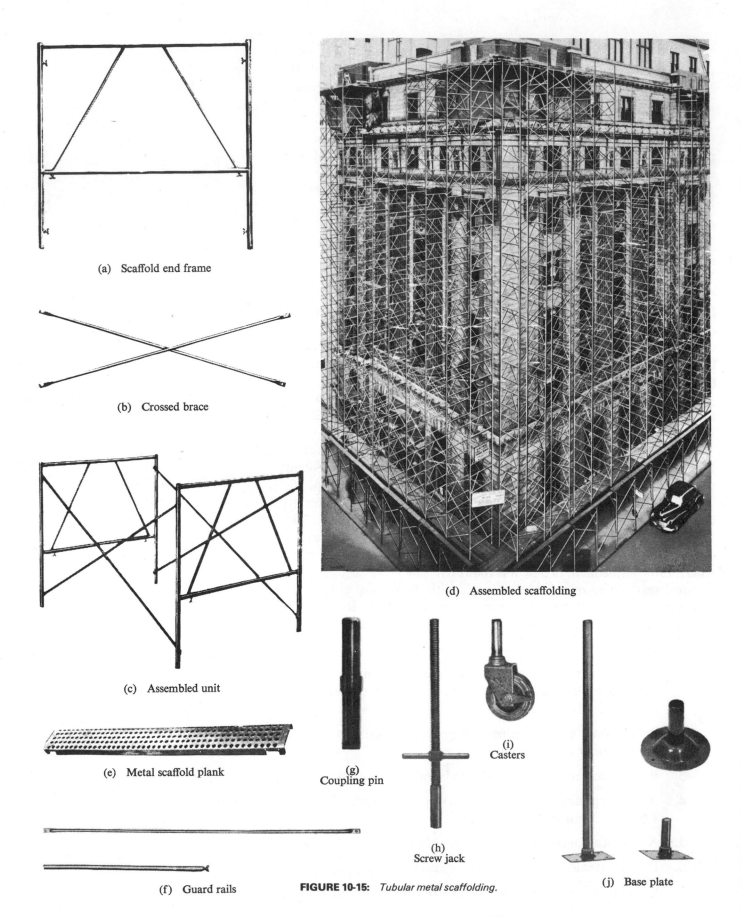

(a) Scaffold end frame

(b) Crossed brace

(c) Assembled unit

(d) Assembled scaffolding

(e) Metal scaffold plank

(f) Guard rails

(g) Coupling pin

(h) Screw jack

(i) Casters

(j) Base plate

FIGURE 10-15: *Tubular metal scaffolding.*

8. Tighten all bolts and wing nuts which are a part of the scaffold.

9. Use horizontal bracing to prevent racking of the structure.

10. All wood planking used on a scaffold should be of sound quality, straight grained, and free from knots.

11. When using steel planks, always fill the space because steel planks tend to skid sideways easily.

12. Handle all rolling scaffolds with additional care.

13. Do not extend adjusting screws to full extent.

14. Horizontal bracing should be used at the bottom, the top, and at intermediate levels of 6 m.

In addition to its many conventional uses, sectional scaffolding may be used as temporary *shoring* or support for various parts of a building under construction, as illustrated in Fig. 10-16.

FIGURE 10-16: *Sectional scaffolding used as shoring.*

Tower Scaffold

Another commonly used type of metal scaffolding is the *tower* scaffold, shown in Fig. 10-17. A standard unit is made up of a pair of metal towers, tied together with both horizontal—*stringer*—braces and crossed braces (see Fig. 10-17). Pairs of towers are then tied together with stringer braces to form a continuous scaffold of any desired length. Each tower supports a *carriage,* on which rests a workman's plank platform or, in the case of scaffolding intended for use by masons, two platforms, one for the tradesmen and one for laborers and materials. A *winch* is attached to each tower to raise the platform to the required height.

The height of these scaffolds can be increased by adding sections to the ends of towers, thus producing scaffolds which will reach to any desired height.

The same rules of safety which apply to the erection and use of sectional scaffolding also apply to the use of tower scaffolds.

FIGURE 10-17: *Tower scaffold (Courtesy, Morgen Manufacturing Co.).*

FIGURE 10-18: *Swing stage scaffold.*

Swing Stage Scaffold

Swing stage scaffolds are platforms, complete with guardrail and toeboard, suspended from the roof of the building by a block-and-tackle system attached to each end. By this means, the men on the platform can adjust the height of the scaffold as required (see Fig. 10-18). Such scaffolds are intended for workmen using only light equipment, working high above the ground.

LADDERS

Several types of aluminum and wooden ladders are used on construction projects. They include *step ladders,* ranging in height from 1.2 to 6 m; *extension ladders,* in lengths up to about 18.25 m; *safety rolling ladders,* usually consisting of three or four steps mounted on rollers; and *single ladders,* usually available in lengths of from 2.4 to 8 m.

A sturdy, reliable single ladder may be made on the job as follows:

1. Choose seasoned, straight-grained stock, preferably fir or Sitka spruce, which is free from knots and other defects which would impair the strength. For ladders up to 4.8 m in length, 38 × 89 mm stock is used; for ladders over that length, 38 × 140 mm material should be used.

2. Taper rails for shorter ladders from 85 mm at the bottom to 65 mm at the top and the larger ones from 140 mm at the bottom to 100 mm at the top. Dress all four sides and bullnose the edges.

3. Cut notches for the cleats on the top edges, 19 mm deep, 75 mm wide for the shorter ladder and 100 mm wide for the longer one (see Fig. 10-19a). Notches must not be more than 300 mm o.c.

4. Cut a cleat not less than 500 mm long for the bottom step. Cleats may be made successively shorter up the ladder so that the top is not more than 100 mm narrower than the base. Dress the cleats on all four sides and bullnose the top edges. Be sure that each cleat fits snugly into its notches.

5. Nail the cleats into place with two nails in each end (see Fig. 10-19b).

Ladders may be reinforced by running a heavy galvanized wire in a groove along the underside of each side rail. The ends must be securely anchored by bringing them over the ends of the rails and providing suitable anchorage on the top edges of the rails (see Fig. 10-19c). Further reinforcement can be provided by running a 6 mm rod with threaded ends behind each cleat through the side rails. Put a washer and nut on each end and tighten them down snugly (see Fig. 10-19d).

278

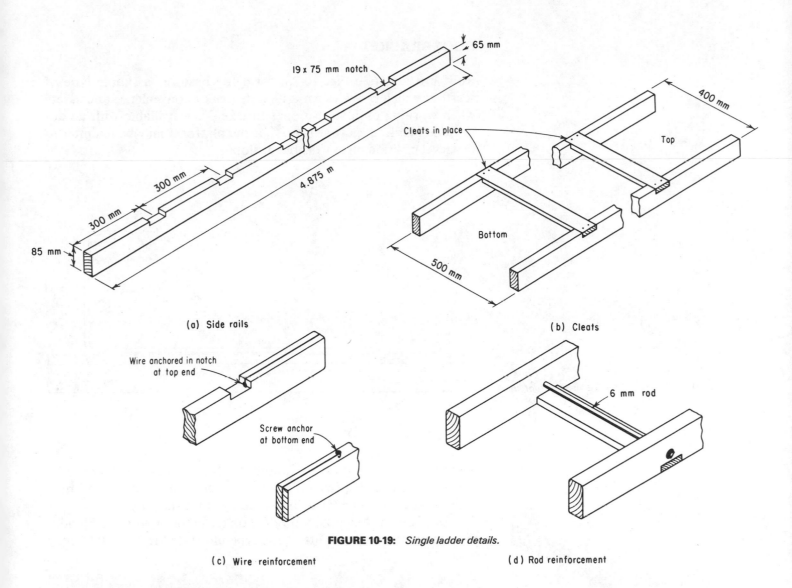

FIGURE 10-19: *Single ladder details.*

(a) Side rails

(b) Cleats

(c) Wire reinforcement

(d) Rod reinforcement

Safety Rules for Ladders

1. Always check a ladder for defects before use.

2. In use, place the ladder so that the distance from its bottom end to the wall is at least one quarter the length of the ladder, unless the top end is secured.

3. Single and extension ladders should extend at least 1 m above the landing against which the top end rests.

4. Check to see that both rails rest on solid, level footing.

5. Equip the bottom ends of the rails with *safety shoes,* if the ladder is to be used on hard surfaces that may allow it to slip.

6. Lubricate locks and pulleys on extension ladders, keep fittings tight and replace worn rope.

7. Do not allow paint, oil or grease to accumulate on ladder rungs or rails.

279

ROOF BRACKET

Roof brackets (see Fig. 10-20) form the base for a simple type of scaffold which provides for a high degree of convenience and safety when working on a steep slope. Brackets are available with an adjustable plank support arm, so that the platform may be maintained in a level position on any degree of slope.

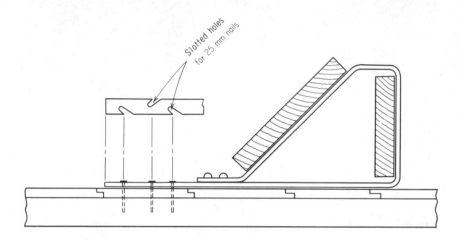

FIGURE 10-20: *Roof bracket.*

MATERIALS HOIST

Some type of equipment is required to lift materials which are to be applied to a building from a scaffold or used on the roof and normally, a *hoist* of some sort will be employed for the purpose.

For relatively low lifts, a *fork lift* on a tractor or front-end loader may be satisfactory or a lift of the type illustrated in Fig. 10-21 may

(a)

(b)

(c)

FIGURE 10-21: *Materials lift (Courtesy, Vermette Machine Co. Inc.).*

FIGURE 10-22: *Elevator-type materials hoist.*

be used. Such a hoist will lift about 225 kg to a height of about 6 m. For greater heights, an *elevator-type materials lift* (see Fig. 10-22), a mobile crane or a tower crane may be necessary.

Approximate imperial equivalents to metric quantities

6 mm	—	¼ in.	1500 mm	—	5 ft	19 × 140 mm	—	1 × 6 in.
19 mm	—	¾ in.	18000 mm	—	6 ft	19 × 184 mm	—	1 × 8 in.
65 mm	—	2½ in.	2400 mm	—	8 ft	38 × 89 mm	—	2 × 4 in.
85 mm	—	3½ in.	3000 mm	—	10 ft	38 × 140 mm	—	2 × 6 in.
550 mm	—	21 in.	2.4 m	—	8 ft	38 × 184 mm	—	2 × 8 in.
750 mm	—	30 in.	6 m	—	20 ft	38 × 235 mm	—	2 × 10 in.
1000 mm	—	3.25 ft	8 m	—	26 ft	38 × 286 mm	—	2 × 12 in.
1200 mm	—	4 ft	18.25 m	—	60 ft		
			225 kg	—	500 lb		

REVIEW QUESTIONS

10-1. Explain the basic difference between a double-pole and a single-pole scaffold.

10-2. **(a)** Name three groups of workmen for whom "light trade" scaffolds are made.

(b) Name three groups for whom "heavy trade" scaffolds are made.

10-3. Carefully draw a diagram of a double-pole scaffold and name each part.

10-4. What is the purpose of a "life line" on a swing stage scaffold?

10-5. What species of lumber, from the standpoint of weight, is best for making ladders?

10-6. (a) What size material should be used for ladders not over 4.875 m length?

(b) What is the accepted taper in the rails of ladders over 4.875 m in length?

(c) What is the maximum spacing of cleats in a ladder?

(d) What is the minimum distance that the bottom end of a free-standing ladder should be from the wall against which it rests?

(e) By how much should a portable ladder project above a landing?

10-7. List three advantages of metal scaffolding over wooden scaffolding.

10-8. Explain why two platforms are often used on scaffolds being used by bricklayers or stone masons.

11

EXTERIOR FINISHING

ORDER OF OPERATIONS

Once the frame of the building has been completed, the next step is to apply the exterior finish. This involves installing window and door frames and outside casings, roofing, exterior paper, cornice work, and the application of whatever is to be used to cover the exterior.

The usual order in which these operations are carried out is as follows: (1) cornice work, (2) roofing, (3) fitting of door and window frames, (4) application of exterior paper, (5) application of exterior finish.

CORNICE WORK

The *cornice* or eave, is formed by the overhang of the rafters and may be *open* or *boxed*. In either case, the work of finishing the eave should be done as soon as the rafters are in place.

Open Eaves

With open eaves, the rafter tails and the underside of the roof sheathing are exposed from below and consequently, the roof sheathing over that section of the roof may be replaced by a better quality of material.

In addition, it is necessary to block off the openings between the rafters above the cap plate and this is done by the use of *windblocks*. These are pieces of 38 mm material with their top edge beveled to the slope of the roof, cut to fit snugly between each pair of rafters (see Fig. 11-1).

With this type of eave, a single fascia may be used over the ends of the rafter tails, as shown in Fig. 11-1.

Boxed Eaves

With boxed eaves, the underside of the roof overhang is enclosed. This may be done by applying a *soffit* to the bottom edge of the rafter tails, as illustrated in Fig. 11-2. In such a case, the *rough fascia,* which supports the outer edge of the soffit between rafters, has both top and bottom edges beveled to the slope of the roof.

An alternative method is to build a frame to which a horizontal soffit may be attached to enclose the eave (see Fig. 11-3). Such a frame is made up of a *lookout ledger,* nailed to the wall, a *rough fascia* over the ends of the rafter tails and *lookouts,* which span between the two and lie alongside each rafter tail (see Fig. 11-3). It may be fabricated on the ground and raised into place as a unit. Proceed as follows:

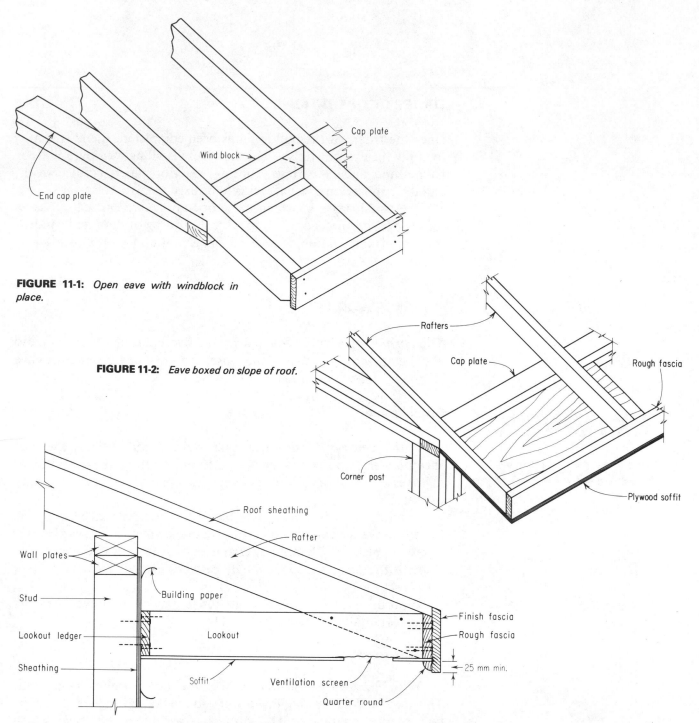

FIGURE 11-1: *Open eave with windblock in place.*

FIGURE 11-2: *Eave boxed on slope of roof.*

FIGURE 11-3: *Boxed eave frame.*

1. Cut the lookout ledger, rough fascia and lookouts to length, using either 19 or 38 × 89 mm material, according to the plan. The lookout ledger and rough fascia lengths will be the wall length plus twice the width of eave or gable overhang, while the lookout length will be the eave overhang less the thickness of the lookout ledger (see Fig. 11-4). Bevel the top edge of the rough fascia to the slope of the roof.

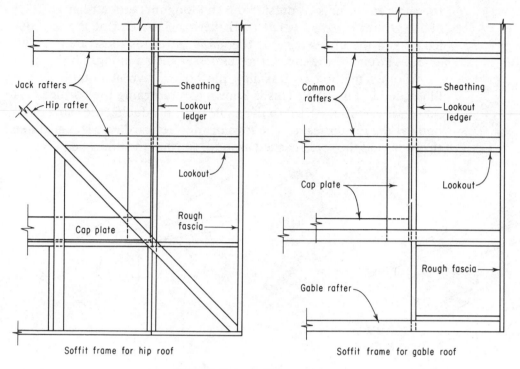

Jack rafters

Hip rafter

Sheathing

Lookout ledger

Lookout

Rough fascia

Cap plate

Soffit frame for hip roof

Common rafters

Sheathing

Lookout ledger

Cap plate

Lookout

Rough fascia

Gable rafter

Soffit frame for gable roof

FIGURE 11-4: *Soffit frame plans.*

2. Lay out the lookout ledger and the rough fascia for lookout positions. They must be offset from the rafter positions by the thickness of the rafter (see Fig. 11-4). In the case of a gable roof, keep the end lookouts back from the ends of the frame by the thickness of a rafter. Assemble the pieces on the ground to form a *soffit frame,* as illustrated in Fig. 11-4.

3. Staple one width of outside building paper along the top of the wall (see Fig. 11-3).

4. Level across from the bottom ends of the rafter tails to the wall at both ends of the building and snap a chalk line at that level. The bottom edge of the lookout ledger will fall on that line.

5. Raise the soffit frame into place, nail the lookout ledger to the wall studs, the rough fascia to the rafter ends and the outer ends of the lookouts to the side of the rafter tails.

6. Cut soffit material (usually 6 mm plywood) to cover the underside of the soffit frame and nail it in place with some type of rust-resistant nails.

7. After the roof sheathing is on, cut the finish fascia to size and shape, as illustrated in Fig. 11-3, and face nail it at rafter ends with long, rust-resistant nails.

In a hip roof building, the end wall soffit frames are made to fit snugly between those on the side walls. When a gable roof is involved,

285

the gable rafter tails fit outside the end lookouts and a filler piece of 38 × 89 mm material is cut to fit between the end of the lookout ledger and the under edge of the gable rafter, as illustrated in Fig. 11-5a. The end of the eave is then closed as shown in Fig. 11-5b.

Another method of finishing the boxed eave at a gable end is illustrated in Fig. 11-6. This is known as "returning the cornice." A set of rafter tails is nailed to the gable wall, producing the same overhang as the regular eave. The tops of the "returns" are shingled like the roof, and the soffit carried around, finishes the underside.

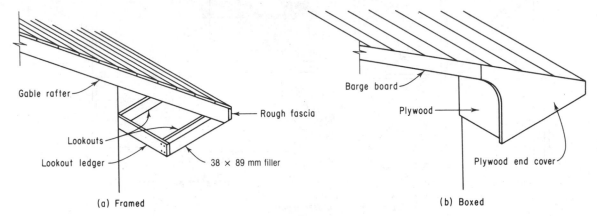

(a) Framed   (b) Boxed

FIGURE 11-5:   *Boxed eave with gable roof.*

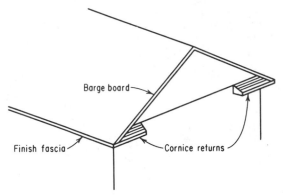

FIGURE 11-6:   *Cornice returns.*

FIGURE 11-7:   *Gable ends with no roof overhang.*

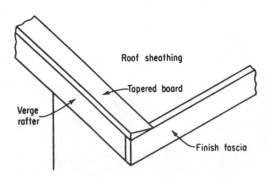

FIGURE 11-8:   *Anti-drip board on roof end.*

Some finishing work must also be done at the gable ends before the roofing is applied. If there is a gable overhang, its underside is lined with 6 mm plywood and *barge boards,* at least 25 mm narrower than the rafters, are used to cover the ends of the sheathing and to act as trim. Their lower ends should be mitred to meet the fascia.

If there is no gable overhang (see Fig. 11-7), *verge rafters,* 50 mm wider than the regular ones, should be nailed to the gable wall, covering the ends of the roof sheathing. A narrow mold may then be added, flush with the top edge of the verge rafters. Finally, a tapered board about 100 mm wide is nailed along the ends of the roof, with its wide edge flush with the outside surface (see Fig. 11-8). This arrangement helps to direct rain water away from the ends of the roof.

Also before the roofing is applied, provision must be made at the lower edges of the roof for the proper direction of rainwater into the eavestrough. One method of doing this is to fasten a sheet metal watershed, like that illustrated in Fig. 11-9, to the edge of the roof, under the roofing. Other methods of providing a watershed are described in subsequent paragraphs.

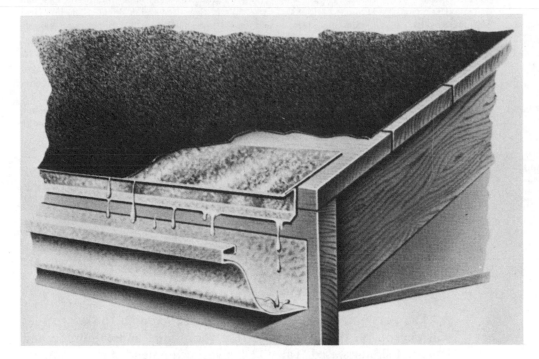

FIGURE 11-9: *Sheet metal watershed for eave.*

ROOFING

The most common type of roofing used on sloping roofs is shingles of one sort or another. These include wood (usually cedar), asphalt, cement-asbestos, and aluminum. Rolled roofing, roofing tile, and sheet metal roofing are also used on sloping roofs. Roofing tile is commonly made from clay, concrete, or cement-asbestos. In recent years plastics have been used for roofing, particularly on roofs of unusual shape that do not lend themselves to the application of more conventional types of material. Builtup roofing is commonly used for flat or nearly flat roofs.

Wood Shingles

Wood shingles are commonly made from cedar, because it changes very little with atmospheric changes and withstands weathering better than most woods.

Cedar shingles are made in a number of grades, both edge and flat grain, as indicated in Table 11-1.

TABLE 11-1: *Western red cedar shingle grades*

Grade	Length	Thickness (at butt)	No. of courses per bundle	Description
No. 1 Blue Label	400 mm (Fivex) 450 mm (Perfections) 600 mm (Royals)	10 mm 11 mm 13 mm	20/20 18/18 13/14	The premium grade of shingles for roofs and side-walls. These top-grade shingles are 100% heart-wood, 100% clear and 100% edge-grain.
No. 2 Red Label	400 mm (Fivex) 450 mm (Perfections) 600 mm (Royals)	10 mm 11 mm 13 mm	20/20 18/18 13/14	A good grade for many applications. Not less than 250 mm clear on 400 mm shingles, 280 mm clear on 450 mm shingles and 400 mm clear on 600 mm shingles. Flat grain and limited sapwood are permitted in this grade. Reduced weather exposures recommended.
No. 3 Black Label	400 mm (Fivex) 450 mm (Perfections) 600 mm (Royals)	10 mm 11 mm 13 mm	20/20 18/18 13/14	A utility grade for economy applications and secondary buildings. Not less than 150 mm clear on 400 mm and 450 mm shingles. 250 mm clear on 600 mm shingles. Reduced weather exposures recommended.
No. 4 Under-coursing	400 mm (Fivex) 450 mm (Perfections)	10 mm 11 mm	14/14 or 20/20 14/14 or 18/18	A utility grade for undercoursing or double-coursed sidewall applications or for interior accent walls.
No. 1 or No. 2 Rebutted-rejointed	400 mm (Fivex) 450 mm (Perfections) 600 mm (Royals)	10 mm 11 mm 13 mm	33/33 28/28 13/14	Same specifications as above but machine trimmed for exactly parallel edges with butts sawn at precise right angles. Used for sidewall application where tightly fitting joints between shingles are desired. Also available with smooth sanded face.

(Courtesy Council of Forest Industries of B.C.)

The portion of shingle which should be exposed to the weather will depend on the steepness of the roof slope and the grade and length of shingles used. Table 11-2 gives recommended maximum exposure, depending on the rise.

TABLE 11-2: *Shingle exposure*

Rise of roof	Maximum exposure recommended for roofs								
	No. 1 Blue Label			No. 2 Red Lable			No. 3 Black Label		
65 to 80 mm	400 mm	450 mm	600 mm	400 mm	450 mm	600 mm	400 mm	450 mm	600 mm
80 mm and steeper	95 mm	105 mm	145 mm	90 mm	100 mm	140 mm	75 mm	90 mm	125 mm
	125 mm	140 mm	190 mm	100 mm	115 mm	165 mm	90 mm	100 mm	140 mm

(Courtesy Council of Forest Industries of B.C.)

The area of roof covered by one bundle of shingles will depend on the shingle exposure and Table 11-3 gives the approximate area covered by one bundle of shingles for various exposures.

TABLE 11-3: *Shingle coverage*

Approximate coverage in m² of one bundle based on the following weather exposures

Length and Thickness	90 mm	100 mm	115 mm	125 mm	140 mm	150 mm	165 mm	180 mm	190 mm	200 mm	215 mm	225 mm
400 mm × 10 mm	1.69	1.88	2.16	2.35*	2.63	2.82	3.10	3.38	3.57‡	3.76	4.04	4.23
450 mm × 11 mm	1.52	1.69	1.95	2.11	2.37*	2.54	2.79	3.04	3.21	3.38	2.64‡	3.81
600 mm × 13 mm	1.14	1.27	1.46	1.59	1.78	1.90	2.09	2.28	2.41*	2.54	2.73	2.85

NOTES: *Maximum exposure recommended for roofs.
†Maximum exposure for double-coursing No. 1 grade on sidewalls.
‡Maximum exposure recommended for single-coursing No. 1 and No. 2 grades on sidewalls.

Approximate coverage in m² of one bundle based on the following weather exposures

240 mm	250 mm	265 mm	280 mm	290 mm	305 mm	315 mm	330 mm	340 mm	355 mm	365 mm	380 mm	390 mm	405 mm
4.51	4.70	4.98	5.26	5.45	5.73†	—	—	—	—	—	—	—	—
4.06	4.23	4.48	4.74	4.90	5.16	5.33	5.58	5.75	6.00†	—	—	—	—
3.04	3.17	3.36	3.55	3.68‡	3.87	4.00	4.19	4.31	4.50	4.63	4.82	4.95	5.14‡

(Courtesy Council of Forest Industries of B.C.)

Decking for Cedar Shingles

Roof decking for wood shingles may be solid or spaced. If the deck is solid, it may be made of shiplap, common boards, or plywood. When plywood is used, it should be 7 mm in thickness when the rafters are 400 mm o.c. and 9 mm on rafters spaced 600 mm o.c..

Spaced sheathing is made up of 19 × 38, 64 or 89 mm boards, spaced on centers equal to the exposure of the shingles.

Paper for Cedar Shingles

Asphalt-impregnated paper should not be used under cedar shingles. It prevents the completed roof from "breathing," that is, from allowing the moisture vapor under the roof to escape. If paper is required, plain or asbestos paper is recommended.

Application of Wood Shingles

Shingles should extend beyond the finish fascia about 25 mm to provide sufficient water shed (see Fig. 11-10). Tack a narrow piece of board 25 mm thick lightly to the fascia as a guide.

The first course of shingles at the eave must be doubled, or, better still, made up of three layers. Lay the first row with shingles 6 mm apart, butts to the guide strip. Use *two nails only* for each shingle, regardless of its width; nails should be not more than 20 mm from the edge of the shingle. The second layer of the first course is laid directly over the first, shingles also spaced 6 mm apart. Be sure that a joint between shingles does not come closer than 38 mm to a joint in the

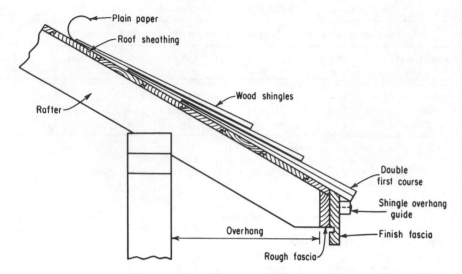

FIGURE 11-10: *Shingle overhang for watershed.*

layer below (see Fig. 11-11). If a third layer is used, it too must have joints offset 38 mm from those underneath.

The second and succeeding courses are laid, with the specified exposure, measured from the butts of the course below. A strip of lumber may be used as a straightedge against which to lay the shingles; a chalk line may also be used as a guide, or a shingling hatchet is sometimes used by expert shinglers to keep the shingles in a straight course (see section on shingling hatchets in Chapter 1). Nails should be placed 19 to 38 mm above the butt line of the next course.

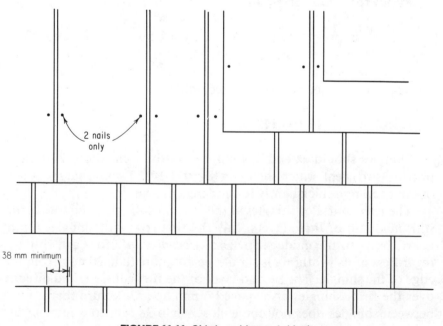

FIGURE 11-11: *Side lap with wood shingles.*

Shingling Ridges and Hips

When ridges and hips are being shingled, the so-called modified "Boston lap" is used for best results. Use edge grain shingles at least 25 mm wider than the exposure used and select them all the same width. For hips, cut the butts at an angle so that they will be parallel to the butt lines of the regular courses (see Fig. 11-12).

Run a chalk line up the roof on each side of the hip center line, at a distance from the center line equal to the exposure. Lay the first shingle to one of the chalk lines and bevel the top edge parallel to the plane of the adjacent roof surface. Now apply a shingle on the opposite side in the same way, beveling its top edge, as shown in Fig. 11-12. Place the nails so that they will be covered by the course above. The next pair of shingles is applied in *reverse order,* and each pair is alternated up the hip.

Ridges are done in much the same way. Start at the ends and work toward the center of the ridge, the last pair of shingles being cut to exposure length.

Shingling Valleys

Valleys have to be *flashed* before they are shingled. A strip of sheet metal—galvanized iron or aluminum—is laid in the valley, extending from 175 to 250 mm on each side of the valley center line, depending on the steepness of the rise. One long edge of each shingle has to be cut at an angle so that it is parallel to the valley center line (see Fig. 11-13). The shingles should be kept back at least 25 mm from the center line in order to leave the valley *open.*

Roof Flashing

Flashing has to be placed around chimneys, dormers or other structures projecting above the roof surface. Along the sides which are perpendicular to the shingle courses, individual flashings must be used, one for each course of shingles. Each is bent at a right angle, so that part of the flashing lies flat on the roof, on top of the shingle, while the other half rests against the side of the chimney or dormer, with the upper edge embedded in a mortar joint or covered by dormer finish.

The upper and lower sides are flashed and counter-flashed—one flashing running under the shingles and the other lying on top of them (see Fig. 11-14).

Chimney Saddle

In order to prevent water from collecting on the *up-roof* side of a chimney which projects through the roof, a *saddle* should be built behind it to shed the water. It should be the same width as the chimney, built like a miniature gable roof (see Fig. 11-15) with flashing at the chimney and in the valleys.

FIGURE 11-12: *Shingling a hip.*

FIGURE 11-13: *Shingling a valley.*

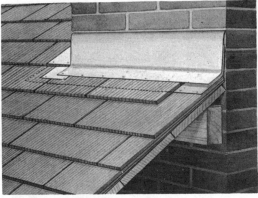

FIGURE 11-14: *Chimney flashing.*

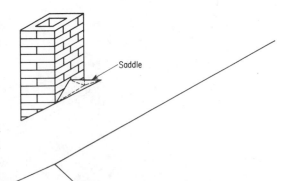

FIGURE 11-15: *Chimney saddle.*

Application of Asphalt Shingles

So-called "asphalt" shingles are made by impregnating heavy felt paper with hot asphalt and covering the upper surface with finely crushed, colored slate. Many types are available, one of the most common being what is known as a *triple-tab* shingle, actually three shingles in one (see Fig. 11-16). Many of these are made with extra thick butt edges to give a more pronounced shadow line.

Laying starts at the center of the roof, and a chalk line should be snapped down the center to act as a guide. Shingles should project beyond the eave to provide a watershed, and, to support the projection, a row of wood shingles must be laid first (see Fig. 11-17). Next, a row of asphalt shingles is laid, backward, on top of the wooden ones; this step is begun by butting two shingles together at the center line. Another layer is laid on top of the first, right way up, with the center of the shingle being laid to the center line. Succeeding courses should reach to the top end of the cutouts in the course below. Nail as specified by the manufacturer.

Individual shingles are used to cap hips and ridges. Fold the shingle over the ridge or hip and nail so that the nails will be covered by the succeeding shingle (see Fig. 11-18).

FIGURE 11-16: *Triple tab asphalt shingles.*

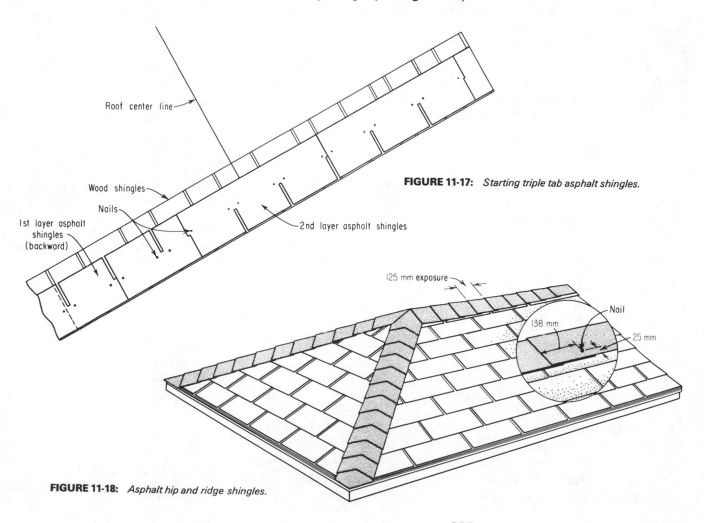

Roof center line

Wood shingles

Nails

1st layer asphalt shingles (backward)

2nd layer asphalt shingles

FIGURE 11-17: *Starting triple tab asphalt shingles.*

125 mm exposure

138 mm

Nail

25 mm

FIGURE 11-18: *Asphalt hip and ridge shingles.*

The final step in laying asphalt shingles is to fasten down the exposed flaps so that strong winds cannot lift and tear them off. This is done with asphalt roofing gum. Lift each shingle up and place a dab of gum under each corner. Press down, and the gum will hold the shingle firmly in place.

Asbestos-Cement Shingles

These rigid, long-lasting, fireproof shingles are made in strips to be applied in horizontal courses. Nail holes are located near the top edge of the shingle so that the following course will cover the nail heads. Care must be taken in nailing to ensure that the nail is tight enough to prevent the shingle from moving, but is not so tight that it will cause it to crack. Figure 11-19 illustrates the appearance of these shingles in place.

FIGURE 11-19: *Asbestos-cement shingles.*

Aluminum Shingles

Aluminum shingles are made in several styles, most of them of the individual, interlocking type. With some, laying is begun from the top, with others, from the bottom of the roof. A baked-on vinyl plastic coating is used on some brands to give a permanent, color-fast finish.

The underlay should consist of 0.75 kg/m² saturated felt, and in locations where there are extremes of climate, a vapor barrier paper should also be used under the shingles.

Most types of aluminum shingles are applied in a diagonal pattern so that the first course must be a half shingle. Edges interlock, and usually one nail is required for each shingle, in the upper corner (see Fig. 11-20). Complete instructions for cutting and applying are available from the various manufacturers. They may be applied over a new roof or over wood or asphalt shingles.

Applied to roofs with a unit rise of at least 65 mm, aluminum shingles will last indefinitely. The metal itself is extremely resistant to weather corrosion and the plastic finish is added protection.

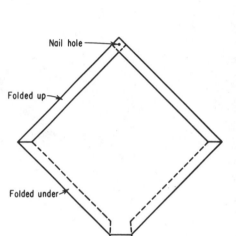

FIGURE 11-20:   *(a) Diagram of aluminum shingle (b) aluminum interlocking shingles in place.*

Builtup Roofing

A description of the application of builtup roofing has already been given in Chapter 8. It should be noted, however, that if there is to be traffic on the roof, preparation must be made for this during the application of the roofing.

While the liquid roofing is still hot, a walk base composed of two 38 × 89 mm pieces laid on the flat, 450 mm apart, is laid along the path intended for traffic. After the gravel has been applied, 19 mm slats are nailed to the base pieces to form a walk.

Rolled Roofing

Rolled roofing is made from very heavy felt paper impregnated with asphalt. One side is coated with finely crushed slate. This type of material is useful for sloped roofs of the more or less temporary variety, but is not recommended for permanent installation.

This roofing comes in rolls, usually 900 mm wide, and is applied horizontally. Start at one end and apply one width across the roof.

Allow the lower edge to fold over the fascia. Nail the top and bottom edges with broad-headed roofing nails, spaced about 150 mm apart. Then apply a band of liquid asphalt roofing gum about 75 mm wide along the top edge and lay the next strip, overlapping the first by at least 75 mm. Nail both edges as before, the lower one being bedded in the asphalt adhesive.

Work up to the ridge from both sides and place the last strip so that it is evenly folded over the ridge, overlapping the last strip on both sides. Any exposed nail heads should be coated with asphalt gum.

Roofing Tile

A number of types of tile are available as roof covering. They include several styles of clay tile, concrete tile, asbestos-cement tile, and slate.

Clay tile has been in use for a long time, and a number of styles or shapes have been developed. Among them are French, Spanish, mission, English, and shingle tile (see Fig. 11-21).

Concrete tile is a more recent product, and, for the most part, shapes resemble some of the clay tile shapes. The two most common are similar to the French and English styles (see Fig. 11-22).

Asbestos-cement roofing tiles are generally made in *corrugated* form, as illustrated in Fig. 11-23, in a standard width and in various lengths ranging from 1800 to 3600 mm.

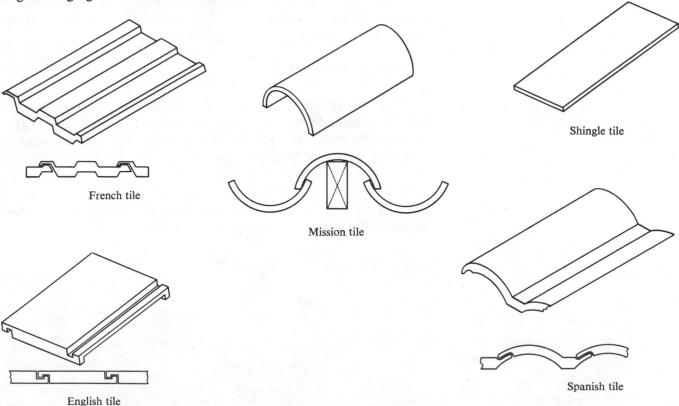

French tile

Mission tile

Shingle tile

English tile

Spanish tile

FIGURE 11-21: *Clay roofing tile.*

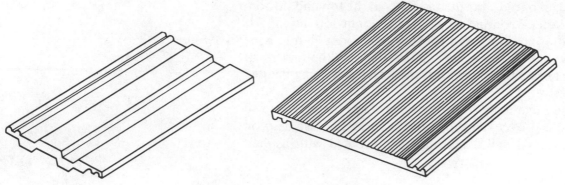

FIGURE 11-22: *Concrete roofing tile.*

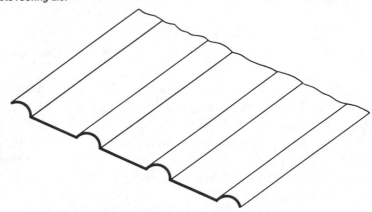

FIGURE 11-23: *Asbestos-cement tile.*

Slate tiles are made from thin slabs of slate, from 9 to 12 mm in thickness, in random widths, with a generally standard length of 600 mm. Holes for nails or wire are predrilled.

Roofing Tile Application

Clay tiles require a strong roof frame because of their weight. For this reason, 38 × 140 mm rafters are recommended, supported between the plate and ridge by purlin studs. In addition, mission tiles require 38 mm furring strips nailed to the roof sheathing and spaced so that a row of tile with the curve *down* can be laid between each pair. A row of tile with the curve up is then laid over each furring strip, lapping the tile on each side, as illustrated in Fig. 11-21. These tile are nailed to the furring strips with copper nails.

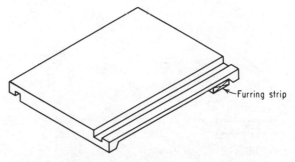

Furring strip

FIGURE 11-24: *English tile on furring strip.*

English tile and concrete tile require horizontal strips nailed to the sheathing. Each tile in a course is laid with the *lug* on the underside above a strip, as shown in Fig. 11-24. Heavy, asphalted felt paper should be laid under the tile and copper nails should be used to fasten them down.

Shingle tile and slate are laid like shingles over solid decking and anchored in place with copper nails through predrilled holes.

Tile edges at gable ends are covered by *rakes,* shaped as illustrated in Fig. 11-25a, while hips and ridges are capped with pieces shaped as shown in Fig. 11-25(b).

Tile are cut with an abrasive wheel mounted on a hand electric saw. Joints and cut edges must be caulked with mortar or an elastic cement.

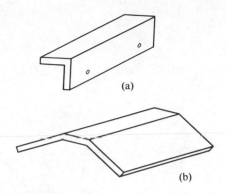

FIGURE 11-25: *Roofing tile accessories.*

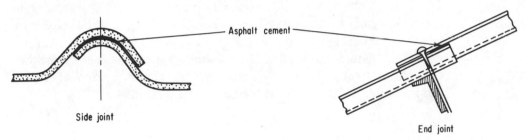

FIGURE 11-26: *Caulked side and end joints for asbestos-cement tile.*

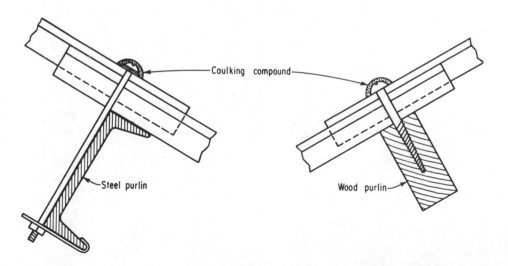

FIGURE 11-27: *Asbestos-cement tile fastened to wood or steel purlins.*

Asbestos-cement tile is laid in horizontal rows on properly spaced purlins. Side laps should be 75 mm or one corrugation, and end laps should be 150 mm. Both side and end laps should be caulked with asphalt cement, as illustrated in Fig. 11-26. The tile is held in place with bolts or screws. Holes for these must be drilled with a twist drill, and the head of the bolt must be covered with a daub of caulking compound (see Fig. 11-27).

WINDOWS

Windows form an important part of a building exterior and a great variety of styles and sizes are manufactured to suit every conceivable purpose. Basically, they consist of one or more panes of *glass* surrounded by a *sash,* which is set into a *frame.* The sash may be wood, aluminum, or steel and the frame also may be made of any one of these three materials, the most common one being wood.

Window Styles

Common window styles include *gliding* windows, in which the sash slide horizontally past one another (see Fig. 11-28) and *double hung,* in which the sash slide vertically (see Fig. 11-29). Another style is the *swinging* window, in which the sash are hinged at either top or bottom (see Fig. 11-30). If the sash swings inward, it is called a *hopper* type; if it swings outward it is an *awning* type. *Casement* windows have the sash hinged at the side (see Fig. 11-31) and in *fixed* windows, the sash does not move in the frame (see Fig. 11-32).

1. Frame
2. Head track
3. Sash

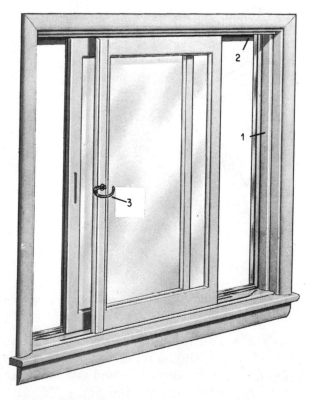

FIGURE 11-28: *Gliding window (Courtesy, Andersen Corp.).*

FIGURE 11-29: *Double hung windows.*

Many windows are made with no sash and consist of a single sheet of glass or two sheets sealed together, set directly into a window frame. The glass may be fixed or two single sheets may glide horizontally. When a large glass unit is fixed in a frame, it is commonly known as a *picture* window (see Fig. 11-33.) If the glass reaches from floor to ceiling, the result is a *window wall* (Fig. 11-34.)

FIGURE 11-30: *Swinging window (Courtesy, Andersen Corp.).*

FIGURE 11-31: *Casement windows (Courtesy, Pella Windows).*

FIGURE 11-32: *Fixed sash.*

FIGURE 11-33: *Picture windows (Courtesy, Pilkington Glass Ltd.).*

FIGURE 11-34: *Window wall (Courtesy, Libby-Owens-Ford).*

Window Manufacture

Modern windows are made in a factory—a millwork plant—and shipped to the construction site, either ready for assembly or, in most cases, already assembled and ready for installation in the openings. Windows with a wood frame will usually have the outside casing in place and be provided with braces or battens to keep them square.

Windows may be made with a variety of combinations of panes in a sash. For example, Figs. 11-35, 11-36, and 11-37 illustrate various combinations available in single and two-sash awning and casement window styles.

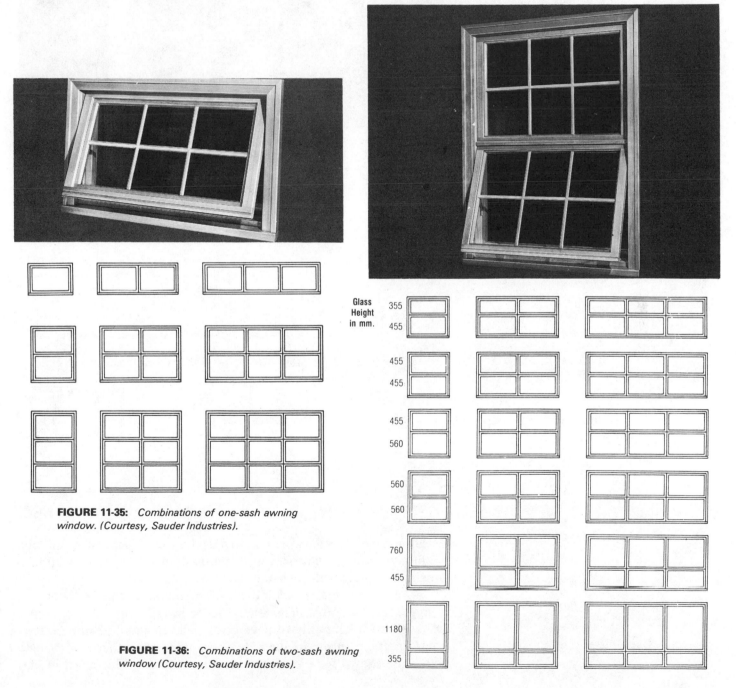

FIGURE 11-35: *Combinations of one-sash awning window. (Courtesy, Sauder Industries).*

Glass Height in mm.

355
455

455
455

455
560

560
560

760
455

1180
355

FIGURE 11-36: *Combinations of two-sash awning window (Courtesy, Sauder Industries).*

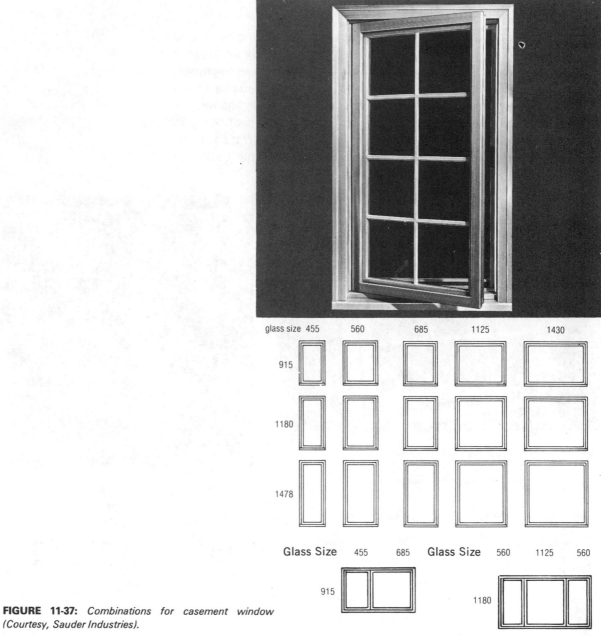

FIGURE 11-37: *Combinations for casement window (Courtesy, Sauder Industries).*

Window Details

Frames for the various window styles vary, depending on the manufacturer, the kind of sash being used and the type of wall into which the window will be installed.

For example, Fig. 11-38 indicates one manufacturer's details for a single, fixed wood sash, intended to be installed in a 38 × 89 mm stud wall, with 7 mm plywood exterior sheathing and 12 mm plasterboard interior finish. In Fig. 11-39, another manufacturer's frame details are shown for a casement window like that illustrated in Fig.

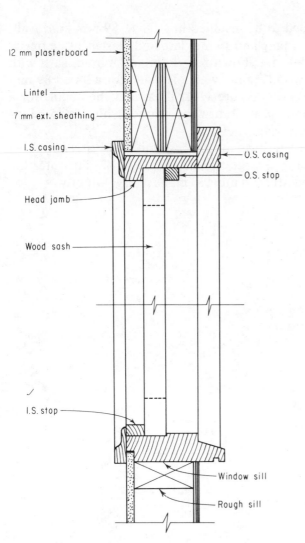

12 mm plasterboard

Lintel

7 mm ext. sheathing

I.S. casing

O.S. casing

O.S. stop

Head jamb

Wood sash

I.S. stop

Window sill

Rough sill

FIGURE 11-38: *Single fixed wood sash.*

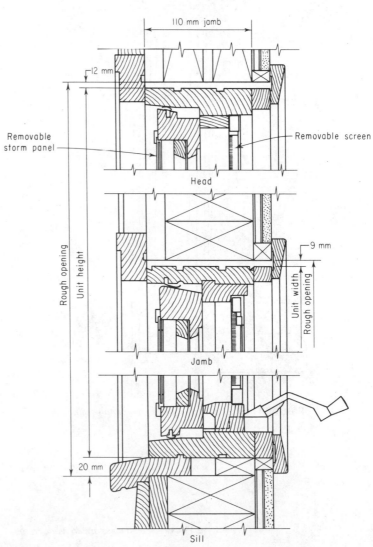

110 mm jamb

12 mm

Removable
storm panel

Removable screen

Head

9 mm

Rough opening

Unit height

Unit width

Rough opening

Jamb

20 mm

Sill

FIGURE 11-39: *Casement window details.*

303

11-37, which is intended to be installed in a 38 × 89 mm stud wall, with 9 mm exterior sheathing and 19 mm lath and plaster inside finish.

In Fig. 11-40, details are shown for gliding aluminum sash with sealed panes, set in a wood frame, which is made for a 38 × 89 mm stud wall with brick veneer. Figure 11-41 illustrates the details for a sealed glass unit without sash, in a wood frame, which is to be installed in a 150 mm brick wall.

Large, multipaned windows may be assembled by *stacking* sash made for this purpose in a large frame. Figure 11-42 illustrates the installation of a number of such units to make a large window.

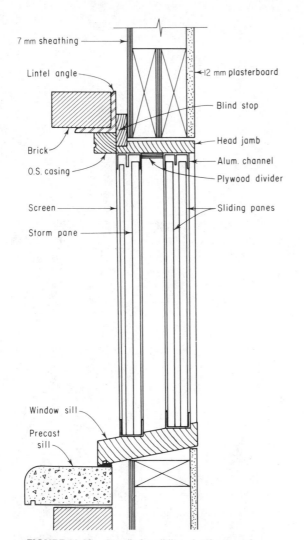

FIGURE 11-40:   *Details for gliding aluminum sash.*

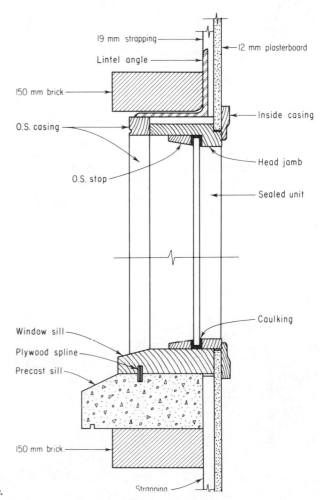

FIGURE 11-41:   *Sealed glass unit in wood frame.*

FIGURE 11-42: *Stacking window units (Courtesy, Andersen Corporation).*

Window Openings

The openings in the wall frame for the installation of windows must be large enough that the frame can be leveled and plumbed. It is therefore necessary to ascertain from the manufacturer either the size of rough opening that is required for the particular style, size and combination of window chosen, or the dimensions of the frame (see Fig. 11-43). If the frame dimensions are given, it is common practice to allow at least 12 mm *on each side* of the frame and 20 mm *above* the head for this purpose.

In residential construction, it is standard practice to frame the top of the rough opening so that the bottom of the header is 2030 mm above the finished floor. When that dimension is used, the height of window and door openings will normally be the same. The height of the bottom of the opening above the floor will depend on the location of the window. In a living room, for example, a common distance is 300 mm above the floor, while in a dining room, it will normally be 750 mm. Kitchen windows are usually over a counter and the standard height for the bottom of the opening for such windows is 1065 mm. In other rooms the height is optional and will depend on the size of windows to be used.

A window story pole may be used to help establish the height of the top and bottom of rough openings above the floor and is also

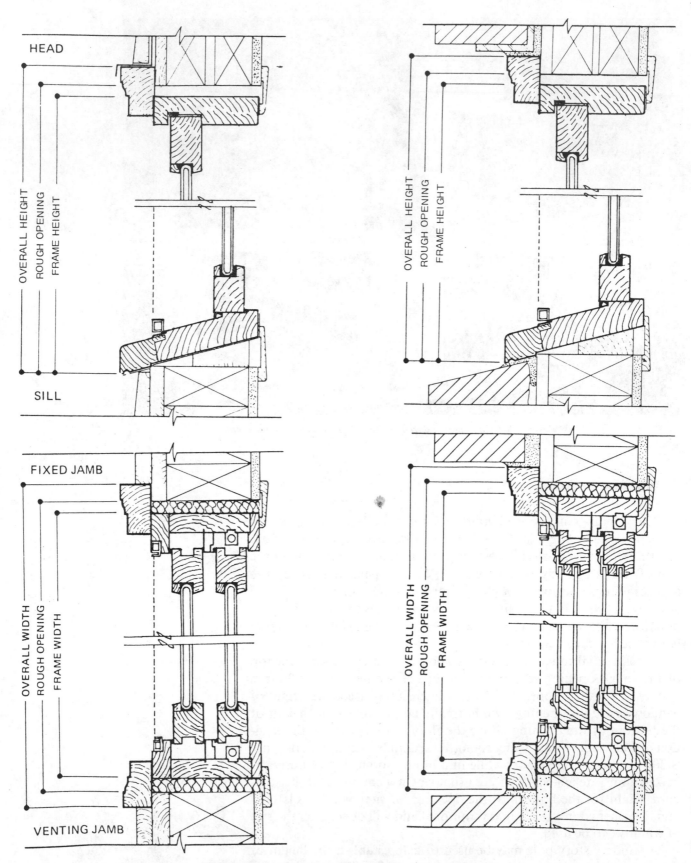

HEAD

OVERALL HEIGHT
ROUGH OPENING
FRAME HEIGHT

SILL

FIXED JAMB

OVERALL WIDTH
ROUGH OPENING
FRAME WIDTH

VENTING JAMB

OVERALL HEIGHT
ROUGH OPENING
FRAME HEIGHT

OVERALL WIDTH
ROUGH OPENING
FRAME WIDTH

FIGURE 11-43: *Window openings (Courtesy, Mason Windows).*

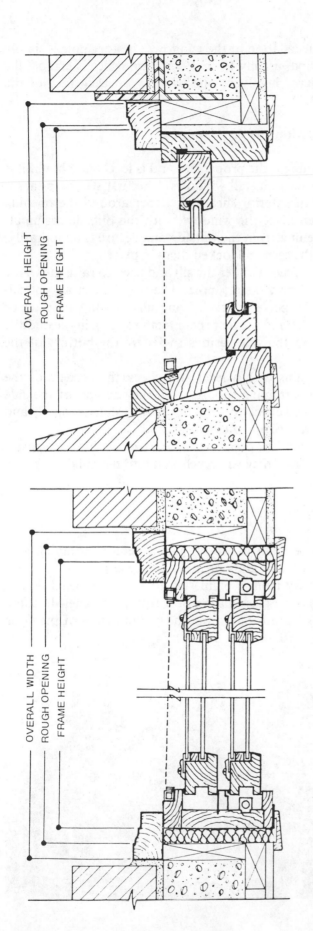

OVERALL HEIGHT
ROUGH OPENING
FRAME HEIGHT

OVERALL WIDTH
ROUGH OPENING
FRAME HEIGHT

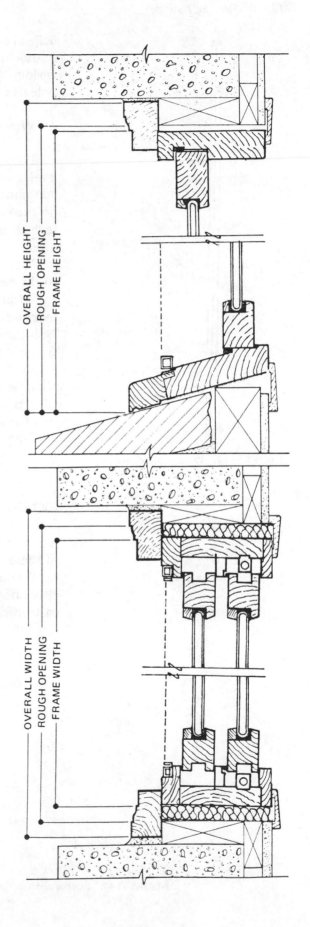

OVERALL HEIGHT
ROUGH OPENING
FRAME HEIGHT

OVERALL WIDTH
ROUGH OPENING
FRAME WIDTH

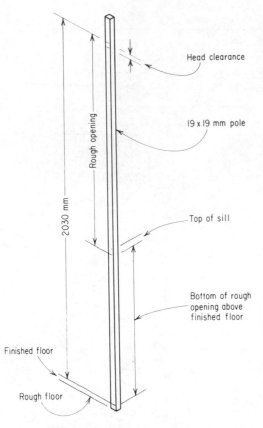

FIGURE 11-44: *Window storey pole.*

helpful during the installation of the windows. A story pole is simply a straight strip of wood, usually 19 × 19 mm, on which is laid out the various vertical heights involved, one window on each face of the pole (see Fig. 11-44).

Window Installation

If the rough opening is the proper size and is level and plumb, it is a relatively easy matter to install windows. The first step is to tack a 200 mm wide strip of exterior sheathing paper around the opening on the outside. Then place the window, with the outside casing attached, into the opening from the outside and secure it temporarily, after having closed the sash and locked them in place.

Wedge blocks are placed under the sill and used to raise the frame to the height marked on the story pole. The wedges can also be adjusted so that the sill is perfectly level. Long sills should have three or more wedges under them to prevent them from sagging in the middle. Nail the lower end of the side casings to secure the bottom of the frame in place.

Plumb the side jams with a level and check the corners of the window frame with a framing square. Nail the top end of the side casings temporarily and check to see that the sash slides properly and that the window hardware operates as it should.

Finally, nail the window permanently in place with noncorrosive nails, long enough so that they will reach well into the building frame.

EXTERIOR DOORS

Exterior doors may be made of wood, glass, metal or combinations of these, such as wood and glass or metal and glass.

Wooden doors vary from a plain slab to ornate paneled doors, either of which may have glass inserts or a full glass panel. In some cases, *sidelights* may be introduced on one or both sides of the door (see Fig. 11-45).

FIGURE 11-45: *Exterior door with sidelights.*

Wooden doors and their frames are made in a millwork plant and may come to the construction site as a complete unit, with the door hinged in the frame and the outside casing attached, or *knocked down,* with the frame pieces cut to size, ready for assembly and the door separate.

Glass doors are usually sliding doors, mounted in an aluminum track, top and bottom, and traveling on nylon rollers. They are frequently used in conjunction with a window wall, as illustrated in Fig. 11-46.

Metal doors are usually a plain slab, mounted in a steel frame, often with a wooden threshold.

FIGURE 11-46: *Sliding glass doors (Courtesy, Pella Windows).*

Door Sizes

A standard size for exterior wooden doors in residential construction is 810 mm wide by 2030 mm high by 45 mm thick, although they may be as large as 900 × 2130 × 45 mm. Common sizes between those two are 810 × 2080 × 45 mm and 860 × 2080 × 45 mm.

Door Frames

Outside door frames, like windows, consist of *heads, jambs,* and *sills.* The heads and jambs are made of 32 mm stock, with a 12 × 45 mm rabbet on the inside edge to receive the door. The sill, which may be made of hardwood for better wearing qualities, is 35 mm stock, with beveled edges and a 45 mm portion of the upper surface dressed flat to fit the bottom of the door.

The details of a given door frame may vary somewhat but in general the construction will be as indicated in Fig. 11-47.

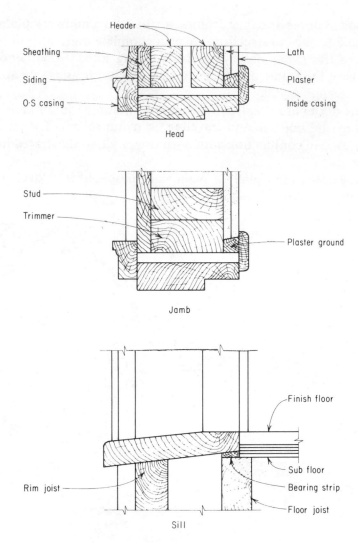

FIGURE 11-47: *Door frame details.*

Door Frame Installation

If the sole plate is still in place in the opening, it must first be cut out, flush with the trimmers. Then a section of the subfloor should be cut away and the top of the rim joist or header joist trimmed off (see Fig. 11-47) so that when it is in place, the top of the sill will be the correct distance above the rough floor—slightly more than the thickness of the finish floor. A beveled bearing strip is cut to support the inner edge of the sill (see Fig. 11-47) and leveled.

If a prehung unit is involved, remove the door from the frame and set it aside. Tack a strip of paper around the outside of the opening, as was done with the window, place the frame in the opening from the outside and secure it temporarily. Check the sill for levelness along its inner edge and shim the bearing strip if necessary. When it is level, nail the bottom ends of the side casings to secure it in place.

Insert wedges between the trimmers and the top end of the jambs and, using a straightedge and level, adjust them until the side jambs are plumb. Place additional wedges between the trimmers and the jambs in at least two more evenly spaced locations between the top and bottom of the jambs and adjust them until the jambs are perfectly straight. Secure the wedges by driving a nail through the jamb and wedge into the trimmer, as illustrated in Fig. 11-48. Wedge the head jamb in a similar manner if necessary, to make sure that it is straight and level. Finally, nail the casing in the same manner as the window casings and secure some type of cover over the sill to protect it during construction.

If a prehung unit is not being used, the *hinge gains* should be cut in one side jamb before the frame is assembled. Check to see whether the door is right- or left-hand (see Chapter 12 for hand of doors) and mark the position of the hinges on the *hinge jamb*. A common position for hinges in residential construction is 175 mm from the top of the door and 275 mm from the bottom, with the third hinge, when required, located midway between the other two. The hinge gain should be cut the exact length of the hinge leaf and normally 30 mm wide and 3 mm deep for 89 × 89 mm butt hinges (see Fig. 11-49).

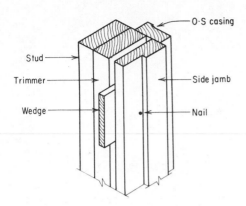

FIGURE 11-48: *Nailing side jamb wedge.*

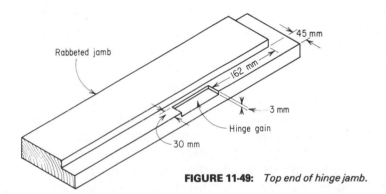

FIGURE 11-49: *Top end of hinge jamb.*

Exterior Door Installation

If a pre-hung unit is involved, rehang the door and check to see that it opens, closes, and locks properly. It may then be desirable to remove the door and replace it with some temporary closure until construction is complete.

If a door has not been installed in the frame, it should be hung at this time. The first step is to cut the door to length. There should be approximately 2 mm clearance between the top of the door and the head jamb and the door should be of such a length that it will fit snugly against the *threshold*—a trim unit used to seal the space between the bottom of the door and the door sill (see Fig. 11-50). Manufacturers provide detailed instructions for installing the threshold. If no threshold is used, the door should just clear the sill—not more than 1.5 mm clearance.

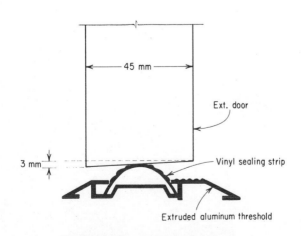

FIGURE 11-50: *Aluminum threshold.*

The door must now be dressed to width, using a jointer plane to keep the edges straight. There should be about 1.5 mm clearance between the door edges and the jambs and the lock edge should be beveled about 5 degrees toward the closing edge.

Set the door in the opening, block it in place at the correct height and mark on it the position of the hinge gains. Take the door down, lay out the hinge gains and cut them exactly the same size as those in the jamb. Separate the leaves of each hinge and install one half of each in the jamb gains and the other half on the door. Hang the door and check to see that it swings freely, opens and closes easily without binding or rubbing and will remain in any open position in which it is placed. (For complete details on cutting hinge gains and installing hinges, see Chapter 12).

Lock Installation

Locks for exterior doors are often more elaborate than interior locks and the installation instructions, contained in the package with the lock, should be followed carefully.

Open the door to any convenient ajar position and fix it there with a wedge placed between it and the floor. Measure up from the floor a distance of 900 mm (optional) and mark a horizontal line on both faces and across the edge of the door, which will be on a level with the center of the knob or thumb latch. Now, following the instructions and using the template provided, mark the centers of the holes required on the faces and edge of the door and drill holes of the proper size. Holes in the face of the door should be bored from both sides to prevent any splintering. In place of the template, a *boring jig* may be used to locate holes in the proper position. Drill holes in the jamb about 15 mm deep at the location of the mortise for the latch bolt and the dead bolt and square the holes out with a chisel.

Lay out the position of the rebates for the lock anchor plate and the striker plate, one on the edge of the door and the second on the jamb, over the mortise just completed and cut them out with a chisel. A *mortise marker* may be used to mark out the rebates. (For details on lock installation, see Chapter 12).

EXTERIOR PAPER

Building paper is applied to the exterior of a frame building for two reasons. One is to provide a moisture-proof barrier on the outside and the other is to give some extra insulation. Need for the latter will, of course, depend on the climate.

A moisture barrier paper is one which has been impregnated with asphalt and is reasonably hard and tough. A good insulating paper, on the other hand, must be soft and porous. This means that it will have little resistance to weathering. If both types are to be used, the insulating paper must be applied first and immediately covered with the asphalted paper.

Apply both horizontally, allowing at least 75 mm of lap. Be sure that the top edge of the last course is tucked under the paper hanging below the cornice. At door and window frames a good lap should be provided over the paper projecting from under the casings.

One point about which you must be particularly careful is that the asphalted paper you use is not also a vapor barrier. Some asphalted papers are also coated with wax to render them vapor proof. You *do not* want a vapor barrier on the outside of the building (see Chapter 12 on vapor barriers).

TYPES OF EXTERIOR WALL FINISH

A great many exterior finishes are used today, particularly for a wood frame. They include *stucco, cedar siding, shake and shingle siding, boards and battens, fiber board siding, aluminum siding, vertical plank, plywood, cement-asbestos siding, composition board siding, rolled siding, masonry finishes.*

Stucco: Stucco finish can be applied directly over a masonry wall, but when a sheathed wood frame is to be stuccoed, wire backing must be applied first. The wire should be of a type that has a relatively small mesh—about 50 mm is satisfactory—and is formed as illustrated in Fig. 11-51. When nailed in place, the main body of the wire stands away from the wall surface, allowing plaster to form all around it.

The wire should be stapled, with the curves to the wall, at least every 200 mm, and therefore the sheathing must be a solid material that will allow such nailing between studs.

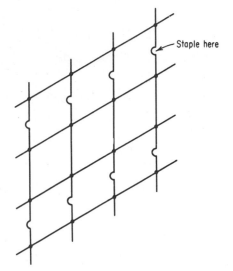

FIGURE 11-51: *Stucco wire.*

Cedar siding: A number of styles of cedar siding are manufactured, but probably the most popular is bungalow siding, available in 140, 184, 235, and 286 mm widths. Each course should overlap the one below from 25 to 38 mm, the exact lap and exposure depending on the width of board being used and the space to be covered.

Under the bottom edge of the first course, nail a beveled furring strip about 25 mm wide and the thickness of the siding at the point of overlap. This furring strip will allow the surface of the first course to have the same slope as that of succeeding courses (see Fig. 11-52).

There are three common methods of fitting bungalow siding at external corners. One is to miter the two meeting ends. Another is

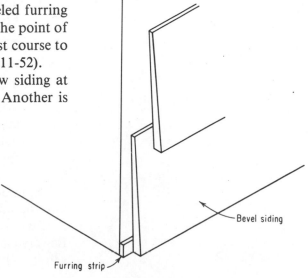

FIGURE 11-52: *Bevel siding in place.*

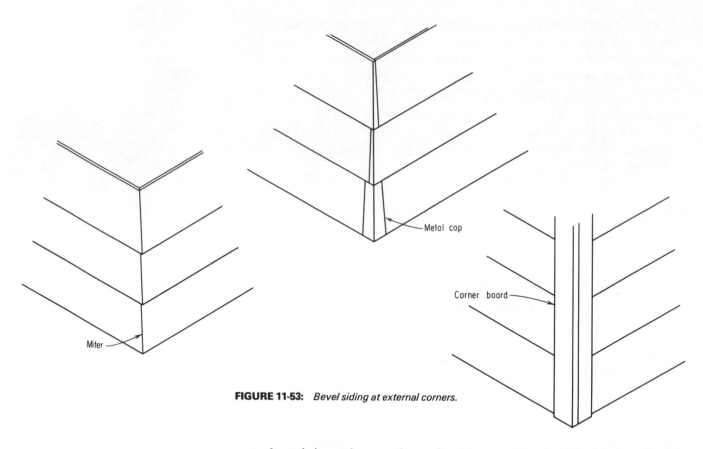

FIGURE 11-53: *Bevel siding at external corners.*

Metal cap

Corner board

Miter

to butt-join and cover the ends with a metal cap. The third method is to butt the siding ends against corner boards (see Fig. 11-53). To get a proper miter joint, proceed as follows:

1. Mark the length required to the corner of the wall on the bottom inside edge and square across the back at this point.

2. Lay off a 45 degree angle across the top and bottom edges from the ends of this line.

3. Join the outer ends of these angle lines across the face of the board.

4. Take off the slope so formed on a sliding T-bevel square and use it to mark all the mitered ends.

5. To make the remaining miter cuts, mark the length on the bottom inside edge, draw a 45 degree angle across the bottom edge, and from its outer end draw the angle with the sliding T-bevel across the face of the board. Cut carefully on both face and edge lines to get the proper miter angle.

At internal corners, nail a 25 × 25 mm strip into the corner and butt the siding ends to it from both sides.

Plan to have butt joints between boards in a course fall on a stud. Be very careful that the ends meet in a perfect joint. Use one 65 mm spiral nail per board at each stud, just above the lap. This sytem of nailing will allow seasonal contraction and expansion without interference. Do not drive the nails so hard as to crack the siding.

To get the proper exposure on each course, make a jig as illustrated in Fig. 11-54. The last course must be ripped to the exact width of the exposure.

Shake and shingle siding: Shakes and shingles are applied to sidewalls in either single or double course. They may be applied directly to walls with solid sheathing, but in other cases, furring strips must first be nailed to the wall, spaced the required amount of exposure (see Fig. 11-55).

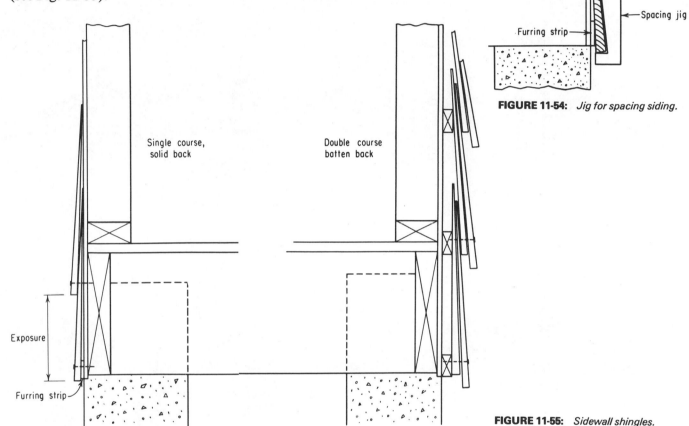

FIGURE 11-54: *Jig for spacing siding.*

FIGURE 11-55: *Sidewall shingles.*

Boards and battens: This is the name given to a type of finish in which square-edged boards are placed vertically on the wall, and the joints between them are covered with narrow strips about 64 mm wide called battens. Boards may be all the same width, two different widths placed alternately, or random widths. Cedar is the best material, either dressed or rough-sawn.

For this type of finish, nail in two rows of blocking, evenly spaced, between the top and bottom plates. Boards can then be nailed at four points. Allow approximately 3 mm between boards. Apply a coat of elastic caulking gum to the inner face of the battens before they are nailed over the joints.

Fiberboard siding: This type of siding is made from wood fiber, pressed into a hard, thin sheet, 6 mm thick and cut into strips 300, 400, and 600 mm wide, in lengths of 1.2, 2.4, and 3.6 m. It may be used as plain lap siding, with a wood strip under the lower edge of each course for a deeper shadow line, or with a special metal mounting strip which also accentuates the shadow line (see Fig. 11-56). With the latter method, a fiberboard starter strip is used at the bottom, and metal caps cover the external corners. Molded sheet-metal wedges are provided to set behind the butt joint of two strips. Full details on any of these methods of application are available from the manufacturer.

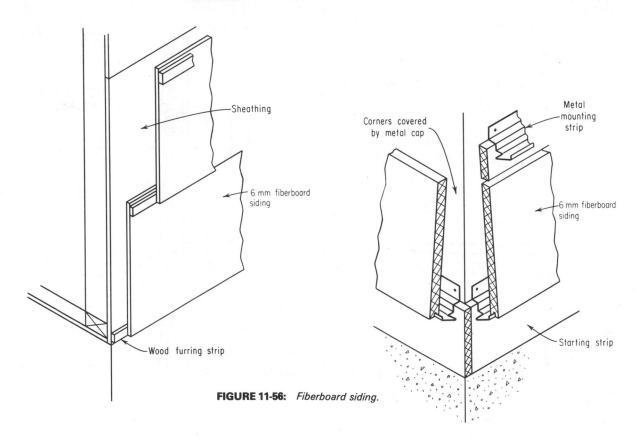

FIGURE 11-56: *Fiberboard siding.*

Aluminum siding: Aluminum siding is made in several forms, two common ones being those illustrated in Fig. 11-57. The type illustrated in Fig. 11-57a is applied from the top down. The top edge of each course is inserted into the fold in the bottom of the one above, and nails are driven through the lower edge. The siding illustrated in Fig. 11-57b is coated with a permanent, dimpled, enamel finish and provides insulation as well as weather protection and finish (see Fig. 11-58).

Vertical plank siding: This type of exterior finish is similar in style to boards and battens. However, the material has a nominal thickness of 50 mm, and, in addition, the planks have tongue-and-grooved

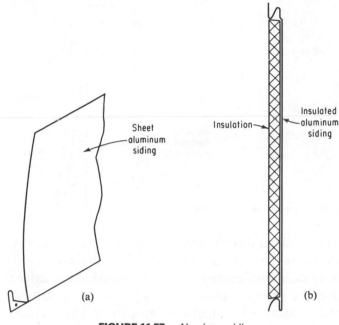

FIGURE 11-57: *Aluminum siding.*

FIGURE 11-58: *House sided with aluminum siding (Courtesy, Aluminum Co. of Canada).*

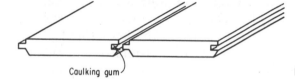

FIGURE 11-59: *Plank siding.*

edges so that battens are not required to cover the joints. It is a good plan to apply a light layer of caulking gum in each groove before the plank is nailed in place. This will insure a weathertight joint (see Fig. 11-59).

Plywood siding: Any exterior grade of plywood is suitable for siding purposes. It may be applied vertically in 1200 × 2400 mm sheets, with the joints covered by battens, or it may be cut in strips and applied horizontally like bevel siding. However, several types of plywood are made particularly for exterior finishing. These include one with a striated surface which is usually applied horizontally in 400 mm wide, overlapping strips, with the striations being vertical (see Fig. 11-60a). Another is made from 19 mm plywood with one surface coated with a smooth plastic coating. This type is applied in horizontal, overlapping strips 300 or 400 mm wide. The plastic coating provides a very smooth paint surface through which the grain of the wood will not show.

Asbestos-cement siding: Siding of this material is made in 300 × 600 mm siding shingles and in long strips—clapboards, 250, 300, or 400 mm wide. Both provide a weather-resistant, fire-resistant exterior that does not require paint, since color is introduced into the

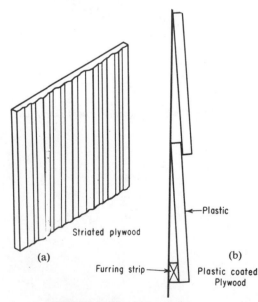

FIGURE 11-60: *Plywood siding.*

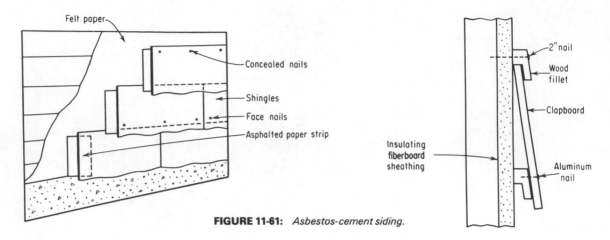

FIGURE 11-61: *Asbestos-cement siding.*

material. Figure 11-61 illustrates the application of each of the two styles. Care must be taken that the exposed nails are corrosion-resistant, preferably cadmium coated, and that the nails are driven firmly enough that the siding is held firmly against the sheathing. However, too much pressure on the nail will cause the siding to crack, since it is a stiff, brittle material. Asphalt-impregnated paper strips are required behind the end joints. These are usually supplied with the siding. Nail holes are predrilled, and the material must be cut with a shear rather than with a saw. The shingles are finished at external corners with alternating lap joints, whereas the clapboards may be mitered, butt-jointed and metal-covered, or butted to corner boards.

Composition board siding: "Composition board" refers to a type of material made from an insulating fiberboard covered with a heavy coating of asphalt. Finely crushed slate, embedded in the asphalt, is formed into patterns of brick, stone, and wood grain. The board is produced in pieces from 600 to 2400 mm long, 400 mm wide. It is applied in horizontal courses over solid sheathing (see Fig. 11-62). Cutting is done with a shear that must be kept clean with kerosene.

Rolled siding: Rolled siding is similar in appearance to composition board, but is produced on heavy paper rather than on rigid board. Consequently, it is packed in rolls—hence, the name "rolled" siding. Apply in horizontal courses over solid sheathing.

Masonry finishes: Masonry finishes which are commonly used over a wood frame include *brick* and *stone veneer* and *ceramic veneer*.

Brick veneering is done in two ways: (1) by facing a wall with a single wythe of brick, nominally 100 mm in thickness and (2) by facing it with a thin layer of brick material approximately 12 mm in thickness.

In the first case, a single wythe of brick is built up outside the sheathed framework; preferably, about 25 mm of space is left between the sheathing and the brick. The brick should rest on the concrete foundation, which must be extended beyond the floor frame to pro-

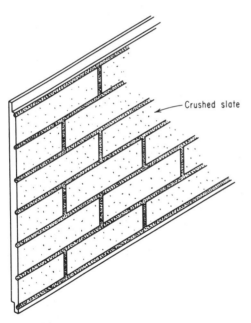

FIGURE 11-62: *Composition board siding (brick imitation).*

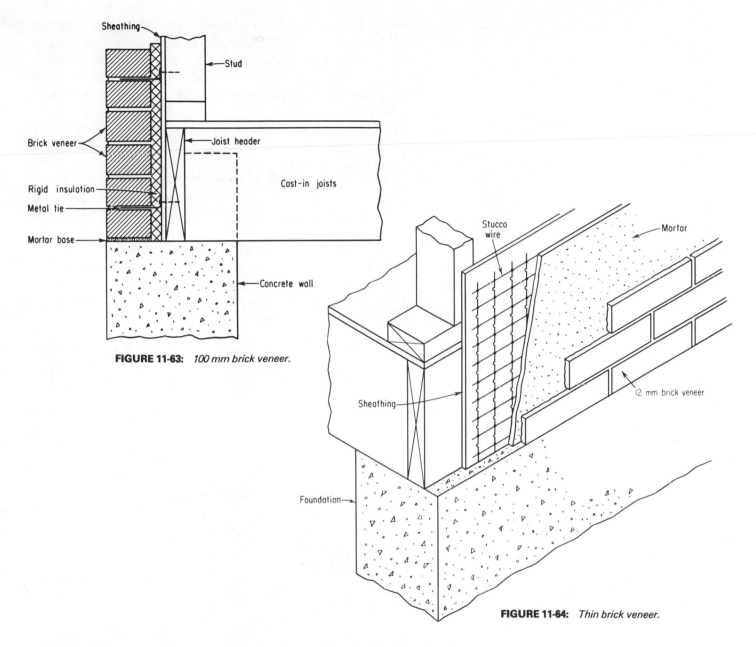

FIGURE 11-63: *100 mm brick veneer.*

FIGURE 11-64: *Thin brick veneer.*

vide a shelf from which to start the brick (see Fig. 11-63). The brick facing is held to the wall by metal ties which have one end nailed to the sheathing and the other laid in a mortar joint between two courses of brick. These should be spaced about 600 mm apart horizontally every six or seven courses. The space between sheathing and brick can be filled with a rigid type of insulation.

The second type of brick facing is set into a mortar base. The wall is prepared as if a stucco finish were to be used. A base coat of plaster is applied over stucco wire and allowed to harden. As the second coat is applied, the brick facing pieces are set into it in the same positions as regular brick would be (see Fig. 11-64) and the joints are dressed after the mortar has partially hardened.

Stone, like brick, can be used in two ways as a veneer over a wood frame. In one, stones, not over 100 mm in thickness, can be laid up in the same way as a single wythe of brick, carried on the concrete foundation and tied to the wall with metal ties. In the other, stone which is available in thin sections, usually not over 19 mm, notably *slate, galena,* or *argillite,* is laid in a mortar bed in the same way as the thin brick veneer is applied, except that the pattern will usually be random rubble.

Ceramic veneer is made from china clay in squares from 100 to 450 mm on a side, about 9 mm thick. The surface is coated with a baked enamel glaze which gives the material a glass-like appearance. Units may be fixed to the wall in a mortar base or they may be cemented to a solid surface with adhesive. In the latter case, the joints have to be filled with a joint cement after the ceramic veneer is in place.

Sometimes two materials are used together to finish an exterior. For example, siding may be used part way up the wall, and the remainder finished with stucco. In such a case it is necessary to use a *drip cap* to divide the two. Be sure that the drip cap is flashed (see Fig. 11-65) before the stucco wire is applied.

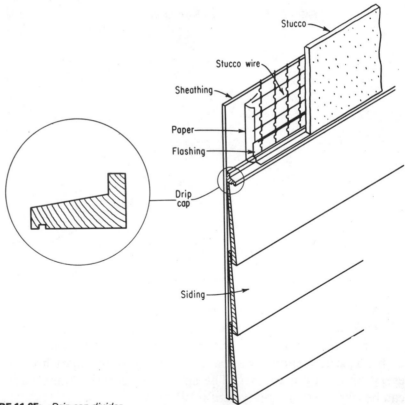

FIGURE 11-65: *Drip cap divider.*

Brick veneer or ceramic veneer and bungalow siding may be used together. In this case, one material will be used to finish all or part of one wall from top to bottom. The other material then is used either on the remainder of that wall or on an adjoining one. The two materials should meet at an external corner or at a vertical dividing piece of the same size as the outside casing (see Fig. 11-66).

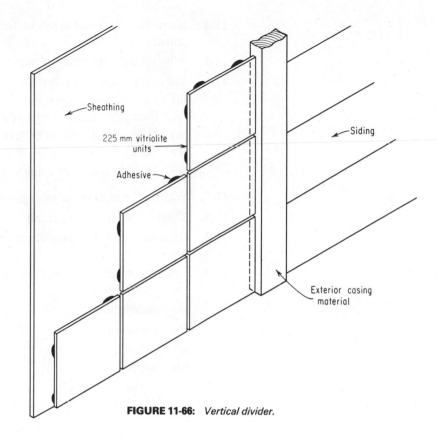

FIGURE 11-66: *Vertical divider.*

Approximate imperial equivalents to metric quantities

6 mm	— ¼ in.	45 mm	— 1¾ in.	810 mm	— 2 ft 8 in.
7 mm	— ⁵⁄₁₉ in.	64 mm	— 2½ in.	1065 mm	— 42 in.
9 mm	— ⅜ in.	89 mm	— 3½ in.	2030 mm	— 6 ft 8 in.
19 mm	— ¾ in.	400 mm	— 16 in.	1.2 m	— 4 ft
25 mm	— 1 in.	450 mm	— 18 in.	0.25 kg/m²—	5 lb/100 ft²
38 mm	— 1½ in.	900 mm	— 3 ft		

REVIEW QUESTIONS

11-1. List five building operations that may be classed under the general heading of "exterior finishing."

11-2. **(a)** What are "wind blocks"?

    (b) Under what circumstances are they used?

11-3. Where is each of the following located:

    (a) barge board?

    (b) verge rafter?

    (c) finish fascia?

11-4. Name five different types of roofing that may be applied to light construction roofs.

11-5. Why should vapor barrier paper not be used under wood shingles?

11-6. Fill in the blanks in each statement below:

(a) Joints in successive rows of cedar shingles should be not less than _____ mm apart.

(b) Each shingle should be fastened with _____ nails only.

(c) Standard exposure for 400 mm shingles is _____ mm.

(d) Proper spacing of shingles in a course is _____ mm.

11-7. What is the primary advantage of aluminum shingles?

11-8. What is meant by "triple tab" asphalt shingles?

11-9. By means of a diagram, illustrate how mission tile are placed on a roof.

11-10. Describe briefly the chief distinguishing characteristic of each of the following window styles:

(a) double hung;

(b) casement;

(c) awning;

(d) hopper.

11-11. What is the purpose of:

(a) wedges under the sill of an exterior door frame?

(b) a drip groove in a door sill?

(c) the door rabbet in the jamb?

11-12. (a) What should be the minimum overlap when applying bevel siding?

(b) What is the purpose of a furring strip under the first course bevel siding?

(c) List three ways of fitting bevel siding at outside corners.

11-13. Outline two advantages of asbestos-cement siding.

11-14. (a) What is meant by "brick veneer"?

(b) Name two types of brick veneer used in exterior finish.

(c) Explain how a brick course is tied to a wood sheathed wall.

(d) Outline two methods of applying ceramic veneer to an exterior wall.

12

INSULATION AND INTERIOR FINISHING

Upon completion of the exterior of the building, attention may then be given to the interior. This part of the job can be done at any time of the year, and it is wise to plan so that interior finishing can be done when the weather does not permit outside work.

First, arrangements must be made to have the wiring, plumbing, heating, and air-conditioning installed. This is necessary for two reasons. One is that a considerable portion of these services will be situated in the walls and partitions and above the ceiling, and the work must be done while the space is open. The other is that heat and power particularly may be required during the finishing operations.

INSULATION

Once these services have been installed, the next step is the placing of insulation in the outside walls and ceiling. Two distinct types of insulation are used, one to insulate against heat loss by conduction and convection, and the other to insulate against heat loss by radiation. For the former purpose, materials are used which contain large numbers of trapped air spaces and are themselves poor conductors of heat. For insulation against radiant heat losses, a material is required that has a smooth, shiny surface—a material which is, in fact, a reflector.

Modern insulators against conduction and convection are made in the form of batts, blankets, rigid slabs, or loose fill, whereas radiant insulators are usually aluminum or copper foil.

Batts are commonly used for insulating in framed walls. They are often made with one surface which is a vapor barrier and usually have flaps along the sides for easy attachment to studs (see Fig. 12-1). Two methods of attaching the batts are used (see Fig. 12-2). To make use of the vapor barrier surface, the flaps must be attached to the edges of studs. The inside finish, nailed over the flaps, seals them together to make the surface vapor-proof. However, if a gypsum board product is to be used on the inside, it is preferable to attach the batts to the sides of the studs. This method allows a tighter fit of the board against the studs, but in such a situation a vapor barrier must be used over the studs.

Batts may also be used between ceiling joists, but it is often more convenient to use loose fill for ceiling insulation. It must be placed after the ceiling has been installed.

Rigid insulation is best suited for application against flat surfaces, such as concrete or masonry walls or a roof deck. It can, however, be cut to fit between studs or applied over the studs, as described in Chapter 5.

Over concrete or masonry walls, rigid insulation is applied with

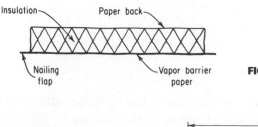

Insulation — Paper back

Nailing flap — Vapor barrier paper

FIGURE 12-1: *Batt insulation.*

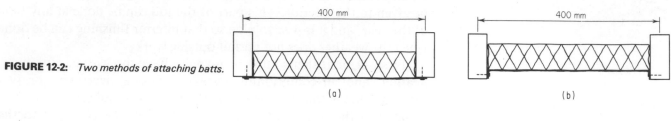

FIGURE 12-2: *Two methods of attaching batts.*

400 mm   400 mm

(a)   (b)

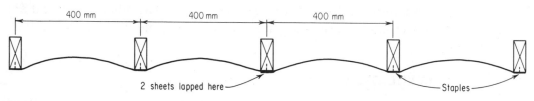

400 mm   400 mm   400 mm

2 sheets lapped here   Staples

FIGURE 12-3: *Reflective insulation draped between studs.*

an asphalt adhesive, while over a wood deck either adhesive, nails or staples may be used.

Reflective insulation is applied in vertical strips. The roll is usually 900 mm wide, so a strip will span two stud spaces. Do not stretch the foil tightly across the studs, but rather allow it to sag back between them. Lap the strips at studs so that the finish material will seal the two pieces together (see Fig. 12-3). Be sure that when insulation has to be cut to fit around electrical outlet boxes, etc., it fits snugly. Open spaces will allow heat to escape.

Vapor Barriers

A *vapor barrier* is an essential component of a building wherever there is a considerable difference between inside and outside temperature and where the inside air has a high moisture content. The moisture vapor, under relatively high pressure, tries to escape to the outside where pressure is lower. If the temperature *in* the wall is low, the vapor will condense there to form water or ice. If the insulation in the wall becomes damp as a result of this condensation, its effectiveness is reduced. In addition, trapped moisture may cause the wood frame to deteriorate.

Vapor barriers must be materials which are impervious to the passage of water vapor. Common ones are waxed paper, polyethylene film, aluminum and copper foil. The latter, properly used, may serve two purposes.

Vapor barriers, like reflective insulations, are applied in vertical strips, lapped on the edge of studs. No *draping* between studs is necessary. Great care must be taken to see that the cover is as complete as possible. Where openings do occur, the vapor barrier must be made to fit tightly around them.

324

INTERIOR WALLS FINISHES

In the past, *lath and plaster* was probably the most popular inside wall and ceiling finishing material. Today, *drywall* (gypsum board) finish is replacing lath and plaster to a large extent and, in addition, *plywood, hardboard, insulating fiberboard, plastic laminates, tile, masonry finishes, wall fabrics,* and *wall paper* finishes are common.

Lath and Plaster

In modern practice, gypsum or metal lath is used as a base for plaster, gypsum lath being commonly used over wood frame. However, before lath is applied, plaster grounds must be placed. These wooden grounds, 19 mm thick, are nailed along the bottom of the walls and around door openings. They act as a guide for the plasterer in getting the plaster straight and of even thickness. Along the wall, they also provide a base to which to nail baseboard. Window and door frames in outside walls act as grounds for those openings (see Fig. 12-4) and door frames in inside walls may be used for the same purpose. A metal molding may also be used as a ground around door and window openings when there is to be no inside casing (see Fig. 12-5).

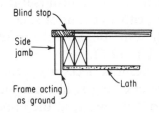

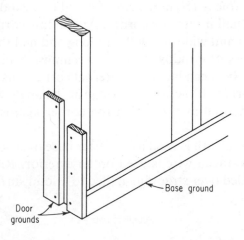

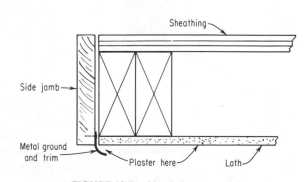

FIGURE 12-5: *Metal plaster ground.*

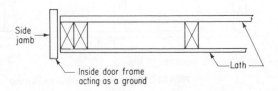

FIGURE 12-4: *Plaster grounds.*

325

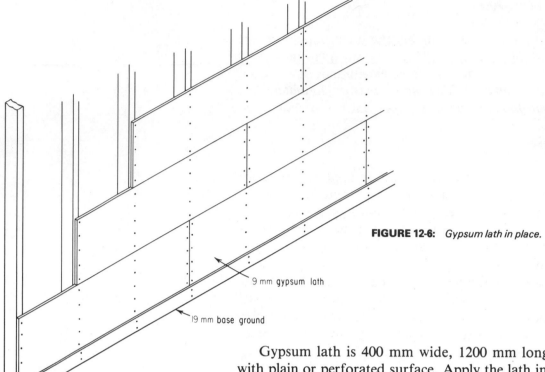

FIGURE 12-6: *Gypsum lath in place.*

9 mm gypsum lath

19 mm base ground

Gypsum lath is 400 mm wide, 1200 mm long, and 9 mm thick, with plain or perforated surface. Apply the lath in horizontal courses, staggering the joints in each succeeding course. It is not necessary to leave a space between them, either at ends or sides. Use 40 mm broad-headed nails, five to each stud. Be careful not to break the paper when driving the nails (see Fig. 12-6).

When lathing is complete, it is necessary to add metal lath reinforcement at points where cracking is likely to occur. These are at internal corners where two walls meet, at the upper corners of windows, and at any point where there is a wide gap between two laths. For the corners, fold a 150 mm strip of metal lath 2400 mm long to a right angle, and nail it into the corner. At window corners, cut strips of lath about 100 mm wide and 300 mm long and nail them diagonally across the corners of window or door openings. Nail strips of lath over wide spaces between laths. At external corners, use metal *corner bead* over the corner. It has a raised ridge at the angle which acts as a plaster ground as well as protecting the corner against damage (see Fig. 12-7).

Expanded metal lath is used as a plaster base over solid backing in the same way as stucco wire is used on an exterior. Ribbed lath (see Fig. 12-8) is applied over strapping nailed to a solid surface.

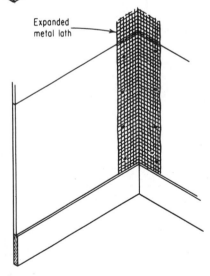

Expanded metal lath

Internal corner

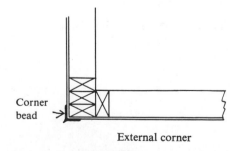

Corner bead

External corner

FIGURE 12-7: *Reinforcing metal lath at corners.*

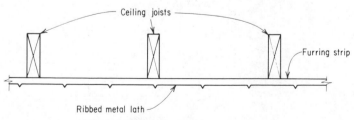

Ceiling joists

Furring strip

Ribbed metal lath

FIGURE 12-8: *Ribbed lath over furring.*

Dry Wall Finish

Dry wall is a term used to describe a finish produced by applying gypsum board to the inside walls and ceiling. This material is made in sheets 1200 mm wide, from 1.2 to 4.8 m in length and in thicknesses of 9, 12, 16, and 25 mm. The 9 and 12 mm thicknesses are most commonly used for interior finishing but the 16 and 25 mm thicknesses are used in some applications and do offer some advantages. The board may be applied in single, double, or triple thickness, the latter two being known as *laminated drywall.*

In single application, 12 mm board is generally used and sheets may be applied horizontally or vertically. In many cases, horizontal application of long sheets will result in a lesser amount of joints to be filled than with vertical application. In horizontal application, backing blocks must be placed between studs at the level at which two sheets will meet. Broad-headed, cadmium-coated, spiral or ringed nails 30 to 40 mm long are used. They should be spaced 225 mm o.c. around the outside edges of the board and 300 mm o.c. on intermediate studs. Use enough force when driving the nails so that a slight depression is made in the surface when the nail is fully driven but, at the same time, care must be taken not to break the paper.

The two-nail system is often used with success. After each nail is driven, a second one is driven about 35 mm away. This serves to draw the board more tightly against the studs or joists and helps to prevent *nail popping.*

The long edges of the board are depressed where two sheets meet, so that a recess appears on the surface that must be filled to hide the joint and to produce a flat surface. To do this, gypsum joint filler and paper tape are used. The tape is about 50 mm in. wide, has *feathered* edges and is perforated to allow filler to come through. The joint filler is mixed with water, allowed to stand for at least one-half hour, and applied with a broad spatula or trowel. The tape is pressed into the first layer of filler applied. Add a little filler over the tape, smooth off the joint, and let it dry. Now give it a light sanding and apply a wider coat, being careful to thin out the edges. Let dry, sand off, and apply a third, still wider coat which, when dry and sanded, should be ready for sizing and painting (see Fig. 12-9).

At internal horizontal and vertical corners, a strip of paper tape is folded into a right angle and set into the angle in a bed of filler. Second and third coats are added and sanded as above (see Fig. 12-10). At external corners a paper-covered metal angle is used (see Fig. 12-11). It is set over the corner in a bed of joint filler, the paper providing the binding surface. The corner is then treated in the same way as other joints.

Much of the taping and joint filling for drywall finish is now done by machine, although, in many cases, nail heads are covered (spotted) by hand (see Fig. 12-9).

At door and window openings, the gypsum board may simply be stopped against the frame if casings are to be used (see Fig. 12-12).

FIGURE 12-9: *Gypsum board joints taped and filled (Courtesy, Westroc Industries Ltd.).*

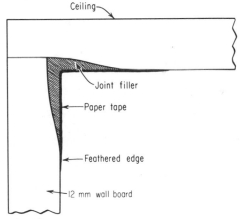

FIGURE 12-10: *Filling and taping internal corner.*

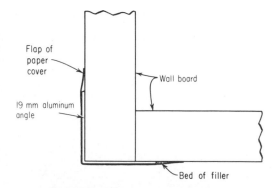

FIGURE 12-11: *Reinforcing external corner.*

327

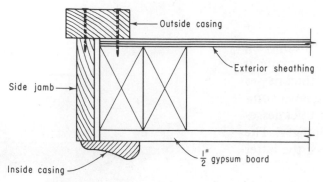

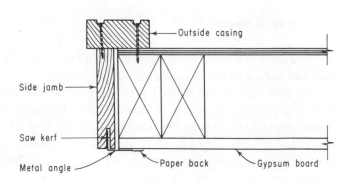

FIGURE 12-12: *Opening trimmed with casing.*

FIGURE 12-13: *Opening trimmed with metal angle.*

When the opening is to be trimmed without casing, again paper-covered metal angles are used. A thin saw kerf is cut into the edges of the frames, and one leg of the angle, with the paper folded around it, is pressed full depth into the kerf. The other leg covers the edge of the gypsum board, and the paper flap is bedded in filler. Finishing is similar to other joints (see Fig. 12-13).

Two-ply laminated dry wall consists of two layers of gypsum board, each usually 9 mm thick. The first is applied vertically over studs, nailed as described above. The second layer is applied horizontally. Sheets should be long enough to reach completely across the wall if at all possible. They are fixed in place by a coating of gypsum cement (joint filler) between the sheets.

The filler should be mixed into a creamy paste and allowed to stand for at least half an hour. It is then remixed and a coating is spread over the back of the sheet to be applied, using a broad, toothed spreader that will give an even distribution of cement. The first coated sheet is then applied to the upper half of the wall, with the upper edge up snug against the ceiling. The board is held in place with double-headed nails, one at each edge and two across the board, at each stud. Later, when the cement is dry, these nails are pulled out and the holes filled. Joints and corners are finished as described for single application. Taping and filling may be done by machine if desired. Also, the junction of wall and ceiling may be finished with a paper-covered gypsum cove molding. It is held in place with gypsum cement and nails.

With either single or double application, board should first be applied to the ceiling and, in either case, only a single application is required. Board may be applied directly to ceiling joists spaced 400 mm o.c. or less, but if spacing is greater than that, the ceiling frame should be *strapped* at right angles to the framing members with 19 mm strapping, at least 38 mm wide and the board applied over the strapping. When two boards butt together at their ends, a small space (about 3 mm) should be left between them so that some joint filler may be forced into the crevice during the taping and filling process, to act as a key for the joint.

A three-ply dry wall lamination is used for making partitions, no studs being used for support. Either 12 or 16 mm board is used for the outside layers, with 25 mm board for the core. A 25 by 25 mm wood strip is nailed to the floor and another to the ceiling on the center line of the partition (see Fig. 12-14). One outside layer is nailed to these, as illustrated in Fig. 12-14. The 25 mm core is cemented to this layer, and the other outside sheet is applied on the opposite side of the furring strip; again, cement is used. A partition built in this way is quite rigid and occupies less space than the conventional, stud-supported one.

Plywood Finishes

A great variety of plywoods is available for interior finishing, both in hardwood and softwood. They may be obtained in plain sheets, in a number of decorative faces, such as simulated driftwood or pressed patterns, and in sheets which have been scored to imitate plank or tile.

Joints between sheets can be treated in several ways. One is to make the edges meet as tightly as possible in an attempt to hide the joint. This is relatively easy with patterned plywoods, but it is difficult with plain sheets, particularly those in light colors. In such a case it is better to chamfer the meeting edges so as to accentuate the joint. Another method of finishing is to use battens over the joints.

Plywoods are nailed with 30 or 40 mm finishing nails or glued in place with high-frequency gluing apparatus. If the gluing process is being used, be careful that the surface of the plywood is not burned. This can happen very easily if the machine is used improperly.

Hardboards

Hardboards are produced in a great variety of face patterns for inside finishing. There are tile and plank effects, wood grain patterns, plastic-covered faces, and boards with baked enamel surface, among others. A very important consideration in applying any of the hardboards, other than those with plastic or enamelled face, is that of pre-expansion. Since these are wood fiber products, they will expand and contract with changes in humidity. Therefore, it is desirable that they be applied while at their maximum size. Otherwise, any expansion on the wall would cause buckling between the studs. To pre-expand hardboards, wet them on the back or screen side and stack them flat, back to back, for 24 hours. Most of the hardboards can be fastened in place with finishing nails, but those with plastic faces must be held by metal moldings.

Insulating Boards

Insulating boards for interior finish are made in regular 1200 by 2400 mm sheets and in various smaller sizes, particularly for use on ceilings. These boards are made from wood fiber, cane fiber, and asbestos fiber. Some are perforated to improve their acoustical qualities.

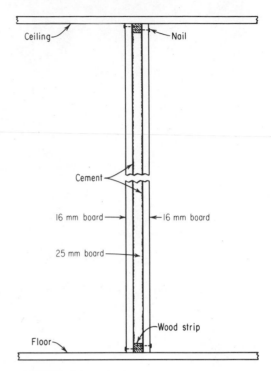

FIGURE 12-14: *Three-ply gypsum board partition.*

Finishing nails are commonly used for fastening these boards because of the ease of hiding the nail head. In wall applications, the nails should be driven at an angle of about 30 degrees to the horizontal. For ceiling application, using the smaller units, cement is commonly used to hold them. Metal channels may also be employed to hold ceiling tile.

Plastic Laminates

Plastic laminates are hard, synthetic materials, commonly made in sheets 1200 by 2400 mm, in thicknesses of 0.75 to 1.5 mm. They are durable and wear-resistant but because of the thickness, must be bonded to other backing materials, such as tempered hardboard, particle board or plywood. Bonding is done with a *contact cement,* that is applied to both the back of the plastic laminate and the face of the backing and allowed to dry before the sheet is placed in position. Bonding is instantaneous and care must be taken to ensure that the sheet is in its proper location before the two coated surfaces are allowed to come into contact. A sheet of paper can be placed over the coating on the backing after it is dry to allow some adjustment to be made in the position of the plastic laminate sheet and then withdrawn to allow the surfaces to come into contact.

For wall application, the material is often prebonded to a backing such as particle board, which may have tongue-and-grooved edges so that the units can be blind-nailed into place. In other cases, metal moldings that are nailed to the sheathing, are used to secure the laminate-faced panels to the wall (see Fig. 12-15).

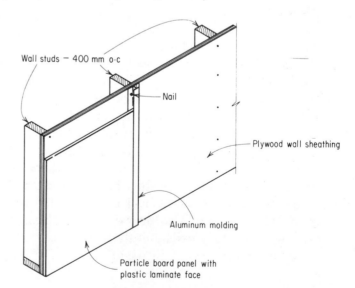

FIGURE 12-15:   *Metal channel to hold plastic laminate panel.*

Tile

For interior finish, 100 by 100 mm tile in plastic, steel, ceramic, or glass are in common use, particularly in bathrooms and kitchens. Plywood or gypsum board forms a suitable base for the tile, which are set in a prepared tile cement. The joints are filled (pointed) after the tile are all in place. A grouting compound especially made for this purpose is used for pointing.

Masonry Finishes

Masonry products have an important place as interior finishes. In addition to brick, tile, concrete block and stone of various types, thin veneers of brick and tile, both real and artificial, are available. These may be fixed to a solid backing by plastic adhesives, the joints being filled with grout after the units are in place.

FLOORING

Flooring materials include: *hardwood; resilient tile* such as linoleum, asphalt, vinyl, vinyl-asbestos, cork and rubber; *sheet flooring; clay tile* and *carpet.* Each has some particular advantages and many require some special preparation.

Hardwood Strip Flooring

Hardwood strip floors are a popular choice for many buildings, with *red and white oak, birch, beech* and *maple* all being used. All are produced in both edge grain and flat grain—*quarter sawn* and *plain sawn.*

Flooring is milled in a number of widths and thicknesses with tongue-and-grooved edges and ends. Standard face widths run from 38 to 89 mm and thicknesses include 9, 12, 20, and 26 mm.

The tongue and groove is placed below the center of the piece to allow for more wear and the bottom surface is hollowed for a tighter fit against the subfloor and for greater resilience (see Fig. 12-16).

Most flooring is made in four grades, determined by the range of color, similarity of grain and the number of defects in the pieces. The finished product is packaged in bundles made up of various lengths from 0.6 m up to the designated length of the bundle.

Hardwood flooring should be laid only after the humidity in the building has been brought to the normal range. The material should be stored in the place for several days before laying in order that it may adjust to the atmospheric conditions. Heat and ventilation are necessary for satisfactory results.

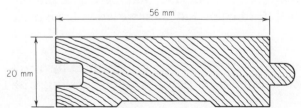

FIGURE 12-16: *Section through hardwood flooring strip.*

Procedure for laying strip flooring over wood subfloor:

1. Plan to lay the floor the long dimension of the building, if possible, and, in any case, lay it at right angles to the floor frame.

2. If the subfloor is shiplap, center match or common boards, it should run diagonally across the floor frame. See that it is adequately nailed.

3. Lay a good-quality, 0.75 kg/m², asphalt-saturated felt paper over the subfloor with 100 mm laps. If the space beneath the floor is cold, paper with vapor-barrier qualities is required.

4. Start the first strip of flooring against an outside wall, unless the area to be covered is large. Place the groove edge to the wall and leave a 12 mm space between floor and wall to allow for expansion (see Fig. 12-17). Make sure that the strip is perfectly straight and then nail it with finishing nails.

5. Succeeding strips are *blind-nailed* (see Fig. 12-18), with flooring nails. The length and spacing of nails depend on the thickness of the flooring. Use 30 mm nails, spaced at 200 mm for 9 mm flooring; 40 mm nails at 250 mm for 12 mm flooring; 55 mm nails at 300 to 400 mm for 20 mm flooring and 75 mm nails at 400 mm for 26 mm flooring. Be sure that each strip is snug against the one behind it and that end joints are tight and square.

6. Use the piece cut off at the end of one strip of flooring to start the next strip, wherever possible. Watch that end joints in successive strips are at least 150 mm apart.

7. After four or five strips have been laid, place a piece of hardwood against the outside edge and strike firmly against it with the hammer to draw up the flooring.

8. When a wide area has to be covered, it is advantageous to start at the center and work both ways toward the outside walls (see Fig. 12-19). In such a situation, be sure that the center strip is straight, then face-nail it and countersink the nails. The holes will later be filled. Now cut a strip of hardwood the thickness of the tongue and twice its width and insert it into the groove of the starting strip. You can now lay flooring in both directions from this double-tongued center strip (see Fig. 12-20).

9. Try to arrange the pieces in the floor so that there is as wide a separation of end joints as possible, and there is as smooth a blending as possible of color and grain variation from piece to piece.

Sanding and finishing hardwood floors are usually done by qualified finishers. They use a drum-type power sander, starting with

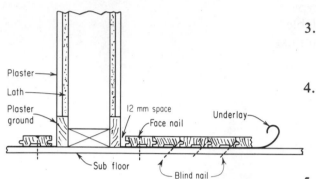

FIGURE 12-17: *Starting flooring at wall.*

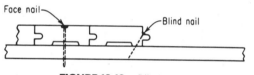

FIGURE 12-18: *Blind nailing.*

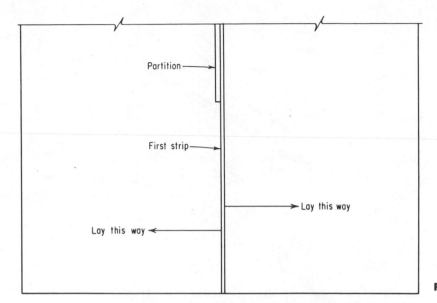

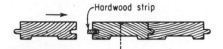

FIGURE 12-20: *Double tongue on centre strip.*

FIGURE 12-19: *Laying flooring from center.*

coarse (No. 2) sandpaper, progressing to medium (No. ½), and finishing with fine (No. 00). Then they use paste filler, rubbing first across the grain and then with it, with a large piece of burlap. Excess filler must be wiped off immediately before it hardens. Oil, shellac, plastic finish, or floor varnish is applied in three coats, and finally, after drying, the surface is waxed.

Wood Floor Over Concrete Base

Wood floors may be laid over a concrete subfloor, although the procedure will vary somewhat depending on whether the concrete slab is suspended or is resting on the earth. If the slab is suspended, with an airspace beneath, a moisture barrier is usually not needed, but for a slab-on-grade floor, a moisture barrier is required between the concrete and the flooring.

Wood strips—*sleepers*—are attached to the concrete slab with asphalt adhesive and nails and they act as a nailing base for the strip flooring.

A satisfactory method of laying strip flooring over a concrete slab-on-grade may be carried out as follows:

1. Clean and prime the floor with asphalt primer.

2. Snap chalk lines down the length of the floor at 400 mm centers.

3. Apply ribbons of the special adhesive required to bond wood to concrete along the chalk lines.

4. Embed random length, 19 by 38 mm or wider, treated wood strips in the adhesive and fasten them in place with 40 mm concrete nails about 600 mm apart or with powder-actuated pins similarly spaced.

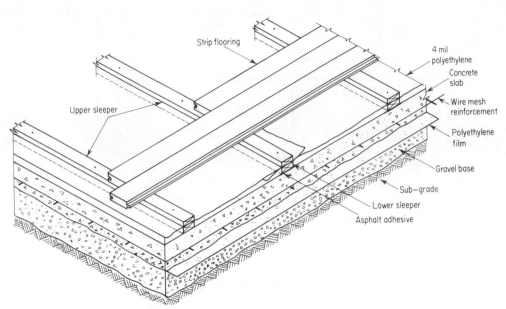

FIGURE 12-21: *Strip flooring over concrete slab.*

5. Lay 4 mil polyethylene film over the sleepers. Joints in the film must be made at a sleeper and the material should overlap at least 100 mm on each side of the sleeper (see Fig. 12-21).

6. Nail another layer of wood strips of the same width over the first, on top of the polyethylene, using 35 mm spiral nails, spaced about 400 mm apart.

7. Apply strip flooring as previously described. If flooring ends are tongue-and-grooved, end joints may fall between sleepers but joints in the succeeding strip must not fall between the same pair of sleepers.

Hardwood Block Flooring

Block flooring consists of small sections of hardwood made either by gluing several short strips of hardwood flooring together—*parquet flooring* (see Fig. 12-22)—or by bonding three thin layers of hardwood together—*laminated flooring*—to form small rectangles or squares with tongue-and-grooved edges, with a maximum size of about 300 by 300 mm.

Both types are laid by the same general methods, although in the case of parquet flooring, allowance must be made for expansion by leaving at least a 20 mm space on all sides between flooring and wall. Both may be blind-nailed in the same way as strip flooring and both may be laid in mastic.

With this method, a thin coat of mastic is first spread over a smooth, level, dry base, to which is applied a layer of 1.5 kg/m² asphalt-impregnated felt paper. A second coat of mastic about 2 mm thick is spread over the paper and the blocks are laid in this top coat. Laying patterns may be square or diagonal.

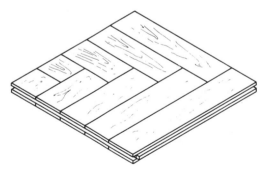

FIGURE 12-22: *Parquet flooring.*

Resilient Flooring

Resilient floor tile of all kinds require a smooth, regular surface in order to give satisfactory service and to maintain a good appearance. In most cases the conventional subfloor does not provide a surface which is smooth and even enough and some type of *underlayment,* such as plywood, particle board or hardboard, must be applied over the subfloor.

Large defects in the subfloor, such as knotholes, should be patched before hardboard is used and the material should be allowed to stand unwrapped in the room for at least 24 hours to adjust to the prevailing humidity conditions. A space of approximately 1 mm should be left between sheets when they are laid to allow for expansion. The end joints in the panels should be staggered and the continuous joints should be at right angles to those in the subfloor.

Plywood and particle board are dimensionally stable products and sheets may be butted against one another when they are laid. They are also rigid enough that they will bridge most defects in the subfloor. Joints should be staggered in the same manner as with hardboard.

Ring-grooved or *cement-coated, tapered-head* nails or divergent staples are used as fasteners for all these underlayment materials, with spacings not over 150 mm on the interior of the panel and 100 mm around the edges for hardboard and up to 200 mm for the interiors and 150 mm around the edges for plywood and particle board.

Procedure for laying resilient tile:

1. Clean the surface thoroughly and check to see that it is smooth and the joints are level. Remove any rough edges with sandpaper or plane.

2. Snap a chalk line down the center of the room in the direction of the long dimension.

3. Lay out another center line at right angles to the main one, using a framing square to get the chalk line in its proper alignment.

4. Spread adhesive over one quarter of the total area, carrying it up to, but not over, the chalk lines. Use the type of spreader recommended by the manufacturer of the adhesive.

5. Allow the adhesive to acquire an initial set. It should be slightly tacky but not sticky and the length of time required to achieve this condition will depend on the type of adhesive.

6. Lay the first tile at the center of the room, with two edges to the two chalk lines (see Fig. 12-23).

7. Lay a row of tile to both chalk lines, being careful to keep the butt joints tight and the corners in line. Lay each tile in position—do not slide it into place.

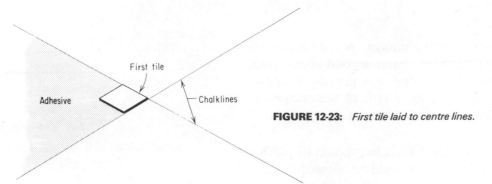

First tile

Adhesive

Chalklines

FIGURE 12-23: *First tile laid to centre lines.*

8. Cut the last tile in each row to fit against the wall, with the cut edge to the wall.

9. Complete the tile laying over that quadrant of the floor and roll the tile if the manufacturer recommends it.

10. Lay the opposite quadrant next and then the other two, in exactly the same manner as the first.

Sheet Flooring

Sheet flooring includes materials such as linoleum and a variety of synthetic products consisting of vinyl or other plastics, sometimes in combination with cork, asbestos or other fibers and various resins. They are produced in rolls from 1.8 to 3.6 m wide, in thicknesses of from 3 to 6 mm, with plain and patterned surfaces.

Some require to be cemented to the floor, while others will hold their position without cement, due to the texture of the material on the underside. All require a smooth base, like that produced by the use of underlayment.

In the case of linoleum, a cushion is required under the material in the form of a layer of soft felt paper. The underlayment is covered with a coating of linoleum cement, into which the felt paper is laid and rolled smooth. Another coating of cement is applied over the paper and the linoleum is laid in it and rolled down.

Clay Tile Flooring

Clay floor tile are burned clay products, similar to brick, made in various dimensions and in thicknesses of from 6 to 24 mm, intended for use over a concrete base floor. The procedure for laying clay floor tile is as follows:

1. Wash the concrete base and saturate it with water.

2. Snap two chalk lines across the floor at right angles to one another, so that the floor is divided into four equal parts.

3. Mix the bedding mortar in the proportion of one part cement to three parts plaster sand, with enough water to make a plastic, workable mixture.

4. Starting at the center of the room, at the intersection of the two lines, apply a layer of mortar the area of one tile and about 12 mm thick and lay the first tile to both lines. Bed the tile firmly and remove any excess mortar around its edges.

5. Continue to lay a row of tile along one of the lines, bedding each one firmly and leaving a 10 mm space between tiles. Remove excess mortar around exposed edges.

6. Lay a row of tile along the second line in the same manner.

7. Lay the remainder of the tile over that section of the floor, keeping the tiles as level as possible and maintaining an even spacing between them.

8. Lay the opposite quarter and then the two remaining ones, in the same manner.

9. After the bedding mortar has set, prepare a grouting mix, using the same proportions of cement and sand but a little more water, for a more fluid mix. Pour the grout over a section of the tiled surface and rub it into the spaces between the tile with a piece of heavy burlap.

10. Rub off the excess grout and when it has set sufficiently, so as not to pull out of the spaces, clean the surface of the title thoroughly.

Carpets

Carpets do not usually require underlayment because normally a rubberized underpad is laid under the carpet as part of the installation. However, the subfloor should be flat and even and cracks and knotholes filled with a reliable crackfiller. Actual carpet installation is normally done by a carpet layer, using specialized equipment for stretching the carpet and holding it in place.

INSIDE DOOR FRAMES

Several different kinds of jamb are used to make inside door frames, as indicated in Fig. 12-24. The flat jamb, 19 mm thick is often saw-kerfed on the back side to minimize cupping. Rabbetted jamb has one edge ploughed out 12 mm deep by 35 or 45 mm wide, depending on the thickness of the door to be used. Hardwood jambs are made in a number of styles, one of which is illustrated in Fig. 12-24e. Steel jambs are made for use in masonry walls (see Fig. 12-24f).

In cases where no casing is to be used around the door frame, a galvanized metal bead is available which can be nailed to the back of the jambs to accommodate lath and plaster wall finish (see Fig. 12-24c). A similar type of trim is used with drywall finish, consisting of a paper-covered aluminum angle, with one leg set into a saw kerf cut in the edges of the jamb (see Fig. 12-24d).

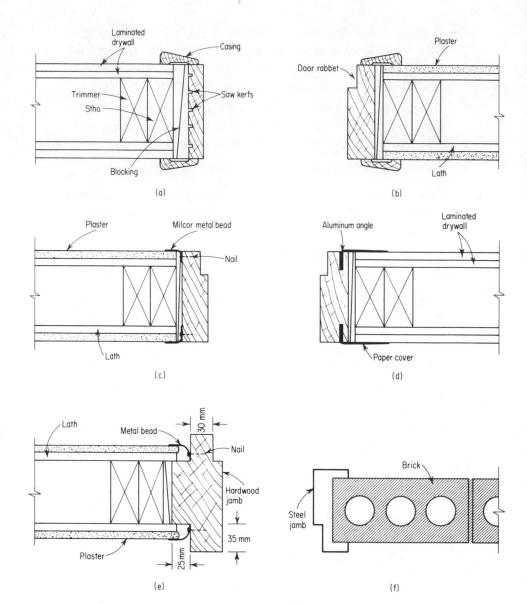

FIGURE 12-24: *Inside door frames.*

Installing Inside Door Frames

In some cases, door frames are cut, sanded, and fitted in a mill-work plant and come to the job ready for assembly. In others, sets of jamb material are supplied, consisting of two side jamb pieces about 2100 mm long and a head jamb piece 900 mm long.

The procedure for installing inside door frames, using precut jambs, is as follows:

1. Check the length of the side and head jamb pieces to make sure that they are correct for the opening.

2. Nail the jambs together, using 65 mm finish or casing nails.

3. Place the frame in the opening with the ends of the side jambs resting on the finish floor and check to see that the head jamb

is level. If it is not, trim the bottom end of the side jamb that is too high.

4. Tack a 19 by 89 mm *spreader,* exactly the same length as the head jamb, across the bottom of the frame, as illustrated in Fig. 12-25.

5. Center the frame in the opening and wedge it in position with double shingle wedges at the top and bottom on both sides. Secure the wedges by nailing through the frame into the trimmer on either side, as illustrated in Fig. 12-26.

6. Complete the blocking by placing pairs of shingle wedges at each hinge location on one jamb, with a third midway between them and one at the lock position and at least one other midway between it and the top on the opposite side (see Fig. 12-27).

7. Adjust the pairs of wedges until the jambs are straight, using a long straightedge to check the straightness, and nail them in place as illustrated.

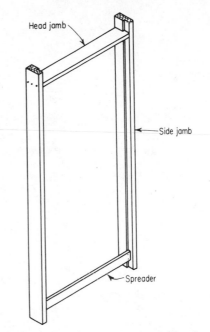

FIGURE 12-25:   *Spreader in place in door frame.*

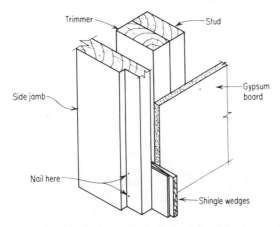

FIGURE 12-26:   *Nailing side jamb wedges.*

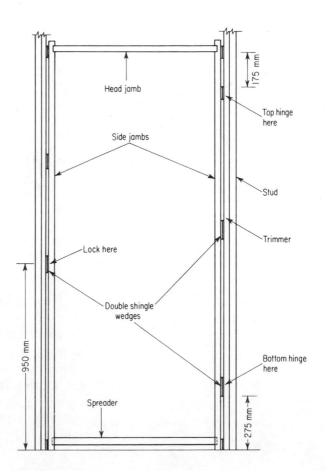

FIGURE 12-27:   *Door frame wedges.*

If the jambs are not precut, they will have to be cut to length, dadoed for the head jamb and the hinge gains cut before the frame is assembled. Proceed as follows:

1. Lay out the two pieces of side jamb material as a pair and check the bottom ends to make sure that they are square.

2. Measure up from the bottom of one side jamb the given height of the door less 12 mm and lay out and cut a dado across the jamb 38 mm wide (see Fig. 12-28). Cut the jamb to length about 20 mm above the dado.

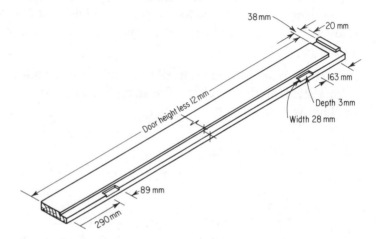

FIGURE 12-28: *Dado and hinge gains cut in side jamb.*

3. Cut the opposite jamb in exactly the same way.

4. Cut the head jamb to the given door width.

5. Hinge gains may be located as illustrated in Fig. 12-28 and cut out by hand, using a chisel and mallet or a *hinge template* may be used to locate them and the cutting done with a hand electric router.

6. Assemble the frame and attach the spreader at the bottom as previously described.

How to Hang an Inside Door

After the inside door frames have been installed, the doors must be *hung,* if prehung units are not being used. Hanging a door involves *trimming* it to fit the opening, *attaching hinges,* and *installing a lockset.* During this operation it is necessary to support the door firmly on edge and this may be done with the aid of a woodworker's vise (see Fig. 1-45) clamped to a sawhorse, or a simple door jack like that illustrated in Fig. 12-29.

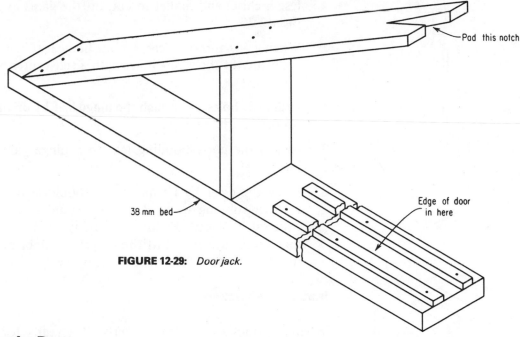

FIGURE 12-29: *Door jack.*

Labels in figure: Pad this notch; Edge of door in here; 38 mm bed

Trimming the Door

1. Use only a door made to fit the size of the opening provided. Doors are made to fit standard openings and a door of any given size should not be cut down to fit a smaller opening.

2. Trim the door to length. Be sure that the top edge is square with the sides and then trim enough from the bottom to make the door the right length. Inside doors should have about 1.5 mm clearance at the top and 16 mm at the bottom.

3. Dress the door to width, using a jointer or a hand electric plane to keep the edge straight. There should be about 2 mm clearance on the lock side and 1 mm on the hinge side. The lock edge should be beveled about 5 degrees towards the closing side.

Attaching Hinges

The first step in attaching hinges is to provide hinge gains on the edge of the door. If a prehung unit is being used, this will have been done in the shop. If a hinge template has been used for the jamb hinge gains, it will also be used for those on the door. In other cases, the gains will be cut by hand.

1. Set the door in the opening and block it to the right height.

2. Mark on the door the position of the hinge gains from those on the jamb.

3. Take the door down, secure it firmly on edge and lay out the positions of the hinge gains on the door edge.

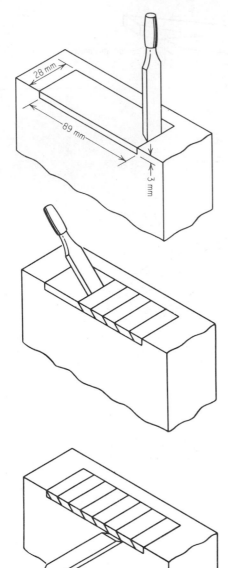

FIGURE 12-30: *Cutting a hinge gain.*

4. Use a chisel and mallet to cut out the gains as illustrated in Fig. 12-30.

5. When gains are complete, set one hinge leaf in each and mark the center of the screw holes with a self-centering punch (see Fig. 12-31).

6. Drill pilot holes and attach the hinge leaf by driving the screws supplied with the hinge.

7. Attach the corresponding leaf to a hinge gain in the door jamb.

8. Hang the door by its hinges. It should swing freely, close without rubbing or binding, and stand in any position in which it is placed. Failure to do any of these things means that some adjustment of the hinges or slight dressing off of the closing edge of the door is necessary.

Installing a Lockset

When the door is hanging properly, it is ready for the lockset. Two types are in common use, mortise locks and cylinder locks. The first is mounted through the edge of the door and the latter through the face.

How to Install a Mortise Lock

1. Measure up 900 or 950 mm from the floor and mark that height on the face and edge of the door (see Fig. 12-32).

2. Measure the thickness and height of the *lock case* and lay out a mortise on the edge of the door with dimensions slightly larger than the height and thickness. Make sure that the layout is centered on the edge of the door and is located so that the center of the knob will fall on the *height-above-floor* line.

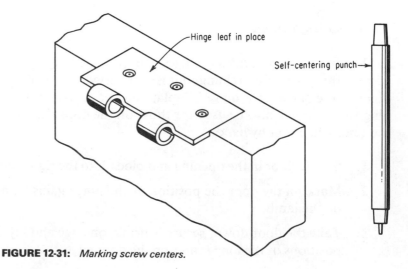

FIGURE 12-31: *Marking screw centers.*

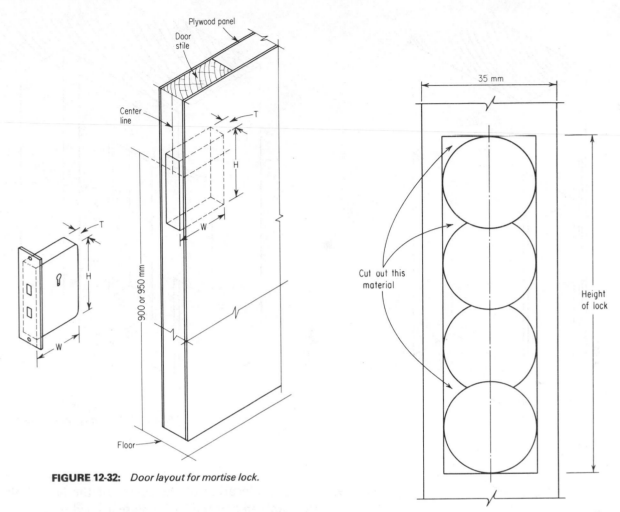

FIGURE 12-32: *Door layout for mortise lock.*

FIGURE 12-33: *Holes drilled for lock mortise.*

3. Select a wood bit with the same diameter as the thickness of the mortise layout and, from the center line, drill a series of holes into the edge of the door, 6 mm deeper than the width of the lockcase (see Fig. 12-33).

4. With a sharp chisel remove the remaining wood around the holes to form a rectangular mortise. Check to see that the lock will fit in the space.

5. Slip the lock into the mortise, and with a marking knife lay out the outline of the lock-mounting plate on the door edge. Cut a gain for the plate as shown in Fig. 12-34.

6. Measure the distance from the face of the mounting plate to the center of the knob shank hole and the keyhole. Lay out these points on the face of the door and drill holes of the size required.

7. Fit the lock into the mortise, drill pilot holes for the lock-mounting screws, and fasten the lock in place.

8. Install knob shank and knobs according to instructions included with the lockset.

343

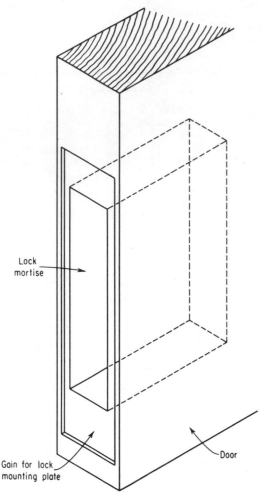

Lock
mortise

Gain for lock
mounting plate

Door

FIGURE 12-34: *Lock mortise complete.*

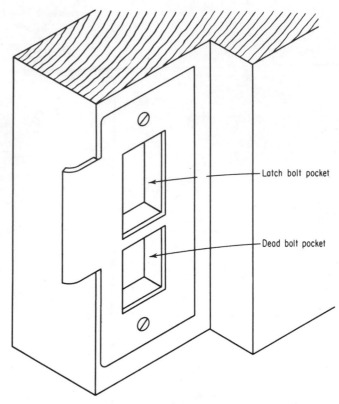

Latch bolt pocket

Dead bolt pocket

FIGURE 12-35: *Strike plate in place.*

9. Mark the location of the center of the latch bolt pocket on the jamb and fit the strike plate accordingly. A gain must be cut into which the strike plate fits and pockets for the latch bolt and dead bolt drilled and squared out (see Fig. 12-35). The strike plate must be positioned laterally so that the latch bolt will just engage when the door is closed and hold the door snugly in the closed position.

How to Install a Cylinder Lock

1. Mark the height of the lock above the floor on the edge and face of the door as before.

2. Use the template usually supplied with this type of lock and, laying it on the line drawn in step 1, mark the centers of holes to be drilled in the face and edge of the door (see Fig. 12-36).

3. Drill the holes through the face of the door and then the one through the edge to receive the latch bolt. It should be slightly deeper than the length of the bolt.

4. Cut a gain for the latch bolt mounting plate, as shown in Fig. 12-37, and install the latch unit.

5. Install exterior knob as described in Fig. 12-38.

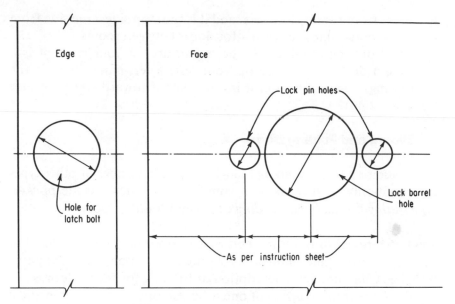

FIGURE 12-36: *Holes for cylinder lock.*

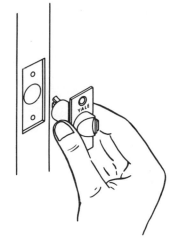

FIGURE 12-37: *Installing latch unit.*

Place exterior rosette with spindle into latch
as shown below. Depress latch, position spindle
and rosette stems correctly. Pass spindle and
stems through holes in latch.

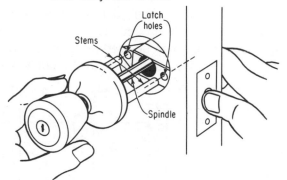

FIGURE 12-38: *Installing exterior knob.*

After exterior knob and rosette is placed,
install interior knob and rosette as shown
below and push rosettes tight against door.
Line up screw holes with stems, insert screws
and tighten until lockset is firm.

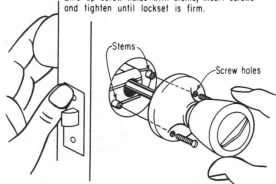

6. Next, install interior knob (see Fig. 12-39).

7. Find the position of the strike plate and install it in the jamb, as described for mortise locks.

FIGURE 12-39: *Installing interior knob.*

The Hand of Doors

The term to describe the direction in which a door is to swing and the side from which it is to be hung is the *hand* of the door. The hand is determined from the outside.

The outside is the street side for entrance doors; it is the corridor side for doors leading from corridors to rooms; it is the room side

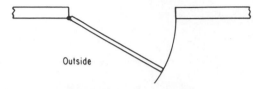

FIGURE 12-40: *Left-hand reverse door.*

for doors from rooms to closets, and it is the stop side—the side from which the butts cannot be seen—for doors between rooms.

Stand outside the door. If the hinges are on your right, it is a right-hand door; if they are on your left, a left-hand door. If the door swings away from you, it is a regular; if toward you, a reverse (see Fig. 12-40).

Sliding and Folding Doors

In addition to conventional hinged doors, a number of other types are commonly used in modern construction. They include *pocket-type sliding* doors, *bypass sliding* doors and *folding* doors.

Pocket-type sliding door: This type of door may be considered to be a space-saver, since it opens by sliding into an opening in the partition. See Chapter 5 for a description of framing for such a door.

The door frame consists of one solid and one split side jamb and a solid head jamb with an apron along each edge to conceal the track. The track is an extruded aluminum product and the rollers are usually nylon for longer wear and silent operations (see Fig. 12-41).

Bypass-type sliding doors: Two doors sliding past one another in an opening are used in this case, so that only half the width of the opening can be utilized at a time. A standard type door frame may be used, with a head jamb long enough to accommodate two doors. The track may be mounted on the underside of the head jamb (see Fig. 12-42) or a split head jamb may be used to recess the track to permit the door to ride flush with the underside of the jamb (see Fig. 12-43).

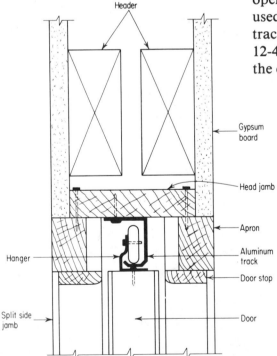

FIGURE 12-41: *Pocket-type sliding door head jamb details.*

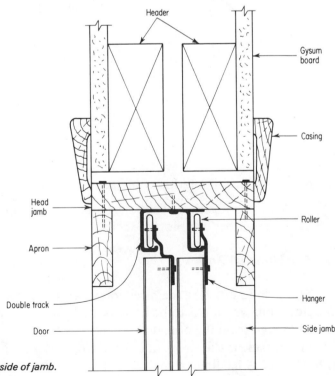

FIGURE 12-42: *Track mounted on underside of jamb.*

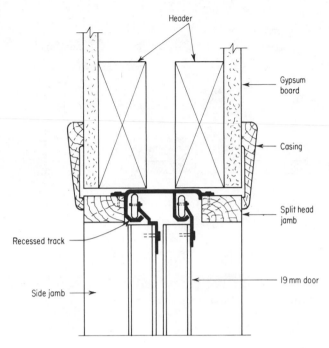

Header

Gypsum board

Casing

Split head jamb

Recessed track

Side jamb

19 mm door

FIGURE 12-43: *Recessed track for sliding doors.*

Folding doors: A folding door unit consists of one or more pairs of doors hinged together at the center and pivoted top and bottom at the outer edge. The pivots fit into *pivot brackets* which are adjustable to provide the proper clearance between the edge of the door and the jamb.

The folding action is provided by the hinges joining pairs of doors together and is guided by a horizontal nylon roller pinned to the traveling edge of the door and enclosed in an overhead track.

WINDOW TRIM

Most of the windows used in modern construction come to the job as a complete unit—frames with the outside casing attached and the sash or glass already installed (see Fig. 11-43). All that is normally required is that the window be *trimmed* on the inside.

In the case of large picture windows, the frame, made for the purpose, is installed first and the glass is then set in place. Depending on the length of the glass, three or more lead, neoprene, or rubber blocks about 6 mm thick are set on the sill, the glass set on them and tilted into place. Temporary stops may be used to hold the glass in place until the permanent ones have been fitted.

Moldings and Trim

These names designate the materials that are used to finish around the base of walls, around windows, doors and other openings. Those with relatively small cross sections are *moldings,* while the larger ones

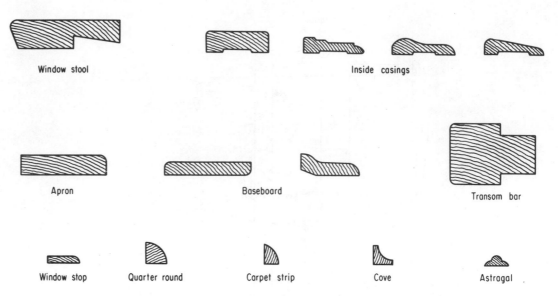

FIGURE 12-44: *Molding and trim sections.*

are *trim materials.* They include *window stool, window and door casing, apron, baseboard, transom bar, window stop, cove mold, quarter round, carpet strip,* and astragal (see Fig. 12-44).

Great care must be taken in cutting these materials and in fitting them into place. A *miter box, coping saw, sharp panel saw, combination square, smooth plane, chisel,* and *marking knife* are essential tools for applying trim. *Butt, miter,* and *coped* joints are all used, and they must be made to fit perfectly.

Door Trim

Casings (see Fig. 12-44) are applied to both sides of interior doors to cover the space between the frames and the wall, to secure the frames to the wall and to hold the jambs in a rigid position and must therefore be nailed to both the jams and the wall frame. The procedure is as follows:

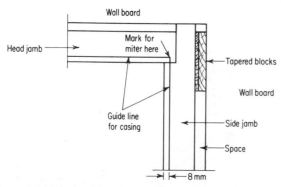

FIGURE 12-45: *Upper right hand corner of door frame with guide line for casing.*

1. Select the necessary pieces and make sure that they are all the same pattern and width.

2. Draw a light pencil line on the jambs 8 mm from the inner edge (see Fig. 12-45).

3. Check the bottom end of each side casing to see that it is square and will sit flat on the finish floor.

4. Set one side casing in place, with its inner edge to the line drawn in step 2 and mark the position of the miter joint at the top (see Fig. 12-45).

5. Use a miter box to make an accurate miter cut through that point.

348

6. Measure and cut the second side casing in exactly the same way.

7. Nail the first side casing temporarily in place.

8. Cut a miter on one end of the head casing to match the one on the side casing already in place.

9. Hold the head casing in place with the two miter cuts together and check to see that they fit perfectly. Then mark the position of the miter cut on the opposite end of the head casing and cut the miter accordingly.

10. Nail the second side casing in place and set the head casing in position. Make sure that both miter joints are close fits.

11. Nail the casing securely, with 35 mm finishing nails into the edge of the jambs and 65 mm nails into the wall frame (see Fig. 12-46).

12. Sand the external corners where side and head casings meet lightly and set the nails.

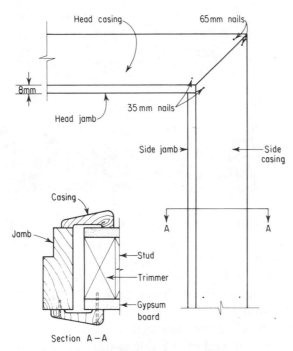

FIGURE 12-46: *Casing nailed in place.*

Window Trim

Windows may be cased on all four sides or, where a window ledge is required, *window stool* and *apron* is applied at the bottom and casing to the two sides and the top (see Fig. 12-47).

The window stool is notched to fit between the jambs (see Fig.

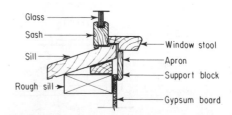

FIGURE 12-47: *Window stool and apron in place.*

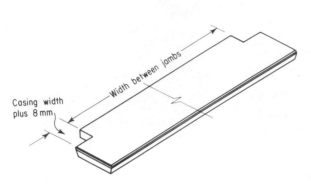

FIGURE 12-48: *Notched ends of window stool.*

FIGURE 12-49: *Window trimmed with stool, apron and casings.*

FIGURE 12-50: *Window cased on four sides.*

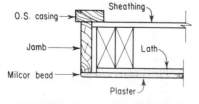

FIGURE 12-51: *Metal bead as trim.*

12-48) and the end projections are cut so that their length will be equal to the width of the casing plus 8 mm. The shape of the edge of the stool is returned around the ends and the stool fitted into place and nailed as shown in Fig. 12-47. A piece of apron is cut about 30 mm shorter than the length of the stool and nailed in place under the stool, as shown in Fig. 12-47.

Side and head casings are then applied in the same way as for doors. The bottom end of the side casings must fit snugly on top of the stool and their outer edges will be in line with the ends of the stool (see Fig. 12-49).

When windows are cased on all four sides, apply the bottom casing first, mitered on both ends, and then proceed with the side casings and the top (see Fig. 12-50).

Many windows are trimmed without the use of casing. This is commonly done by using a paper-backed metal angle set into a saw kerf in the jamb (see Fig. 12-3) when a dry wall finish is applied or a curved metal bead which is nailed over the lath, when walls are plastered (see Fig. 12-51).

Another method of trimming door and window openings is to use the edge of the door or window frame as the trim. This is best suited to dry types of finish. Frames are made (Fig. 12-52) and are installed in the same way as other types, and the edges of the wall finish are slipped into place as shown.

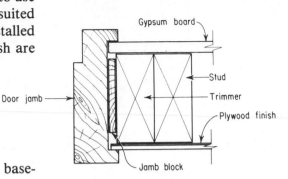

FIGURE 12-52:　*Self-trimmed door jamb.*

BASEBOARD, QUARTER ROUND, AND CARPET STRIP

When the floors have been laid and the doors trimmed, the baseboard and carpet strip, if required, can be installed. Two types of baseboard are illustrated in Fig. 12-44—one plain and the other molded; the same basic procedures are used in applying any type.

The first step is to find and mark the location of the wall studs so that the baseboard may be nailed to them. Then try to select pieces which will be long enough to reach across the spans involved, if possible. Otherwise it is necessary to join two pieces together with a miter joint (see Fig. 12-53). The joint must come on a stud and should be made with precision so that the joint will be as inconspicuous as possible.

At door casings, butt the end of the baseboard to the casing with a tight, square joint. At inside corners, butt the end of the baseboard on one wall against the adjoining wall. The end of the meeting piece must be coped to fit against the other (see Fig. 12-54). To get a coping line, trace the shape of the baseboard on either the front or the back of the piece to be coped. Use a coping saw and undercut slightly from front to back in order to get a tight fit at the outside face. Pieces meet at outside corners with a 45 degree miter joint. Carefully mark the length to the corner of the wall on the inside edge of the baseboard, and cut the miter *out* from this point (see Fig. 12-55).

When plain baseboard is used, carpet strip may be added at the bottom. At the end where baseboard meets a door casing, the end of the carpet strip is mitered, as shown in Fig. 12-56. At an inside corner, the end of one piece is butted against the baseboard and the end of the meeting piece is *coped* to fit over it (see Fig. 12-57). To cope the end, first cut a 45 degree miter and then follow the curved line of the

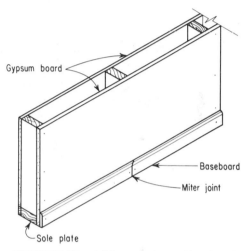

FIGURE 12-53:　*Joining two pieces of baseboard.*

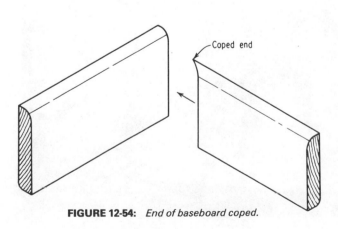

FIGURE 12-54:　*End of baseboard coped.*

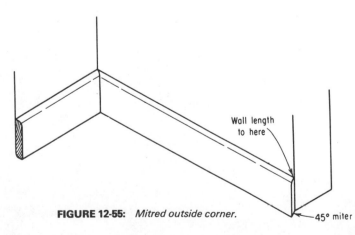

FIGURE 12-55:　*Mitred outside corner.*

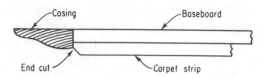

FIGURE 12-56: *Carpet strip meets casing.*

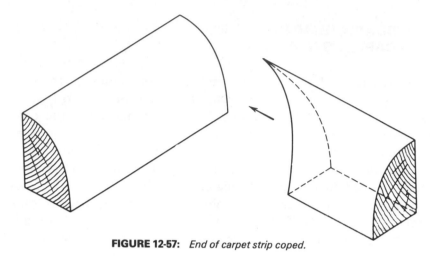

FIGURE 12-57: *End of carpet strip coped.*

miter cut with a coping saw, undercutting slightly to produce a tight fit. At outside corners, the ends of the two meeting pieces are mitered at 45 degrees.

CABINETWORK

The final finishing work usually consists of installing kitchen and bathroom cabinets, closets and wardrobes, built-in features such as dressing tables or desks (see Fig. 12-58) in bathroom, bedroom or library, mantels, room dividers, counters, display racks, booths, etc. Such items may be *custom-built* in a cabinet shop for a specific installation, *mass-produced* in components in a millwork factory or *built on the job* by the carpenter.

FIGURE 12-58: *Built-in library desk.*

Cabinetwork Drawings

The building plans usually include some details of the built-in cabinetwork. The floor plan will show the location of the units, while elevations, drawn to a larger scale, will provide detailed dimensions. Figure 12-59 illustrates a typical drawing of a kitchen cabinet, upper and lower sections. Detailed sizes of drawers and doors, facing widths and overhangs may be scaled from the drawing.

When cabinets are to be built on the job, it is usually helpful to draw a *full scale layout* of each of the various sections involved on plywood or heavy paper. these will be *section views,* both horizontal and vertical, in which each member and the various clearances that may be required are shown full size. These layouts are useful when cutting end or partition panels or doors to size, locating joints and determining the size and location of drawer parts, etc., which are not included in the original drawings.

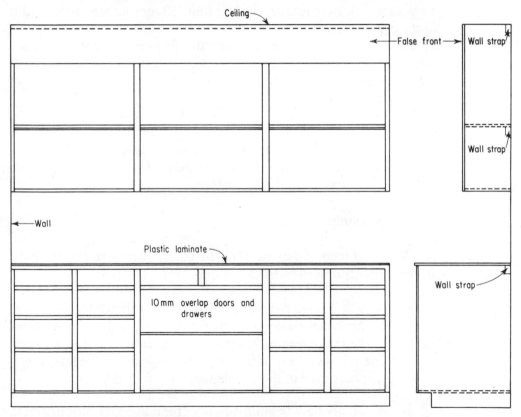

FIGURE 12-59: *Kitchen cabinet drawing (scale − 1 mm = 12 mm).*

Standard Sizes

A number of dimensions and material sizes common in cabinetwork are relatively standard and the finish carpenter should be familiar with them.

The counter section of a kitchen cabinet is normally 900 mm high and 600 mm deep, with a countertop overhang of about 25 mm. The

353

toespace at the bottom will be approximately 75 × 89 mm (see Fig. 12-59). The vertical distance between the counter and the *wall* (upper) section will vary from 375 to 450 mm, unless the wall section is located over a sink or the cooking surface of a stove, in which case the minimum distance allowed is 600 mm. The usual overall depth of the wall section is 300 mm.

In bathrooms and dressing rooms, the top of a built-in vanity or dressing table should be 750 to 775 mm high, with the depth depending on the type of wash basin fixture, where applicable. Otherwise, the depth is normally 525 to 550 mm. Knee room should be provided under a wash basin, approximately 600 mm high.

In bedrooms and dressing rooms, the minimum clear depth for clothes closets will be 600 mm and shelves in such closets should be 1650 mm above the floor, in order to allow a clothes bar to hang 1500 mm above the floor.

Drawers in kitchen or other cabinets should not usually extend over 450 mm in width, with depths ranging from 75 to 300 mm in most cases. Drawer length will be about 50 mm less than the width of the counter top.

Doors in wall sections of cabinets should normally not exceed 450 mm in width, while those in lower sections may be up to 600 mm wide. Doors exceeding these widths will usually prove to be inconvenient in the open position.

End and partition panels in cabinets, shelves, doors, drawer fronts, and counter tops should be made from 14 or 17 mm plywood or particle board, and the cabinet base cover, drawer sides and backs from 12 mm material and drawer bottoms from 6 mm plywood. Facings will normally be 19 mm material.

Basic Framing

When cabinets are being built in place, there are several basic framing procedures to be followed.

1. A 19 × 38 mm strap is attached to the wall in a level position, 19 mm below the level of the counter top, with its length equal to the *inside length* dimension of the cabinet. Draw a plumb line from the ends of the strap to the floor. These lines represent the inside of the end panels.

2. A cabinet base is built, usually from 38 × 89 mm material, with its length equal to the length of the wall strap and its width 106 mm less than the width of the counter top. It is nailed in place between the plumb lines drawn in step one (see Fig. 12-60).

3. The end panels are cut next, the length equal to the height of the top of the wall strap and the width 44 mm less than the counter top width. The bottom front corners must be notched to match the width and depth of the toe space (see Fig. 12-61).

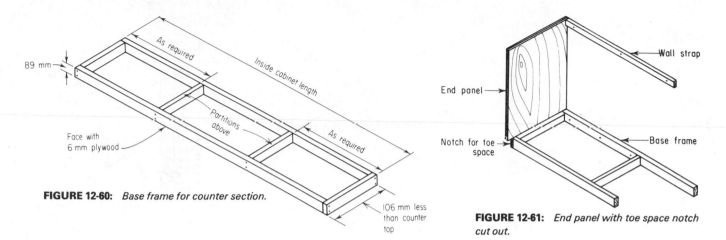

FIGURE 12-60: *Base frame for counter section.*

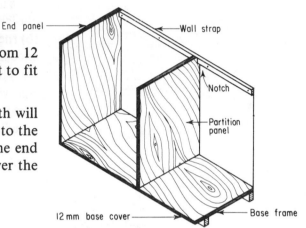

FIGURE 12-61: *End panel with toe space notch cut out.*

4. The base cover can now be applied. It will be made from 12 mm plywood, the same width as the end panels and cut to fit snugly between them.

5. Partition panels are cut to size and installed. The length will be the distance from the top surface of the base cover to the top of the wall strap and the width equal to that of the end panels. The top back corner must be notched to fit over the wall strap (see Fig. 12-62).

Facings

With the base frame members in place, the facing strips are applied to the front edges of the basic frame. The horizontal members are called *rails* and the vertical members, *stiles*.

If the ends of the cabinet are not exposed, the top rail can be applied first, flush with the top end of the panels, its length equal to the distance from outside to outside of the panels. If the ends are exposed, the two outside stiles should be attached first and the top rail cut to fit between them. One method of making the joint between top rail and stile is illustrated in Fig. 12-63. Intermediate stiles are applied next and then the rails which form the dividers between drawers are cut to fit between them. One method of making the joint between divider rail and stiles is shown in Fig. 12-64.

Drawers

Drawers are made with two general types of front—*flush* and *overlapping.* flush drawers close so that the drawer front is flush with the facings around it and must be carefully fitted for good appearance. Overlapping drawers are made with a 10 × 10 mm lip around the edge of the drawer front, so that when the drawer is closed, the lip overlaps the edge of the facings around the opening, allowing more freedom in fitting (see Fig. 12-58).

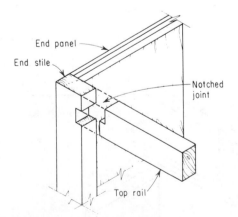

FIGURE 12-62: *Partition panel with notch cut for wall strap.*

FIGURE 12-63: *Top rail-to-stile joint.*

355

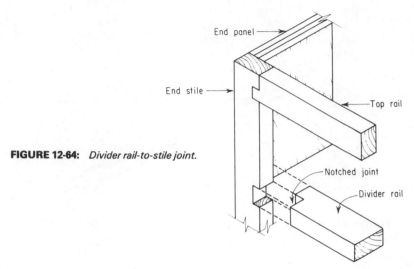

FIGURE 12-64: *Divider rail-to-stile joint.*

End panel

End stile

Top rail

Notched joint

Divider rail

Various construction techniques are used in making drawers, the choice depending on: (a) whether the drawer is flush or overlapping, (b) the type of drawer guide to be used, and (c) the carpenter's preference as to the type of joints to be used.

The front will normally be 19 mm plywood, the sides and back 12 mm material and the bottom 6 mm plywood or hardboard. Figure 12-65 illustrates some drawer joint and assembly details and Fig. 12-66, an assembled overlapping front drawer.

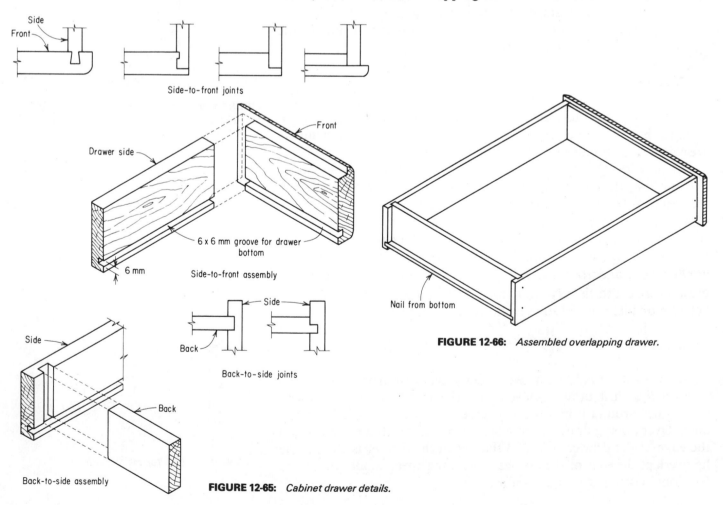

Side

Front

Side-to-front joints

Front

Drawer side

6 x 6 mm groove for drawer bottom

6 mm

Side-to-front assembly

Side

Back

Side

Back

Back-to-side joints

Side

Back

Back-to-side assembly

FIGURE 12-65: *Cabinet drawer details.*

Nail from bottom

FIGURE 12-66: *Assembled overlapping drawer.*

Drawer Guides

Drawers must be guided during opening and closing and held in an approximately horizontal position when open. Types of drawer guide include *corner* guide, *side* guide and *center* guide. When corner guides are used, an additional member, a *kicker*, must be added above the drawer to keep it level when it is open. Figure 12-67 illustrates a typical corner guide assembly and kicker location.

Side guides consist of narrow strips approximately 10 × 12 mm, fixed to the side of the drawer opening, which fit into grooves cut in the sides of the drawer. They not only guide the drawer but hold it in a level position as well (see Fig. 12-68).

A center guide is located on the bottom of the drawer and consists of a grooved *guide bar* attached to the drawer bottom and a *runner* attached to the dividing rail. A kicker is also necessary with this type of guide (see Fig. 12-69). Center guide drawer hardware is also available for the same purpose.

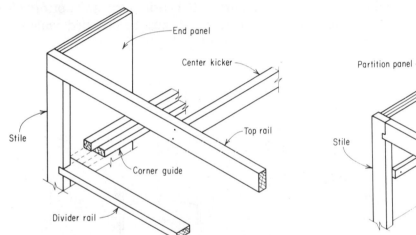

FIGURE 12-67: *Corner guide and kicker details.*

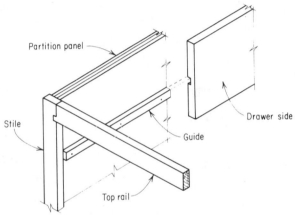

FIGURE 12-68: *Side guide for cabinet drawer.*

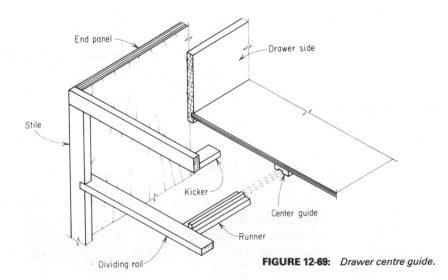

FIGURE 12-69: *Drawer centre guide.*

357

Wall Cabinets

The construction of wall cabinets is a relatively simple procedure. Side panels of 19 mm plywood are cut to size, rabbetted at both ends for the bottom shelf and cabinet top and dadoed to receive the ends of intermediate shelves (see Fig. 12-70). Narrow straps glued under the back edge of the top and one intermediate shelf are used to fasten the cabinet to the wall. After assembly, the cabinet is secured in place and the facings installed.

Revolving Shelves

In the corners of L-shaped and U-shaped counter sections of cabinets there will be a considerable amount of space which will be inaccessible by the conventional type of cabinet door. That space can be made available by the use of *carousel shelving*—circular shelves which turn on a central shaft, with bearings top and bottom. The unit is available as a hardware item and must be installed while the counter section is being framed (see Fig. 12-71).

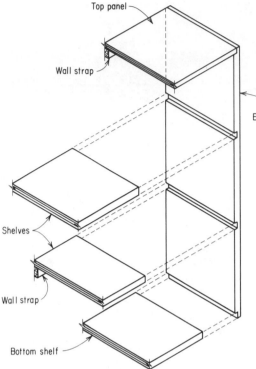

FIGURE 12-70: *Wall cabinet assembly.*

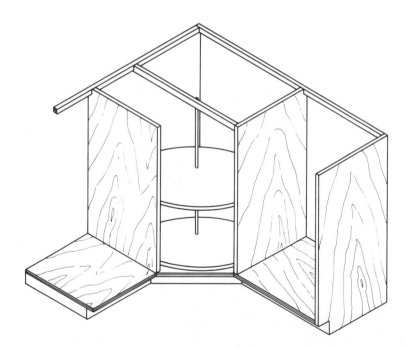

FIGURE 12-71:*Carousel shelving in place.*

Counter Tops

The top of the counter section is generally made from 16 or 19 mm plywood or particle board, cut wide enough to allow for a 25 mm overhang at the front (see Fig. 12-59). It is fixed in place by glue and by nailing through the top into the edges of panels, top rail, and wall strap.

Most counter tops are covered with some type of plastic laminate which is attached to the counter surface with *contact cement*. The cement is applied to the back of the laminate and the surface of the counter and allowed to dry before the material is set in place. Care must be taken to ensure that the topping is in the proper position before contact is made because adhesion between the two surfaces is instantaneous.

Exposed counter edges are covered first. After the strip is in place, the top edge is dressed flush with the counter top. The top sheet must be cut to fit snugly against the wall and overhang the front edge slightly. Cement is applied to both meeting surfaces and allowed to dry. When the sheet is ready for installation, the dried cement on the counter surface may be covered with paper but the cement *must be dry* before this is done so that the paper will not stick to the surface. The laminate sheet can then be laid on the paper, adjustments made in position and the paper removed, allowing the two cement surfaces to contact. Full contact should be insured by tapping the surface with a wooden mallet or rubber hammer. The slight overhang can then be removed with a coarse file or with a special cutter available to fit a router.

Sinks

One important item in cabinet building is the installation of a sink and it is common practice to wait until the plastic laminate top is on before installing it.

The first step is to mark the shape of the sink rim in its proper location on the counter top and cut a hole slightly larger than the sink rim in the top.

The sink is held in place by a special frame, the same shape as the sink, having a cross section as illustrated in Fig. 12-72. One lip of the frame rests on the counter top, the other on the sink rim, and the web projects down into the opening.

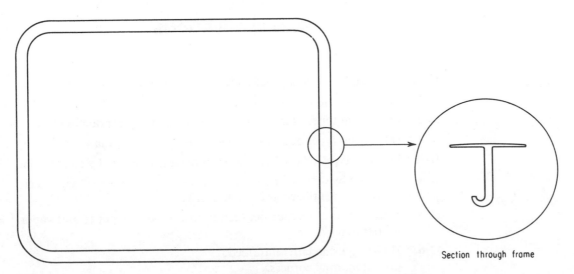

Section through frame

FIGURE 12-72: *Sink frame.*

359

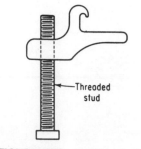

FIGURE 12-73: *Sink frame clip.*

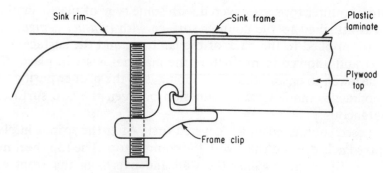

FIGURE 12-74: *Sink frame in place.*

The sink is placed in the opening, temporarily supported and the sink frame fitted over it. To ensure a watertight fit, a light bead of caulking compound should be run all around the edge of the hole before the sink frame is set down. Then, from the underside, clips such as the one shown in Fig. 12-73 are used to secure the sink in place, as illustrated in Fig. 12-74.

Approximate imperial equivalents to metric quantities

1.5 mm	—	1/16 in.	150 mm	—	6 in.
3 mm	—	1/8 in.	225 mm	—	9 in.
9 mm	—	3/8 in.	400 mm	—	16 in.
12 mm	—	1/2 in.	900 mm	—	36 in.
16 mm	—	5/8 in.	1200 mm	—	48 in.
19 mm	—	3/4 in.	2100 mm	—	7 ft
25 mm	—	1 in.	2400 mm	—	8 ft
35 mm	—	1 3/8 in.	75 × 89 mm	—	3 × 4 in.
40 mm	—	1 1/2 in.	19 × 89 mm	—	1 × 4 in.
65 mm	—	2 1/2 in.	0.75 kg/m²	—	15 lb/ft²
100 mm	—	4 in.			

REVIEW QUESTIONS

12-1. **(a)** Explain how heat is lost from a building by conduction.

   (b) How is it lost by radiation?

12-2. **(a)** What types of material prevent heat loss by conduction?

   (b) What types of material prevent heat loss by radiation?

12-3. List four types of insulation used to prevent heat loss by conduction.

12-4. Illustrate by diagram how batts are installed between studs, if their cover is to be utilized as a vapor barrier.

12-5. What is the difference between moisture barrier paper and vapor barrier paper?

12-6. How is gypsum lath reinforced:
   (a) at internal corners.
   (b) at external corners.

12-7. Explain what is meant by a "laminated dry wall finish."

12-8. Illustrate four methods of treating joints between sheets of plywood used as interior finish.

12-9. Explain how "pre-expanding" of hardboards is carried out.

12-10. **(a)** List four types of hardwood flooring in common use.

 (b) Why is the bottom surface of hardwood flooring strips concave?

 (c) Why is 12 mm space left between flooring and wall?

 (d) What is meant by "blind" nailing?

12-11. What is the basic difference between a mortise lock and a cylindrical lock?

12-12. **(a)** Where is the strike plate located?

 (b) What is the normal height of a door knob from the floor?

 (c) What is a hinge "gain"?

12-13. **(a)** How is the hand of a door determined?

 (b) If a door swings from the outside toward you, with the hinges on the left hand, it is a _____ door.

12-14. Name six commonly used "trim" materials.

12-15. What is meant by "coping" a joint in trim?

12-16. Give the usual dimensions for:

 (a) height of toe space under kitchen counter section.

 (b) height of counter section above floor.

 (c) distance between upper and lower sections of kitchen cabinets.

 (d) maximum drawer width.

13

POST-AND-BEAM CON-STRUCTION

The post-and-beam method of framing consists essentially of a framework made up of *beams, posts,* and *decking,* supported on a foundation. It dates back over a long period of time to early Greek structures and has been used in traditional Japanese homes, in Tudor homes in Britain and in English and American Colonial homes.

The method differs from conventional framing in the size and spacing of the framing members. Whereas conventional framing uses *joists, studs,* and *rafters,* usually spaced 400 mm o.c. (see Fig. 13-1), post-and-beam construction uses larger members with much larger spacings (see Fig. 13-2). The beams are used for the floor and roof frame, while the posts produce the wall frame and support the roof structure. Horizontal spaces between beams are normally spanned by plank decking, although conventional joist construction may be used between beams (see Fig. 13-3). The spaces between posts are filled with prefabricated wall panels, glass panels (see Fig. 13-4), supplementary framing and sheathing or masonry panels.

In contrast to conventional framing, in which the framework is hidden by exterior sheathing and inside finish, the post-and-beam frame is very frequently left exposed for architectural effect (see Fig. 13-5).

A combination of post-and-beam with conventional framing may also be used and, indeed, this combination may well provide the lateral stability which must be specially provided for in a complete post-and-beam structure (see Fig. 13-6).

This system has its limitations, of course. In the first place, the plank floors are intended for uniformly distributed loads; where concentrated loads occur, extra framing is required beneath them. Secondly, insulation normally placed in the ceiling frame or in stud walls must be incorporated into the building in a different manner. Insulation applied to the outside of a roof deck must be of the rigid variety; if it is applied inside, it must be a material which can become a part of the interior finish. In walls, the insulation must be introduced in the infill panels. Electrical wiring may be more difficult to hide but hollow or spaced beams may provide one partial solution to this problem.

Post-and-beam, though similar in style, should not be confused with *heavy timber construction* (see Fig. 13-7). In building codes, *heavy timber* is classified by itself as a structural material, with appropriate stress ratings and specific minimum sizes are required for beams, columns and other components. Figure 13-8 illustrates typical post-and-beam framing, with the wall in one corner framed with conventional framing to provide lateral stability.

FIGURE 13-1: *Conventional framing.*

FIGURE 13-2: *Post-and-beam construction.*

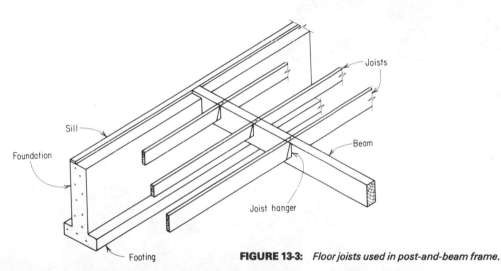

Joists

Sill

Foundation

Beam

Joist hanger

Footing

FIGURE 13-3: *Floor joists used in post-and-beam frame.*

FIGURE 13-4: *Glass panels in post-and-beam frame.*

FIGURE 13-5: *Exposed post-and-beam frame.*

FIGURE 13-6: *Combination post-and-beam and conventional construction.*

FIGURE 13-7: *Heavy timber construction.*

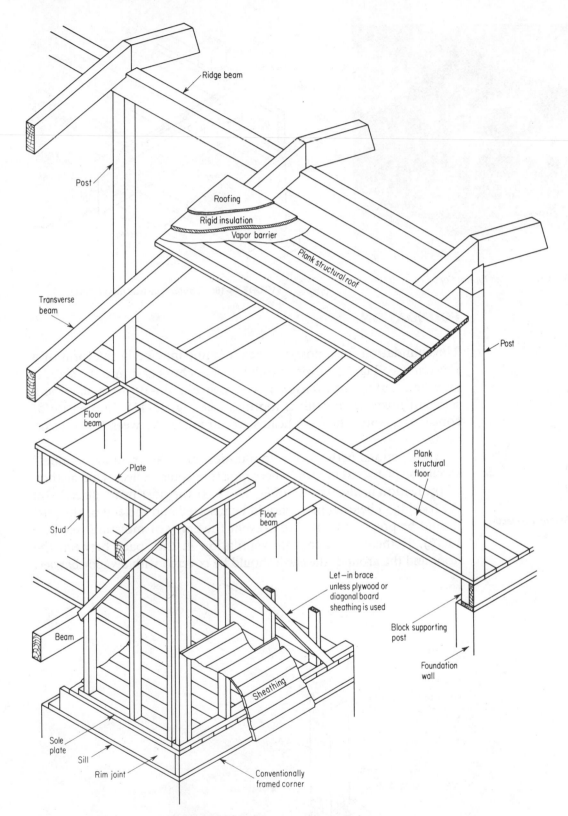

Ridge beam

Post

Roofing

Rigid insulation

Vapor barrier

Plank structural roof

Transverse beam

Post

Floor beam

Plate

Plank structural floor

Stud

Floor beam

Let–in brace unless plywood or diagonal board sheathing is used

Beam

Block supporting post

Foundation wall

Sheathing

Sole plate

Sill

Rim joint

Conventionally framed corner

FIGURE 13-8: *Typical post-and-beam frame.*

365

FIGURE 13-9: *Flat slab foundation.*

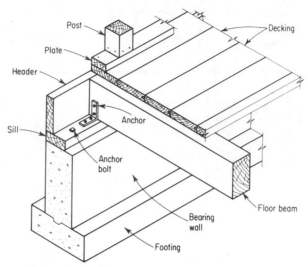

FIGURE 13-10: *Continuous wall foundation.*

FOUNDATION

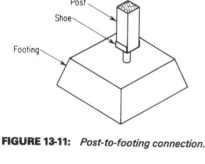

FIGURE 13-11: *Post-to-footing connection.*

The foundation for a post-and-beam frame may be in the form of a *flat slab* (see Fig. 13-9) with special post anchors cast into the slab. It may be a *continuous masonry wall* (see Fig. 13-10) or it may be a series of *posts* on individual footings (see Fig. 13-11). In the case of continuous walls, the floor beams are supported between the walls on posts.

Connections between the foundation and the framing members should be protected in areas where moisture could collect. One method of protection is illustrated in Fig. 13-11. If the post bears directly on the footing, a bearing plate should be inserted and the end of the post should be pressure-treated to prevent the entry of moisture (see Fig. 13-12). If there is inadequate ventilation in the space between the floor and the ground, the earth should be covered with a vapor barrier.

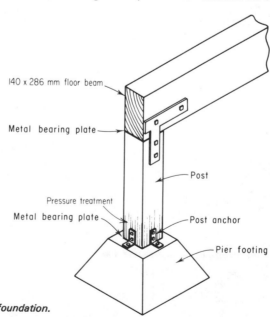

FIGURE 13-12: *Pier and post foundation.*

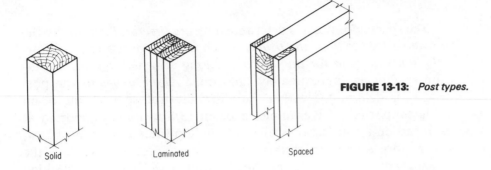

FIGURE 13-13: *Post types.*

Solid   Laminated   Spaced

POSTS

Post Types

The type of post used will vary, depending on its location, on the length required, the load to be supported, and the availability of material. It may be a solid member—either a *sawn* or a *glue-laminated timber* or, if the load is light, it may be a *spaced member,* as illustrated in Fig. 13-13.

Post Sizes

Solid posts will normally be at least 89 × 89 mm in cross section, with one dimension equal to the width of the beam which rests on top. Where two beams meet on a post, the dimension of the bearing surface parallel to the beams should be at least 140 mm. For a small post, this may be provided by adding *bearing blocks* to the sides of the post, as illustrated in Fig. 13-14.

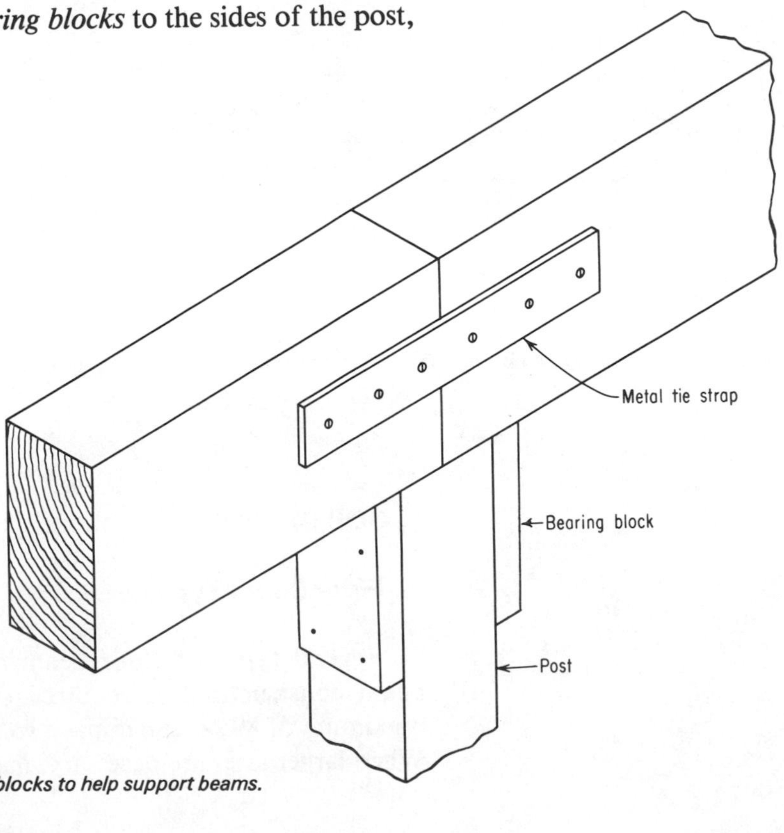

Metal tie strap

Bearing block

Post

FIGURE 13-14: *Bearing blocks to help support beams.*

Post Spacing

The spacing of posts is determined by *architectural design,* by the *allowable free span of the beams* which they support and the *allowable limits of span for the decking.* Along an exterior wall, a common spacing is approximately 1200 mm. *Along a beam,* the post spacing is determined within the allowable free span of the beam being supported. For example, a beam 13.8 m long, supported at each end on a foundation wall, with an allowable free span of 3 m, will require four supporting posts. In the opposite dimension, the spacing will be determined by the allowable free span of the decking being used.

Post Anchors

The method of anchoring posts in place depends on the type of base to which they are to be secured. Posts will usually be anchored to a concrete base by means of a shoe or by two metal angles, as illustrated in Figs. 13-11 and 13-12. If posts rest on a wooden beam or plate, they may be secured by nailing or by metal anchor straps (see Fig. 13-15).

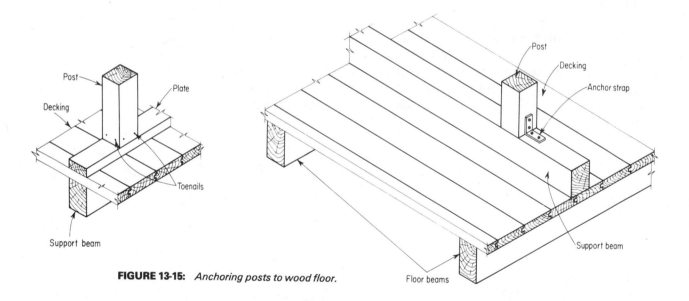

FIGURE 13-15: *Anchoring posts to wood floor.*

FLOOR BEAMS

Floor Beam Types

Several types of floor beam are available for use in post-and-beam construction. If required sizes are small—up to a probable maximum of 89 × 286 mm—a *solid timber* beam is the likely choice. When larger sizes are necessary, *laminated beams* will usually be more

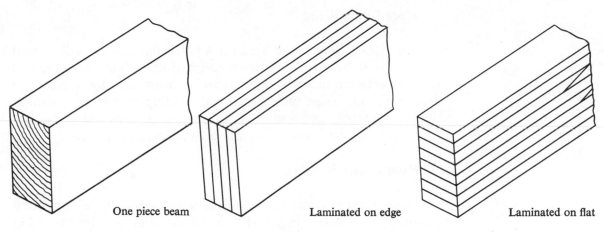

One piece beam   Laminated on edge   Laminated on flat

FIGURE 13-16: *Solid beams.*

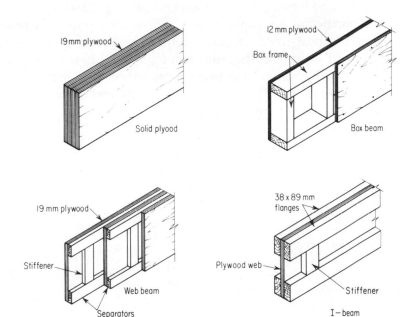

19 mm plywood

Solid plyood

12 mm plywood

Box frame

Box beam

19 mm plywood

Stiffener

Web beam

Separators

38 x 89 mm flanges

Plywood web

Stiffener

I – beam

FIGURE 13-17: *Plywood beam types.*

economical. These may have the components laminated together on *edge* or on the *flat* (see Fig. 13-16), the latter being more common.

Floor beams may also be made from plywood or a combination of plywood and lumber. Four types are made—*solid plywood* beams, *web* beams, *box* beams, and plywood *I-beams*.

A solid plywood beam consists of strips of plywood of the proper width nailed or glued together. A web beam is made by separating strips of plywood with horizontal strips of solid lumber, with or without vertical stiffeners (see Fig. 13-17). A box beam is made by first constructing a frame of 38 × 89, 140 or 184 mm material, as may be required and covering the frame on both sides with a plywood skin, nailed and glued in place (see Fig. 13-17). The I-beam is made by gluing lumber *flanges* to the top and bottom edges of a plywood web, to form the type of beam illustrated in Fig. 13-17.

Floor Beam Sizes

The size of floor beam used for a particular project will depend on the load to be supported, the amount of deflection permitted and the span between supports. Sizes must be determined by reference to available beam design tables, the local building code or by consultation with a recognized authority. In the case of plywood beams, information on sizes is available from plywood manufacturers.

Floor Beam Framing

Floor beam ends carried by a foundation wall may be supported on top of the wall (see Fig. 13-10) or rest in a *beam pocket* formed in the top of the foundation. In the case of a beam pocket, a metal *bearing plate,* set in grout, should be used in the bottom of the pocket to provide solid bearing for the beam end (see Fig. 13-18).

Floor beams are supported at intermediate points by posts, and beam and post must be tied together by some type of connector, usually a T-strap, like that shown in Fig. 13-12. In situations in which the post is *continuous,* the beam is carried on it by means of a *framing anchor* (see Fig. 13-19). In such cases, the end of the beam must be notched to fit over the anchor.

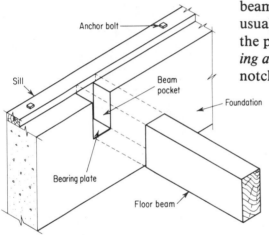

FIGURE 13-18: *Beam pocket.*

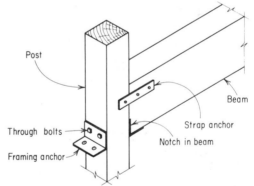

FIGURE 13-19: *Beam anchored to continuous post.*

ROOF BEAMS

Types and Sizes

The roof frame in post-and-beam construction consists of a *ridge beam* and *transverse beams,* which span from the ridge to the wall plates (see Fig. 13-8) or a ridge beam and one or more *longitudinal beams,* parallel to the ridge, on either side of it (see Fig. 13-20).

The ridge beam and longitudinal beams will usually be the same type of beam used in the floor frame and will be designed for size according to the load that they must support. The transverse beams may also be one of those types, though smaller in size, due to the lighter load, or they may be *spaced beams,* like that illustrated in Fig. 13-21.

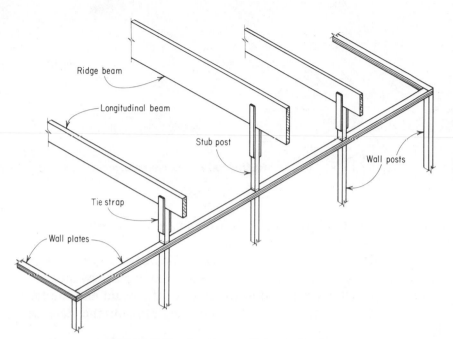

FIGURE 13-20: *Roof frame with longitudinal beams.*

FIGURE 13-21: *Spaced roof beam.*

Roof Frame Connections

A ridge beam or longitudinal beam may be supported at its ends by stub posts resting on the end wall plates (see Fig. 13-20), or continuous posts in the wall frame may be utilized to support it (see Fig. 13-22). In either case the beam and post must be tied together by *straps* running up the sides of the post and overlapping the beam, as shown in Fig. 13-22.

Transverse beams may be carried on top of the ridge (see Fig. 13-23), in which case they will be tied together with a metal strap over the top or a metal gusset across the joint, as shown in Fig. 13-23. They may also be supported on the sides of the ridge beam by means

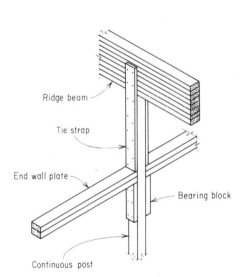

FIGURE 13-22: *Continuous post supporting ridge beam.*

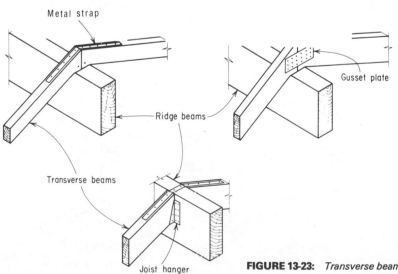

FIGURE 13-23: *Transverse beam connections at ridge.*

371

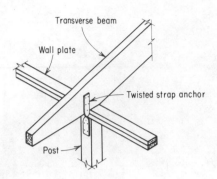

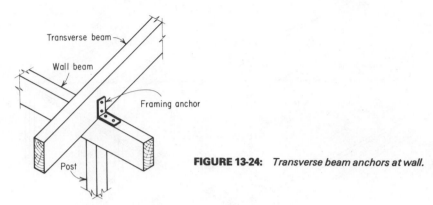

FIGURE 13-24: *Transverse beam anchors at wall.*

of joist hangers (see Fig. 13-23), in which case two opposing beams will be tied together with a metal strap.

At the plate or wall beam, the lower ends of transverse beams must be cut to fit the flat surface and are secured in place by means of twisted strap anchors attached to the sides of the beam and the face of the post or by metal angles fastened to the beam and the plate (see Fig. 13-24).

Exposed Beam Finishes

A variety of techniques are used to trim the underside of exposed beams. They will vary somewhat, depending on whether the beam is solid or spaced and on whether it is made of solid timber or plywood. Figure 13-25 illustrates a number of commonly used methods.

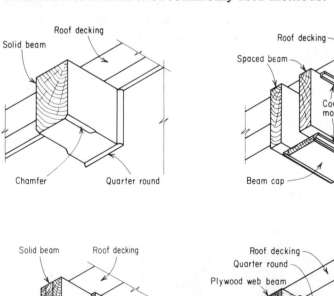

FIGURE 13-25: *Finishes for exposed beams.*

The ends of overhanging beams that are exposed to the weather are subjected to rapid and extreme fluctuations in moisture content as moisture penetrates or leaves the end grain of the wood. These ends should be sealed with an impenetrable sealer or covered with wood caps to prevent deterioration and eventual decay.

FLOOR AND ROOF DECKS

Floor and roof decks may consist of exposed planking or conventional joist construction, although plank decks lend themselves to post-and-beam construction and are used extensively.

Planks

Floor and roof planks will be 38, 64, or 89 mm material of various species, notably fir, southern pine, spruce or cedar, *tongue-and-grooved, double tongue-and-grooved* or *grooved for spline* (see Fig. 13-26).

Plank Spans

Several methods are used for laying planks, including *simple span, two-span-continuous, multiple-span-continuous* and *controlled-random pattern* (see Fig. 13-27), and the amount of deflection occurring in the planks between supports depends on the method. For example, using the two-span-continuous method, the deflection will be about 41 percent of that occurring in the simple span, for the same load. Controlled-random pattern method will produce about 77 percent of the deflection that occurs with the simple span method.

Tongue-and-groove

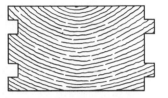
Double tongue-and-groove

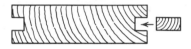
Grooved for spline

FIGURE 13-26: *Types of planking.*

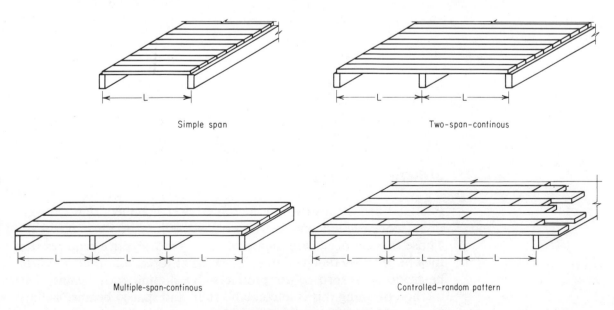

Simple span

Two-span-continous

Multiple-span-continous

Controlled-random pattern

FIGURE 13-27: *Deck-laying patterns.*

Plank Installation

Planks used for decking should be in a dry condition—that is, they should contain not more than 15 percent moisture, in order to avoid unsightly gaps between planks as the wood dries.

The plank thickness will be determined by the load to be imposed and the spacing of the beams, while the width, in many codes, will be restricted to a maximum of 184 mm. Lengths should be chosen to conform to the plank span pattern chosen. In the case of controlled-random pattern, random length decking can be used.

Planks 140 mm or less in width should be fastened to each beam with two nails, while 184 mm planks should have three nails per beam. Nails should be twice as long as the nominal thickness of the plank.

Projecting ends of roof planking should be protected by capping with a 38 mm fascia, as indicated in Fig. 13-28 and trimmed with a narrower piece of 19 mm material.

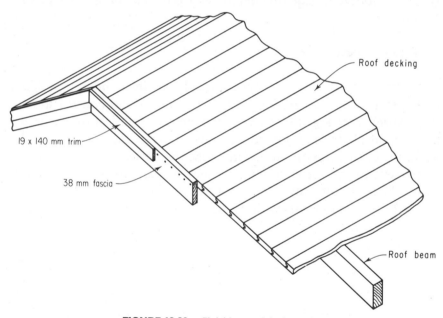

FIGURE 13-28: *Finishing roof deck overhang.*

JOINTS

Post-and-beam construction contains fewer members than conventional construction and therefore fewer joints between members. Those that do occur are important and good practice requires that they be properly designed to resist external forces and that provision be made to absorb *thrust* produced by sloping roof beams. One method of doing this is to combine solid and spaced beams, as illustrated in Fig. 13-29.

374

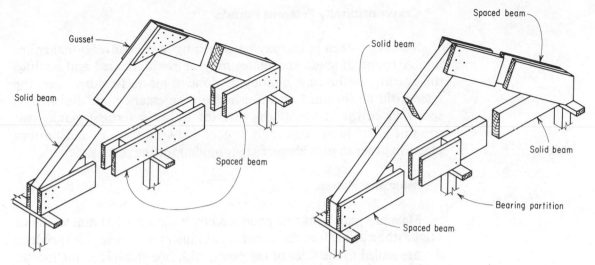

FIGURE 13-29: *Arrangement of beams to counteract thrust.*

CURTAIN WALLS

The spaces between posts and between top plate and roof deck in post-and-beam construction may be enclosed in a number of different ways but in each case the material forms a *curtain wall*—it encloses space but carries no structural load.

Among the types of curtain wall used are: *glass, masonry, conventionally framed panels,* and *sandwich panels.*

Glass Curtain Wall

Glass curtain wall is usually in the form of thermopane units that may be installed directly into the opening or frames containing the panes may be custom-made to fit.

When glass is installed directly between posts, the first step is to install a tapered *sill* at the bottom of the opening, that will overhang to the outside in the same manner as a conventional window sill. If required, *dividers* may be used to divide the space into smaller areas. Inside stops are nailed in place, the panes installed and the outside stops installed to secure the pane. A bead of caulking compound should be placed behind the outside stop to seal the joint against air infiltration (see Fig. 13-30).

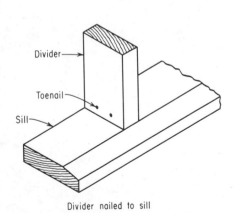

Divider nailed to sill

FIGURE 13-30: *Sill, dividers and stops.*

Conventionally Framed Panels

Spaces between posts may be closed by using conventional framing. A frame of studs and plates may be prefabricated and set into the opening or the framing may be done in place. In either case, the frame will be sheathed and finished on the exterior and finished as specified on the inside. If the exterior finish is vertical plank, two rows of *girts* should be evenly spaced between the top and bottom plates in order to provide sufficient nailing for the planks.

Masonry Panels

Masonry panels may be produced by building a 100 mm wythe of brick, stone or tile into the opening, as illustrated in Fig. 13-31. Metal ties are nailed to the sides of the posts, with one end laid in the mortar joints in the masonry.

The masonry finish may also be in the form of a thin veneer over a sheathed wood frame, applied as described in Chapter 11.

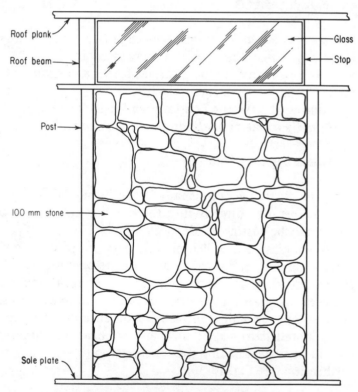

FIGURE 13-31: *Masonry panel in post-and-beam frame.*

Sandwich Panels

A sandwich panel consists of two outer skins of thin plywood or other types of building board, with a layer of some type of rigid insulation cemented in between them, as illustrated in Fig. 13-32. Panels may be square-edged and installed in the openings with *stops,* as glass would be or they may be made with a *flange* on the inside and installed as illustrated in Fig. 13-33. Caulking should be applied behind the stops or the flange for a tight seal.

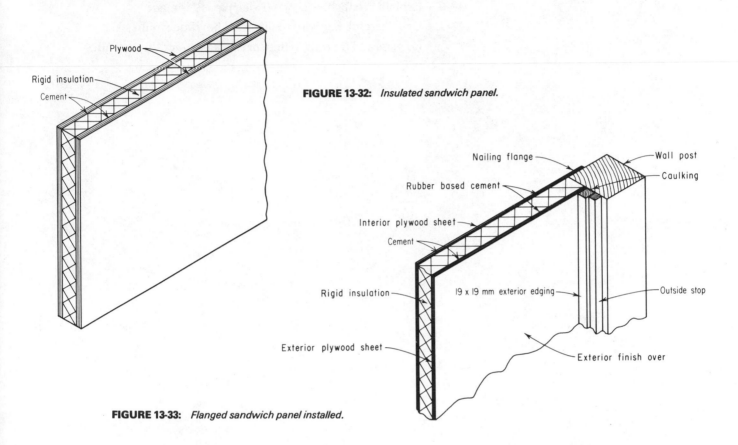

FIGURE 13-32: *Insulated sandwich panel.*

FIGURE 13-33: *Flanged sandwich panel installed.*

Approximate imperial equivalents to metric quantities

19 mm	—	¾ in.	400 mm	—	16 in.	38 × 89	—	2 × 4
100 mm	—	4 in.	1200 mm	—	4 ft	38 × 140	—	2 × 6
140 mm	—	6 in.	3 m	—	10 ft	38 × 184	—	2 × 8
184 mm	—	8 in.	13.8 m	—	46 ft	38 × 235	—	2 × 10
						38 × 286	—	2 × 12

REVIEW QUESTIONS

13-1. Outline the major differences between post-and-beam and conventional framing.

13-2. List three of the main advantages that you see in post-and-beam construction over conventional framing. Explain why you think each of these is important.

13-3. By means of diagrams, illustrate the difference between tongue-and-grooved planking and splined planking.

13-4. Explain what is meant by a "curtain wall."

13-5. Outline two methods of forming a sloping roof with post-and-beam construction.

13-6. Explain briefly how a "sandwich panel" is made.

13-7. Draw careful diagrams to illustrate how you would fix:

(a) glass and (b) sandwich panels in a post-and-beam wall.

The basic materials involved in masonry construction are *brick, stone, structural tile* and *concrete block,* together with the *mortar* used to bind them together. Brick and stone have been primary building materials since time immemorial, while the other two made their appearance in more recent times, the first concrete blocks being molded in the 1880's.

Increasing use is being made of all these materials and no discussions of light construction would be complete without a description of the basic methods of using them in modern buildings.

CONCRETE BLOCK CONSTRUCTION

'Concrete block' is the name given to a type of masonry unit made from a mix of fine aggregate and cement, with or without color added. A very dry mix is used and the blocks are molded under pressure by a vibrating machine, like that illustrated in Fig. 14-1.

A great variety of blocks are available, in a wide range of *types, shapes, sizes,* and *surface textures,* each for a specific purpose. Figure 14-2 illustrates some of the common shapes used in building construction.

Concrete block can be used for *basement walls,* for *exterior* and *partition walls,* for *foundation piers* and for *curtain walls* in steel or reinforced concrete frame buildings. Regardless of the use to which the blocks are to be put, a basic requirement for good results, both from the standpoint of structural stability and good appearance, is good mortar.

Mortar

Mortar serves a number of purposes, the main one being to *join the masonry units together* into a strong, well-knit structure. In addition, mortar is required to produce *tight seals between units,* to *bond to steel reinforcement, metal ties and anchor bolts,* to *provide a bed* which will accommodate variations in the size of units and to *provide an architectural effect* by the various treatments given to mortar joints in exposed walls.

Masonry mortar is composed of one or more *cementatious materials* (normal portland cement, masonry cement and hydrated lime), clean, well-graded *masonry sand,* and enough *water* to produce a plastic, workable misture. In addition, *admixtures* (accelerators, retarders and water-reducing agents) may be added for some special purpose.

A number of mortar types are recognized, based on strength and composed of varying amounts of cement and hydrated lime, by

MASONRY CON-STRUCTION

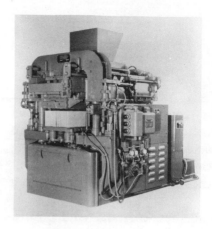

FIGURE 14-1: *Concrete block-making machine.*

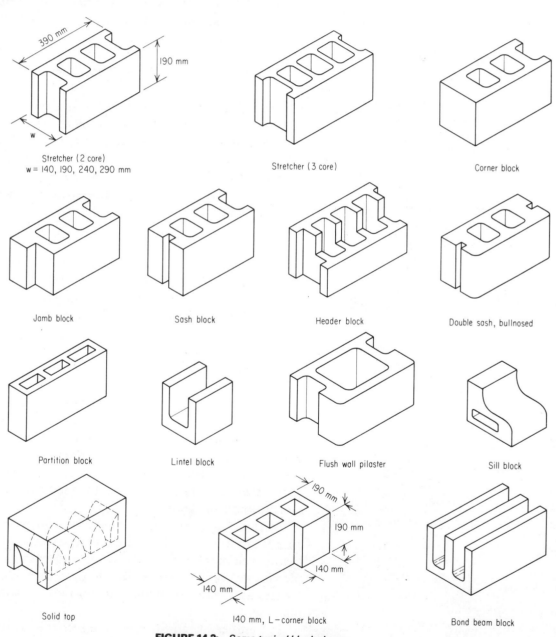

Stretcher (2 core)
w = 140, 190, 240, 290 mm

Stretcher (3 core)

Corner block

Jamb block

Sash block

Header block

Double sash, bullnosed

Partition block

Lintel block

Flush wall pilaster

Sill block

Solid top

140 mm, L-corner block

Bond beam block

FIGURE 14-2: *Some typical block shapes.*

volume. Table 14-1 indicates these types and the proportions of ingredients in each case.

TABLE 14-1: *Mortar types by cement and lime proportions*

		Parts by volume		
Specification	*Mortar type*	*Portland cement*	*Masonry cement*	*Hydrated lime or lime putty*
	M	1	1	—
		1	—	¼
	S	½	1	—
		1	—	over ¼ to ½
For plain masonry ASTM C270 CSA A179	N	—	1	—
		1	—	over ½ to 1¼
	O	—	1	—
		1	—	over 1¼ to 2½
	K	1	—	over 2½ to 4
For reinforced masonry ASTM C476	PM	1	1	—
	PL	1	—	¼ to ½

(Courtesy Portland Cement Association)

In order to obtain good workability and allow the development of the maximum strength possible, mortar ingredients must be thoroughly mixed. Whenever possible, the mixing should be done by machine, except when only a small quantity of mortar is required.

Mixing time should be from three to five minutes after all ingredients have been added. A shorter mixing time may result in poor-quality mortar, while a longer mixing time may adversely affect the air content of mortars made with air-entraining cements.

If the mortar becomes stiff because of water evaporation, it may be *retempered* by the addition of a little water and thorough remixing. However, if the stiffness is due to partial hydration, the material should be discarded. Mortar should be used within two hours after the original mixing, if the temperature is above 26 °C, or within three hours if the temperature is below that point.

Two methods are used for applying mortar to concrete masonry units. One is to apply the mortar to the two long edges only. This is known as *face-shell bedding* (see Fig. 14-3). The other is to apply mortar to the cross webs as well as the face shells and this is known as *full mortar bedding* (see Fig. 14-4).

FIGURE 14-3: *Face-shell bedding.*

FIGURE 14-4: *Full mortar bedding.*

Laying Blocks

The first step in laying blocks is to locate accurately the positions of the corners of the building on the footings and establish the line of the outside of the wall. This can be done by taking the dimensions from the plans and snapping chalk lines on the footing to indicate

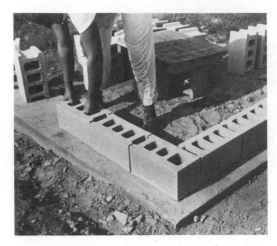

FIGURE 14-5: *Test lay-up for spacing.*

the corners and building lines. Then the first course may be laid without mortar to ascertain what spacing is required between blocks (see Fig. 14-5), although in general, that spacing should be 10 mm, in order to maintain a 400 mm module, center-to-center of mortar joints.

Now remove the blocks, spread a full bed of mortar long enough to accommodate at least three blocks and lay the corner block, making sure that it is *to the line, plumb,* and *level.* Butter the ends of the face shells of the second block, bring it over its final position and set it down into the mortar bed, while at the same time pressing it against the previously laid block so as to insure a tight vertical joint (see Fig. 14-6).

Now butter the ends of several blocks, as shown in Fig. 14-7, so that they can be laid up in quick succession. After several blocks have been laid each way, use a straightedge and level to make sure that the blocks are *aligned,* brought to the *correct level,* and *plumb,* as illustrated in Fig. 14-8.

After the first course is laid, build up the corners as shown in Fig. 14-9. Use a story pole to insure that the bedding joints are maintained at the same thickness for each course, so that the four corners will remain level with one another. A story pole is simply a long, slim strip of wood on which the height of each block plus its mortar joint is laid out (see Fig. 14-10). Use the straightedge and level frequently to make sure that the corners are plumb and level (see Fig. 14-11).

FIGURE 14-6: *Full mortar bed for first course.*

FIGURE 14-7: *Mortar on block ends.*

FIGURE 14-8: *Block aligning, levelling and plumbing.*

FIGURE 14-9: *Building up corners.*

FIGURE 14-10: *Using a storey pole.*

FIGURE 14-11: *Plumbing and levelling corners.*

FIGURE 14-12: *Line from corner to corner.*

FIGURE 14-13: *Line holder in place.*

FIGURE 14-14: *Mechanical mortar spreader.*

When the corners have been built up, the walls are completed between them. To do so, a line is run from corner to corner, along the top edge of the course to be laid (see Fig. 14-12). The line is held by a *line holder* (see Fig. 14-13) attached to each corner and adjusted so that the line is at the correct height—level with the top of the block. The line is then drawn as tight as possible to provide a horizontal guide for the blocks in the course.

The bed joint mortar is then laid, either by hand or by machine (see Fig. 14-14) and the ends of enough blocks buttered to complete the course (see Fig. 14-3). Set each block carefully and tap it down till it comes to the line (see Fig. 14-12).

FIGURE 14-15: *Vertical edges buttered.*

FIGURE 14-16: *Closure block set in place.*

FIGURE 14-17: *Removing excess mortar extruded from joint.*

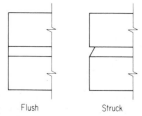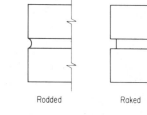

Flush   Struck   Rodded   Raked

FIGURE 14-18: *Tooled mortar joint styles.*

FIGURE 14-19: *Forming a rodded joint.*

The final block in each course is the *closure* block. Butter all the edges of the opening (see Fig. 14-15) and the four vertical edges of the closure block. Set it carefully into place (see Fig. 14-16) and make sure that the mortar is pressed firmly into the joint. Finally, remove any extruded mortar that appears, on both the exterior and interior faces of the wall (see Fig. 14-17).

After the mortar is set hard enough that it can just be dented by the thumb nail, the joint may be *tooled*—shaped and compacted. Several styles of joint are made, including *flush, struck, rodded,* and *raked* (see Fig. 14-18), all of which are watertight if properly done. Figure 14-19 illustrates a tool being used to produce a rodded joint.

It is sometimes necessary to use short lengths of block to complete a course. These will usually be cut from a block with an abrasive wheel, though, in some cases, the cutting is done by hand. The piece is introduced into the wall in exactly the same way as a whole or half block (see Fig. 14-20).

FIGURE 14-20: *Short piece of block built into wall.*

FIGURE 14-21: *Setting anchor bolt in block wall.*

Plate Anchored to Block Wall

When a wooden plate is to be fastened to the top of a block wall, anchor bolts are used. They should be 12 mm in diameter, 450 mm long, and not more than 1.2 m apart. Lay a piece of metal lath over the cell in which the bolt will be set, two courses below the top of the wall, as shown in Fig. 14-21. When the wall is complete, fill the cell with concrete and set the bolt in place so that at least 50 mm project above the wall.

Control Joints

Movements do occur in masonry walls from various kinds of stresses, and if these are not controlled, cracking will occur in step fashion along the mortar joints. To control these movements and eliminate cracking, *control joints* are used. These are continuous vertical joints built into the masonry wall at critical points (see Fig. 14-22). The joint should first be laid up with mortar like any other vertical joint but the bond between blocks on either side of the joint should be minimized. This may be done by inserting pieces of asphalt-impregnated paper between blocks (see Fig. 14-23). To provide lateral

FIGURE 14-22: *Constructing control joint.*

FIGURE 14-23: *Bond breaker at control joint.*

385

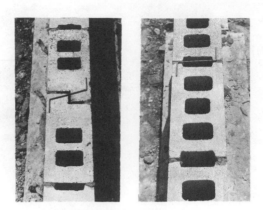

FIGURE 14-24: Control joint lateral tie.

FIGURE 14-25: Raking and caulking control joint.

support, metal ties are laid across the joint, in every second horizontal course, as shown in Figure 14-24. Later, the control joint is raked out about 20 mm deep and the groove filled with caulking compound (see Fig. 14-25).

Intersecting Walls

Two methods are used to joint two intersecting walls. One is to butt the cross wall against the inner face of the other, in which case, whole and half blocks are required alternately, as the start of each course (see Fig. 14-26a). In the other a *chase* (recess) is built into the main wall and the blocks of the cross wall are set into it (see Fig. 14-26b). In either case, a control joint is involved at the intersection and the two walls should be tied together with metal straps or by wire mesh laid across the junction (see Fig. 14-27).

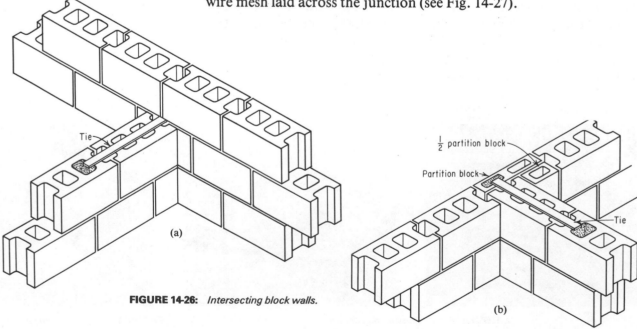

FIGURE 14-26: Intersecting block walls.

FIGURE 14-27: *Ties for intersecting walls.*

Lintels

The wall load over door and window openings in block construction must be supported by a horizontal member which spans the opening and is carried on solid bearing at each end. Such a member is called a *lintel* and it may be provided by two different methods. One is to use a precast concrete lintel, designed for the span, with its ends resting on the block at each side of the opening (see Fig. 14-28).

The other method involves the use of *lintel blocks,* illustrated in Fig. 14-2. They are laid across the top of the opening and filled with reinforced concrete. Lintel blocks must be supported until the concrete has hardened and this may be done in one of two ways. One is to set the window frame in place and use it to support the blocks, as illustrated in Fig. 14-29. The other is to provide a temporary support, as shown in Fig. 14-30, which will be removed when the concrete has reached its design strength.

Floors Supported on Block Walls

Wood floors on block walls are usually supported by wooden floor joists resting on a *sill plate* anchored to the top of the wall. The plate is anchored by bolts set in *grout* cast into the block cores (see Fig. 14-21).

FIGURE 14-28: *Precast lintel in place.*

387

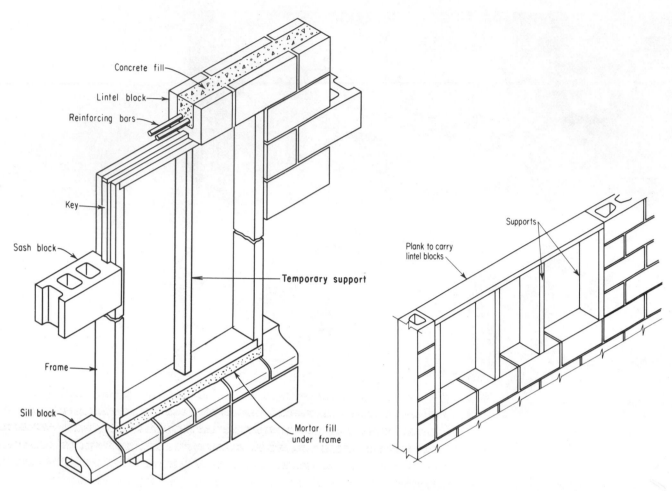

FIGURE 14-29: *Window frame supporting lintel blocks.*

FIGURE 14-30: *Temporary support for lintel blocks.*

Concrete floors may consist of a solid *flat* slab, like that illustrated in Fig. 14-31 or a *ribbed* slab, formed as shown in Fig. 14-32.

When a flat slab is specified, the outer rim may be formed by a course of 100 mm solid blocks, laid on top of the regular blocks and set flush with the outside face of the wall (see Fig. 14-31). The slab form will consist of a plywood deck supported from below on posts or shores.

A ribbed slab consists of a series of narrow, reinforced ribs, of various widths and depths, depending on the span of the building, supporting a relatively thin floor slab. Ribs are frequently spaced 600 mm o.c..

Ribbed slabs are formed in various ways. In Fig. 14-32, the voids between ribs are being formed by using special floor blocks, 600 mm long, carried on the planks used to form the bottom of the ribs. A cross section of the finished ribbed floor is illustrated in Fig. 14-33.

Pilasters

A pilaster is a type of *column,* incorporated into a block wall for the purpose of providing additional lateral support and/or providing a larger bearing surface for beam ends carried on the wall.

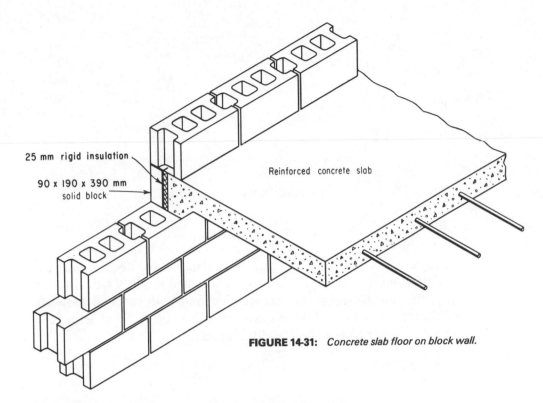

25 mm rigid insulation

90 x 190 x 390 mm
solid block

Reinforced concrete slab

FIGURE 14-31: *Concrete slab floor on block wall.*

FIGURE 14-32: *Forming a ribbed concrete floor slab.*

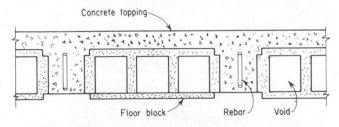

Concrete topping

Floor block   Rebar   Void

FIGURE 14-33: *Section through ribbed floor slab.*

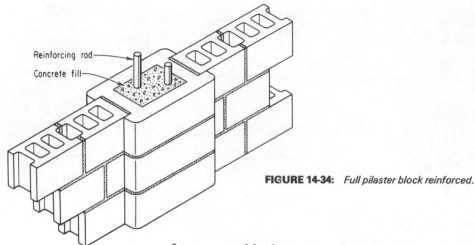

FIGURE 14-34: *Full pilaster block reinforced.*

In concrete block construction, the pilaster is formed by means of a *pilaster block,* one type of which is illustrated in Fig. 14-2. Another type, the *full pilaster block,* projects beyond both faces of the wall, as illustrated in Fig. 14-34. Pilaster blocks may be filled with reinforced concrete to give them additional strength.

Coping Blocks

When the top of a concrete block wall projects above a flat roof to form a *parapet,* it must be protected against moisture penetration. This protection is provided by capping the wall with coping blocks (see Fig. 14-35). The blocks are set in a bed of mortar, and the joints between blocks are filled with mortar. When the joint mortar is hard enough, it must be raked out about 19 mm deep and the joint caulked with a good grade of caulking compound.

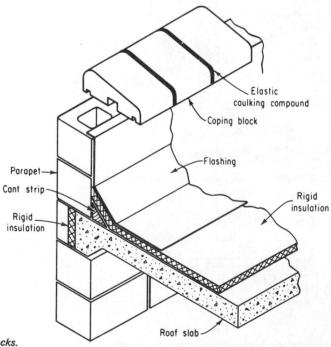

FIGURE 14-35: *Wall capped with coping blocks.*

390

(a)

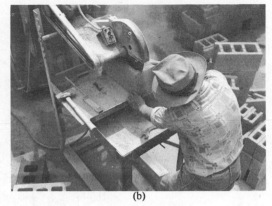
(b)

FIGURE 14-36: *Cutting concrete blocks.*

Cutting Concrete Blocks

Concrete blocks are usually made in half sizes, as well as full-length units. However, it is sometimes necessary to cut a block to fit a particular location. This can be done in two ways. The block can be scored on both sides with a chisel, as shown in Fig. 14-36a, and broken cleanly along the score lines. Blocks may also be cut with a masonry saw (Fig. 14-36b). This saw is particularly useful when only a portion of the block is to be cut away.

Window and Door Frames in Block Walls

A number of methods are used to set wood window and door frames into a concrete block wall. One method is to set the frame on *sill blocks,* as illustrated in Fig. 14-29. In place of sill blocks, a precast concrete sill may be installed at the bottom of the opening (see Fig. 14-37) and the frame set on it. A wood sill may be used for the same purpose, as illustrated in Fig. 11-43d. Frames with no slope on their sill may be set directly on the blocks at the bottom of the opening.

Wood frames may be held in place by a *key* which is fastened to the outside of the frame and fits into the notches in the sash block framing the sides of the opening.

Metal straps, with one end nailed to the side jambs of the frame and the other laid in the mortar joints between the blocks along the sides of the opening, may also be used to anchor frames.

FIGURE 14-37: *Precast window sill.*

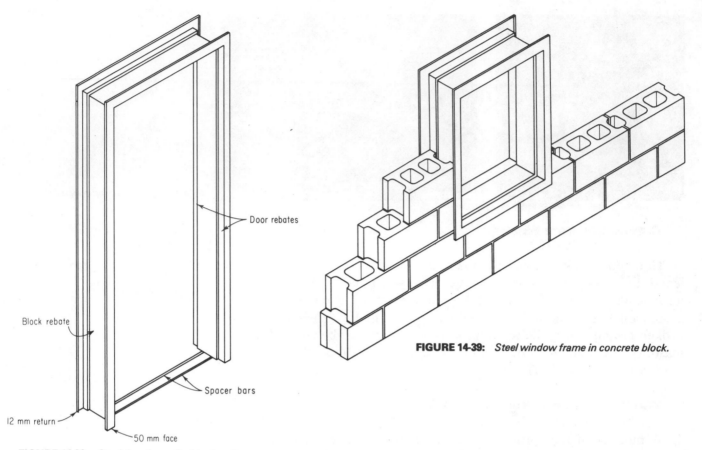

Door rebates

Block rebate

Spacer bars

12 mm return

50 mm face

FIGURE 14-38: *Steel door frame for block wall.*

FIGURE 14-39: *Steel window frame in concrete block.*

Steel window and door frames are commonly used in block construction (see Fig. 14-38). Flanges on their inner and outer edges form rebates into which standard width blocks will fit (see Fig. 14-39).

Cavity Walls

A cavity wall is constructed using two thicknesses (wythes) of block, separated by a continuous air space (see Fig. 14-40) and tied together by wire ties embedded in the mortar joints in every second course.

When required, the space between the wythes can be filled with loose fill or rigid insulation for added protection against heat loss through the wall. If loose fill insulation is to be introduced, it is good practice to keep the inner faces of the walls free from protruding ridges of mortar, which could later interfere with the flow of loose fill insulation into the space. This can be done by the use of a *cleanout bar*—a strip of board slightly narrower than the width of the space between wythes. It has a light wire attached to each end and rests on a row of wire ties in the cavity. When the two following courses have been laid, the bar is raised by means of wires, bringing with it any mortar which has extruded from the joints or has dropped into the cavity (see Fig. 14-41).

When rigid insulation is specified, it is placed in the cavity as the blocks are being laid.

FIGURE 14-40: *Cavity wall with cross ties.*

392

FIGURE 14-41: *Cavity clean-out bar.*

Reinforced Block Walls

Block walls may be reinforced either vertically or horizontally and either single-wythe or cavity walls may be reinforced.

To reinforce single-wythe walls vertically, the reinforcing bars are introduced into the cores at the specified spacing and those cores are filled with a high strength concrete grout, with a relatively high slump of from 125 to 150 mm. Two-core block are preferred to three-core because of the ease in placing reinforcement and grout and special shaped units have been developed for use in single-wythe, reinforced block construction. They are *open-end blocks* and *H-blocks,* both illustrated in Fig. 14-42. The advantage of these units is that they can be laid around vertical steel, rather than having to be threaded down over the rods.

Reinforcement is placed in the cavity of cavity wall construction and the entire space between wythes is filled with grout.

Horizontal reinforcing is accomplished by making one complete course of block into a reinforced concrete beam at a specified level in the wall. Such a beam is known as a *bond beam.*

Several methods are used to construct a bond beam, one of which is to use bond beam blocks, illustrated in Fig. 14-2. A complete course of these is laid in a full mortar bed, with the corner blocks being mitered to allow continuous reinforcing around the corners. Reinforcing bars are placed in the block channels (see Fig. 14-43), which are

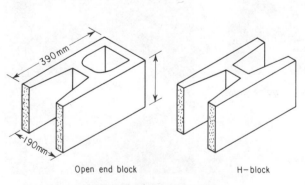

Open end block   H−block

FIGURE 14-42: *Special blocks.*

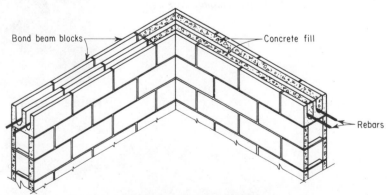

FIGURE 14-43: *Bond beam.*

(a)

(b)

subsequently filled with concrete. Further courses of block may then be added in the usual way above the bond beam.

A bond beam may also be made by forming and casting an all-concrete beam, the same width as the blocks and any desired height.

Watertight Block Walls

To ensure that block walls below grade will be watertight, they must be parged and sealed. Parging consists of applying two 6 mm coats of plaster, using the same mortar that was used for laying the blocks (see Fig. 14-44). Dampen the wall before applying the plaster in order to get a better bond. The first coat should extend from 150 mm above the grade line down to the footing. When it is partially set up, roughen with a wire brush and then allow it to harden for at least 24 hours. Before the second coat is applied, the wall should be dampened again and the plaster kept damp for 48 hours.

In poorly drained soils, the plaster should be covered with two coats of an asphalt waterproofing, brushed on (see Fig. 14-45).

In heavy, wet soils, the wall may be further protected by laying a line of drainage tile around the outside of the footing to prevent a buildup of moisture in the area. Such a technique is illustrated in Fig. 14-46. The joints in the tile should be covered with the strips of asphalt-impregnated building paper and the tile covered with about 300 mm of coarse gravel before the backfilling is done.

(c)

FIGURE 14-44: *Parging block wall.*

FIGURE 14-45: *Waterproofing below grade.*

FIGURE 14-46: *Laying drainage tile.*

Protection of Block

Concrete block require some protection both *before* and *after* laying. Block should be laid *dry* and must therefore be protected from wetting by rain or snow, by being kept in an enclosed space or by some type of cover, such as that illustrated in Fig. 14-47. Block should also be kept from getting too cold just prior to laying and may require a heated enclosure for that purpose.

After blocks are laid, the mortar should be protected from drying out too quickly in hot weather and this may be accomplished by covering newly laid block with a tarpaulin, dampened if necessary (see Fig. 14-48).

In cold weather, block structures should be kept at a reasonable temperature—10 °C or better—for several days until the mortar has had an opportunity to harden properly. This may be done by some type of space heater (see Fig. 14-49).

FIGURE 14-47: *Block protected from rain.*

FIGURE 14-48: *Block structure protected from drying out.*

FIGURE 14-49: *Space heater for cold weather construction.*

BRICK CONSTRUCTION

The basic ingredient is *clay,* finely ground, mixed with water, molded and burned in a kiln to form *brick*—one of the oldest building materials known to man.

Sizes and shapes of units have changed considerably over the years and there is still some variation from one area to another. But as a result of consultation and cooperation among planners, designers, manufacturers, and governmental authorities, a great deal has been accomplished in the way of standardization of brick sizes and in the application of the principle of *modular coordination* to the manufacture of brick.

Brick Shapes

The best known shape is the *common brick,* universally recognized as a brick shape with a generally accepted set of dimensions. In addition, a number of other shapes have been developed, some regionally, some for a special purpose and some for reasons of economy. Included in these are *Roman, Norman, Giant, Titan or TTW* (through-the-wall), *Monarch* and *Saxon (see Fig. 14-50). Each shape has a* range of widths in which it is normally produced.

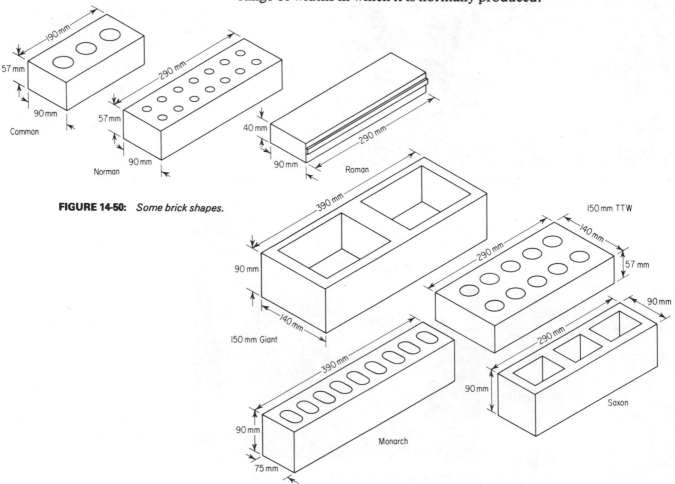

FIGURE 14-50: *Some brick shapes.*

Brick Sizes

It has been customary to designate unit masonry products by their *nominal* dimensions (sizes by which they are named) but their actual or *modular* dimensions are such that, measured center-to-center of mortar joints of specified thickness, the dimension will conform to a standard planning module.

Under the SI metric system, the recognized planning modules are 100, 300, and 600 mm, with the internationally recognized *planning grid* being a square 600 × 600 mm. Under this sytem the recognized module for brick is 100 mm.

The nominal metric size for common brick is 100 × 67 × 200 mm, which means that, using standard 10 mm mortar joints, the modular size of common brick will be 90 × 57 × 190 mm. Thus one brick length, two brick widths or three brick thicknesses will equal 200 mm—2 modules. Three common brick modular lengths or nine thicknesses fit into the 600 × 600 mm planning grid (see Fig. 14-51). Nominal and modular sizes for a number of brick shapes are given in Table 14-2.

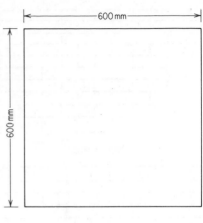

Standard metric grid

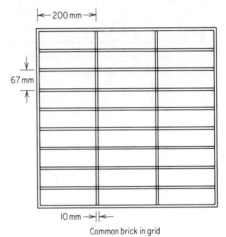

10 mm →|←
Common brick in grid

FIGURE 14-51: *Planning grid.*

TABLE 14-2: *Nominal and modular brick sizes (mm)*

Brick shape	Nominal size	Modular size
Common	100 × 67 × 200	90 × 57 × 190
Norman	100 × 67 × 300	90 × 57 × 290
Roman (standard)	100 × 50 × 300	90 × 40 × 290
Roman (king)	100 × 67 × 400	90 × 57 × 390
Giant (100 mm)	100 × 100 × 400	90 × 90 × 390
Giant (150 mm)	150 × 100 × 400	140 × 90 × 390
Giant (200 mm)	200 × 100 × 400	190 × 90 × 390
Giant (300 mm)	300 × 100 × 400	290 × 90 × 390
TTW (150 mm)	150 × 67 × 300	140 × 57 × 290
TTW (200 mm)	200 × 67 × 300	190 × 57 × 290
75 mm brick	75 × 67 × 200	75 × 57 × 190
Monarch	75 × 100 × 400	75 × 90 × 390
Saxon	100 × 100 × 300	90 × 90 × 290
Hollow	100 × 200 × 400	90 × 190 × 390

Brick Terminology

Course types: Brick may be laid with four different exposures. One is with the long edge horizontal. This is called a *stretcher.* Another is with the end horizontal—a *header.* A third is with the long edge vertical—a *soldier,* and the fourth, with the end vertical, is a *rowlock* (see Fig. 14-52).

FIGURE 14-52: *Types of brick course.*

Stretcher

Header

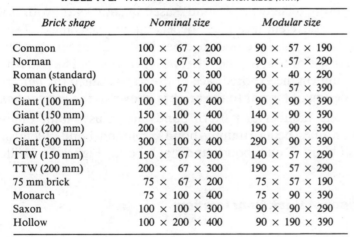

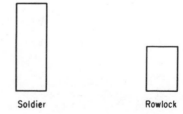

Soldier

Rowlock

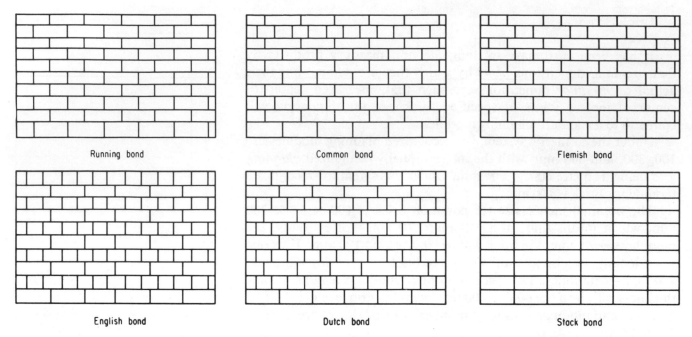

Running bond   Common bond   Flemish bond

English bond   Dutch bond   Stack bond

FIGURE 14-53: *Typical pattern bonds.*

Brick bond: The word "bond" used in connection with brick may have three different meanings, depending on the context. The method by which the units are tied together in a wall, either by overlapping or by the use of ties, is called the *structural bond.* The pattern formed by the units in the exposed face of the wall is called the *pattern bond;* the adhesion of mortar to the brick is known as the *mortar bond.*

A great number of pattern bonds are in use, some of the more common ones being running bond, common bond, Flemish bond, English bond, Dutch bond, and stack bond. Figure 14-53 illustrates these.

Types of Brick Construction

Brick may be used in walls in a number of ways in light construction. One is to use it as a *veneer* over a wood frame, concrete block, or structural tile backup wall. Another is to build a *conventional* brick wall, which will be at least 190 mm thick. A third method is to use *TTW brick, 140 mm wide,* a method widely accepted for single walls of limited height. Another is to build *cavity walls,* with brick for both exterior and interior wythes. In buildings having a skeleton frame of wood, steel or reinforced concrete, brick may be used as a *curtain wall* to close in the spaces between framing members.

Brick Veneer

Over wood frame: A single wythe of brick, 90 mm thick, is often used to face a sheathed wall, framed in wood. Both the building frame and the brick wythe must be supported on the foundation wall (see

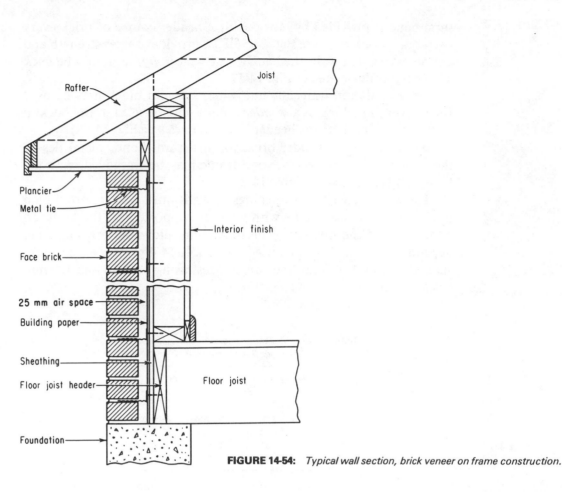

FIGURE 14-54: *Typical wall section, brick veneer on frame construction.*

Labels on figure:
Rafter
Joist
Plancier
Metal tie
Interior finish
Face brick
25 mm air space
Building paper
Sheathing
Floor joist header
Floor joist
Foundation

Fig. 14-54) and a 25 mm space should be left between brick and sheathing.

The brick must be anchored to the frame by noncorrosive metal straps, not less than 0.4 mm thick and 22 mm wide, spaced in accordance with Table 14-3.

TABLE 14-3: *Brick veneer tie spacing (mm)*

Horizontal spacing	Maximum vertical spacing
400	600
600	500
800	400

Over concrete block: 100, 150, or 200 mm block may be used as a backup wall for a 90 mm brick veneer face, depending on the width of the foundation. In the case of a block foundation, the cores in the top course of blocks should be filled with grout (see Fig. 14-55).

Then, with 200 or 250 mm wide foundation walls, it is common practice to lay a header course of brick (see Fig. 14-55) and build up the wall with 100 mm backup blocks and a brick veneer face. Struc-

FIGURE 14-55: *Starting brick veneer wall on 250 mm block foundation.*

FIGURE 14-56: *Header brick for structural bond.*

tural bond is provided by introducing a header course of brick every two courses of block (see Fig. 14-56). To provide greater strength and a more watertight wall, the back of the veneer wythe should be *back plastered,* as illustrated in Fig. 14-57.

For foundation walls 300 mm wide, 200 mm block may be used for backup, in which case *header blocks* may be used in the backup wall to accommodate the header brick courses (see Fig. 14-58).

Instead of using header brick for structural bond, metal ties of the same type as used for a wood frame may be employed, with the tie spacing regulated by Table 14-2.

The brick veneer over openings in walls must be supported by a *lintel,* usually a steel angle with its ends supported on the brick on either side of the opening. The maximum allowable opening span depends on the size of lintel used and Table 14-4 gives the maximum span allowed for various lintel angle sizes, using both 75 and 100 mm brick veneer.

FIGURE 14-57: *Back plastering facing brick.*

TABLE 14-4: *Maximum opening span allowed for various lintel angle sizes*

Lintel angle size (mm)	75 mm brick	100 mm brick
89 × 76 × 6 mm	2540 mm	—
89 × 89 × 6 mm	2565 mm	2465 mm
100 × 89 × 6 mm	2820 mm	2690 mm
125 × 89 × 6 mm	3300 mm	2515 mm
150 × 89 × 6 mm	3725 mm	3555 mm

Conventional Brick Wall

The conventional brick wall is made by using headers and stretchers in various combinations or patterns, as illustrated in Fig. 14-59 and will be at least 190 mm in thickness. Walls of this type may be used as the load-bearing walls in buildings of two storys or more. In such cases, the exterior walls of the bottom storys of two-story buildings and all the walls of three-story buildings must not be less than 190 mm thick.

150 mm Brick Walls

Solid brick walls in one story buildings and the top story of two-story buildings may be constructed of 140 mm brick, provided that the wall is not over 2.74 m high at the eaves and not more than 4.57 m high at the peaks of the gable ends. Through-the-wall (TTW) brick (see Fig. 14-50) are normally used for this type of construction.

On the inside surface, the wall may be *furred out* with 38 × 38 mm members and interior finish applied to them. This furring allows for application of a vapor barrier, makes for easy installation of electrical facilities and provides space for the introduction of insula-

FIGURE 14-58: *Header blocks with brick headers.*

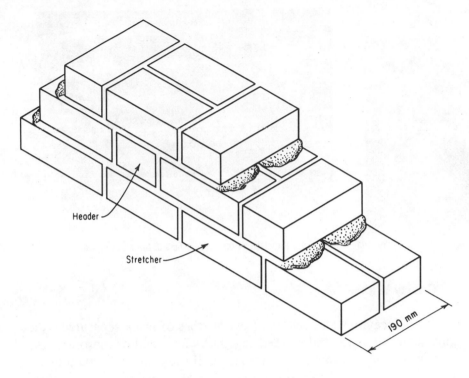

FIGURE 14-59: *Typical TTW brick construction methods.*

tion. However, it is possible to plaster directly to the inside face of the brick or face brick may be used, in which case no other finish is required.

A 200 mm foundation wall is adequate but the details of construction will depend on the type of floor being used. Figure 14-60 illustrates two typical methods of construction using TTW brick.

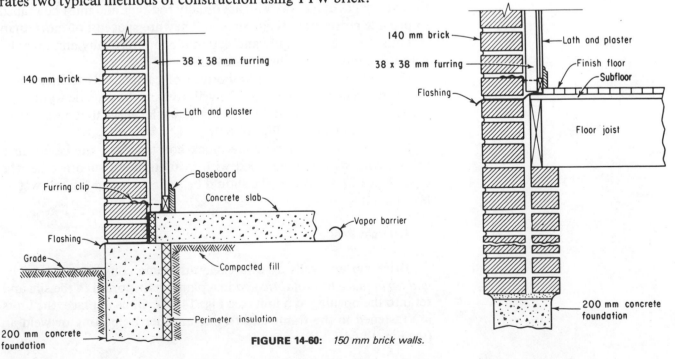

FIGURE 14-60: *150 mm brick walls.*

401

FIGURE 14-61: *Flashing at base of cavity wall.*

FIGURE 14-62: *Weephole in brick cavity wall.*

Cavity Walls

A brick cavity wall consists of two wythes of brick separated by a continuous air space and bonded together with metal or masonry ties. Each wythe must be at least 90 mm thick if the joints are *raked* or 75 mm thick if unraked joints are used. The air space must be not less than 50 mm or more than 75 mm wide if metal ties are used and not less than 75 mm or more than 100 mm wide if masonry ties are used.

The minimum thickness of cavity walls above the foundation must not be less than 250 mm for the top 7.6 m and not less than 350 mm for the remaining lower portion, when 90 mm wide units are used. In cases where 75 mm units are used, the wall height above the foundation must not exceed 6.1 m.

The ties commonly used to provide the structural bond between the two wythes of a cavity wall are usually rod-type and must be shaped to provide a drip near their centers. They are spaced not more than 900 mm apart horizontally and 450 mm apart vertically and must be within 300 mm of openings in the wall.

Flashing is provided at the bottom of cavity walls to direct any moisture which collects within the wall toward the outside wythe (see Fig. 14-61) and *weepholes* in the outside wythe allow that moisture to drain to the outside (see Fig. 14-62).

As was the case in concrete block construction, the cavity in a brick cavity wall may be filled with insulation. In such a case, the outer face of the inner wythe should be sealed with an asphalt waterproof coating.

Curtain Walls

Brick curtain walls used in skeleton frame construction may be *laid up in place* or *prefabricated* in a plant, transported to the site and set into the opening as a unit (see Fig. 14-63). Once in place, the units are fastened to the frame and to one another by bolting or welding (see Fig. 14-64).

FIGURE 14-63: *Prefabricated brick walls ready for installation.*

FIGURE 14-64: *Welding sections of prefabricated brick wall together.*

Laying Brick

One of the primary requisites for a good brick structure is good mortar. To be able to fulfil its purpose, mortar must possess a number of important qualities, both in the *plastic* stage and after it has hardened.

In the plastic stage, the important qualities are *workability, water retentivity,* and a *consistent rate of hardening.* Hardened mortar must have *good bond, durability,* good *compressive strength,* and *good appearance.*

Good workability is the result of a combination of factors, including the *quality of aggregate* used, proper *grades of aggregate,* the use of a small quantity of *hydrated lime or lime putty* (see Table 14-1), the use of *masonry cement,* the *amount of water* used, proper *mixing facilities, consistency,* and *flowability,* the ability of the mortar to *retain water, adhesion qualities,* and *setting time.*

Mortar with good workability should *slip readily on the trowel, spread easily* on the masonry unit, *adhere to vertical surfaces,* and *extrude readily* from joints as the unit is being placed, without dropping. The consistency must be such that the unit can be properly bedded but its weight and the weight of following courses will not cause further extrusion of the mortar.

The ability of a mortar to retain water—its *water retentivity*—is very important because loss of water will result in premature stiffening of the mortar, which will prevent it from achieving a good bond and watertight joints.

The causes of poor water retentivity in mortar are likely to be *poorly graded aggregate, oversized aggregate, too short a mixing time,* or the *wrong type of cement.* The addition of an air-entraining agent and increased mixing may also improve the water retentivity.

In order to obtain good masonry construction, it is essential that all mortar joints be completely filled as the bricks are being laid.

403

Failure to do so will result in voids through which water can penetrate. Not only will water pass through the wall to mar the interior finish, but water in the wall may dissolve salts from the brick and then deposit them on the surface as *efflorescence* when it returns to the outside and evaporates. In addition, water in the wall may freeze and cause deterioration in the wall itself.

Mortar for the bed joint should be spread thickly, with a shallow furrow down the center of the bed (see Fig. 14-65). There will then be enough excess mortar in the bed to fill the furrow and allow some mortar to be extruded at the joint when the bricks are bedded to the line. The bed mortar should be spread over only a few bricks at a time so that water will not evaporate before the bricks are laid and thus result in poor adhesion. Figure 14-66 illustrates mortar which has good adhesion qualities.

Care must be taken that all vertical joints in both stretcher and header courses are completely filled with mortar. To obtain a full head joint in a stretcher course, apply plenty of mortar to the end of the brick being placed, so that when it is set, mortar will be extruded at the top of the head joint (see Fig. 14-67). To ensure full vertical cross joints in header courses, spread mortar over the entire side of the header brick to be placed, as illustrated in Fig. 14-68. When the brick is set, mortar should be extruded from the face and the top of the joint (see Fig. 14-68).

FIGURE 14-65: *Furrowed bed joint.*

FIGURE 14-66: *Mortar with good adhesion.*

FIGURE 14-67: *Full head joint.*

FIGURE 14-68: *Buttering and setting header brick.*

Closures in both stretcher and header courses need careful attention. Mortar should be spotted on the sides or ends of both bricks already in place, and both sides or ends of the brick to be placed should be well buttered. Then set the closure brick without disturbing those already in place (see Fig. 14-69).

Tooling the mortar joint compacts the mortar, making it more dense, and helps to seal any fine cracks between brick and mortar (see Fig. 14-70). A number of styles of joint are used, similar to those used in concrete block (see Fig. 14-18).

FIGURE 14-70: *Before and after tooling joint.*

FIGURE 14-69: *Setting closure brick.*

STRUCTURAL TILE CONSTRUCTION

Clay tile is made from the same basic material and by the same general process as brick, but the units are hollow. This makes for a lighter structure and at the same time provides dead air space insulation.

Tile is made in three grades: dense, semiporous, and porous. Dense tile are used in load-bearing capacities, and semiporous and porous tile are used in non-load-bearing locations.

Tile in all three grades are made in a variety of shapes and sizes, for many purposes. Among them are facing tile, wall tile, partition tile, furring tile, floor tile, and backer tile (see Fig. 14-71).

Tile in walls may be laid up in either side or end construction. Side construction means that the tile are laid with the cells horizontal; in end construction the cells are vertical. End construction will result in greater compressive strength but less resistance to lateral stresses. In side construction there is a greater area in mortar bond, and, therefore, greater resistance to lateral pressure but reduced compressive strength.

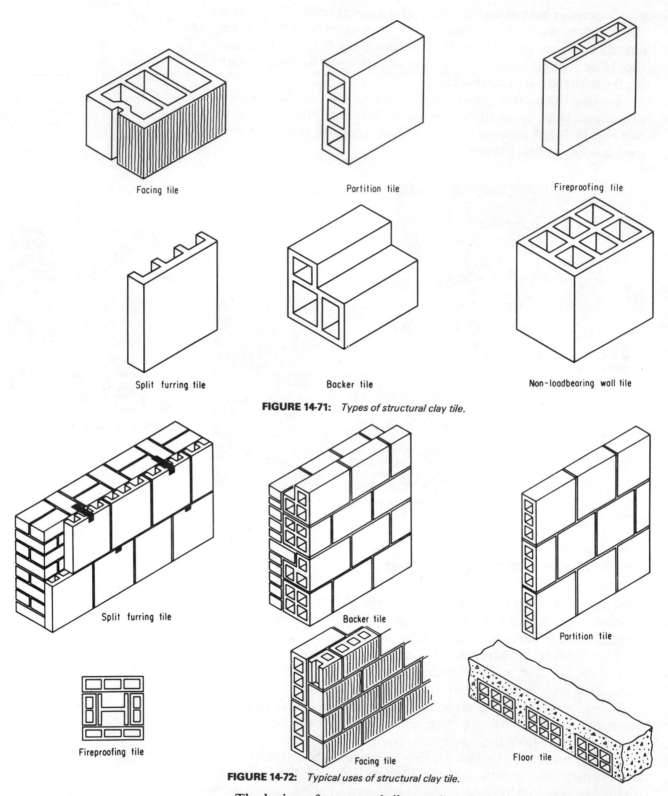

FIGURE 14-71: *Types of structural clay tile.*

FIGURE 14-72: *Typical uses of structural clay tile.*

The laying of structural tile requires the same careful attention to workmanship as does bricklaying. Bed joints are usually divided, and full head joints should be used on both the inner and outer faces.

Figure 14-72 illustrates some typical uses of different types of structural tile.

406

STONE CONSTRUCTION

In modern light construction, stone is used almost entirely as a veneer —an exterior facing over a wood frame or unit masonry structural wall or as an interior decorative material, used for fireplaces, mantels, feature walls, and finish floors.

Stone for this purpose is available in two forms. One is a small stone block, commonly known as *ashlar,* usually 50, 75 or 100 mm thick, with regular or irregular face dimensions. Stones will usually not exceed 600 mm in length, while the height will vary from 100 to 300 mm. The other is a thin, flat slab, from 12 to 25 mm thick, with either regular or random face dimensions.

Ashlar veneer is applied in the same way as brick veneer. The stone must rest on the foundation (see Fig. 14-54) and is bonded to the wall with metal ties, with one end nailed to a wood frame backup wall or laid in the mortar joints of a unit masonry wall. If the stones are cut to specific dimensions, they can be laid with regular course lines and the result is known as *coursed ashlar.* But if the face dimensions are irregular, the result will be *random ashlar,* illustrated in Fig. 14-73.

Thin slabs of stone—slate, galena or argillite—are fixed to the wall in a bed of mortar. (See Chapter 11, Masonry Finishes).

FIGURE 14-73: *Random ashlar stone veneer.*

PRECAST CONCRETE SLAB CONSTRUCTION

Precast roof slabs and precast beams and columns for industrial buildings have been used for many years, and the use of precast concrete panels for the walls of lighter buildings has become increasingly popular.

In this type of construction, known as *tilt-up* construction, the panel is cast on a flat, solid surface at the site and, when cured, is tilted up into place. The surface used is usually the previously cast and cured concrete floor slab for the building.

Side forms for the tilt-up panel are laid out on the floor and fixed in place with powder-actuated pins or bolts previously cast in place. Forms or frames for openings in the wall are positioned and fastened down. Then the surface is covered with some type of bond-breaking material to prevent the panel from adhering to the floor. The required reinforcing and the anchor plates to hold the panel in position are placed and the panel cast and finished as specified (see Fig. 14-74). When it is sufficiently cured, the panel can be tilted up into position and the bottom bolted or welded in place.

Slabs may be made to be fastened together, edge to edge, upon erection or they may be set with a space between each pair and concrete columns later cast around the column edges (see Fig. 14-75).

Approximate imperial equivalents to metric quantities			
6 mm	— ¼ in.	90 mm	— 3⅝ in.
10 mm	— ⅜ in.	100 mm	— 4 in.
12 mm	— ½ in.	125 mm	— 5 in.
20 mm	— ¾ in.	150 mm	— 6 in.
25 mm	— 1 in.	190 mm	— 7⅝ in.
50 mm	— 2 in.	400 mm	— 16 in.
57 mm	— 2²⁄₂₄ in.	450 mm	— 18 in.
67 mm	— 2⅔ in.	600 mm	— 24 in.
75 mm	— 3 in.	1.2 m	— 4 ft

FIGURE 14-74: *Casting tilt-up panel.*

408

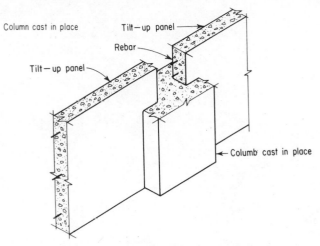

FIGURE 14-75: *Column cast around panel edges.*

REVIEW QUESTIONS

14-1. Outline the primary purpose of mortar used in masonry construction.

14-2. What are the basic ingredients of a good mortar?

14-3. Under what circumstances is it not necessary to use hydrated lime in mortar?''

14-4. Explain what is meant by ''retempering'' mortar.

14-5. What is the purpose of building up the corners of block walls first?

14-6. List four types of mortar joints that may be used in masonry work.

14-7. Describe how a ''control joint'' is made in block masonry.

14-8. What is the purpose of a control joint?

14-9. Describe two methods of bonding two intersecting block walls together.

14-10. What is the purpose of a ''lintel'' in masonry construction?

14-11. Give two reasons for using pilasters in masonry construction.

14-12. For what purpose is a coping block used?

14-13. Outline two advantages of cavity walls in masonry construction.

14-14. What is the purpose of a ''bond beam'' in a block wall?

14-15. Describe three methods of fastening interior finishing material to the inside surface of a brick wall.

14-16. Outline two basic differences between brick and structural tile.

14-17. By means of a diagram, illustrate a method of making a precast concrete wall panel.

14-18. Outline briefly a method for applying 20 mm stone veneer to the exterior of a structural clay tile backup wall.

INDEX

8236454

EDUCATION